DATE DUE

SEP 4 1987 4141	
NOV 6 1988	
NOV 2 4 1988	
JUL 2 4 1991	
APR 2 7 1992	
MAR 2 3 1994	

BRODART, INC.   Cat. No. 23-221

CHILDREN'S RIGHTS IN THE PRACTICE OF FAMILY LAW

edited by
Barbara Landau, Ph.D., LL.B., LL.M.

CARSWELL
Toronto   Calgary   Vancouver
1986

Canadian Cataloguing in Publication Data

Main entry under title:

Children's rights in the practice of family law

ISBN 0-459-39040-6

1. Children - Legal status, laws, etc. -
Canada.   2. Parent and child (Law) - Canada.
3. Children's rights - Canada.   4. Domestic
relations - Canada.   I. Landau, Barbara.
KE512.C49 1986   346.7101'7   C86-091365-1

CONTRIBUTORS

Nicholas M.C. Bala, B.A., LL.B., LL.M., Associate Professor, Faculty of Law, Queen's University, Kingston, Ontario.

Richard F. Barnhorst, Legal Advisor, Ontario Ministry of Community and Social Services, Toronto, Ontario.

Janne M.N. Burton, Student-at-Law, Toronto, Ontario.

David A. Cruickshank, B.A., LL.B., LL.M., Director of Professional Legal Training, Continuing Legal Education Society of British Columbia, Vancouver, British Columbia.

Bernard M. Dickens, Ph.D., LL.D., Professor, Faculty of Law and Faculty of Medicine, University of Toronto, Toronto, Ontario.

Barbara Landau, Ph.D., LL.B., LL.M., Barrister and Solicitor, Toronto, Ontario.

H. Allan Leal, O.C., Q.C., Vice Chairman, Ontario Law Reform Commission, Toronto, Ontario.

J.W. Mohr, Professor, Osgoode Hall Law School, York University, Toronto, Ontario.

Judith Patricia Ryan, M.S.W., LL.B., LL.M., Barrister and Solicitor, Toronto, Ontario.

Allan Q. Shipley, Counsel, Policy Development Division, Ministry of the Attorney General (Ontario), Toronto, Ontario.

Michael S. Wald, Professor of Law, Director of the Stanford Center for the Study of Youth Development, Stanford, California.

The author wishes to express her gratitude to Professor Bernard M. Dickens for the preparation of the Foreword to this book.

PREFACE

The very existence of a book devoted to children's rights is a reflection of the increased importance given to the status, rights and obligations of children, separate and apart from both their parents and the State. The balance of interests of children, parents and the State has had a tremendous impact on our legislative philosophy and on the extent to which children, particularly young adolescents, are permitted or even encouraged to participate in serious decisions affecting their future. This book reviews a number of recent or proposed legislative reforms in terms of the underlying policy considerations and the impact on children's rights. I gratefully acknowledge the excellent contribution of all of the authors toward an increased sensitivity to children's issues and in many cases toward major substantive changes in our laws.

In addition, I extend my thanks to Simone Johnston and Maureen Holder, both of whom offered tremendous organizational talent, skilled typing, persistence and encouragement that made this difficult project happen. I am particularly indebted to my family, my husband Sy Landau for his tolerance of my many adventuresome projects and my children Daryl and Niki Landau who constantly reminded me of the importance of children's rights both in our family and in the broader community.

Barbara Landau
Toronto, Ontario
June, 1986.

FOREWORD

The challenge of what the law can do and should do with and for children will probably never be satisfactorily resolved. Evolving perceptions and new experiences shape changing attitudes and determine positions taken by individuals, institutions and governmental administrations along a continuum of possible viewpoints. The issues are complicated by the developmental progression of children into adolescents who want increasingly to participate in decision-making procedures that affect them, and to behave like adults before their legal time. This book brings together a number of related chapters that address developments in Canadian law on children's interests. Recent changes, particularly in legislation of federal and provincial governments, make this a timely occasion to study modern children's law in principle, in detail, and in prospect.

Michael S. Wald's opening chapter proposes a basic framework for analysis, identifying different types of claims that seem to rely on the concept that children have legal rights. Claims to rights to protection and also to autonomy may appear to conflict with each other and need to be explicated and distinguished. Adults have the power and the responsibility to make decisions for themselves. They take risks, bear the burdens and suffer the consequences of making poor choices. To deny adults that power and responsibility is to be paternalistic, and to demean them. Children are entitled to their guardians' protective paternalism, however, since they lack the hindsight, foresight and insight to be reliable decision-makers and to be left to the consequences of their decisions. The point at which their right to autonomy supersedes their right to protection against risk of error is unavoidably contentious. It is determined by subjective philosophy and by empirical data derived from scientific study of developing capacity of children and adolescents to see the world as it is seen by adults. Personal philosophies of persons in positions of authority such as, for instance, legislators, judges and mental health professionals are informed to different degrees by apparently objective information about children's capacities, and by a sense of what rights it is appropriate for children and adolescents to exercise.

The application to children of legal rights persons enjoy under Canada's new Charter of Rights and Freedoms is considered in chapter 2 by Nicholas Bala and David A. Cruickshank. The Charter in general came into effect in April 1982, but the highly significant section 15 came into force only three years later. Section 15(1) provides that: "Every individual is equal before and under the law and has the right to the equal protection and benefit of the law without discrimination . . . based on . . . age or mental or physical disability." In the next few years, the Charter will be authoritatively interpreted by the Supreme Court of Canada, and by provincial Courts of Appeal. All concerned with children's interests have to be aware of the techniques of interpretation the courts may apply, and the implications of the decisions they will reach. The authors selectively review key sections of the Charter in sequence, addressing relevant Canadian judgments and the comparative United States jurisprudence in order to clarify issues to be resolved by the courts.

More specific and closer to where and how children live is the following chapter by Barbara Landau, which addresses minors' consent to medical care, mental health treatment and residential care. Underlying these issues is the contest that may exist between parents and children over who controls children's health, environment and other influences that will fundamentally affect children's futures. A third party, not necessarily mediating between parents and children but often pursuing its own agenda reflecting its own philosophy, is the State itself. The decision to remove children from their parents' homes is often made by courts when they apply provincial legislation. In passing legislation authorizing alternative placement of children for medical and mental health care, the provinces follow principles inspired by a vision of children's welfare that parents have not shared or have violated. Decision-making processes are particularly significant in a legal review of how children are to be protected, because facts may be elusive, medical and psychiatric categories may be uncertain, and diagnoses and prognoses made in good faith are liable to irreducible error. In the inexact art of medical and psychiatric care, reliance is placed on estimations of the truth, even when they are based on scientifically precise measurements. Determination of whose decision is to prevail is therefore a determination of whose liability to error will influence a child's future.

Chapter 4 by Allan Q. Shipley discusses Ontario's recent reform of children's custody law. While specific to a single province, this chapter offers materials relevant to prospective custody law reform elsewhere in Canada. Originating in recommendations of the Ontario Law Reform Commission made in 1973, the province's Children's Law Reform Act and the Children's Law Reform Amendment Act, 1982, are the latest expression of governmental philosophy on the proper guardianship of children. Implications of the concept of legal "guardianship" are explored, relating "custody" to "guardianship" and distinguishing physical custody of the person from legal custody of the person's property interests. The Act's principles and processes of making custody decisions are fully explained. The chapter includes a discussion of parents' joint custody of a child, but in chapter 5 Judith P. Ryan expands on this issue. She suggests that, despite the restrictive view courts have taken of this concept, it warrants a second look that is considerably more favourable. Including both analysis and advocacy, this chapter contrasts doctrine and experience in the United States with that in Canada, and argues that the higher courts' approach to joint custody has got off to a false start and should be brought back to its starting blocks and be prepared to set off again. Judith Ryan reviews the background social work literature extensively and critically and explores what is significant.

An unfortunate consequence of a court's actual or anticipated child custody decision may be one parent's abduction of a child and removal to another jurisdiction. H. Allan Leal addresses the legal problems that arise in this event, focussing on the Hague Convention on the Civil Aspects of International Child Abduction, concluded in 1980. In chapter 6, the distinguished author considers the impact of the Convention on Ontario's legislation in a way that permits reflection on the legislation and case law established in other Canadian jurisdictions. Further, while the Convention limits itself to civil law aspects of and approaches to the problem, the chapter also touches on relevant criminal law provisions and the role that the police may play. The provisions and mechanisms of the Convention are explained through their consequences in provincial and territorial law, but the author also considers the obligations of Canada, as a ratifying party on behalf of certain provinces, to give effect to the Convention on the return of abducted children.

Nicholas Bala asks in chapter 7 whether the federal Young Offenders Act introduces a new era in juvenile justice for adolescents suspected of committing criminal offences. He considers that it does, consistently with the Act's history and intentions. As much criticism of the Act's operation since it was proclaimed into force in 1984 is unaware of or unsympathetic to its reforming purposes, the author performs a useful function in reviewing the Act's inspiration and principles before he considers its central provisions. Avoiding the Act's legalistic details, the author gives an overview of its characteristic contours, indicating both achievements and implementation problems in the Act. Balancing this study of how Canadian law now deals with juveniles suspected of committing crimes, is Richard F. Barnhorst's succeeding chapter on consequences of suspected offences committed against the young. He addresses recent reforms in Canadian child protection legislation, giving attention to the different principles and processes of legislative authorization of judicial action. The method of law reform itself is isolated for special consideration to show how it affects the particular provisions that have been adopted in various Canadian jurisdictions. The chapter gives separate attention to relevant legal principles, establishment of grounds for involuntary legal intervention in families, initiation of court proceedings, interim custody of children while proceedings are pending, the range of dispositions courts may make on finding that children are in need of protection, and accountability mechanisms for child protection agencies and the courts themselves.

Addressing a more specific concern in child protection law in chapter 9, Janne M.N. Burton considers legal doctrinal and evidentiary issues in a criminal case alleging sexual abuse of children. This topic is placed in Part III of the book, considering future directions in the law, because the author presents a critical analysis of the existing criminal justice system, drawn from the perspective of the child victim of sexual assault, and proposes preferred alternatives. The chapter therefore does not promote other perspectives, notably that of the person accused of committing such an offence who may invoke not only the presumption of innocence, protected for instance by the Charter of Rights and Freedoms, but also the right of critical confrontation with a hostile witness such as a child alleging that an assault occurred. The approach the author takes is accordingly not unbalanced or unanalytical, but is overtly adversarial and argumentative. It gives special weight to the ignored vulnerability and embarrassment that sexual abuse victims experience as witnesses, and inquires whether Canadian court procedures are now part of the solution or part of the problem of sexual abuse of children. The author applies anecdotal and more scientific data to consider the effect of laws of evidence on the likelihood that convictable suspects of abuse will be charged and convicted, and proposes alternative legal processes, protective of victims, that would maintain and perhaps increase that likelihood without doing violence to principles of legal due process.

In chapter 10, Bernard M. Dickens considers the quite different topic of artificial or asexual reproduction. The chapter considers legislative responses to the relatively new reproductive practice of artificial insemination by sperm donation, artificial reproduction by ovum or embryo donation made possible through techniques of *in vitro* ("test tube") fertilization and *in vivo* (in the body) fertilization followed by recovery and transplantation of the resulting embryo, and the application of reproductive techniques in surrogate motherhood agreements. It is initially pointed out that these techniques have developed as medical responses to the growing incidence of infertility in our society, and to improved means to predict a couple's natural reproduction of a genetically handicapped child. General legal attitudes to artificial reproduction are reviewed, and regulatory legislative models are considered in outline before the author discusses general conceptual approaches to possible new legislation. Some more specific, transcending legal issues in the control of asexual reproduction are identified, and more particular legal problems are addressed that are raised by sperm, ovum and embryo donation, *in vitro* fertilization and surrogate motherhood.

In conclusion, J. (Hans) W. Mohr philosophically considers the future of the family, the law and the State, drawing together perceptions of many social developments and phenomena. The author observes the schizophrenia with which we assert at the same time that the family is the basic unit and building block of society, but that it is also the location of wife battering and abuse of children, and the source of interpersonal discord and individual emotional and mental health distress. The modern revolution in family law is considered as a reflection rather than a source of social change, only legitimating the *de facto* reforms in family functioning that have already occurred. The author explains past and present myths about how families function, and offers his reasons for confidence that the family as a social unit has a future, despite the absence of coherent social and legal policies for its protection. His confidence lies more in people themselves than in the formal institutions of the State or the laws, more in the rational, human instinct for fairness than in governmental or legal romanticism about what families ought to be. He argues for the rehumanization of law.

TABLE OF CONTENTS

TABLE OF CASES

TABLE OF STATUTES

CANADA

ALBERTA

BRITISH COLUMBIA

MANITOBA

NEW BRUNSWICK

NEWFOUNDLAND

NOVA SCOTIA

ONTARIO

PRINCE EDWARD ISLAND

QUEBEC

OTHER JURISDICTIONS

part I

CHILDREN'S RIGHTS

1

CHILDREN'S RIGHTS: A FRAMEWORK FOR ANALYSIS*

Michael S. Wald

I   Categories of Rights

   1.   Rights Against the World

   2.   Protection from Inadequate Care

   3.   Adult Legal Status

   4.   Rights Versus Parents

II   Conclusion

The question of what rights should be given children is now being debated in courts, legislatures and scholarly and popular journals.[1] Increased societal concern over individual rights, the recognition of child abuse as a major problem, the loss of faith by many in juvenile courts, schools and other institutions dealing with children, and the changing structure and role of families have all played a part in the emergence of a movement to give children more "rights".[2]

---

*This research was supported, in part, by funds from the Boys Town Center on Youth Development at Stanford. I wish to thank Cheryl French, Tom Grey, Charles Halpern, Susan Halpern, John Kaplan and Catherine Lewis for their helpful comments on earlier drafts.

 1 Among the most important court cases are *In re Gault*, 387 U.S. 1 (1967) (juvenile court procedures); *Ginsberg v. N.Y.*, 390 U.S. 629 (1968) (first amendment); *Tinker v. Des Moines Sch. Dist.*, 393 U.S. 503 (1969) (first amendment); *Goss v. Lopez*, 419 U.S. 565 (1975) (school expulsion); *Erznoznik v. Jacksonville*, 422 U.S. 205 (1975) (first amendment); *Bellotti v. Baird*, 428 U.S. 132 (1976) (abortion); *Carey v. Population Services, Int.*, 431 U.S. 678 (1977) (access to contraceptives); *Ingraham v. Wright*, 430 U.S. 651 (1977) (corporal punishment); *In re Roger S.*, 19 Cal. 3d 921 (1977) (civil commitment). The literature is becoming quite extensive. Among the most influential works are: R. Farson, *Birthrights* (1974); H. Foster, *A Bill of Rights for Children* (1974); J. Holt, *Escape from Childhood* (1974); Institute of Judicial Administration — American Bar Association (IJA-ABA), *Juvenile Justice Standards Project, Standards Relating to Rights of Minors*, tentative draft (1977); Geiser, "The Rights of Children" (1977), 28 Hastings L.J. 1027; Goldstein, "Medical Care for the Child at Risk: On State Supervision of Parental Autonomy" (1977), 86 Yale L.J. 645; Hafen, "Children's Liberation and The New Egalitarianism: Some Reservations About Abandoning Youth to Their Rights" (1976), B.Y.U.L. Rev. 605; "The Rights of Children", Special Issue (pp. 131-32) (1973-74), 43 Harv. Educ. Rev. 481, 44 Harv. Educ. Rev. 1. The issue has received a good deal of press as well. See, e.g., "Children's Rights: The Latest Crusade", *Time*, 25th December 1972, at 41; "Drive for Rights of Children", *U.S. News & World Report*, 5th August 1974, at 42.

 2 See Margolin, "Salvation v. Liberation: The Movement for Children's Rights in a Historical Context" (1978), 25 Soc. Prob. 441, for a discussion of the forces leading to the "children's rights movement". See also Geiser, *ibid.*

The idea of children having rights is, in many ways, a revolutionary one. Historically, children have been under the control of their parents, and to a lesser degree, the state.[3] Presumed by law to lack the capacity of adults, children are denied full participation in the political, legal and social processes.[4] In lieu of most rights, the state affords children special protection.[5]

Today, however, many people consider this control, and the special protection that accompanies it, to be harmful, even oppressive,[6] to children. At the extreme, some children's rights advocates call for a total change in policy. For example, teacher and author John Holt advocates that children of any age be given the right to vote, to work for money, to choose what type of education they want, and to be free from corporal punishment.[7] Psychologist Richard Farson goes even further. He argues that the issue of self-determination is at the heart of "children's liberation".[8] To Farson, children's rights can only be realized when all children have total freedom to decide for themselves what is best for them, including the right to sexual freedom, financial independence, and the right to choose where they shall live. Therefore, he argues for the elimination of both state and parental control of children.[9]

While most advocates do not go this far, respected experts from many disciplines argue that we need to adopt a "Bill of Rights" for children to assure their well-being. The type of rights suggested range from broad claims such as

---

3 The discussion in this chapter focuses on the status of children in the United States. The degree of autonomy given to children and the relative role of state and parent varies from society to society. Unfortunately, the anthropological and historical literature provide relatively little information about children's rights in different cultures or times.

4 Jeremy Bentham stated the traditional view of the law over 100 years ago: "The feebleness of infancy demands a continual protection. Everything must be done for an imperfect being, which as yet does nothing for itself. The complete development of its physical power takes many years; that of its intellectual faculties is still slower. At a certain age, it has already strength and passions, without experience enough to regulate them. Too sensitive to present impulses, too negligent of the future, such a being must be kept under an authority more immediate than that of the law. . . ."
See J. Bentham, *Theory of Legislation* (1840), at 248.

5 It is questionable whether children actually get special protection. Adult treatment of children has always been a mixed bag. While children are thought of as special, deserving of extra help and care, they have also been viewed and treated as chattels. Infanticide, severe misuse of children in factories and selling of children into marriage are just some examples of the ways children have been treated like property. Institutions, like juvenile courts, designed to protect children have often harmed them instead: see E. Ryerson, *The Best Laid Plans* (1978).

6 Even the media uses the term oppression: see Finefrock, "Our Last Oppressed Minority — Children", *San Francisco Examiner*, 30th November 1978, at 1.

7 Holt, *supra*, n. 1, at 18 *passim*.

8 Farson, *supra*, n. 1, at 27.

9 *Ibid.*, *passim*.

the right to grow up free from poverty and discrimination, to be born a wanted child, and to grow up nurtured by affectionate parents, to more specific rights, such as the right of children to choose their custodians upon divorce, to decide whether or not to have an abortion, to get medical care without parental consent or knowledge and to live on their own if they can support themselves.[10] Some advocates make distinctions by age; many do not.[11] Most advocates also assert that children must have access to counsel to effectuate their rights. A number of legal organizations funded to provide free legal services to children are already raising issues of children's rights.[12]

Not everyone shares the views of children's rights advocates, however. Among the most prominent proponent of limited rights and expanded parental control is Yale Law Professor Joseph Goldstein. He argues that:

> To be a *child* is to be at risk, dependent, and without capacity to decide what is "best" for oneself.

> To be an adult is to be a risktaker, independent, and with capacity and authority to decide and to do what is "best" for oneself.

---

10 One of the first Children's Bill of Rights is found in the United Nations Declaration of the Rights of the Child reprinted in B. Gross and R. Gross, *The Children's Rights Movement* (1977), at 333. See also H. Foster, *supra*, n. 1. A constitutional amendment to assure children's rights has been proposed by S. Soman, *Let's Stop Destroying Our Children* (1975). The amendment would include the right to:
   — physical safety and health care before and after birth;
   — the basics of life itself, including love;
   — learn and be educated;
   — enjoyment, play, laughter;
   — the same constitutional protections as anyone else;
   — understanding, tolerance, acceptance on the part of all adults;
   — adult models demonstrating consideration, integrity, ethics and, most especially, compassion;
   — a peaceful, nonracist world where violence, massacres and wars are considered obsolete; and
   — his or her own identity.
   Even the children have joined in. A recent conference of educators, held at Columbia Teachers College, invited a group of 9 to 16-year-olds to address them on the issue of children's rights. The children made more limited claims than their elder advocates. They asked for freedom from corporal punishment, the end of placement of children in large penal or mental institutions, and the end of child pornography. Their position was summarized by 9-year-old Cristy, who said, "Children should have civil rights, just like women and other people get, because, you know, civil rights isn't only for grownups, it is for children, too." "Last Oppressed Minority Speaks Up", *N.Y. Times*, 17th June 1977, A at 24.

11 Compare Farson and IJA-ABA, *Standards*, both *supra*, n. 1.

12 Among the organizations suing on behalf of children are the National Youth Law Center, the ACLU Juvenile Rights Project, and the Children's Defence Fund: see Campbell, "Children's Rights Drive is Centered in Courtroom", *N.Y. Times*, 31st October 1976, at 26.

> To be an *adult who is a parent* is to be presumed in law to have the capacity, authority, and responsibility to determine and to do what is good for one's children.[13]

Others, who fear that expansion of the notion of children's rights will undermine the family structure to the detriment of children and society as a whole, have expressed similar views.[14]

To date, neither legislatures nor courts have developed a coherent philosophy or approach when addressing questions relating to children's rights.[15] Different courts and legislatures have been willing to give some new rights to children, while denying them others, without explaining the difference in outcome.[16]

The absence of a coherent theory is not surprising. The status of children in society raises extremely perplexing issues. The demand for children's rights calls into question basic beliefs of our society. Implementation of many of the rights being claimed for children could involve substantially altering the role of the state towards parents and children and the role of parents towards children. Most legal and social policy is based on the beliefs that children lack the capacity to make decisions on their own and that parental control of children is needed to support a stable family system, which is crucial to the well-being of society.[17] These views are widely held and, at least for young children, seem intuitively correct.[18] On the other hand, our society is unwilling to treat children merely as the property of adults. Given our commitment to individual liberty, there needs to be substantial reason for treating any class of individuals in a special way. Therefore, it is necessary to examine closely the claims of children's rights advocates in order to see whether the existing legal structure should be altered.

This article does not attempt to delineate what specific rights, if any, children should be given. Instead, it tries to provide a framework for analyzing the concept of "children's rights" and to isolate some of the issues that must be resolved in order to make sound policy decisions.[19] In order to assess the need

---

13 Goldstein, *supra*, n. 1, at 645.

14 See, e.g., Hafen, *supra*, n. 1.

15 For example, many states allow minors the right to abortion without parental permission or guidance, while others demand such permission. For a summary of various state laws relating to children's rights, see A. Sussman, *The Rights of Young People* (1977).

16 See Sussman, *ibid.*, for a comparison of which rights each state gives to, and denies, children. Compare *Bellotti v. Baird*, 428 U.S. 132 (1976), with *Ingraham v. Wright*, 430 U.S. 651 (1977).

17 Statements about the importance of family are commonplace in judicial opinions regarding family or children's rights: see, e.g., *Wisconsin v. Yoder*, 406 U.S. 205 (1972). However, the reasons our family structure is critical to the well-being of the state are rarely articulated.

18 These intuitive views are supported by child development research: see nn. 71-76, *infra*.

19 The article addresses policy decisions at both the legislative and judicial level. Although much of the activity concerning children's rights has focused on the courts, it may well be that legislative, rather than judicial, resolution is more appropriate for many issues.

for further extension of children's rights, it is first necessary to separate the various types of claims being made on behalf of children. By lumping a wide range of claims under the heading "children's rights", proponents of expanded rights broaden their appeal while masking significant differences in the desirability or undesirability of granting specific rights to children.[20] In addition, assuming that children should have some additional rights, the means of achieving and enforcing various rights depends on the type of "right" being advocated.[21]

I CATEGORIES OF RIGHTS

There are four different types of claims under the general rubric of children's rights. While there is some overlap among the categories, each has special characteristics relevant to analyzing whether children should be given such rights. The categories are: (1) generalized claims against the world, for example, the right of freedom from discrimination and poverty; (2) the right to greater protection from abuse, neglect or exploitation by adults; (3) the right to be treated in the same manner as an adult, with the same constitutional protections, in relationship to state actions; (4) the right to act independently of parental control and/or guidance.

1. Rights Against the World

The first category, claims for rights such as the right to freedom from poverty, to adequate health care, to adequate housing and to a safe community are frequently found in proposed "Children's Bills of Rights".[22] In many respects, these types of claims are the most important "rights" that could be given to children. They lie at the heart of a child's well-being. It is now well established that factors such as nutrition and medical care can greatly affect a child's physical and mental development from the time of conception onward.[23]

---

20 Many advocates do lump the classes together, without distinction. See Soman, *supra*, n. 10.

21 Means of enforcement are of particular concern to lawyers, who think in terms of legal remedies. Many non-lawyer proponents of children's rights have not given much thought to implementation. See, e.g., Soman, *supra*, n. 10. The failure to think about implementation is not limited to non-lawyers, however. See Foster, *A Bill of Rights for Children* (1974).

22 This type of protection can be thought of as "welfare" or "positive" rights. See Michelman, "In Pursuit of Constitutional Welfare Rights: One View of Rawls' Theory of Justice" (1973), 121 U.Pa.L. Rev. 962, 966, 997.

23 See generally K. Keniston, *All Our Children* (1977); U.S. Dept. of Health, Education & Welfare, E. Grotberg (ed.), *200 Years of Children* (1977), chapters 2 and 3. This does not mean that nutrition or medical care are dispositive, just that they can have a big influence. Children are quite resilient and often can overcome deficits: see Werner, Bierman and French, *Kauai's Children Come of Age* (1977).

In addition, poverty, neighbourhood conditions and discrimination seem to contribute to delinquency, school and mental health problems.[24] To the extent that children are denied equal access to adequate nutrition, housing, medical care and schooling, they may be effectively denied equal opportunity in our society. In a society committed to both equal opportunity and individualism, the moral force of such claims is very great.

On the other hand, these claims are not of great significance in terms of reordering the legal and social status of children. First, the rights in this category are not meant to benefit only children, they are not claims for legal rights now given adults but denied children. These are rights that would and should benefit all people if they were available to children.[25]

Moreover, making the world a better place for children will not alter the status of children in the manner Holt, Farson or the numerous lawsuits attempting to establish legal rights for children seek. Providing children with adequate income or health care does not entail giving them more autonomy or self-determination — quite the opposite. Demands for such rights recognize that children cannot provide for themselves and need the care and guidance of adults. Thus, these claims might be better thought of as protections due, rather than rights of, children.[26]

In fact these claims generally are not for things traditionally thought of as legal "rights", that is, entitlements enforceable by court order. Courts cannot order that the world be free of poverty or that all children have adequate health care.[27] Only the legislative process can provide all children with these goods and it cannot guarantee a "right" to them.

Properly classifying these "rights" as protections tells us where to focus claims and how to defend them. Because the claims are basically moral and social goals, they should be addressed to legislatures, not courts. The debate

---

24 We do not know the "causes" of these problems, but there is a high correlation between the factors enumerated and these problems. Other factors are certainly important as well: see Pierce, "Poverty and Racism as they Affect Children" and Berlin, "It Can be Done: Aspects of Delinquency, Treatment and Prevention" in I. Berlin (ed.), *Advocacy for Child Mental Health* (1975).

25 Some of these "rights" could be given solely to children, through special medical programs, school breakfast and lunches, etc. It may be that children should have a special claim to such goods since they are more dependent than adults, and perhaps more likely to be affected by deprivations. They are also a more politically appealing group for redistribution purposes. However, by not giving adults such goods as well, we impair their ability to care for their children.

26 See Geiser, "The Rights of Children" (1977), 28 Hastings L.J. 1027 at 1039-44.

27 Courts can given children some such rights, especially if there is any legislative basis: see Michelman, *supra*, n. 22, at 991-97 and 1003-1015.

should centre on defining the obligations society has towards both adults and children, not on questions of the status of children and parents or on the capacity of children for independent decision making.

2. Protection from Inadequate Care

The second category of rights encompasses claims that the state should more actively protect children from harm by adults, especially their parents. Over the past 15 years, concern over child abuse, plus increased evidence that early child rearing can affect a child's school readiness and performance, has led many commentators to advocate, in the name of children's rights, increased state monitoring of the adequacy of the parental care.[28] In general, these commentators have argued for broadening the definition of child neglect, in order to ensure that parents rear their children properly. The most expansive definition would include "any act of commission or omission by individuals, institutions, or society as a whole . . . which deprive children of equal rights and liberties, and/or interfere with their optimal development".[29]

In many respects, this category of "rights" is closely analogous to the category of general rights just discussed.[30] The need for more "rights" is based on the premise that children lack the capacity to care for themselves and therefore need adult protection, care and guidance. Our society, as most societies, has given the power and duty to rear children primarily to their parents.[31] The power is great, although it has never been without limits. Because society assumes that children cannot raise themselves, that the type of rearing they receive will affect their life chances, and that children, as individual human beings, are not merely chattels subject to total parental control, all states have established some minimal standards for parental conduct[32] and have assumed some child rearing activities, most notably schooling.[33] Those advocating more

---

28 These trends and the issues they raise are discussed in Wald, "State Intervention on Behalf of 'Neglected' Children: A Search for Realistic Standards" (1975), 27 Stan. L. Rev. 985.

29 D. Gil, *Violence Against Children*, 3d ed. (1973), at 202. Insofar as definitions like Gil's apply to "society as a whole" they are addressing category one as well as category two "rights".

30 The rights in both groups are designed to ensure that children receive adequate care from adults until such time as they can care for themselves. The distinction lies in the fact that the first category requires the state to directly provide goods to the child to ensure the child a given quality of life, while the second category only requires the state to monitor whether adults, especially parents, are actually harming children.

31 A few countries or cultures have adopted more communal child rearing methods, such as the kibbutz in Israel. While the relative role of state and parent must be addressed in deciding how to cope with child abuse, it is unlikely that the U.S. will move in any significant way towards communal child rearing, although some subgroups in society may do so.

32 See Wald, *supra*, n. 28.

33 Given our society's commitment to parental freedom, the state has not assumed total control of

rights for children would require a higher level of minimum parental care than current standards require,[34] just as they would require the state to provide a higher level of state services to children and help to parents through expansion of the rights included in category one.

Again, however, claims in this area are of a very different nature than the assertion that children should have more autonomy or independence. They do not change the status of children. The intervention advocated entails substituting one adult decision-maker for another, rather than giving children the choice of deciding whether they like the conditions in which they find themselves. Generally, it is adults, not children, who invoke the protection process.[35]

In fact, children's views often are disregarded when giving them more protection.[36] Thus, if parents allowed their children to appear in pornographic movies, few children's rights advocates, let alone legislators or the general public, would allow the situation to continue, even if the child said, "I'm enjoying myself and making good money. Leave me alone." They would "protect" children in spite of their "rights" or "autonomy". Neither do we ask physically abused children whether they want to remain with their parents if we cannot protect them from further physical harm. We assume that children in these situations are not capable of protecting their own long-range interests.

In addition to protection from parental abuse or inadequate care, a number of other claims for increased protection of children come within this category of "rights". For example, those adults who advocate, in the name of children's rights, putting controls on television violence or on the quality of children's food are not asking whether children like violent programs or enjoy eating Captain Crunch Chocolate Flakes; they are asserting that such fare is not in a child's

---

schooling. Although all parents must ensure that their children receive a certain amount and type of education, they can do so in schools of the parents' choice, if they are able to pay for them. Some parents may even be able to limit the amount, as well as influence, of education: see *Wisconsin v. Yoder*, 406 U.S. 205 (1972) (Amish parents can end their children's formal schooling at eighth grade).

34 One group of children's rights cases has focused on the adequacy of care given to children under state care: see, e.g., *N.Y. State Assn. for Retarded Children, Inc. v. Rockefeller*, 357 F. Supp. 752 (N.Y. Dist. Ct., 1973). Conceptually these are not a separate class of rights; instead they can be seen as an extension of abuse and neglect laws to the state when it assumes guardianship of a child. The key issue is the level of such care. The greater resources available to the state make it appropriate to demand a higher level of care than we demand of parents.

35 Older children do sometimes initiate abuse proceedings.

36 Courts often solicit older children's views in abuse or neglect proceedings. Young children usually are not consulted. Even when children have lawyers to represent them, the lawyers frequently see their role as deciding what is best for the child, not advocating the child's position: see Areen and Mlyniec "Representing Juveniles In Neglect, PINS, and Delinquency Cases", in District of Columbia Bar Association, *District of Columbia* (1975).

interest, regardless of the child's views.[37] At least in my family, my children would consider this a significant interference with their rights. Implementation of such controls would actually reduce, rather than increase, the rights of choice many children now have.

Thus, these claims, like those in category one, are appropriately viewed as protections, not rights. Because the protections in this category are more specific and generally focus on whether parents are harming a child, the claims are more easily subject to judicial, as well as legislative, resolution.[38] The critical questions for debate should centre on the appropriate role of parents and the state in child rearing.[39] It is necessary to decide what level of adult care is essential for children and how this can be best provided. This is an issue that divides "children's rights" advocates, since some people who work with children believe that less, rather than more, state interference is the way to best protect children.[40] It must also be decided what role the child should have in defining an acceptable environment.[41]

---

37 Opponents of regulation of commercials or cereal makers usually are defending parents' rights, not children's. They argue that control of television watching and food buying should be in the hands of parents, not government.

38 Social work agencies and courts are responsible for protecting children from inadequate parental care. They are expected to apply specific standards in evaluating the adequacy of parental care. Through the use of services to the parents or foster care, these agencies are supposed to ensure that children receive adequate care.

39 See Wald, *supra*, n. 28, for a discussion of the various issues that must be considered in this debate.

40 Compare, e.g., Bourne and Newberger, "Family Autonomy or Coercive Intervention? Ambiguity and Conflict in the Proposed Standards for Child Abuse and Neglect" (1977), 57 B. U. L. Rev. 670, and Wald, *supra*, n. 28.

41 The question of the role of the child in defining abuse or neglect is a very troublesome one. The problem can arise even in cases where society in general believes the parent to be abusive, such as in cases of incest. The child may not view the relationship as harmful. How much weight should be given the child's views? Protectionists would protect; it is not clear what liberators would say.

Even more difficult are instances where older children want to leave their home because of parent-child conflict or because they find the home a difficult place to live. Home environments can be bad for children without falling into the abuse or neglect range. If the child is able to earn a living and is willing to be independent, emancipation is possible. However, emancipation is unrealistic for most people under 18, since they are unemployable. It must then be asked whether the state would provide them with state supported alternative living arrangements.

When the home situation does not amount to abuse or neglect but the child finds the situation intolerable, the policy questions involve category four disputes, i.e., parent-child conflicts.

It may be difficult to draw the line between neglect and family conflict in many instances. Thus, the two categories overlap.

While there has been some increase in the past few years in the "rights" afforded children with regard to state services and parental care — or more accurately put, there has been some effort to better protect children's interests — implementation of these rights has not affected the status of children in society. If these claims were the full extent of the children's rights movement, the debate over children's rights would be relatively limited. Since 1967, however, the children's rights movement has focused on two other categories of rights. These categories — the right of children of certain ages to be treated similarly to adults with regard to constitutional claims, and the right to act independently of parents — raise fundamental issues regarding the role assigned to children in our society.

3. Adult Legal Status

The third category of rights, that is, the right of children to fuller adult legal status in terms of state policies, has been the focus of the greatest amount of legislative and judicial activity. Historically, age alone has been accepted as a sufficient basis for withholding certain privileges from children.[42] Among the adult rights they lack are the rights to vote, marry, drive, drink alcoholic beverages, work, express themselves and read what they please. Children are subject to compulsory education, a form of coercion that would be unconstitutional if attempted with adults. In addition, children have been denied due process protections in proceedings where adults would be entitled to such protections.[43] The special treatment of children has been justified on the basis of the minor's incapacity or lack of maturity or because of special protections children purportedly receive.[44]

Beginning with the U.S. Supreme Court decision in *In re Gault*,[45] which provided due process procedural protections to minors charged with crimes in a juvenile court, the right of minors to adult legal status or protections has gradually increased. For example, the U.S. Supreme Court has ruled that children have a right to some due process protections before being expelled from school[46] and that school children are entitled to some first amendment free-

---

42 Throughout this chapter I use the term children rather than minors. The term obviously lumps a disparate group. While it may be reasonable to lump all persons falling below the age of majority for purposes of providing children protection, issues of autonomy generally involve older children, primarily adolescents. In fact, the term "minors" is often used in discussing the type of issues raised in categories three and four. The semantic difference may reflect real differences in how we perceive young people depending on the issue under consideration.

43 For example, children do not enjoy full adult rights in proceedings which deprive them of liberty, such as juvenile delinquency or civil commitment proceedings.

44 See Ryerson, *The Best Laid Plans* (1978).

45 387 U.S. 1 (1967).

46 *Goss v. Lopez*, 419 U.S. 565 (1975).

doms, such as the right to wear armbands or distribute literature.[47] Among the legislative reforms are new juvenile court codes which give children rights similar to adults in delinquency and school expulsion proceedings.

In granting children these rights, the courts and legislatures have not arrived at any consistent theory of why they should grant children some rights and not others. In many instances the courts also have stopped short of placing the minor on equal footing with an adult in the same situation. For example, children still do not have full adult rights in delinquency proceedings and may be subjected to corporal punishment at school.[48]

It is in this area that children's rights advocates make their strongest claim. The special treatment of children rests on assumptions about their incapacity to act in an "adult" manner or on the necessity to protect them from factors that might impair their growing into autonomous, productive citizens. To the extent that the assumptions of incapacity are invalid or that changes in our social structure and in the rate of development of adolescents call into question constraints placed on children, these constraints should be eliminated.[49]

Such an action has already taken place, on an immense scale, by the lowering of the age of majority from 21 to 18 in most states. In so doing, the legislatures determined that people at 18 have the capacity to exercise all rights of citizenship and/or do not need the special protections given younger people.[50] Eighteen, however, should not be a magic age. Various states already use widely disparate standards in granting rights to children at different ages. For example, the minimum age for marriage ranges from 14 to 21; for driving the age range varies from 13 to 17.[51] Similar disparities exist in other areas such as contract law, work laws and compulsory schooling ages.[52] Different conditions among the states may, in some instances, justify disparities. For example, it may

---

47 *Tinker v. Des Moines Sch. Dist.*, 393 U.S. 503 (1969).

48 *Ingraham v. Wright*, 430 U.S. 651 (1977).

49 Children now reach puberty earlier than in the past: see Tanner, "Physical Growth", in P. Mussen (ed.), *Manual of Child Psychology* (1970), vol. 1, at 146-47. Children are exposed to television which may provide them with more information (and misinformation) than they have had in past times. On the other hand, people started full-time work much earlier in the past, which may have prepared (entitled?) them for adult roles earlier. There is virtually no literature describing the capacities of children at different times in history. But see P. Aries, *Centuries of Childhood* (1962).

    The rationale for given restrictions can also change: see, e.g., the discussion of child labour laws in R. Mnookin, *Child, Family, State* (1978), at 646-67.

50 Not all legislatures have lowered the age of majority and some "rights", such as the right to drink alcoholic beverages, still may be withheld even after a person reaches the age of majority. See Sussman, *The Rights of Young People* (1977), at 220-23.

51 Sussman, *ibid.*, at 229-30.

52 *Ibid.*, at 245-46.

be that younger people can drive more safely in primarily rural states. In many instances, however, states have adopted age constraints arbitrarily without any basis in developmental or sociological differences.

The question of age discrimination should be examined from both a constitutional and a legislative perspective. At the constitutional level, the basic question is whether a given discrimination based on age is rationally related to differences in the capacities of people under a certain age or to the special needs of children.[53] In deciding this question the courts must also determine whether age is a "suspect classification", which would require states to meet a high burden of proof in order to justify differential treatment of children.[54]

In determining the rationality of a given restriction, it must be recognized that any given age will be arbitrary to some degree. People mature at different times so that not all 13-year-olds are the same. The difficulty of making decisions on a case-by-case basis may justify selection of some age as a cut-off point for granting specific rights.[55] However, the courts should determine both whether any age restriction is necessary in order to achieve a legitimate state interest and whether the specific classification chosen is reasonable in light of existing data of the capacities of children at different ages.[56] Since most restrictions were enacted years ago, the courts should determine whether their rationales remain valid.[57]

Depending on the standard of review employed by the courts, a number of present restrictions may be unconstitutional. Courts have already invalidated many restrictions. For example, courts have struck down school regulations limiting speech by students, as well as school hair and dress codes. Other decisions provide children with the right to counsel and other constitutional protections when the state is seeking to deprive them of liberty, and the right of

---

53 *Ibid.*, at 220-46.

54 Advocates of total liberation argue that no age related disabilities are rational: see Farson, *Birthrights* (1974) and Foster, *A Bill of Rights for Children* (1974). However, the evidence from developmental psychology belies their assertions: see n. 59 and accompanying text, *infra*. While it is therefore tempting to dismiss their claims outright, this should not be done. Instead, their claims should be treated as a challenge to prove the basis for existing restrictions and to abandon those that do not withstand scrutiny.

55 A specific cut-off age, even if somewhat arbitrary, may be preferable to a system which requires case-by-case determination of "maturity" or "capacity". Case-by-case determination is only viable if there are objective ways to measure capacity. Otherwise there is too great a possibility of discrimination. Case-by-case determination can also be very costly.

56 For a discussion of some of the constitutional law considerations, see Garvey, "Child, Parent, State, and the Due Process Clause: An Essay on the Supreme Court's Recent Work" (1978), 51 S.C.L. Rev. 769.

57 See n. 49, *supra*.

access to contraceptive devices and to abortions.[58] The rationality of the present age limits on the exercise of other rights, such as the right to contract, marry, or vote, also may not withstand judicial scrutiny.

Legislative re-evaluation of existing restrictions is also needed. Such review should extend into areas that may be outside the realm of judicial review. Given society's commitment to equality under law, legislatures should examine closely the accuracy of prevailing assumptions about the capacities of children and should analyze the skills needed for specific rights, for example, voting, marrying or reading "obscene" literature. It should be determined whether existing age limits continue to make sense (if they ever did) in light of changes in children's development and our social structure. Only through such an analysis can the claim of Holt, Farson and other children's liberators be confidently rejected or accepted.

Such a review is not likely to totally eliminate the incapacities of childhood. Many restrictions are undoubtedly sound. Children are not adults in their mental abilities, judgment, or work capacity.[59] Adequate preparation for participation in society may require a period of forced learning. This does not mean, however, that existing age limits are sensible. While the reasons for disenfranchising a 1-year-old are clear, the justification is less obvious with regard to 16-year-olds.[60] Upon analysis, a legislature may conclude that a different age limit is appropriate in some areas and that age restrictions should be abandoned and new criteria adopted in other areas.[61]

For some rights it may be sensible to give control to parents, rather than to the state. Many states already make some rights contingent upon parental approval, for example the right of children to marry. Requiring parental guidance or approval can alleviate concerns about a child's capacity to make wise decisions.[62]

---

58 See the cases cited in n. 1, *supra.*

59 Most researchers interested in child development have not examined the capacities of children to make decisions with regard to such activities as voting, marrying, driving or reading "obscene" material. A thorough review of the literature on adolescent decision making is found in C. Lewis, "Three Studies of Adolescent Decision-Making", unpublished Ph.D. dissertation. Stanford University (1979).

Of course, criteria for "good" decision making in these areas must be established before we can examine whether children of various ages are capable of making "good" decisions.

60 See Schrag, "The Child's Status in the Democratic State" (1975), 3 Political Theory 441, for an analysis of the capacities required for voting.

61 This analysis should be on a "right"-by- "right" basis.

62 The fact of parent-child unity in asserting a claim for rights is significant since in such situations family privacy and autonomy is being preserved. Deference to parents is especially justified in cases where the "right" is denied on the theory that it is good for the child (e.g., limits on access to contraceptives), as opposed to cases where the right is denied for the good of society

In deciding whether to give children more rights, it also must be recognized that the notions of rights and responsibilities are closely related. There is currently a growing movement to hold children more responsible for their criminal actions.[63] If children are to be held responsible for their acts, perhaps they should be given rights commensurate with their responsibilities. On the other hand, those arguing for additional rights must decide whether they are willing to accept the imposition of responsibility on children as well.

4. Rights Versus Parents

Perhaps the most controversial and the most complex questions make up the fourth category of claimed rights, that is, the right of children to act independently of their parents prior to emancipation.[64] It is one thing to argue, for example, that a school, without compelling reasons, should not be able to dictate to children and their parents the length of children's hair. It is quite another to argue that children who want long hair should have a right, enforceable by court order, not to cut their hair if their parents want it cut.[65]

In order to develop a framework for analyzing claims in this category, it is useful to examine the types of claims currently being asserted. Again, the extreme view asserts that all children, of any age, should be free to make their own decisions, ranging from what to eat and when to go to bed to whether to have an operation. Fortunately, most court cases have involved issues of greater

---

(driving? voting?). The U.S. Supreme Court seems to have indicated that in some areas state limitations are unreasonable but parental control may be acceptable: see *Carey v. Population Services, Int.*, 431 U.S. 678 (1977).

   Legislatures have made the same decision with regard to some rights, e.g., marriage. Children under a certain age are allowed to exercise these rights only with parental permission.

   However, some rights might be the minors' regardless of parental views, e.g., the right to counsel in delinquency proceedings.

63 See IJA-ABA, *Juvenile Justice Standards Project, Standards Relating to Dispositional Procedures*, tentative draft (1977).

64 The issue of emancipation involves both category three and four rights. By selecting an age of majority each legislature determines the general age of emancipation. However, it may be that certain children are ready for emancipation, i.e., freedom from parental control prior to the general age of majority. Such freedom, however, may not be accompanied by full adult status, e.g., emancipation does not entitle the minor to vote. Emancipation may even be partial, i.e., for specific rights, such as access to medical care.

   In deciding whether to allow case-by-case emancipation, the legislature must formulate standards for determining that a minor is ready to be emancipated and decide what institution should make the determination. It must also decide whether emancipation only involves freedom from parental control or should entail complete adult status.

65 The question of rights versus parents has been an especially troublesome and divisive issue among people concerned with children's rights: see Uviller, "Children Versus Parents: Perplexing Policy Questions for the ACLU" in O. O'Neill and W. Ruddick (eds.), *Having Children* (1979), at 214.

magnitude than bedtime. The major questions centre on whether a parent should be able to control the medical care a child receives, including whether a child should have an abortion, whether the parent should be able to determine what school the child attends, the material the child reads or views, and the place where a child shall live.

Historically, all such decisions were within the parents' domain, unless a given decision endangered the child in a manner covered by abuse and neglect laws. Recently, however, courts and legislatures have altered the extent of parental control. For example, a number of legislatures have granted children the right to get medical care, especially care related to pregnancy or contraception, without parental permission or knowledge.[66]

The expansion of rights can take several different forms. The right to act independently can be given solely to the child or the child may be required to seek approval for his or her action, or to challenge the parental decision, in a court or other agency. For example, some states have given a child the right to have an abortion, whenever the child wants, without parental consent or even knowledge. Other states do not leave the final decision to the child. Instead, the child may petition a court to order the abortion in cases of parent-child dispute. In other instances, children must inform their parents of given actions, even if the children have the ultimate decision.

Thus, if decision-making authority is removed from the realm of parental discretion, it must be decided who will be given the authority — the child or an adult other than the parents. In determining whether to remove the decision-making authority from the parents, five factors must be considered: (a) whether the child can make such decisions adequately; (b) if not, whether other decision makers, or decision-making processes, are likely to arrive at better decisions than the parents; (c) whether the state can really remove the decision-making power from the parents; (d) the costs of removing the decision from the parents in terms of family autonomy and family privacy (both valued goals in our society); and (e) the cost of *not* giving the decision to the child. For some specific issues, it also must be considered whether there are parental interests, such as in being able to visit a child not in one's custody, which may equal or exceed the child's interest in autonomy. In addition, if the decision is given solely to the child, it must be decided whether the parents should be informed of the child's actions.

Analyzing claims from this perspective, it is apparent that it is unrealistic to treat certain claimed rights, designed to give children autonomy, as legally enforceable rights. Children, as members of family units, cannot enjoy total autonomy over their lives, even if they are capable of making all decisions.

---

66 See Sussman, *The Rights of Young People* (1977), at 24-38.

While a legislature could declare that children, while living with their parents, have the right to decide when to go to bed, when to bathe and what to eat, it would not be realistic to expect such a declaration to have operative consequences. Allowing courts to enforce such rights would be enormously costly, and not very effective. It would be a waste of resources for courts to hear such disputes. Moreover, it would be very difficult to enforce such orders. For example, if a parent orders a child to bed and the child refuses, can a court order the parent to let the child stay up? If the parents do not follow the court order, will they be sent to jail? Will the parents be forbidden from enforcing their request by cutting off allowance, setting a curfew, not buying Christmas presents, or giving the child a spanking? With regard to these decisions, Farson's concept of total independence is just unrealistic unless we are prepared to place an outside monitor in every home to eliminate the authority parents have stemming from their greater strength and economic power.[67]

Of course, analysis need not stop at this level. One could ask whether children are capable of making such decisions without harming themselves. Clearly infants cannot. We know little about how older children would make such decisions. As a practical matter most older children probably enjoy substantial autonomy in many such areas, anyway. The impact of total autonomy on parental willingness to provide and sacrifice for children might also be explored. But such analysis seems unnecessary in light of the practical reasons militating against giving children total autonomy in these areas. Debate over such issues can be left in the philosophical or rhetorical arenas.

Most children's rights advocates do not go as far as Farson or Holt, of course. Instead of focusing on minor decisions like bedtime or clothing, they argue that some types of decisions, such as whether to have an abortion, receive drug, alcohol or medical care, go to a certain school or participate in religious exercises, use contraceptives, or enter a mental hospital, either should be entirely in the hands of the child or, at least, be subject to the ultimate control of a court, rather than the parents.[68]

---

67 Giving children such rights might have substantial symbolic value. Husbands and wives each can act independently in such matters but they could not enforce these "rights" in a court. Adults either use power or negotiation to do what they want or to get a divorce. While some people advocate allowing children to divorce their parents, see "Expert Proposes Child 'Divorce' of Parents", *Los Angeles Times*, 17th November 1978, Pt. 1-B, at 7, this is unrealistic unless the child can be independent. It is not very likely that a large number of children can be so.

   The symbolic value may be important if we want to alter family power relationships. Of course, many children are able to obtain such rights from their parents without legal backing. Parents may go along willingly or grudgingly. It is probably best to leave the internal workings of families to "power politics" and reserve state action for only very serious situations.

68 The ability to exercise category three "rights", e.g., voting, driving, counselling, also falls into this more significant area of rights.

There are a number of good reasons for giving children additional rights in these areas. First, such rights are most likely to be exercised by older children, who have the greatest claim to individual autonomy. Moreover, failure to give children certain rights might be harmful to them. For example, parents may place a child in a mental hospital because they do not like his or her behaviour or they may refuse to allow a daughter to receive an abortion although she may be psychologically damaged by bearing the child. Similarly, requiring parental involvement in some of these decisions may lead some children to forego actions that would benefit them. For example, teenagers who have a drug or alcohol problem or who are sexually active may refuse to seek out counselling or contraceptive information if their parents must learn of their actions.[69]

Giving children the right to make such decisions does not entail the same problems as giving them the right to decide on bedtime or bathing. It would not involve courts in the minutia of day-to-day living decisions. Some rights, for example the right to receive certain medical care, if given exclusively to the child, could be exercised without parental knowledge. Monitoring of a limited class of conflicts, for example, conflicts over civil commitment, would not place undue burdens on the courts or other agencies and generally would not require on-going involvement with the family.[70]

However, there are many countervailing considerations. Before giving children a specific right it is necessary to determine whether children are likely to have the capacity to make the decision for themselves. For example, do we believe that a child of a given age (or maturity level, if we can develop a means of determining maturity levels) is capable of deciding whether to have an operation (including abortions), to go to one school rather than another, or to use contraceptives? To analyze this question we must determine what types of skills a person needs to make a given decision and to what degree children of any given age possess the requisite abilities.

The exploration of these questions should begin with the research regarding the intellectual, social and moral development of children.[71] This research

---

69 It is unclear whether teenagers are, in fact, discouraged by parental consent requirements: see Torres, "Does Your Mother Know. . . .?" (1978), 10 Fam. Planning Perspectives 280.

70 Spelling out children's rights in the medical or contract area may be extremely important in terms of giving guidance to third parties, such as doctors or merchants, who deal with children. Their actions often are constrained due to the uncertain legal status of children: see IJA-ABA, *Juvenile Justice Standards Project, Standards Relating to Rights of Minors*, tentative draft (1977), at 1-6, 50-85 and 104-119.

71 This research is summarized in Lewis, *supra*, n. 59. Among the major works are W. Damon, *The Social World of the Child* (1977); J. Conger (ed.), *Contemporary Issues in Adolescent Development* (1975); J. Conger, *Adolescent and Youth: Psychological Development in a Changing World* (1973); E. Douvan and J. Adelson, *The Adolescent Experience* (1966); E. Erikson, *Childhood and Society* (1963); J. Piaget, *The Moral Judgment of the Child* (1932); L. Kohlberg and E. Turiel (eds.), *Moralization, The Cognitive Development Approach* (1973).

documents, contrary to the assertions of total liberators, that younger children, generally those under 10-12 years old, do lack the cognitive abilities and judgmental skills necessary to make decisions about major events which could severely affect their lives.[72] These limitations are developmental, not just a result of more limited experience or social expertise. Younger children are not able to think abstractly, have a limited future time sense, and are limited in their ability to generalize and predict from experience.

The research regarding older children is more limited and therefore offers less guidance for legislation. In both moral and cognitive development, many people seem to reach adult levels between 12 and 14.[73] However, there is little evidence regarding adolescents' decision-making capacity with regard to issues such as abortion, use of medical care, or choice of education.[74] It does appear that the ability to reason improves throughout adolescence. This may reflect greater social experience, but there may be biological reasons as well.[75]

Some researchers and clinicians assert that the decision-making capabilities of adolescents are limited in other ways. It is argued that adolescents must struggle with both dependence and independence needs which may cause an adolescent to act in a way which meets some immediate psychological needs, but which may be adverse to long-term interests, as the child would define those interests.[76] For example, a 12-year-old may wish to keep a baby in order to feel more "grown-up" or to compensate for rejection by parents or peers, without any realistic assessment of her capabilities at child rearing or the impact that having a child would have on her development. Similarly, teenagers may resist necessary psychiatric treatment because they feel it is an imposition of adult values.

Clinicians also claim that adolescents benefit from having parental restraints available. Such restraints allow adolescents to challenge authority and to explore new areas with the realization that "wise" parents will stop them if they act in harmful ways.[77] While parents often do not act wisely, removing the

---

72 See, e.g., Damon, *ibid.*

73 See Piaget, *supra*, n. 71, and Kohlberg and Turiel, *supra*, n. 71. With regard to some types of moral development the age may be much earlier: see Darley, Klosson and Zanna, "Intentions and Their Contexts in the Moral Judgments of Children and Adults" (1978), 49 Child Dev. 66.

74 Lewis, *supra*, n. 59, in her dissertation, interviewed pregnant girls aged 13 to 18 who were faced with the decision whether to have the child. She found that older girls did tend to consider a larger number of factors and consult more people but no clear-cut decision-making differences emerged along age lines.

75 It may well be that children's problem solving capacities reflect the limited role they are given in society and that if they were given more responsibility they would have the ability to make sound decisions: see Skolnick, "The Limits of Childhood: Conceptions of Child Development and Social Context" (Summer 1975), L. & Contemp. Prob., at 66.

76 See D. Elkind, *Children and Adolescents: Interpretive Essays on Jean Piaget* (1970), at 101.

77 These views have been expressed to me in conversations with a number of mental health

authority structure may be more detrimental than unwise parental actions.

This brief summary is not meant to be exhaustive. Moreover, it is unlikely that developmental psychology can provide any firm conclusions about adolescent decision making at this time. However, in deciding whether to give adolescents more autonomy, it is necessary to utilize the best existing data and to assess the likely costs of giving adolescents greater autonomy.

Even if adolescents could make some (or all) decisions without harming themselves significantly, we still might not give autonomy to children because of its disruption of the family system.[78] The loss of family harmony and the potential destruction of family autonomy are major concerns of those opposed to more children's rights in the family context.

These concerns need careful scrutiny, however. Opponents of children's rights fail to explain how giving children some autonomy to make major decisions threatens our family system.[79] As discussed below, the family system may be threatened if courts are given authority to intervene in cases of family disputes.[80] However, if the ultimate authority to decide on an abortion, on other medical care, on schooling[81] or on religion resides in the child, no outside intervention is necessary. Family privacy remains.

What is the threat to the family then? Giving children decision-making power could generate family conflict, thereby worsening the situation for all family members. Since "divorce" by either side often is impossible or undesirable,[82] such conflict can continue for long periods or may lead to the child's

---

professionals.

    Even when autonomy is presumably given directly to the child, the effect may be to turn the decision over to an adult, such as a lawyer, doctor or counsellor. Young children, and even adolescents, often have great difficulty acting independently. In many cases where I have represented children, my clients wanted me to make the decisions for them. Unlike adult clients, children rarely tell you what they want. Instead, they ask "What should I do?" In fact, decision-making authority may be extremely traumatic for children.

78 Home and family disruption are not the only concerns. Children are unable to utilize some rights because they lack money. For example, the right to medical care is only valuable if it is provided free or for the limited number of children with income.

79 The impact of the law on changing social attitudes and customs is highly debatable. The law generally follows changes in values rather than generates them. All discussions about the impact on our family system are highly speculative and no data are presented documenting changes caused by the recent grants of autonomy to children.

80 See nn. 100-101 and accompanying text, *infra*.

81 Choice of school could become a major issue if proposals to use school vouchers in lieu of compulsory attendance at a given school are adopted. School vouchers could be used to buy a variety of kinds of education. It would then have to be decided who has the right to use the voucher — parent or child: see J. Coons and S. Sugarman, *Education By Choice: The Case for Parental Control* (1978).

82 Divorce, by emancipation, is impossible because most children do not have the resources, and

running away. On the other hand, children who are resentful of parental decision making may also generate family conflict.

Parental retaliation is also possible. We cannot prevent parents from cutting allowances, setting curfews, and so on, as a means of enforcing their authority even if the child has the legal right to autonomy. This may be a cost children are willing to pay for exercising autonomy, especially since parents already exercise such powers, and children have no legal redress.

Perhaps the most legitimate concern is that if parents lose ultimate authority they will be less willing to assume responsibility for the child. Among the major reasons for supporting family-based child rearing, is the substantial evidence that children thrive best in an environment where a small number of adults, strongly committed to their well-being, nurture and guide them.[83] Among the commitments of parenthood is the willingness to put the child's well-being ahead of the parents'. There is evidence that an increasing number of parents feel unwilling or unable to make this commitment.[84] For example, in a recent survey of American families a large number of parents expressed the belief that parents should not sacrifice in order to give their children the "best".[85] Many of these parents expressed doubts about their capability of controlling or guiding their children.[86] If such commitment is deemed important, it must be determined whether giving children more autonomy will affect adults' willingness to assume parent functions.[87] It must be recognized, how-

---

ability, to live independently. This would still be true even if we eliminated child labour laws, since most children do not have marketable skills.

"Divorce" would only be feasible if the state were willing to assume care of children or if the state compelled parents to pay for their children to live elsewhere. Historically laws dealing with "status" offenders, i.e., children beyond the control of their parents, did allow parents to divorce their children by turning them over to the state. This approach is now being widely rejected: see IJA-ABA, *Juvenile Justice Standards Project, Standards Relating to Noncriminal Behavior*, tentative draft (1977).

Whether the state should provide alternative living situations for children who cannot get along with their parents is an extremely troubling problem. There is no problem, however, if both the parent and child agree to an alternative living situation and are willing to pay for it.

Even if children were allowed to divorce their parents prior to emancipation, they would still have to remain under adult supervision until they were capable of living on their own and supporting themselves.

83 See J. Goldstein, A. Freud and A. Solnit, *Beyond the Best Interests of the Child* (1973), at 9-52 (hereinafter cited as Goldstein, Freud and Solnit).

84 "Raising Children in a Changing Society" in *General Mills American Family Report, 1976-77* (1977).

85 *Ibid.*, at 10.

86 *Ibid.*, at 16.

87 Traditionally families have played a central role as a stabilizing and socializing force in our society. This role is said to be critical to the development of the child. While the "decline of the family" has been blamed for many of society's ills, there is little research supporting such

ever, that the legal system and the granting or withholding of legal rights may have little to do with how parents view their role. Other forces in society are likely to be far more important.[88]

Finally, it must be decided whether in some situations the costs of not giving the child autonomy exceed any costs in terms of weakening families. For example, forcing a girl to have (or not have) an abortion or discouraging children from getting drug counselling or birth control information by requiring parental permission before the child can obtain such services, may be very harmful to some children. It has been argued that if children faced with such problems are unwilling to talk with their parents, there is not much of a family relationship to preserve anyway.[89]

These concerns may be decisive, especially for specific issues, such as abortion. An analysis much more thorough than the courts or legislatures have made so far is necessary, however, before we can conclude that children should have greater autonomy.

The preceding analysis focuses on claims that autonomy ought to be given to the child. This is not the only option, however. It may be that in cases of parent-child conflict a court or other agency should have to resolve the dispute. The U.S. Supreme Court seems to have supported this approach with regard to teenagers' abortions.[90] Other courts have become involved in disputes ranging from whether a parent can place a child in a psychiatric hospital[91] to whether a teenager should have to accompany her parents on a round-the-world trip.[92]

The option of referring such disputes to courts or to "child development experts"[93] is attractive to many legislators. "Experts" frequently are involved in deciding whether a child is abused or neglected, who should have custody of a child and what to do with delinquents. In all these instances they have to decide what is in a child's best interest; so why not let them decide cases of parent-child conflicts?

---

assertions. Assertions of autonomy by children need not necessarily result in less parental commitment.

88 See n. 79, *supra*.

89 See, e.g., P. Wald, "Making Sense Out of the Rights of Youth" (1976), 55 Child Welfare 379 at 383-84.

90 See *Bellotti v. Baird*, 428 U.S. 132, 147 (1976).

91 See *In re Roger S.*, 19 Cal. 3d 921 (1977).

92 The Hennepin County, Minnesota Juvenile Court was willing to intervene in this dispute and arrange to have the girl stay with an aunt: *In re Lee Anne G.*, Hennepin County Dist. Ct. — Juvenile Division, 11th August 1972 (unreported).

93 The legal system relies heavily on professionals from other disciplines — especially psychiatry, psychology and social work — in making decisions about children. While these professionals have expertise in treating children with problems, it is questionable whether they are expert in determining what is best for a child: see Wald, "State Intervention on Behalf of 'Neglected' Children: A Search for Realistic Standards" (1975), 27 Stan. L. Rev. 985 at 992.

There are many reasons not to allow court intervention in such cases, however. In fact, many commentators question whether courts should continue to have authority even in areas such as custody disputes.[94] First, disputes between parents and children cannot be settled by reference to any existing statutes or principles of law. Instead, they involve making value judgments about appropriate family relationships. Inevitably, such decisions will be based on the personal values and biases of the decision maker, not on legal grounds. In other areas where judges have such discretion, they often make decisions based on their own moral or social values or life-style preferences.[95] Personal predilections, which vary from judge to judge, would undoubtedly become decisive in a court's views regarding whether to grant an abortion, to allow a child to use contraceptives, or to attend a particular school. Moreover, since judges are not trained in child development, are not chosen from a wide cross section of racial, ethnic or cultural backgrounds,[96] and frequently are not subject to public control, it must be questioned why they should be allowed to make decisions about a child's best interest or about how a family should function.[97]

Similar concerns may dictate against giving these decisions to other professionals. Except in extreme situations, there is no scientific method for determining a child's best interest. We get no consistent answers from Drs. Spock, Ginott, Salk or Brothers. Most experts have not even faced questions of the sort raised by children's rights issues. We could expect value judgments to play just as large a role as in the decisions of judges, regardless of the profession involved.

Moreover, courts, doctors, lawyers and other professionals frequently just drop in and then drop out of the child's life. Yet the child's problems may be ongoing. For example, a girl who gets an abortion may need counselling after the abortion, either with regard to the psychological impact of the abortion or to future sexual behaviour. No professional can ensure that the child will continue to consult them.[98] So long as the child continues to function as part of the

---

94 See Goldstein, Freud and Solnit, *supra*, n. 83, at 63, n. 12; Mnookin, "Child-Custody Adjudication: Judicial Functions in the Face of Indeterminacy" (1975), 39 L. & Contemp. Prob. 226.

95 See Mnookin, *supra*, n. 79, at 260-61. One widely known example is the Iowa Supreme Court decision in *Painter v. Bannister*, 258 Iowa 1390 (1966), where the court opted for grandparents who provided "a stable, dependable, conventional middle-class midwestern background", rather than the father, whose home would be "unstable, unconventional, arty, Bohemian and probably intellectually stimulating".

96 Females are not well represented, either.

97 It is questionable, in any case, whether any type of training exists which would enable judges to make such decisions.

98 Some proposals would have the professional decide whether the child is a "mature minor" capable of giving "informal consent": see American Academy of Pediatrics, "A Model Act Providing for Consent of Minors for Health Services" (1973), 51 Pediatrics 293. Obviously, this

family, it will still be the parents who bear primary responsibility for providing help, guidance and support for the child. Parents may not be able to perform these roles adequately if they do not know about critical events in the child's life, such as abortions or psychiatric counselling.[99] Even a helpful professional who is willing to make the kind of commitment to a child that most parents are willing to make cannot be certain that the child will remain available, since either the parents or the "helper" may leave the area.

Finally, we must again consider the broader implications for the family system if courts or experts become the ultimate decision makers. As discussed previously, this might deter parents from assuming important parental roles. While many factors influence the role a parent assumes, one of these factors might well be society's view of the role of parents. At least one commentator has argued recently that turning over major decision making to professionals is extremely detrimental to society.[100] He claims that parents will not be able to act autonomously, and children will be harmed as a result, if parents are made to believe that only professionals know what is best for children. If we want to bolster the family, parents have to want to perform traditional functions, and they must be able to feel confident that they can perform these functions. While no data are provided to support such claims, we might want to search for evidence and analyze the logic of the claims before abandoning traditional structures.

One other cost of court intervention is also relevant. Just the fact of turning over such disputes to courts or agencies outside the family may, in and of itself, have negative implications. Our society is already very litigious. We have, in recent years, placed a great deal of emphasis on protecting individual rights. One benefit of staying out of such disputes may be in the message that family problems should be worked out within the family.

Of course, all these supposed advantages of family decision making assume that parents will be willing to make such decisions.[101] Perhaps we have

---

is not giving autonomy to children; it is being given to the professional. Can professionals make better judgments than parents?

99 Difficulties like unwanted pregnancies are frequently recurring problems for the child. Yet doctors who perform an abortion may do little to prepare the girl for avoiding future unwanted pregnancies.

100 See, e.g., C. Lasch, *Havens In a "Heartless" World* (1978). See also Goldstein, "Medical Care for the Child at Risk: On State Supervision of Parental Autonomy" (1977), 86 Yale L.J. 645, for a strong condemnation of court involvement.

101 A policy protecting family (parental) autonomy does not mean children should be totally excluded from decision making. Parents should be encouraged to include their children in the decision-making process. The findings from researchers like psychologist Diana Baumrind indicate that including children in family decisions contributes to their positive growth in areas such as the development of autonomy, flexibility and self-esteem: see Baumrind, "Some Thoughts on Children" in S. Cohen and T. Comiskey (eds.), *Child Development Contemporary Perspectives* (1977).

passed the point where this can be assumed to be true of most parents. If large numbers of parents are disinterested in their children, that circumstance may justify giving more autonomy to children, or even to other institutions. Recent changes in family structure, which result in parents being less available to their children, may also affect the ability of parents to perform these roles.[102]

In addition, some decisions by parents may have such potentially negative consequences for almost all children that we should subject such decisions to review. The decision to place a child in a mental hospital may be one such decision.[103] Requiring such review would alter the roles of the state and parents in control of child rearing. Requiring review is analogous to expanding the definition of abuse and neglect, and proposals to require review should be analyzed in the manner recommended for category two cases.[104] Instead of viewing state review of commitment decisions as protecting a child's right to liberty, it is more appropriate to see the state acting in its protective functions, ensuring that parents are providing adequate care.[105]

II CONCLUSION

The foregoing analysis raises, rather than resolves, questions.[106] The questions are difficult ones; their resolution requires data about child development which are not currently available. Far more articulation of the assumptions underlying the positions of both opponents and advocates of children's rights also is necessary before we can begin to intelligently define the appropriate scope of both the rights and protections to which children should be entitled.

---

102 See National Academy of Sciences, *Toward a National Policy for Children and Families* (1976), chapter 2.

103 This is the argument being made in cases of civil commitment: see *Bartley v. Kremens*, 402 F. Supp. 1039, reversed on other grounds, 431 U.S. 119 (1977). Similar decisions might be the decision to sterilize a child or to force an abortion.

104 It is also possible to leave the decision to the child, of course.

105 Questions of appropriate medical care, including hospitalization in a psychiatric facility, are among the most difficult for courts to handle: see Wald, *supra*, n. 93, at 1028-33, and Goldstein, *supra*, n. 100.

106 Moreover, not every type of children's rights claim falls within one of the four categories. The most significant exception involves the role of children in the custody process. Among the issues are: should children have a right to choose their custodian upon divorce? Does it have to be one of the parents? Should this differ depending on whether the parents are in agreement or disagreement about custody? Should children have to visit a non-custodial parent?

At least in cases of parental disagreement these issues do not fit any category. (Where the parents agree it then becomes a parent-child dispute.) The key questions turn on the child's capacity to make such decisions and, in the case of visitation, the balancing of the adult's needs with the child's. In these latter cases it should be recognized that we do not require adults to visit their children. Why should it be different for children (perhaps because the adult is paying support?).

The need for an interdisciplinary approach is critical. At present persons from different disciplines often talk past one another. Common framing of questions and attempts at data gathering should help significantly in clarifying and resolving issues.

Finally, it must be recognized that the proposed analysis, especially the analysis of parent-child conflicts, could be rejected entirely. The analysis assumes that the capacity of children for decision making and the impact of autonomy on family structures are relevant to deciding whether children should have more rights. These assumptions need not be accepted. Other commentators have approached the subject as a moral issue. They believe children should have autonomy because they are independent individuals. Giving parents control of children can be viewed as treating children as property. As one commentator concluded "in the final analysis the . . . justification . . . for . . . honouring children's rights is that it is right and fair".[107] One must wonder, however, whether such an approach is, in effect, a case of abandoning children to their rights.[108]

---

107 See P. Wald, "Making Sense Out of the Rights of Youth" (1976), 55 Child Welfare 379 at 392.

108 This term is borrowed from Hafen, "Children's Liberation and The New Egalitarianism: Some Reservations About Abandoning Youth to Their Rights" (1976), B.Y.U.L. Rev. 605.

2

CHILDREN AND THE CHARTER OF RIGHTS*

Nicholas Bala and David Cruickshank

---

*This is a substantially revised version of a paper by Bala, "Families, Children and The Charter of Rights", presented at a Continuing Legal Education Program of the Law Society of Upper Canada, on 6th June 1985.

I INTRODUCTION

The Canadian Charter of Rights and Freedoms has been in effect since April 1982, and it is now clear that this constitutional document is having a profound effect on our legal system, and indeed on Canadian society. Initially, some judges were taking a quite cautious approach to the Charter, typified by the remarks of Zuber J.A. of the Ontario Court of Appeal in *R. v. Altseimer* that:

> . . . the Charter does not intend a transformation of our legal system or the paralysis of law enforcement.[1]

More recently, however, the Supreme Court of Canada has made it clear that the Charter is to be given a broad purposive interpretation. The Supreme Court has stated that the Acts of both the executive and the legislative branches of government are to be regulated by the Charter,[2] and has invoked the Charter for such diverse purposes as striking down the Lord's Day Act,[3] rendering invalid warrantless searches under the Combines Investigation Act,[4] and requiring a hearing before the denial of refugee status under the Immigration Act.[5] In *Hunter v. Southam Inc.*, Dickson J. stated:

> The task of expounding a constitution is crucially different from that of construing a statute. . . . A constitution . . . is drafted with an eye to the future. Its function is to provide a continuing framework for the legitimate exercise of governmental power and, when joined by a *Bill* or a *Charter of Rights*, for the *unremitting protection of individual rights and liberties*. Once enacted, its provisions cannot easily be repealed or amended. It must, therefore, be capable of *growth and development over time to meet new social, political* and *historical realities often unimagined by its framers*. The judiciary is the guardian of the constitution and must, in interpreting its provisions, bear these considerations in mind. Professor Paul Freund expressed this idea aptly when he admonished the American courts "not to read the provisions of the Constitution like a last will and testament lest it become one". . . .
>
>   . . . recently, in *Minister of Home Affairs v. Fisher*, [1980] A.C. 319, dealing with the Bermudian Constitution, Lord Wilberforce reiterated at p.328 that a constitution is a document "sui generis, calling for principles of interpretation of its own, suitable to its character", and that as such, a constitution incorporating a *Bill of Rights* calls for:
>
> ". . . a generous interpretation avoiding what has been called 'the austerity of tabulated legalism', suitable to give individuals the full measure of the fundamental rights and freedoms referred to."

---

1 (1982), 29 C.R. (3d) 276 at 282 (Ont. C.A.).

2 *Operation Dismantle Inc. v. R.* (1985), 18 D.L.R. (4th) 481 (S.C.C.).

3 R.S.C. 1970, c. L-13. See *R. v. Big M Drug Mart Ltd.* (1985), 18 D.L.R. (4th) 321 (S.C.C.).

4 R.S.C. 1970, c. C-23. See *Hunter v. Southam Inc.*, [1984] 2 S.C.R. 145.

5 S.C. 1976-77, c. 52. See *Singh v. Min. of Employment & Immigration* (1985), 17 D.L.R. (4th) 422 (S.C.C.).

> Such a *broad, purposive analysis*, which interprets specific provisions of a constitutional document in the light of its larger objects, is also consonant with the classical principles of American constitutional construction enunciated by Chief Justice Marshall in *M'Culloch v. Maryland*, 17 U.S. (4 Wheat.) 316 (1819). It is, as well, the approach I intend to take in the present case.[6]

Thus far, the primary impact of the Charter has been in the area of what can broadly be defined as criminal law, the laws and practices which render illegal certain forms of individual behaviour. But it is clear that the Charter will significantly influence other relationships between individuals and the state. Section 15 of the Charter, the equality rights provision, came into effect on 17th April, 1985, and while the effect of this section has yet to be fully measured by the courts, it seems destined to have a major impact on a broad range of legal and social issues.

For a number of reasons, the courts have been relatively slow to invoke the Charter in cases where the relationship of families, children and the state are involved, even though this is an area where the potential impact of government actions on individual lives is enormous. One reason for this may stem from the lack of effective argument by the Bar;[7] another reason is the lack of resources for arguing this type of case.[8] Further, there may be a belief on the part of judges that since state action in this area is viewed as being "intended" to promote the welfare of families or the "best interests" of children, it should not be subject to constitutional scrutiny.

It is not surprising that many of the cases where advocates for children have successfully raised the Charter have involved criminal proceedings, such as those under the Juvenile Delinquents Act, and its replacement, the Young

---

6 *Supra*, n. 4, at 155-56. Emphasis added.

7 Responsibility does not rest solely with the practising Bar. While legal academics have devoted considerable attention to the Charter of Rights, comparatively scant attention has been paid to the question of the impact of the Charter on family. See, however: Bala and Redfearn, "Family Law and the 'Liberty Interest': Section 7 of the Canadian Charter of Rights" (1983), 15 Ottawa L. Rev. 274; and Thompson, "The Charter and Child Protection: The Need for a Strategy" (1985), forthcoming in Can. J. Fam. L.

8 It is evident that litigants with more extensive resources are among those in the best position to make use of the Charter, and particularly to pursue extensive appeals. Thus, corporations like Southam Inc. and Big M Drug Mart Ltd. have been among the first to argue Charter cases in the Supreme Court of Canada. Some groups, most notably those raising "women's issues" and "peace issues" have organized to raise funds specifically for Charter litigation. Advocates for children and parents may be constrained by limited resources in pursuing Charter arguments through the courts. It is, however, possible that advocates for children will in some cases benefit from the new program of government funding for challenges under s. 15 (equality rights) and s. 28 (sexual equality) of the Charter; this fund is being administered by the Canadian Council on Social Development.

Offenders Act.[9] There are clear indications, however, that the Canadian courts are prepared to accept the applicability of the Charter in other contexts. As will be discussed in this chapter, the Charter has been effectively invoked by counsel in a range of other cases, including ones involving truancy, child protection and adoption. The relevance of the Charter to many situations involving families and children is clear if one appreciates that when assessing whether state action is unconstitutional, one must consider not only its intent, but also its effect. Mr. Justice Dickson emphasized this point in *R. v. Big M. Drug Mart Ltd.* (the Lord's Day Act case):

> In my view, both purpose and effect are relevant in determining constitutionality; either an unconstitutional purpose or an unconstitutional effect can invalidate legislation. All legislation is animated by an object the Legislature intends to achieve. This object is realized through the impact produced by the operation and application of the legislation. Purpose and effect respectively, in the sense of the legislation's object and its ultimate impact, are clearly linked, if not indivisible. Intended and actual effects have often been looked to for guidance in assessing the legislation's object and thus, its validity.[10]

In *Re M.B.*, a Nova Scotia case involving "unmanageability" under child welfare legislation, Daley Fam. Ct. J. adopted this approach.[11] The judge acknowledged that while the legislation was a "treatment tool", its effect was to place a child in a training school — an environment where he was in effect "incarcerated". Although child welfare legislation was involved, it had "penal consequences", and hence the Charter was applicable. In this case there had been a failure to give adequate notice of the proceedings to the boy, and thus s. 7 of the Charter was violated and the complaint was dismissed.

This chapter will provide a section-by-section consideration of the provisions of the Charter, discussing cases where the Charter has been applied to protect the rights of parents or children, and suggesting situations where such

---

9 Juvenile Delinquents Act, R.S.C. 1970, c. J-3, repealed by the Young Offenders Act, S.C. 1980-81-82-83, c. 110, s. 80. See, e.g., *R. v. M.J.R.*, [1983] W.D.F.L. 737 (Ont. Prov. Ct.) (s. 11(*d*) of the Charter invoked to prevent use of prior "caution" at disposition hearing); *R. v. V.T.W.* (1982), 30 C.R. (3d) 193 (N.S. Fam. Ct.) (s. 11(*e*) of Charter invoked to obtain bail under Juvenile Delinquents Act); *R. v. D.E.M.* (1984), 13 W.C.B. 397 (Ont. Prov. Ct.) (Charter s. 8, used to exclude unlawfully seized marijuana); *R. v. K.S.* (1982), 8 W.C.B. 502 (Ont. Prov. Ct.) (s. 10(*b*) of Charter right to retain counsel infringed and statement excluded); *R. v. I.C.V.*, [1985] W.D.F.L. 2087 (Ont. Prov. Ct.), *per* Main Prov. J. (ss. 7, 8, 9, and 10(*b*) invoked to quash assault charge after unlawful arrest); and *R. v. R.L.* (1985), 47 C.R. (3d) 278, reversed 22nd April 1986 (Ont. C.A.) (ss. 11(*f*) and 15 invoked to guarantee young person charged under Young Offenders Act right to jury trial).

10 *Supra*, n. 3, at 350.

11 *Re M.B.* (1984), 65 N.S.R. (2d) 181 (Fam. Ct.); for a contrary approach, see *Re S.B.* (1983), 3 C.C.C. (3d) 390 (B.C.C.A.), where a juvenile facing indefinite committal to training school under the Juvenile Delinquents Act was denied the right to a jury trial under s. 11(*f*) of the Charter as he was not subject to "punishment", but rather to "treatment".

arguments ought to be made in the future. In some cases Canadian courts and legislatures recognized and protected familial rights even before the Charter came into force; in these situations the Charter gives important constitutional recognition and protection to existing rights. In other cases it is clear that the Charter is expanding the scope of protected interests. Affording "constitutional" protections to families and children may create rights which will disturb some governments or parents. It must, however, be recognized that the Charter was drafted with the express purpose of protecting individuals from unjustified discrimination or unwarranted intrusion in their lives.

II CONSTITUTIONAL SIGNIFICANCE OF THE CHARTER: SECTIONS 52 AND 33

Supreme Law of Canada: Section 52

> 52.(1) The Constitution of Canada is the supreme law of Canada, and any law that is inconsistent with the provisions of the Constitution is, to the extent of the inconsistency, of no force or effect.

Notwithstanding Clause: Section 33

> 33.(1) Parliament or the legislature of a province may expressly declare in an Act of Parliament or of the legislature, as the case may be, that the Act or a provision thereof shall operate notwithstanding a provision included in section 2 or sections 7 to 15 of this Charter.
>
> (2) An Act or a provision of an Act in respect of which a declaration made under this section is in effect shall have such operation as it would have but for the provision of this Charter referred to in the declaration.
>
> (3) A declaration made under subsection (1) shall cease to have effect five years after it comes into force or on such earlier date as may be specified in the declaration.
>
> (4) Parliament or the legislature of a province may re-enact a declaration made under subsection (1).
>
> (5) Subsection (3) applies in respect of a re-enactment made under subsection (4).

Section 52 of the Constitution Act, 1982 makes clear that the Charter (Pt. I of the Constitution Act, 1982) is the "supreme law of Canada". If there was any doubt that it is the role of the courts to strike down laws inconsistent with the Charter, that doubt is resolved by s. 24(1), which permits application to the courts for an appropriate remedy for violation of the Charter. Even without s. 24, it is clearly the role of the courts to interpret and apply the Charter.

Furthermore, the mandate of s. 52 is unambiguous. Unlike the Canadian Bill of Rights, which only grants the courts the power to construe and apply the Bill so as to not "abrogate, abridge, or infringe . . . rights or freedoms",[12] the

---

12 R.S.C. 1970, App. III, s. 2.

Charter gives the courts the power to declare a law to be "of no force and effect". This should remove the problem experienced by the courts in the early interpretation of the Canadian Bill of Rights. There was some uncertainty whether the Bill was merely a canon of construction or actually an instrument for rendering inconsistent laws inoperative.[13] Clearly the authority found in s. 52 of the Constitution Act, 1982 is a judicial power to declare a law unconstitutional or without legal effect. This power arises from the fact that the Charter is constitutionally entrenched, while the Bill of Rights was merely a piece of federal legislation. This means that an interpretation and application of the Charter can only be overturned by judicial overruling or a constitutional amendment. In some cases, the "notwithstanding" provision of s. 33 of the Charter can be used to avoid future compliance with the Charter.

Quebec enacted a single provincial law which declared all of s. 2 and ss. 7-15 of the Charter to be of no effect in regard to matters within the province's sphere of jurisdiction, but this law has been declared invalid.[14] While it seems likely that other governments will be reluctant to take the politically sensitive step of overriding the Charter through invoking s. 33, Saskatchewan utilized this provision in connection with legislation prohibiting civil servants from going on strike.

Further, s. 52 leaves it open to a court to "read down" a statute to an application (or non-application) that does not offend the Charter. This option arises from the words "to the extent of the inconsistency" in s. 52. A variation of "reading down" is the judicial declaration that a law "does not extend" to the challenged behaviour. An example of the exercise of this power occurred in the pre-Charter case of *McKay v. R.*[15] where a restrictive municipal by-law was held not to extend to a political candidate's signs in a federal election. The by-law, in its general terms, remained in force, but it did not apply to the signs in question. Such an option comes within the words "to the extent of the inconsistency."

III APPLICATION OF THE CHARTER: SECTION 32

32.(1) This Charter applies

(a) to the Parliament and government of Canada in respect of all matters within the authority of Parliament including all matters relating to the Yukon Territory and Northwest Territories; and

---

13 See *R. v. Drybones*, [1970] S.C.R. 282; and *A.G. Can. v. Lavell; Isaac v. Bedard*, [1974] S.C.R. 1349. Ironically, with the Charter in effect, the courts have been much more willing to invoke the Bill of Rights to strike down legislation: see, e.g., *Singh v. Min. of Employment & Immigration, supra*, n. 5.

14 *Alliance des Professeurs de Montreal v. A.G. Que.* (1985), 21 D.L.R. (4th) 354 (Que. C.A.).

15 [1965] S.C.R. 798.

(b) to the legislature and government of each province in respect of all matters within the authority of the legislature of each province.

(2) Notwithstanding subsection (1), section 15 shall not have effect until three years after this section comes into force.

Section 32 declares that the Charter applies to all matters "within the authority" of both levels of government.

It is now clear that the Charter applies not only to legislative acts, but also to acts of the executive[16] and such quasi-governmental agencies as Ontario's children's aid societies. There is, however, some doubt about whether the Charter would apply to such "private" matters as an agreement between a private child care agency and parents.[17]

The extension of the Charter to administrative action is of considerable importance. Indeed, if the history of the Bill of Rights in the United States is repeated, the courts will relatively rarely be involved in scrutinizing and striking down statutes. But administrative action taken under law could be a field of frequent litigation.

Although enforcement of rights will be outlined later, it should be noted here that s. 24(1) is not limited to striking down laws that are unconstitutional. It allows for the control of administrative action under law as well.

One result of the broader view of "government" is that judicial acts also come within the application of the Charter. Thus it seems that the Charter can be invoked to modify or limit the effect of common law rules. This view is reinforced by the use of the expression "any law" in s. 52.

IV REASONABLE LIMITS: SECTION 1

1. The *Canadian Charter of Rights and Freedoms* guarantees the rights and freedoms set out in it subject only to such reasonable limits prescribed by law as can be demonstrably justified in a free and democratic society.

Section 1 guarantees the rights set out in the Charter, but stipulates that none of these rights are absolute. They are subject to "reasonable limits" demonstrably justified in a free and democratic society, which requires the courts to *balance* the rights of individuals against other social concerns. These limits cannot be judicially invented. They must already be "prescribed by law". This includes common law limitations that are still in force.[18]

---

16 See *Operation Dismantle Inc.*, *supra*, n. 2.

17 See B. Slattery, "Charter of Rights and Freedoms — Does it Bind Private Persons" (1985), 63 Can. Bar Rev. 148; see also *Blainey v. Ont. Hockey Assn.*, Ont. C.A., 17th April 1986 (not yet reported); and *Peg-Win Real Estate Bd. v. Winnipeg Real Estate Bd.*, [1985] 4 W.W.R. 758 (Man. Q.B.).

18 Robin Elliot, "Overview of the Charter", in *Materials on the Canadian Charter of Rights and Freedoms*, Continuing Legal Education Society of B.C. (1982), at 36.

The most challenging task of interpretation will be to determine whether the limits on rights are "reasonable" and "demonstrably justified in a free and democratic society". It could be said that Parliament or a legislature, democratically elected, passed a limiting law; therefore, it is automatically "reasonable" and "justified". As Elliot points out, this leaves the courts no interpretive task and no legal test at all; furthermore, it runs counter to the legislative history of s. 1.[19]

A couple of Supreme Court of Canada decisions, *R. v. Oakes*[20] and *R. v. Big M Drug Mart Ltd.*[21] have helped to define s. 1 of the Charter. It is clear from these decisions that s. 1 will not be used to easily override constitutionally protected rights. In *Oakes*, Dickson C.J.C. offers the following statement on the function of s. 1:[22]

> It is important to observe at the outset that s. 1 has two functions: first, it constitutionally guarantees the rights and freedoms set out in the provisions which follow; and second, it states explicitly the exclusive justificatory criteria (outside of s. 33 of the Constitution Act, 1982) against which limitations on those rights and freedoms must be measured. Accordingly, any s. 1 inquiry must be premised on an understanding that the impugned limit violates constitutional rights and freedoms — rights and freedoms which are part of the supreme law of Canada. As Wilson J. stated in *Singh v. Min. of Employment & Immigration* . . .

> ". . . it is important to remember that the courts are conducting this inquiry in light of a commitment to uphold the rights and freedoms set out in the other sections of the *Charter.*"

> A second contextual element of interpretation of s. 1 is provided by the words "free and democratic society". Inclusion of these words as the final standard of justification for limits on rights and freedoms refers the court to the very purpose for which the Charter was originally entrenched in the Constitution: Canadian society is to be free and democratic. The court must be guided by the values and principles essential to a free and democratic society, which I believe embody, to name but a few, respect for the inherent dignity of the human person, commitment to social justice and equality, accommodation of a wide variety of beliefs, respect for cultural and group identity, and faith in social and political institutions which enhance the participation of individuals and groups in society. The underlying values and principles of a free and democratic society are the genesis of the rights and freedoms guaranteed by the Charter and the ultimate standard against which a limit on a right or freedom must be shown, despite its effect, to be reasonable and demonstrably justified.

> The rights and freedoms guaranteed by the Charter are not, however, absolute. It may become necessary to limit rights and freedoms in circumstances where their exercise would be inimical to the realization of collective goals of fundamental importance. For this reason, s. 1 provides criteria of justification for limits on the rights and freedoms guaranteed by the Charter.

---

19 *Ibid.*, at 38.

20 (1986), 50 C.R. (3d) 1 (S.C.C.).

21 [1985] 2 S.C.R. 295.

22 *Supra*, n. 20, at 27-28.

The standard to be met by a party seeking to invoke s. 1 is also set out in *Oakes:*[23]

> To establish that a limit is reasonable and demonstrably justified in a free and democratic society, two central criteria must be satisfied. First, the objective, which the measures responsible for a limit on a Charter right or freedom are designed to serve, must be "of sufficient importance to warrant overriding a constitutionally protected right or freedom": *R. v. Big M Drug Mart Ltd.* . . . The standard must be high in order to ensure that objectives which are trivial or discordant with the principles integral to a free and democratic society do not gain s. 1 protection. It is necessary, at a minimum, that an objective relate to concerns which are pressing and substantial in a free and democratic society before it can be characterized as sufficiently important.
>
> Second, once a sufficiently significant objective is recognized, then the party invoking s.1 must show that the means chosen are reasonable and demonstrably justified. This involves "a form of proportionality test": *R. v. Big M Drug Mart Ltd.* . . . Although the nature of the proportionality test will vary depending on the circumstances, in each case courts will be required to balance the interests of society with those of individuals and groups. There are, in my view, three important components of a proportionality test. First, the measures adopted must be carefully designed to achieve the objective in question. They must not be arbitrary, unfair or based on irrational considerations. In short, they must be rationally connected to the objective. Second, the means, even if rationally connected to the objective in this first sense, should impair "as little as possible" the right or freedom in question: *R. v. Big M Drug Mart Ltd.* . . . Third, there must be a proportionality between the *effects* of the measures which are responsible for limiting the Charter right or freedom and the objective which has been identified as of "sufficient importance".

The limitations of s. 1 of the Charter are particularly likely to be significant in matters concerning children and family life. For example, it is recognized that children will, in some cases, lack the capacity to exercise Charter rights. Thus, while s. 3 of the Charter guarantees every citizen of Canada the "right to vote", it would not be difficult to "demonstrably justify" the need to deprive children of the right to vote, although there might be some disagreement as to the age and circumstances under which young people should be free of this deprivation.

While s. 1 is obviously a most important limitation on the rights enshrined in the Charter, it must be invoked with caution lest it be used to justify almost any infringement of the Charter and totally destroy its effect. There is a particular need for a careful application of s. 1 in cases involving children and family interests, where generalized notions of promoting welfare or best interests may be used to attempt to justify virtually any state restriction of rights. The need for caution was recognized by Thomson Prov. J. in *T.T. v. Catholic Children's Aid Society of Metropolitan Toronto*,[24] where he acknowledged: "I am concerned that the courts not make too easy reference to the nature and goals

---

23 *Supra*, n. 20 at 30.
24 (1984), 39 R.F.L. (2d) 279 at 296 (Ont. Prov. Ct.).

of child protection proceedings in support of major interference with basic natural justice protections [as guaranteed by the Charter of Rights]". Fortunately, a number of recent higher court decisions recognize and emphasize that a litigant seeking to invoke s. 1 faces a real and substantial burden.

An example of a case making a fairly expansive statement concerning the use of s. 1 of the Charter is *Re S.M.B. and Children's Aid Society of Metropolitan Toronto.* Jehovah's Witness parents sought termination of a wardship order made to ensure that their child received a blood transfusion, arguing that the wardship order infringed their rights of freedom of religion, protected under s. 2 of the Charter. Walmsley A.C. Prov. J. commented in *obiter dicta:*

> . . . with respect to those under a disability, such as children, or mental incompetents, there is a valid power to intervene. It seems to me that the Child Welfare Act, coming as it does between parents and children and interfering with parental rights, is a good example of this type of legislation. In fact, in this case we have really three competing rights: we have rights of children; we have rights of parents; we have religious rights, either as they apply to parents or in the abstract. But we have to remember that under the Canadian Charter of Rights and Freedoms . . . any one of these three rights may be subject to reasonable limitations. In s. 1 of the Canadian Charter of Rights and Freedoms . . . I am absolutely convinced in my own mind that the limitation of parental rights in the field of child protection would be considered to be such a reasonable limitation, according as it does with common sense and according, as it does, with the tradition that I have mentioned.[25]

It seems clear that the authority of the state to protect children in life threatening situations where parents refuse to provide medical care is a "reasonable limit[s] . . . demonstrably justified in a free and democratic society". It is submitted, however, that the words used by Walmsley A.C. Prov. J. appear to give s. 1 a far broader scope than is necessary or justified. It seems clear that there are circumstances in which the restriction of parental rights in the field of child

---

25 (1983), 36 R.F.L. (2d) 80 at 83 (Ont. Prov. Ct.). See also *Shingoose v. Sask. Min. of Social Services* (1983), 149 D.L.R. (3d) 400 (Sask. Q.B.); *Re K.K.; K.K. v. Sask. Min. of Social Services* (1982), 31 R.F.L. (3d) 334 (Sask. Q.B.). See, e.g., in the United States *Raleigh Fitkin-Paul Morgan Memorial Hosp. v. Anderson*, 201 A. 2d 537 (N.J. S.C., 1964), cert. denied 377 U.S. 985 (1964) (transfusion for pregnant Jehovah's Witness woman to save unborn child); and in Canada *Re D.* (1982), 30 R.F.L. (2d) 277 at 281 (Alta. Prov. Ct.), where Catonio Prov. J. remarked:

"As between the state's right to safeguard the health and welfare of children and the rights of parents to freely practice their religion, the former must prevail. If a responsible adult refuses to accept a blood transfusion for himself or herself on religious grounds, the state should not and will not intervene, but when medical treatment, that is, a blood transfusion, is withheld from the offspring of the adult, the state must and has valid legislation to intervene."

See, however, *Re L.D.K.; C.A.S. of Metro. Toronto v. K.* (1985), 48 R.F.L. (2d) 164 (Ont. Prov. Ct.), *per* Main Prov. J., where the court refused to find a Jehovah's Witness child whose parents refused chemotherapy, which involved blood transfusions, in need of protection. The girl was suffering from acute leukemia, and the court concluded the decision of the girl and parents should not be overturned by the state.

protection might not be a "reasonable limit". The limited nature of s. 1 of the Charter is made clear in a number of higher court decisions which have restricted the scope of this provision.

The need for caution in interpreting s. 1 of the Charter was emphasized in a recent decision of the Supreme Court of Canada, *Singh v. Minister of Employment and Immigration*, where Wilson J. stated:

> The question of the standards which the court should use in applying s. 1, is, without a doubt, a question of enormous significance for the operation of the Charter. If too low a threshold is set, the courts run the risk of emasculating the Charter. If too high a threshold is set, the courts run the risk of unjustifiably restricting government action. It is not a task to be entered upon lightly.[26]

If a right protected by the Charter is infringed, the onus is upon the party seeking to uphold the s. 1 limitation. As stated in *Re Southam Inc. and R.* by MacKinnon A.C.J.O.:

> Section 1 guarantees those rights and, although the rights are not absolute or unrestricted, makes it clear that if there is a limit imposed on these fundamental rights by law, the limits must be reasonable and demonstrably justified in a free and democratic society. The wording imposes a *positive obligation on those seeking to uphold the limit* or limits to establish to the satisfaction of the court by evidence, by the terms and purpose of the limiting law, its economic, social and political background, and, if felt helpful, by references to comparable legislation of other acknowledged free and democratic societies, that such limit or limits are reasonable and demonstrably justified in a free and democratic society.[27]

The Ontario Court of Appeal in *R. v. Bryant* has emphasized that the s. 1 limits on freedoms are to be no broader than is necessary to achieve the desired results. Blair J.A. stated:

> The standard by which the reasonableness of the limitation of the Charter right must be assessed is that the court must be satisfied that a valid legal, social or other objective is served *by the limitation of the right and that the limitation is restricted to that which is necessary for the attainment of the desired objective.*[28]

In the same decision Houlden J.A. indicated how the s. 1 burden might be satisfied. The following are some of the more common ones:

> an examination of the rationale and purpose of the legislation;
>
> comparable legislation in other free and democratic societies, including judicial interpretation of such legislation;
>
> international conventions and agreements on the same or similar subject matter;

26 (1985), 17 D.L.R. (4th) 422 at 467 (S.C.C.).

27 (1983), 41 O.R. (2d) 113 at 124 (C.A.). Emphasis added.

28 (1984), 42 C.R. (3d) 312 at 323 (Ont. C.A.). Emphasis added. See also *R. v. Big M Drug Mart*, *supra*, n. 21.

judicial decisions of other Canadian courts on the same legislation;

the calling of oral evidence; and

the argument of counsel.[29]

An interesting case involving the applicability of s. 1 is *Re Southam Inc. and R.*[30] Southam challenged ss. 38 and 39 of the Young Offenders Act which prohibit publication of identifying information involving young offenders and create a discretionary power in a Youth Court Judge to exclude members of the public from the proceedings. It was accepted that these provisions violated freedom of the press, as protected by s. 2(*b*) of the Charter of Rights, but the court accepted this as a "reasonable limit" under s. 1. In this case, to satisfy the s. 1 onus, the Crown had expert witnesses — psychiatrists, a psychologist, a criminologist and a policy analyst — testify about the potential harm to young persons from public identification. The court accepted that there would be cases where there would be no harm, but that most young persons would be harmed by such publicity, and further that it would be "virtually impossible" for a judge to identify in advance which young persons would likely be harmed. The court held that the "protection and rehabilitation" of young persons were "social values of superordinate importance" justifying the restrictions on freedom of the press and expression. In coming to this conclusion, the court was prepared to accept a general limit prohibiting reporting of identifying information for all persons involved in Youth Court proceedings, even though this protection might be overly broad as it would not be required by all young persons.

Although the court did not discuss the issue, there are clearly cases where general limits are justifiable, but there will be others where individualized decision making is necessary. A general limit was justifiable in this case because of the nature of the issue (a limited restriction on freedom of the press) and because of the difficulty in readily identifying which young persons should or should not be protected. If a limitation severely restricted an individual freedom, like "liberty or security of the person", it is submitted that such a general limitation based on mere convenience would not be sufficient. The issue of general as opposed to specific limitations will be considered again later in this chapter. There might, however, be specific situations where a court might make an individualized decision and declare s. 38 of the Young Offenders Act inoperative for the purposes of the particular proceeding without declaring it unconstitutional for all purposes.[31] For example, if a case should arise under the

---

29 *Ibid.*, at 315-16.

30 (1984), 14 D.L.R. (4th) 683 (Ont. H.C.).

31 See *Re Moore and R.* (1984), 45 O.R. (2d) 3 at 9 (H.C.), where Ewaschuk J. stated:
"In deciding that the carefully crafted dangerous offender provisions accord with public standards of decency and propriety, I gauge those provisions not on the "worst case scenario"

Young Offenders Act in which a young person wanted to have identifying information published, perhaps because it involved a "political issue", the court might declare s. 38 inoperative for that single case.

V FUNDAMENTAL FREEDOMS: SECTION 2

> 2. Everyone has the following fundamental freedoms:
>
> (*a*) freedom of conscience and religion;
>
> (*b*) freedom of thought, belief, opinion and expression, including freedom of the press and other media of communication;
>
> (*c*) freedom of peaceful assembly, and
>
> (*d*) freedom of association.

The U.S. Supreme Court in *Wisconsin v. Yoder*,[32] held that parental freedom of religion included the right of Amish parents not to send their 14-year-old son to a secular public school, notwithstanding compulsory attendance laws. This decision was followed in a case invoking the freedom of religion provision of the Alberta Bill of Rights by Mennonite parents who sent their child to an "unapproved" Mennonite school.[33] However, in a more recent Alberta case, *R. v. Powell*,[34] Litsky Prov. J. refused to apply s. 2(*a*) of the Charter in a case where fundamentalist Christian parents, who were purporting to educate their children at home, were charged with violating compulsory school attendance laws. The court observed that while religious benefits and convictions are constitutionally guaranteed, religious expression or practices are not always so protected. It may well have been significant in *Powell* that the court concluded that the homestudy program was "mere puffery and is in reality a smokescreen for teaching *only* religious philosophy and hardly anything

---

to the Crown, but on what I consider to be an "average" or "normal" dangerous offender, and where all the statutory conditions have been met. In assessing Charter applications, it is generally socially unrealistic to consider only the possible worst case where such case is not before the court. Indeed, it is only too easy for the creative legal imagination to concoct bizarre examples that never come to court. Where the worst case comes before the court, then the preferable practice is not to invalidate otherwise valid legislation but to hold it inoperative in the particular case. . . . This also is the general American approach in dealing with constitutional challenges."

To a similar effect, see *R. v. Jones* (1984), 13 C.C.C. (3d) 261 (Alta. C.A.).

32 406 U.S. 205 (1972). In his dissenting judgment, Justice Douglas raised the issue of whether the child has an independent constitutional right and should be consulted in a case such as this.

33 *R. v. Wiebe*, [1978] 3 W.W.R. 36 (Alta. Prov. Ct.). Alberta Bill of Rights, S.A. 1972, c. 1 [now R.S.A. 1980, c. A-16].

34 (1985), 39 Alta. L.R. (2d) 122 (Prov. Ct.).

else".[35] If the parents had been effectively educating their children, s. 2(*a*) of the Charter might have been invoked to protect their right to do this outside the public school system.

It may be that "freedom of association", guaranteed in s. 2(*d*), could be raised in cases where government denies parents access to a child in care or detention. In *Re J.; Catholic Children's Aid Society of Metropolitan Toronto v. S.*, Nasmith Prov. J., stated: "Surely the association among family members including parents and children comes under s. 2(*d*)".[36] The judge relied on ss. 2(*d*), 7 and 15 of the Charter to find that legislation which absolutely prohibited post-adoption access between biological parents and their children would be unconstitutional. Clearly any substantive right to enjoy a parent-child relationship will be subject to "reasonable limits" which would include termination of such a relationship where its continuation would be harmful to the child. In *Re J.* the legislation was apparently considered unconstitutional to the extent that there was no opportunity for a judicial determination of whether denial of such visitation would be in the child's best interests.

VI MOBILITY RIGHTS: SECTION 6

> 6.(1) Every citizen of Canada has the right to enter, remain in and leave Canada.
>
> (2) Every citizen of Canada and every person who has the status of a permanent resident of Canada has the right
>
> (*a*) to move to and take up residence in any province. . . .

Section 6(1) could, for example, be raised by a person who is required to surrender a passport under s. 38(3) of Ontario's Children's Law Reform Act,[37] as part of an order to prevent unlawful removal of a child from the province. Section 6(2) of the Charter could be used as a basis for challenging an order of custody or access which requires that a child remain in a particular jurisdiction. In most cases such limitations upon mobility will be accepted as being "reasonable limits . . . demonstrably justified in a free and democratic society" to ensure that a child's best interests are protected and that a relationship is maintained with the parents.[38]

---

35 *Ibid.*, at 130.

36 (1985), 48 R.F.L. (2d) 371 (Ont. Prov. Ct.). For an apparently contrary decision, see *Shingoose v. Sask. Min. of Social Services, supra*, n. 25, where the court appeared to reject an argument that s. 2(*d*) of the Charter could be relevant to a wardship proceeding.

37 R.S.O. 1980, c. 68, s. 38(3) [en. 1982, c. 20, s. 1].

38 See *Re K.K.; K.K. v. Sask. Min. of Social Services* (1982), 31 R.F.L. (2d) 334 (Sask. Q.B.), where s. 1 of the Charter was invoked to deny a 13-year-old ward of a child welfare agency the right to determine which province she was to reside in.

VII LIFE, LIBERTY AND SECURITY OF THE PERSON: SECTION 7

7. Everyone has the right to life, liberty and security of the person and the right not to be deprived thereof except in accordance with the principles of fundamental justice.

Section 7 is potentially one of the most significant provisions of the Charter for children and parents and deserves careful consideration.

1. "Liberty and Security of the Person": Section 7

Some judges and academic commentators have suggested that "liberty and security of the person" have a narrow meaning. According to this view "liberty" means essentially "freedom from arrest or restraint", and "security of the person" is restricted to protection of the physical integrity of the individual.[39] However, a convincing argument can be made that the concepts of "liberty" and "security of the person" have a much broader meaning, and increasingly Canadian courts seem willing to accept such arguments.

In the United States, the courts have long held that the concept of "liberty", protected by the requirements of due process in the Fifth and Fourteenth Amendments, extends far beyond mere freedom from imprisonment or other physical restraint. In 1923, in *Meyer v. Nebraska*, Mr. Justice McReynolds of the United States Supreme Court, stated that the term "liberty"

Without doubt . . . denotes not merely freedom from bodily restraint, but also the right of the individual . . . to marry, establish a home and bring up children . . . and, generally, to enjoy those privileges long recognized at common law as essential to the orderly pursuit of happiness by free men.[40]

The U.S. Supreme Court affirmed this approach in 1973 in *Roe v. Wade*, with Mr. Justice Stewart in a concurring opinion, offering a broad summary of the meaning of "liberty":

"This 'liberty' is not a series of isolated points pricked out in terms . . . the freedom of speech, press, and religion; the right to keep and bear arms; the freedom from unreasonable searches and seizures; and so on. It is a rational continuum which, broadly speaking, includes a freedom from all substantial arbitrary impositions and purposeless restraints . . . and which also recognizes, what a reasonable and sensitive judgment must, that certain interests require particularly careful scrutiny of the state needs asserted to justify their abridgment." . . . In the words of Mr. Justice Frankfurter, "Great concepts like . . . 'liberty' . . . were purposely left

---

39 See *R. v. Operation Dismantle Inc.* (1983), 3 D.L.R. (4th) 193 at 200, affirmed on other grounds 18 D.L.R. (4th) 481 (S.C.C.). See also, e.g., Garant, "Fundamental Freedoms and Natural Justice" in Tarnopolsky and Beaudoin (eds.), *The Canadian Charter of Rights and Freedoms: Commentary* (1982), 257 at 263-70.

40 262 U.S. 390 at 399 (1923).

to gather meaning from experience. For they relate to the whole domain of social and economic fact, and the statesmen who founded this Nation knew too well that only a stagnant society remains unchanged."

Several decisions of this Court make clear that freedom of personal choice in matters of marriage and family life is one of the liberties protected by the Due Process Clause of the Fourteenth Amendment.[41]

The Utah Supreme Court surveyed a number of leading American decisions[42] on the scope of parental rights to raise their children free from undue state interference, and offered the following rationale for the protection of parental rights:

... the parental liberty right at issue . . . is fundamental to the existence of the institution of the family, which is "deeply seated in this Nation's history and tradition" . . . and in the "history and culture of Western civilization". . . .

This recognition of the due process and retained rights of parents promotes values essential to the preservation of human freedom and dignity and to the perpetuation of our democratic society. The family is a principal conservator and transmitter of cherished values and traditions. . . . Any invasion of the sanctity of the family, even with the loftiest motives, unavoidably threatens those traditions and values.

For example, family autonomy helps to assure the diversity characteristic of a free society. There is no surer way to preserve pluralism than to allow parents maximum latitude in the rearing of their children, as defined by official dogma. Conversely, there is no surer way to threaten pluralism than to terminate the rights of parents who contradict officially approved values imposed by reformers empowered to determine what is the "best interest" of someone else's child.[43]

Clearly, American jurisprudence supports the view that "liberty", as referred to in s. 7 of the Charter of Rights, is a broad concept and includes the right to enjoy family relations without unreasonable state interference.

The concept of "security of the person" does not appear in the American constitution, and though it is used in s. 1(*a*) of the Canadian Bill of Rights, it has never been subject to judicial interpretation in that context. In *Singh v. Minister of Manpower and Immigration*, Wilson J. of the Supreme Court of Canada observed that "security of the person" is capable of a "broad range of meaning", but concluded that for the case before the court it was sufficient to recognize that it at least encompassed "freedom from the threat of physical punishment or suffering as well as freedom from such punishment itself".[44]

---

41 410 U.S. 113 at 168-69 (1973).

42 Some of the leading American decisions include: *Meyer v. Nebraska, supra,* n. 40; *Moore v. East Cleveland,* 431 U.S. 494 (1977); *Pierce v. Soc. of Sisters,* 218 U.S. 510 (1925); *Prince v. Massachusetts,* 321 U.S. 158 (1944); *Wisconsin v. Yoder, supra,* n. 32; and *Santosky v. Kramer,* 455 U.S. 745 (1982).

43 In *Re J.P.,* 8 F.L.R. 2515 at 2516 (Utah S.C., 1982).

44 (1985), 17 D.L.R. (4th) 422 at 459-60 (S.C.C.).

In *R. v. X.*[45] Linden J. appeared to accept the proposition that the concept of "security of the person" in the Charter includes the protection of the "physical, mental and social well-being" of the person. If this approach is adopted, then the protection of "security of the person" may also require protection of familial relationships.

It also seems fair to say that even before the Charter was in force Canadian courts consistently recognized the fundamental importance of the family, and the need to protect parents from improper interference. In 1970 in *Re Mugford*, Schroeder J.A. of the Ontario Court of Appeal, in affirming a decision to terminate permanent state wardship of a child, stated:

> One cannot over-estimate the importance to a child of living, moving, and having its being in an environment shared by its own blood kin where it will enjoy the warmth and affection of the mother who gave it birth. These are but a part of the intangible values which flow from a custom deeply rooted in our way of life against which superior material advantages which a child may enjoy in the home of strangers in blood cannot accurately be measured on the most delicately balanced scales. The law is on the side of the natural parents unless for grave reasons, endangering the welfare of the child, the Court sees fit not to give effect to the parents' wishes.[46]

In *Re Chrysler*, decided in 1978, Karswick Prov. J. refused to make a wardship order and returned a young child home to the custody of her parents under agency supervision. The court emphasized that even though there might be some risk involved in sending a child back home to a purportedly neglectful parent, that risk

> . . . must still give way to the greater risk of the irreparable harm that can be inflicted upon a child and the danger to society of the serious undermining of the parents and the family if a C.A.S. [Children's Aid Society] is permitted to act in an arbitrary way. . . .[47]

Canadian judges have been prepared to protect parents from interference by the state or others, in particular interpreting legislation in such a way as to maximize the rights of natural parents threatened with loss of custody of their

---

45 (1983), 43 O.R. (2d) 685 at 688 (H.C.). See also *Joplin v. Chief Constable of Vancouver Police Dept.* (1982), 4 C.R.R. 208 at 212 (B.C.S.C.); and *Kahlon v. Min. of Employment & Immigration*, [1985] O.L.W. 524-014 (Fed. T.D.).

46 [1970] 1 O.R. 601 at 609, affirmed [1970] S.C.R. 261 (sub. nom. *C.A.S. of Ottawa v. Mugford*). Though some recent decisions, like *K.K. v. G.L.* (1985), 16 D.L.R. (4th) 576 (S.C.C.), emphasize that the "best interests" of the child take precedence to parental rights, it must be remembered that these decisions do not involve the *state* as a litigant, but rather are contests between biological parents and "psychological parents".

47 (1978), 5 R.F.L. (2d) 50 at 59 (Ont. Prov. Ct.); for another example of the same judicial approach, see *Re Gonyea* (1979), 3 Fam. L. Rev. 66 (P.E.I.S.C.). For a somewhat different view, however, see *C.A.S. of Ottawa-Carleton v. D.J.L.* (1980), 15 R.F.L. (2d) 102 (Ont. Prov. Ct.).

children. It can be argued that this special judicial concern, a part of our common law tradition of protecting the individual, should be reflected in the interpretation of the concepts of "liberty" and "security of the person" in s. 7 of the Charter of Rights.

A number of recent Canadian decisions clearly support the view that liberty is to be broadly interpreted. For example, in *R. v. Morgentaler* the Ontario Court of Appeal acknowledged:

> Some rights. . . . are so deeply rooted in our traditions and way of life as to be fundamental and could be classified as part of life, liberty and security of the person. The right to choose one's partner in marriage, and the decision whether or not to have children, would fall in this category, as would the right to clothe oneself, take medical advice and decide whether or not to act on this advice.[48]

In *Re R.A.M.; Children's Aid Society of Winnipeg v. A.M.*[49] a 13-year-old boy was made a permanent ward of the children's aid society. As part of an appeal, counsel for the boy applied to a higher court for an order that counsel be appointed under child protection legislation and that the boy be made a party to the proceeding. Matas J.A. of the Manitoba Court of Appeal, sitting alone, made the order sought, relying in part on s. 7 of the Charter; he concluded that the boy's "liberty and security would be affected by a permanent order". Unfortunately the decision does not offer much discussion of why s. 7 is applicable to such proceedings. The decision of Matas J.A. was reversed by a full panel of the Manitoba Court of Appeal in a very brief oral judgment made on strictly procedural grounds; the panel expressed no views on the applicability of s. 7.

In another child protection case, *T.T. v. Catholic Children's Aid Society of Metropolitan Toronto*, a parent was challenging an order to produce the child before the court as required by s. 21(*b*) of Ontario's Child Welfare Act. Although the application was dismissed, Thomson Prov. J. stated:

> If one accepts, *as I do,* that *security of the person includes the right to individual privacy* or *family autonomy* . . . and that one of the *liberty interests to be protected is the parental right* to be *free from state intervention.* . . . then it can be argued that an order which requires a parent to produce her child before a court does violate, to some degree, the rights set out in s. 7. . . . this is an argument more easily made when dealing with the more intrusive step of apprehending the child without any prior authorization.[50]

Perhaps the most encouraging support for the broad interpretation of s. 7 comes from statements of Madame Justice Wilson in the Supreme Court of Canada in *Singh v. Minister of Employment and Immigration*, where she states:

---

48 (1985), 52 O.R. (2d) 353 at 377 (C.A.).

49 (1983), 37 R.F.L. (2d) 113 at 121, reversed on other grounds 39 R.F.L. (2d) 239 (Man. C.A.).

50 39 R.F.L. (2d) 279 at 293-94 (Ont. Prov. Ct.). Emphasis added. The Child Welfare Act, R.S.O. 1980, c. 66 was repealed by the Child and Family Services Act, S.O. 1984, c. 55, s. 208.

> Certainly, it is true that the concepts of the right to life, the right to liberty and the right to security of the person are capable of a broad range of meaning. The Fourteenth Amendment to the United States Constitution provides in part ". . . nor shall any State deprive any person of life, liberty, or property, without the due process of law . . .". In *Board of Regents of State Colleges v. Roth* (1972), 408 U.S. 564 at p.572, Stewart J. articulated the notion of liberty as embodied in the Fourteenth Amendment in the following way:

>> "While this Court has not attempted to define with exactness the liberty . . . guaranteed [by the Fourteenth Amendment], the term has received much consideration and some of the included things have been definitely stated. Without doubt, it denotes not merely freedom from bodily restraint but also the right of the individual to contract, to engage in any of the common occupations of life, to acquire useful knowledge, to marry, establish a home and bring up children, to worship God according to the dictates of his own conscience, and generally to enjoy those privileges long recognized . . . as essential to the orderly pursuit of happiness by free men. . . . In a Constitution for a free people, there can be no doubt that the meaning of "liberty" must be broad indeed. . . ."

> The "single right" theory advanced by counsel for the Minister would suggest that this conception of "liberty" is too broad to be employed in our interpretation of s. 7 of the Charter. Even if this submission is sound, however, it seems to me that it is incumbent upon the court to give meaning to each of the elements, life, liberty and security of the person, which make up the "right" contained in s. 7.[51]

Although these remarks were probably only *obiter dicta*, and supported by only three of the six judges who decided the case, the general approach of *Singh* seems to indicate that the highest court in Canada may take a broad interpretation to s. 7.

Much of the jurisprudence in this area, both Canadian and American, refers to the need to protect the "family unit". It is possible, however, to distinguish at least two different, yet interrelated, interests. One is *familial integrity* — or an interest in upholding the family as an independent, autonomous unit in society; either a parent or child may base claims on this interest. The other is parental authority — a *parental* right to enjoy family life and control various aspects of a child's life, free from unnecessary state interference. Though conceptually distinct, and not always necessarily harmonious,[52] the courts and

---

51 *Supra*, n. 44, at 458-59 (S.C.C.).

52 Robert Keiter, "Privacy, Children and Their Parents: Reflections on and Beyond the Supreme Court's Approach" (1982), 66 Minn. L. Rev. 459, identifies three distinct interests. This American author writes, at 492-93:

"When the interests of parent and child collide, however, it is not clear that the constitutional principles underlying these decisions necessarily support legislative reinforcement of parental child rearing prerogatives. Three distinct, yet interrelated constitutional principles emerge. . . to limit the state's authority. . . to regular family matters — parental authority in child rearing, family privacy and family institutional integrity. These principles are neither synonymous nor necessarily harmonious with each other. This becomes particularly evident when each principle is individually evaluated as a basis for a state legislative decision requiring

legislatures have at times given recognition and protection only to a right of parental authority, though sometimes justifying this on the basis of promoting familial integrity.[53]

The common law has viewed the parents as the child's natural guardians and has given them a broad range of rights in regard to their child. At common law, parents have the right to custody and control of their child, to direct their child's education and religious training, to discipline their child and to make health care decisions regarding the child. In various Canadian jurisdictions, some of these rights have been modified and codified by statute.[54]

The protection of parental rights is based, at least in part, on a belief that parents will act to promote their child's interests, and hence a protection of these rights will promote a child's welfare. Further, as parents in our society have primary responsibility for the care of the children that they brought into the world, this necessitates giving parents a very significant set of rights in regard to their children. It is also recognized that even well-intentioned state involvement in a child's life may not be beneficial. The resources of the state to care for and control children are inevitably limited, and so it is felt presumptively best to leave a child in its natural environment, particularly since any change is bound to have a disruptive effect upon a child. Perhaps most fundamentally, parental rights are viewed as "natural rights". It is accepted as a basic tenet of our culture and way of life that parents have a "right" to control and care for their children; this right is inextricably bound to our view of a society based on the primacy of the individual.

---

parental involvement in situations implicating children's constitutional . . . interests. The concept of parental authority certainly serves as a legitimate state interest underlying a legislative decision to reinforce the parental role. The concept of family privacy, however, suggests that state intrusion into the family in any guise, even to support the parental role, is undesirable. The principal of family institutional integrity, which recognizes the fundamental importance of the family unit to all members, also mitigates against any form of state legislative interference that might jeopardize the family as a unit. Therefore, when the state . . . chooses to reinforce parental authority in real or potential child conflict situations, it may be overlooking or disregarding other important interests, each with a vulnerable constitutional status in its own right."

53 See Laurence H. Tribe, *American Constitutional Law* (1978), at 986-87:
". . . although the [U.S. Supreme Court] has spoken of recognizing a 'private realm of family life which the state cannot enter' without compelling justification. . . . Such 'exercises of familial rights and responsibilities' . . . prove to be *individual* powers to resist governmental determination of who shall be born, with whom one shall live, and what values shall be transmitted."

54 For a discussion of the scope of parental rights at common law and under legislation, see Bernard Dickens, "The Modern Function and Limits of Parental Rights" (1981), 97 L.Q. Rev. 462; Walder G.W. White, "A Comparison of Some Parental and Guardian Rights" (1980), 3 Can. J. Fam. L. 119; and J.M. Eekelaar, "What are Parental Rights?" (1973), 89 L.Q. Rev. 210.

Later in this chapter it will be argued that children also have constitutional rights which they can assert on their own. Of course none of these rights is absolute. It will be necessary to consider the various constitutional issues which arise when these rights have to be balanced against each other and against societal interests.

2. "In Accordance with the Principles of Fundamental Justice": Section 7

Section 7 of the Charter does not afford an absolute guarantee to "liberty and security of the person". Rather, it provides that a person shall not be deprived of "liberty and security of the person" (which it has been argued includes a right to enjoy familial relations) *except* "in accordance with the principles of fundamental justice". The proper interpretation of the term "principles of fundamental justice" has aroused considerable controversy.

Many judges and commentators have felt that the "principles of fundamental justice" simply embodied the concept of procedural due process — a right to be treated in accordance with the requirements of natural justice. For example, in *Re Mason and R.*, Ewaschuk J. stated:

> Section 7 of the Charter provides minimal procedural safeguards, in relation to federal and provincial legislation and conduct. . . . It is . . . undoubted that s. 7 was intended to guarantee procedural due process. (*i.e.*, natural justice) and not substantive due process. . . .[55]

The concept of procedural due process is a flexible one, with the exact nature of the procedural rights granted depending upon the nature of the proceedings.[56] However, procedural due process would generally include the following:

the right to have the decision made by a person who is free of bias or a reasonable apprehension of bias, and who has heard all the evidence and argument;

the right of each party whose rights may be affected to notice thereof with sufficient information concerning the allegations against him to enable him to make adequate reply;

the right to a genuine hearing at which each party affected is made aware of the allegations against him and is permitted to answer;

---

55 (1983), 43 O.R. (2d) 321 at 323 (H.C.). See also *R. v. Hayden* (1983), 8 C.C.C. (3d) 33 (Man. C.A.); *Re Jamieson and R.* (1982), 3 C.R.R. 193 (Que. S.C.), *per* Durand J.; and *Latham v. Solicitor Gen. of Can.* (1984), 12 C.C.C. (3d) 9 (Fed. T.D.).

56 See, e.g., *Howard v. Presiding Officer of Inmate Disciplinary Ct. of Stony Mountain Institution* (1985), 57 N.R. 280 (Fed. C.A.). For the American approach to how "much process is due", see *Mathews v. Eldridge*, 424 U.S. 319 (1976).

the right of each party to cross-examine witnesses giving evidence against his interest;[57]

the right to be represented by counsel, and perhaps even the right to state appointed counsel for an indigent litigant whose "liberty or security of the person" is in jeopardy;[58]

the right to make a reasonable request for an adjournment so as to permit a party affected properly to prepare and present his case.

Some courts and commentators, however, have gone beyond this and, borrowing from American jurisprudence, have argued that the "principles of fundamental justice" also include a notion of "substantive due process", thus allowing the courts to strike down laws which are in some sense substantively unfair in depriving a person of liberty or security of the person. Applying the doctrine of "substantive due process" courts review the content of the law, and not simply its procedural aspects.

---

57 See, e.g., *Re U.S. and Smith* (1984), 44 O.R. (2d) 705 (C.A.), where it was held that in an extradition hearing, given the nature of the proceedings, the Charter did not require that the accused fugitive be given an opportunity to cross-examine on affidavits.

58 In Canada, under the Bill of Rights, the courts held that the right to "retain and instruct counsel" did not include the requirement that if the accused was unable to afford counsel, legal services should be provided at public expense: *Re Ewing and R.* (1974), 49 D.L.R. (3d) 619 (B.C.C.A.). In the United States, however, an accused's Sixth Amendment right to "have the assistance of counsel for his defence" includes the right to have counsel provided at state expense where the accused faces possible imprisonment and is unable to afford counsel: *Gideon v. Wainwright*, 372 U.S. 335 (1963). In *In re Gault*, 387 U.S. 1 (1967), the due process provisions of the American Constitution were interpreted to require that a juvenile facing committal to training school also be provided with counsel. In *Lassiter v. Social Services Dept. of Durham County*, 452 U.S. 18 (1981), it was held that since a parent faced a potential loss of a "liberty interest" in a termination of parental rights proceeding, in many circumstances due process and "fundamental fairness" required that indigent parents in such cases have counsel provided by the state.

In *R. v. Powell* (1984), 30 Alta. L.R. (2d) 83 (Prov. Ct.), Litsky Prov. J. held that the procedural due process provisions of the Canadian Charter of Rights, and s. 11 (*d*), which guarantees the right of an accused in a criminal case to a "fair trial", required that indigent parents facing a truancy charge were to have counsel provided by the state. Litsky Prov. J. stated, at 92:

"The court surely cannot expect lay people to become legal pundits navigating this case with provocative points of fact and law. . . . Matters such as adducing evidence, presentation of argument, and cross-examination on evidentiary points all constitute procedural processes not within the professional purview of the Powells".

If the approach of *Powell* is followed, it may be possible for indigent parents and children in protection proceedings, facing possible loss of familial relations, vital aspects of their "liberty and security of the person", to argue that they too are entitled to state appointed counsel. See also *Deutsch v. L.S.U.C. Legal Aid Fund* (1985), 48 C.R. (3d) 166 (Ont. H.C.), where Craig J. held that a trial judge might invoke ss. 7 and 11(*d*) to direct that counsel be provided to a criminally accused person.

The Supreme Court of Canada has recently ruled that s. 7 of the Charter of Rights extends beyond procedural due process and has a substantive element as well. In *Re Constitutional Question Act; Reference re S. 94(2) of the Motor Vehicle Act*, the court considered provincial legislation which created an absolute liability offence, having a minimum sentence of seven day's imprisonment, for any person driving while prohibited from doing so or while his licence was suspended, regardless of whether or not the accused knew of the prohibition or suspension. The court noted the potential unfairness of an absolute liability offence in these circumstances and invoked s. 7 of the Charter to strike down the law.

Writing for a majority of the court, Lamer J. wrote:

> In other words, the principles of fundamental justice are to be found in the basic tenets of our legal system. They do not lie in the realm of general public policy, but in the inherent domain of the judiciary as guardian of the justice system. . . .
>
> . . . they represent principles which have been recognized by the common law, the international conventions and by the very fact of entrenchment in the Charter, as essential elements of a system for the administration of justice which is founded upon a belief in the dignity and worth of the human person and the rule of law.
>
> Consequently, the principles of fundamental justice are to be found in the basic tenets and principles, not only of our judicial process, but also of the other components of our legal system.[59]

Madam Justice Wilson defined the principles of fundamental justice as "the basic, bedrock principles that underpin a system".[60] In *Re Potma and R.*, an earlier decision of the Ontario Court of Appeal, Robins J.A. remarked:

> This is not to suggest that "the principles of fundamental justice" now recognized by the Charter of Rights and Freedoms are immutable. "Fundamental justice", like "natural justice" or "fair play", is a compendious expression intended to guarantee the basic right of citizens in a free and democratic society to a *fair procedure*. The principles or standards of *fairness* essential to the attainment of fundamental justice are in no sense static, and will continue as they have in the past to evolve and develop in response to society's changing perception of what is *arbitrary, unfair or unjust*.[61]

More recently, in *R. v. Morgentaler*, the Ontario Court of Appeal concluded that:

> . . . in applying the principles of fundamental justice the Court is not limited to procedural review but may also review the substance of legislation. . . . such substantive review should take place only in exceptional cases where there has been a marked departure from the norm

---

59 [1985] 2 S.C.R. 486 at 503, 512.

60 *Ibid.*, at 530.

61 (1983), 41 O.R. (2d) 43 at 52 (C.A.). Emphasis added.

of civil or criminal liability resulting in the infringement of liberty or in some other injustice. We reiterate that the policy and wisdom of legislation should remain first and foremost a matter for Parliament and the Legislatures.[62]

In *Morgentaler*, the Ontario Court of Appeal refused to rule that s. 251 of the Criminal Code,[63] governing Canada's abortion law, violated s. 7 of the Charter, but accepted that s. 7 has a substantive element.

It is thus clear that the words "in accordance with the principles of fundamental justice" require that a person be afforded procedural due process before forfeiting aspects of his "liberty" or "security of the person". However, it clearly means more than this. Although it seems improbable that Canadian courts will quickly undertake the broad substantive reviews of legislation which have been the hallmark of some American constitutional jurisprudence, they appear ready to move cautiously beyond the procedural core of s. 7. This may well mean that laws which deprive individuals of opportunities to enjoy aspects of a familial or parental relationship may be struck down if they are viewed as "arbitrary, unfair or unjust".

VIII PARENTAL RIGHTS: SECTION 7

Section 7 of the Charter of Rights stipulates that no person shall be deprived of liberty or security of the person "except in accordance with the principles of fundamental justice". It has been argued above that this constitutional provision should protect the right to enjoy family life, as an aspect of the "liberty and security of the person". In this part of the chapter, some suggestions will be offered about who may invoke these rights and about some situations in which parental rights under the Charter of Rights may be violated. In the following part there is a discussion of the nature of the constitutional rights a child may have, and of how parental rights are to be balanced against the rights of a child and the interests of the state.

1. Unwed Fathers

In some pre-Charter judicial decisions, such as *Children's Aid Society of Metropolitan Toronto v. Lyttle*,[64] the courts showed a concern with ensuring that fathers of children born out of wedlock have a right to notice of and participation in legal proceedings at which the fate of their children is to be decided, but Canadian legislatures have sometimes shown much less concern for the parental rights of unwed fathers.

---

62 (1985), 52 O.R. (2d) 353 at 385.

63 R.S.C. 1970, c. C-34, s. 251 [am. 1974-75-76, c. 93, s. 22.1].

64 [1973] S.C.R. 568.

For example, until recently Manitoba's Child Welfare Act defined a child in need of protection to include "a child born to parents not married to each other whose *mother* is unable or unwilling to care for him".[65] No legislative mention was made of the ability of the father of a child born out of wedlock to care for the child. In several provinces, a child born out of wedlock can still be adopted without the biological father having to consent or even being notified of the proposed adoption, but a mother's consent is always required[66] (unless the child is a ward of the state or a court order is made dispensing with a mother's consent).

It is clear that legislation which discriminates against unwed fathers can be challenged as a violation of the equality rights provisions of s. 15 of the Charter, but a strong challenge can also be made to such legislation on the ground that it violates rights protected under s. 7 of the Charter. In the United States it is common in claims involving familial or parental rights for the courts to give effect to both the Equal Protection (that is, gender discrimination), and Due Process clauses of the Fourteenth Amendment. The fact that legislation affects a fundamental "liberty interest", the right to enjoy a familial relationship, strengthens the Equal Protection argument.[67]

In *Stanley v. Illinois*[68] the U.S. Supreme Court declared unconstitutional state legislation that made a child born out of wedlock a ward of the state upon

---

65 S.M. 1974, c. 30 (also C.C.S.M., c. C80), s. 16(*f*) [re-en. 1982-83-84, c. 55, s. 6]. In *C.A.S. of Winnipeg v. Sinclair; Prince v. C.A.S. of Winnipeg* (1980), 5 Man. R. (2d) 170 (C.A.), this legislative provision prompted Huband J.A. to remark, at 175:

"The natural mother has a *prima facie* right of custody against all others, including the putative father, and that right can be interfered with only where there are serious and important reasons affecting the welfare of the child to warrant such interference. A putative father has no comparable rights, either as against the mother, or against the Children's Aid Society which claims guardianship with the mother's apparent approbation.

. . . a putative father has few rights, if any, relative to custody of a child."

66 See for example, the Adoption Act, R.S.B.C. 1979, c. 4, s. 8 [am. 1980, c-11, s. 26; c-36, s. 1]; and the Family Services Act, R.S.S. 1978, c. F-27, ss. 2, 52. See also the brief comments of J.G. McLeod, "Annotation to *Re J.R.M.*" (1982), 28 R.F.L. (2d) 131 at 132, which support the view that an unwed father may have rights under s. 7 of the Charter in regard to the adoption of his child. In *Re L.T.K.* (1982), 31 R.F.L. (2d) 424 (Man. Co. Ct.), an unwed father tried to argue that the failure to give him notice of an adoption application concerning his child was "cruel and unusual treatment" and hence in violation of s. 12 of the Charter. The judge did not deal with the argument on its merits since the application was commenced prior to the Charter coming into force and the judge decided that the Charter was not "retroactive". If the father's case was based on s. 7 of the Charter, could he have argued that his rights were "procedural", and hence could be applied after the Charter came into effect?

67 See, e.g., *Zablocki v. Redhail*, 434 U.S. 374 (1978), where Equal Protection and Due Process clauses were both invoked to strike down legislation restricting the rights of persons with child support obligations to remarry; see also *Stanley v. Illinois*, 405 U.S. 645 (1977), dealing with the rights of the fathers of children born out of wedlock.

68 *Ibid.*

the death of his mother. The court recognized that the state has a right — indeed a duty — to protect minor children, and that many children born out of wedlock might be in need of protection upon the death of their mothers. But the court emphasized that an unwed father has a substantial "liberty interest" in raising his child, and held that the state could not deprive him of this interest on the basis of a mere presumption that unwed fathers are unfit parents. Due process, said the court, demanded that the father have a hearing to determine *his* fitness as a parent.

In Canada it would seem that a constitutional challenge can be made under s. 7 and s. 15 of the Charter to adoption or child protection legislation which denies an unwed father the right to reasonable notice or to be heard before a decision is made concerning his child. Clearly the "principles of fundamental justice" require notice and an opportunity to participate in a hearing. The key to making a successful constitutional challenge depends upon demonstrating that an unwed father has a substantial, constitutionally protected interest in such a proceeding. If it is accepted that in general "liberty" or "security of the person" includes a right to enjoy familial relationships, it may be difficult to deny an unwed father constitutional protection for this right, particularly a father who has established a meaningful relationship with the child in question.

It is not adequate to simply presume that all unwed fathers should be denied parental rights without notice or a hearing. Of course, when a case involving the welfare of a child is decided on its substantive merits, it may be that the parental rights of an unwed father will be curtailed or terminated. Unwed fathers often have little contact with their offspring, but this does not mean that all such men should be denied the right to participation in legal decisions concerning their children. As noted in *Stanley v. Illinois*:

> Procedure by presumption is always cheaper and easier than individualized determination. But when as here, the procedure forecloses the determinative issues of competence and care, when it explicitly disdains present realities in deference to past formalities, it needlessly risks running roughshod over the important interests of both parent and child.[69]

This notion that Charter rights cannot be ignored on the grounds of "administrative convenience" has received significant judicial support in the recent Supreme Court of Canada decision of *Singh v. Minister of Employment and Immigration* where Wilson J. observed:

> Seen in this light I have considerable doubt that the type of utilitarian consideration brought forward by Mr. Bowie [counsel for the Minister] can constitute a justification for a

---

69 *Ibid.*, at 656-57. For a very interesting discussion of *Stanley* and the constitutional difficulties surrounding use of conclusive presumptions, see Laurence H. Tribe, "Childhood, Suspect Classifications, and Conclusive Presumptions: Three Linked Riddles" (1975), 39:3 Law & Contemp. Prob. 8.

limitation on the rights set out in the Charter. Certainly the guarantees of the Charter would be illusory if they could be ignored because it was administratively convenient to do so. No doubt considerable time and money can be saved by adopting administrative procedures which ignore the principles of fundamental justice but such an argument, in my view, misses the point of the exercise under s. 1. The principles of natural justice and procedural fairness which have long been espoused by our courts, and the constitutional entrenchment of the principles of fundamental justice in s. 7, implicitly recognize that a balance of administrative convenience does not override the need to adhere to these principles.[70]

The argument against discriminating against unwed fathers, as opposed to unwed mothers, in terms of rights to notice and participation in a proceeding, is reinforced by s. 28 of the Charter, which provides that the "rights and freedoms" referred to in the Charter, including those in s. 7, are "guaranteed equally to male and female persons". Further, s. 15, the equality rights provision, strengthens the position of unwed fathers; are they not subject to discrimination on the basis of sex?

Of course, the rights in the Charter are not absolute, but rather, as set out in s. 1, are subject "to such reasonable limits prescribed by law as can be demonstrably justified in a free and democratic society". Thus, it would not seem necessary to extend to all unwed fathers a full panoply of procedural rights. In Ontario, the Child and Family Services Act has definitions of "parent" for the purposes of protection and adoption proceedings[71] which include a biological father who has established or formally acknowledged his paternity. It would seem to be a "reasonable" limitation to only protect the rights of unwed fathers who can be identified with reasonable effort, though it may be argued that the legislative definitions do not go far enough. As Steinberg U.F.C.J. commented in a recent case:

> My concern, however, is whether the result in this case, and the many others of its ilk, is just for men, who for no fault of their own are unaware of the birth of their children and are kept in ignorance of the fact by virtue of a restrictive definition of "parent" under the Child Welfare Act. . . .
>
> Justice is generally not served when persons' interests are litigated upon without their knowledge. Some legislation is required to ensure, *where reasonable and practical*, that prior to the placement of a child for adoption:
>
> (a) The biological father is made aware of the birth of the child; and
>
> (b) He has an opportunity to present to a court an alternative plan for his child.[72]

---

70 (1985), 17 D.L.R. (4th) 422 at 469 (S.C.C.).

71 Ss. 37(1)(*d*) and 131(1).

72 *Re A.* (1984), 42 R.F.L. (2d) 221 at 223-24 (Ont. U.F.C.). See, however, *Lehr v. Robertson*, 9 F.L.R. 3077 at 3080-3081 (U.S.S.C., 1983), where it was held that "the mere existence of a biological link does not merit equivalent [constitutional] protection". If the father fails to establish a relationship with his offspring, the "Constitution will not automatically compel a state to listen to his opinion of where the child's best interests lie".

It may be that even without legislative action, the Charter requires courts to act as Steinberg U.F.C.J. advocates.

In summary, it has been argued that an aspect of the "liberty and security of the person" of an unwed father is his right to enjoy a relationship with his child. This does *not* mean that he cannot be deprived of custody of his child, or have the relationship to his child severed through child protection proceedings or adoption. But it does mean that, subject to such "reasonable limits" as may be "demonstrably justified in a free and democratic society", he can forfeit this aspect of his liberty only "in accordance with the principles of fundamental justice". Further, as will be discussed below, any legal treatment which discriminates against parents on the basis of sex (that is, treats fathers worse than mothers), will be constitutionally suspect and subject to challenge under ss. 15 and 28 of the Charter.

2. Rights of Foster Parents and Relatives

In Canada, until relatively recently, those who voluntarily agreed to care for the children of others, whether at the request of the biological parents or the state after children were made state wards, had very few, if any, legal rights in regard to the children. The legal custodian, whether a biological parent or a stage agency, could simply remove the child without notice and without any sort of a hearing. In the past few years, some courts and legislatures[73] have come to grant some significant legal recognition to the care-giving "psychological parents" of the child.

In the United States there have been a number of reported decisions in which foster parents have claimed that they were entitled to procedural due process under the Fourteenth Amendment before their relationship to a child in their care is severed. It is clear that in many instances foster parents will have no right to constitutional protections as the relationship to the child is not strong enough and there is no reasonable expectation of any stable relationship

---

73 See e.g. *Re Moores and Feldstein*, [1973] 3 O.R. 921 (C.A.) (persons having *de facto* care of a 4-year-old child almost since birth awarded custody over biological mother). This judicial concern for "psychological parents" has recently gained substantial judicial support in the Supreme Court of Canada in *K.K. v. G.L.* (1985), 16 D.L.R. (4th) 576 (S.C.C.). In legislative terms see, e.g., the Family Law Act, S.O. 1986, c. 4, s. 1(1)(" 'parent' includes a person who has demonstrated a settled intention to treat a child as a child of his or her family, except under an arrangement where the child is placed for valuable consideration by a person having lawful custody"); and the Child and Family Services Act, s. 39(3) (foster parent having care of child on behalf of child protection authority for six continuous months has right to notice of protection hearing, to make representations, to be represented by counsel, and to take further part in the proceedings with leave of the court) and s. 57(7). See also Child Welfare Act, S.A. 1984, c. C-8.1, s. 21(1)(*d*).

forming.[74] In *Rivera v. Marcus,* however, the court was prepared to extend a range of due process protections to a foster mother, who was a blood relative of the child, before allowing removal by the welfare department which had legal custody. The court stated:

> . . . there would appear to be instances in which a liberty interest should be recognized where long term family relationships evolve out of foster home placements. It seems clear that, as with a biological parent and child, strong, loving emotional and psychological ties can develop among members of a long term foster family. Any arbitrary state interference with those ties surely can result in harsh and lasting consequences to the foster child and to the foster family members. In these special circumstances, it would seem that a pre-removal hearing which comports with constitutional standards may be required.[75]

The courts in the United States have seemed most prepared to protect foster parents in situations where a child welfare agency plans to move the child to another foster home or to an adoptive placement. On the other hand, at least in situations where a foster parent gains care of the child through the intervention of an agency, the interests of the foster parents "must be substantially attenuated where the proposed removal from the foster family is to retun the child to his natural parents".[76] The existence of a relationship between the foster parent and the child will not be permitted to weaken the claim of natural parents in their relationship with the state child welfare agency.

In some circumstances, foster parents in Canada may well be able to argue that they too have a right not to be deprived by state action of the care of a child with whom they have established a stable relationship, "except in accordance with the principles of fundamental justice". The recognition of such procedural rights would be in accord with the tentative legislative and judicial steps which have been taken in this country, and with the growing body of evidence supporting a child's need for stable relationships with his "psychological parents".[77] In *B.M. v Alberta; B.M. v. Director of Child Welfare,*[78] foster parents made just such an argument; Veit J. of the Alberta Court of Queen's

---

74 See e.g. *Kyees v. Tippecanoe County Dept. of Pub. Welfare*, 600 F. 2d 693 (C.A. 7th Circ., 1979).

75 8 F.L.R. 2270 at 2271, affirmed 9 F.L.R. 2178 (C.A. 2nd Circ., 1982).

76 *Smith v. Organization of Foster Families for Equality and Reform*, 97 S. Ct. 2095 at 2111 (1977), *per* Brennan J.

77 See, e.g., Goldstein, Freud and Solnit, *Beyond the Best Interests of the Child* (1973). See also *W. v. C.A.S. of Sarnia-Lambton*, [1982] W.D.F.L. 1373 (Ont. Prov. Ct.), *per* Kent Prov. J. for a case where foster parents and a child in care sought to challenge the actions of the children's aid society; and see *D.B. v. Dir. of Child Welfare for Nfld.* (1982), 30 R.F.L. (2d) 438 (S.C.C.), where the court invoked its *parens patriae* jurisdiction to protect the rights of prospective adoptive parents when a child was arbitrarily removed by the adoption authorities after almost six months in their care.

78 (1985), 45 R.F.L. (2d) 113 (Alta. Q.B.).

Bench seemed to view their argument sympathetically, but ultimately decided in their favour by involving the court's *parens patriae* jurisdiction and without determining the constitutional issue.

There may be other circumstances in which individuals, other than the biological parents but who have an interest in the child, may be able to invoke the Charter to at least gain access to the courts. For example, in some situations grandparents of a child in the care of a state agency might make such claims under s 7.

IX CHILDREN, PARENTS AND THE STATE: SECTION 7

1. The Status of Childhood

Children have limited intellectual, physical, social, psychological and economic resources. They are born in a state of total dependence requiring constant care. As children mature, they gradually acquire the capacity to care for themselves. At some point they are deemed fully capable of caring for themselves and legally become adults. At birth a child is not capable of exercising any rights on his own behalf; his parents, some other person or agency, or the state must exercise all rights on behalf of the child. Upon becoming an "adult", the former "child" acquires a full range of legal and citizenship rights, to be exercised on his own. In regard to certain matters, a child may acquire legal rights and responsibilities before becoming an adult.

A child has a particular legal "status". In recognition of the child's limited development, there are certain legal obligations, privileges and incapacities ascribed to this status by operation of law. The common law and legislation provide that children are legally incapable of making various decisions which affect their lives, though for some matters children who are older may have certain rights denied younger children. In general, parents have a presumptive right to exercise a broad degree of control over their children, making decisions regarding such matters as place of residence, health care, discipline, education, religious training and even marriage.[79] As outlined above, at least in regard to some of these matters, parents can argue that they have a constitutionally protected "interest", and exercise rights in regard to their children subject to state intervention only "in accordance with the principles of fundamental justice".

The state also recognizes the status of childhood by exercising direct control over children, for example through school attendance laws and young

---

79 See the articles by Dickens, White and Eekelaar, *supra*, n. 54, dealing with the extent of parental rights.

offenders legislation. Further, at some point, the state is prepared to intervene and protect children *from* their parents, either through criminal law (for example prosecutions resulting from situations of child abuse), or by invoking child protection legislation and, if necessary, removing a child from parental care. As well, the state recognizes the status of childhood by specifically denying children certain rights guaranteed to others. As noted earlier in the discussion of s. 1 of the Charter, this section can easily be invoked to deny children certain constitutionally guaranteed rights on the basis of immaturity. At least for children below a certain age or level of maturity, mobility rights and the right to vote would fall into this category. In other cases it may not be so clear that s. 1 should be invoked to deny children constitutional rights.

Our concern here is to consider what constitutionally protected interests a child may assert against the state and his parents, and then to discuss some of the very difficult issues which arise when the state becomes involved in interfering with parental interests to protect a child from his parents. Later in this chapter consideration will be given to whether s. 15 of the Charter can be invoked by children to show that they have been unreasonably discriminated against on the basis of age.

2. Child Versus State

There are a number of situations in which the state becomes directly involved in controlling the behaviour of young persons and limiting their "liberty or security of the person".

The most obvious example of state control over the behaviour of young persons is the Young Offenders Act. This legislation makes the substantive criminal law applicable to "young offenders". Under this Act, it is the young person who is the accused and who faces a potential threat to his liberty and a restraint on his freedom. Section 3(e) of the Young Offenders Act guarantees a young person all the rights and freedoms of the Charter of Rights. It was accepted that even under the Juvenile Delinquents Act, with its treatment oriented philosophy, juveniles were entitled to invoke the Charter to ensure that their rights were protected.[80] This is consistent with the approach in the United States where courts have held that juveniles are entitled to a broad range of due process constitutional rights, though in view of the nature of the delinquency proceedings, they are denied certain rights guaranteed adults, such as the right to a trial by jury.[81]

---

80 See, e.g., cases cited *supra*, n. 9.

81 See *In re Gault*, 387 U.S. 1 (1967), and *In re Winship*, 397 U.S. 358 (1970), for cases granting juveniles rights. In *McKeiver v. Pennsylvania*, 403 U.S. 528 (1971), a juvenile charged with a delinquency was held not to be constitutionally entitled to a jury trial. In Canada the courts have

In young offenders proceedings, it is the child (using the term in its generic sense) who is a party to the proceedings; the parents are not parties. It is the child who faces sanction and a loss of "liberty" if a conviction is registered, and so it is entirely justifiable that the youth is granted constitutional protections in such proceedings.[82]

There are other proceedings in which a child faces a loss of "liberty" but for which Canadian courts and legislatures thus far failed to afford full rights of participation and constitutional protections. In a child protection proceeding, it can be argued that a child faces a loss of "liberty and security of the person". The proceeding may result in committal to the care of a state agency until adulthood. Such committal will involve removal from a child's natural family which may in itself be viewed as a deprivation of "liberty and security of the person", as familial relationships are threatened. The child may be placed in a group home or other facility in which his movements and activities are controlled, and in some provinces may actually be placed in a correctional institution in which juvenile offenders are placed.[83] In Ontario, s. 40 of the Child and Family Services Act specifically refers to the fact that a child may be "apprehended" and "detained", which clearly suggests that a loss of physical "liberty" may also be involved in such a situation. In many jurisdictions, the grounds for finding a child in need of protection may effectively overlap with those which form the basis of a charge under the Young Offenders Act;[84] this also suggests that a child's "liberty" is at stake in a protection proceeding. These impositions on "liberty" through state action may well be justified, but only if this is done "in accordance with the principles of fundamental justice".

---

come to the same conclusion; *R. v. S.B.* (1983), 32 R.F.L. (2d) 432 (B.C.C.A.); and *R. v. D.T.* (1983), 37 C.R. (3d) 29, affirmed 39 C.R. (3d) 95 (Ont. C.A.); and *R. v. R.L.*, Ont. C.A., 22nd April 1986 (not yet reported).

82 In *In re Gault, ibid.*, the U.S. Supreme Court held that a boy charged with a delinquency has a range of constitutional rights. Justice Fortas remarked, at 27:
"It is of no constitutional consequence — and of limited practical meaning — that the institution to which he is committed is called an industrial school. The fact of the matter is that, however euphemistic the title, a 'receiving home' or an 'industrial school' for juveniles is an institution of confinement in which the child is incarcerated for a greater or lesser time. His world becomes a 'building with whitewashed walls, regimented routine and institutional hours. . .' Instead of mother and father and sisters and brothers and friends and classmates, his world is peopled by guards, custodians, state employees, and 'delinquents' confined with him for anything from waywardness to rape to homicide."

83 For example, in s. 2(*n*) of the Saskatchewan Family Services Act: "place of safety" is defined to include a "correctional institution for boys or girls. . . but does include a jail, prison, police station, lock-up or guardroom unless used temporarily and in an emergency". In Ontario, see s. 37(1) and s. 96 of the Child and Family Services Act.

84 For a general discussion of the relationship and overlap between protection and delinquency proceedings, see Reva Landau, "Status Offences: Inequality Before the Law" (1981), 39 U. T. Fac. L. Rev. 150 at 160-67; and Bala, Lilles and Thomson, *Canadian Children's Law: Cases, Notes and Materials* (1982), at 471-78.

The principal parties to a protection hearing are the parents and the state. Some provinces, however, provide that in certain circumstances children are given rights of notice and participation in protection hearings.[85] In other Canadian jurisdictions, however, there are no such rights. It may well be that a child who has the capacity and interest to participate in a protection proceeding but who is denied the right to notice and participation may be able to challenge the proceedings as violating his "liberty" and "security of the person" under s. 7 of the Charter.[86] Though in some situations parents may be viewed as "natural guardians", protecting the rights of their children from the state, in many proceedings the parents may lack the inclination or ability to protect their child's rights; their views or interests may be antithetical to those of their child. The child with capacity should be able to participate in the proceedings in his *own* right. Arguments in this regard may be reinforced by reference to s. 15 of the Charter: is denial of the right to participate in such proceedings demonstrably justified in a free and democratic society?

The argument put forward here about the effect of a protection proceeding on a child's rights under s. 7 of the Charter was apparently accepted by Matas J.A. of the Manitoba Court of Appeal in *Re R.A.M.; Children's Aid Society of Winnipeg v. A.M.*[87] In this case, a 13-year-old was made a permanent ward of the children's aid society. He did not appear and was not represented at the wardship hearing; though the boy recognized it would not be appropriate for him to return home, he expressed a desire to live with an aunt. The boy apparently was not told of his right to make his wishes known to the court and to be represented by counsel. The boy had counsel retained for a delinquency proceeding and when counsel learned of the wardship order an appeal was launched by the boy. In a preliminary motion in regard to the appeal an application was made for an order appointing counsel for the child and adding the child as a party to the protection

---

85 See, e.g., Ontario, Child and Family Services Act. ss. 38, 39 — children 12 and over presumptively given rights of notice and participation; under 12 with discretion of the court. See also s. 60(4) of the Ontario Child and Family Services Act and Alberta's Child Welfare Act, s. 21(1)(*c*), which give children 12 and over certain rights of participation.

86 In *W. v. C.A.S. of Sarnia-Lambton, supra*, n. 77, *per* Kent Prov. J., foster parents and a 9-year-old Crown ward, acting through counsel, sought to have the child found in need of protection as against the child protection agency. Under Ontario's Child Welfare Act, s. 38(1), only a child of 12 or more could apply for a review of a Crown wardship order. Counsel for the child argued that, "to deny the child an opportunity for a review of her case under s. 38 because of an apparently arbitrary age requirement would mean she herself would have no legal recourse in this court under the Act [Child Welfare Act], which is contrary to the Canadian Charter of Rights and Freedoms to live with the security of the person, and the right not to be deprived thereof except in accordance with the principles of fundamental justice, and also to her rights under s. 8 wherein everyone has a right to be secure against unreasonable seizure. . . ." The court did not rule on this issue.

87 (1983), 37 R.F.L. (2d) 113, reversed on other grounds 39 R.F.L. (2d) 239 (Man. C.A.).

proceeding. Manitoba legislation[88] expressly allowed a judge to order that a child be represented. In making the order that the boy should be represented, Matas J.A. quoted s. 7 of the Charter and stated:

> The premise of Ms. Burka's [counsel for the boy] argument is that the principles of fundamental justice are at least equivalent to the principles of natural justice; *audi alteram partem* applies and all children, regardless of age, are entitled to be present at a hearing and to be represented by counsel.

> It is not necessary to hold that counsel should be appointed in all cases of applications for permanent guardianship. . . .

> Nor do I think it is necessary to decide the extent of the applicability of the section with respect to age, nor to enter upon a full discussion of the inherent biological and human constraints applicable to children, nor to consider the reasonableness of s. 7 as it applies to children generally (s. 1 of the Charter). Taking into account the age of the applicant and his apparent level of understanding, it is my judgment that he comes within the ambit of s. 7. I have concluded that his liberty and security would be affected by a permanent order.

> An important factor leading to this conclusion is the relationship of these proceedings to those under the Juvenile Delinquents Act. It is taken for granted that R. [the boy] has the capacity to instruct counsel in the juvenile proceedings. I see no reason for thinking he cannot do so here. Coincidentally, there is an overlap in the two matters. As I have mentioned above, the suggested disposition in the juvenile proceedings is a committal to the society. That is very close to the appointment of the society as R.'s permanent guardian.[89]

---

88 Child Welfare Act, s. 25(7) [am. 1979, c. 22, s. 26; 1984, c. 15, s. 12], (7.1) [en. 1979, c. 22, s. 27; am. 1984, c. 15, s. 12] provides:
   "25(7) The judge shall advise those persons affected by a hearing under this section that they have the right to be represented by legal counsel; and in the case of a child if the judge is of the opinion that the child should be represented by counsel he may order that legal counsel be provided to represent the interests of the child.
   "25(7.1) In determining under subsection (7) whether representation of the child is desirable, the judge or master shall, in addition to all other relevant considerations, have regard to,
   "(*a*) any difference in the views of the child and views of the child caring agency or of a parent of the child;
   "(*b*) any difference in the interests of the child and the interests of the child caring agency or of a parent of the child;
   "(*c*) the nature of the proceedings, including the seriousness and complexity of the issues and whether the child caring agency is requesting that the child be removed from the home of a parent of the child;
   "(*d*) the capacity of the child to express his or her views to the court; and
   "(*e*) the views of the child regarding separate representation, where such views can reasonably be ascertained. . . ."

89 *Supra*, n. 87, 37 R.F.L. (2d) at 121-22. See also *Roe v. Conn*, 417 F. Supp. 769 (Ala. Dist. Ct., 1976) (in a child neglect proceeding a child was constitutionally entitled to have state appointed counsel); and *In re D*, 547 P. 2d 175 (Or. C.A., 1976), cert. denied 429 U.S. 907 (1976) (court need not appoint counsel for child in *all* termination proceedings).

The decision of Matas J.A. was reversed by a full panel of the Manitoba Court of Appeal on procedural grounds as the boy had not brought his application by a next friend; the brief decision of the full panel does not deal with the applicability of the Charter to this situation.

A recent Nova Scotia decision also recognized that children may invoke s. 7 of the Charter in situations jeopardizing their "liberty" but not arising as strictly criminal prosecutions. In *Re M.B.* a complaint was made against a 14-year-old ward alleging that she was "unmanageable" and hence, pursuant to s. 55 of Nova Scotia's Children's Services Act, could be committed to a "place of safety". Daley Fam. Ct. J. noted that:

> A place of safety in this context is only a more recent term for what were formerly called training, industrial, correctional or reform schools, all places of incarceration. . . . It was my finding that given the nature of the section and the penal consequences, that [sic] the standard of proof to be applied is the criminal standard. . . .
>
> . . . to suggest that there should be a different standard and that the Charter should not have any application to s. 55 just because it is a treatment tool, is not proper. If the child stands to be deprived of her liberty by committal to a place of safety, i.e. here the Nova Scotia School for Girls, then the principles of fundamental justice must apply.[90]

In *Re M.B.* the judge invoked s. 7 of the Charter to dismiss the complaint; it was so vague that the child would not know what behaviour, or lack of it, was to be addressed in defending herself and hence was threatened with a loss of liberty which was not in accordance with the principles of fundamental justice.

There may be a number of other circumstances where a child may have the intellectual capacity and legal right to directly challenge state actions as violating his constitutional rights. For example, perhaps a child at school who is subject to corporal punishment or suspension administered by a teacher or principal — an agent of the state — can argue that his "liberty" or "security of the person" has been violated without regard to the "principles of fundamental justice". In defining these rights, the courts may be influenced by the age of the child and also by whether the student's parents approve or disapprove of this type of punishment.[91]

---

90 65 N.S.R. (2d) 181 at 183, 185 (Fam. Ct.). Children's Services Act, S.N.S. 1976, c. 8.

91 See Anderson, "Will Charter Usher in New 'Schoolhouse Law'?", O.L.W. 1st November 1985, at 4. In *Baker v. Owen*, 395 F. Supp. 294, affirmed without opinion 423 U.S. 907 (1975), it was held that a student was constitutionally entitled to certain minimal procedural protections before receiving corporal punishment. In *Ingraham v. Wright*, 430 U.S. 651 (1977), the Supreme Court of the United States affirmed that school children do have a "liberty interest" requiring constitutional protection before corporal punishment, though it appeared to set quite a low standard for due process, saying, at 683, its requirements were "satisfied by. . . preservation of common law constraints and remedies". In *Goss v. Lopez*, 419 U.S. 565 at 581 (1975), the Supreme Court held that a high school student facing a ten-day suspension was threatened with a violation of a "liberty interest" and entitled to "notice of the charges. . . and an opportunity to present his side of the case".

3. Child versus Parent

As discussed above, a parent is given a broad range of powers at common law and by legislation to make decisions regarding the life of his child and to effectively discipline and control his child. It has been argued in this chapter that these parental rights are an aspect of "liberty" or "security of the person" as the terms are used in s. 7 of the Charter of Rights. The issue to be explored now is whether there are circumstances in which a child will be able to assert that his "liberty" or "security of the person" is being infringed by his parents' decisions or conduct, and hence is entitled to some constitutional protections against their actions.

Clearly the "liberty" and "security of the person" interests of a child as against his parents are subject to extensive limitations. It would seem easy to demonstrably justify as reasonable a law which allows parents to determine where their 9-year-old child will reside. It is part of the concept of parental "liberty" that parents are entitled to make these decisions, at least as long as the child is not being harmed. In *Tischendorf v. Tischendorf*, the Minnesota Supreme Court ruled that once a court has decided in an access dispute that it is in the child's best interest to visit his father in Germany, the boy has no constitutional right to stay in the United States. The court commented:

> While children do possess constitutional rights, some of those rights may not become operative unless it can be demonstrated that the child can exercise them intelligently.[92]

There are clearly many situations in which children lack the intellectual or emotional maturity to make decisions about their lives. However, there may be circumstances in which a child may seek to make a decision about his own life, and in which to deny this right to the child is to infringe upon the child's "liberty", "security of the person" or other constitutionally guaranteed right. In a recent American case, a 12-year-old boy was ultimately permitted to claim political asylum, despite his parents' desire to have him return with them to the Soviet Union. The court observed that at age 12 he was "near the lower end of an age range in which a minor may be mature enough to assert individual rights that equal or override those of his parents", but that these rights "grow more compelling with age".[93]

---

92 8 F.L.R. 2566 (Minn. S.C., 1982). In *Re K.K.; K.K. v. Sask. Min. of Social Services* (1982), 31 R.F.L. (2d) 334 at 336 (Sask. Q.B.), it was held that a 13-year-old girl could not involve the mobility rights guaranteed by s. 6(2) of the Charter as these rights were subject to "the reasonable limit of the legal guardian's right, prescribed by law, to determine where that child shall live".

93 *Polovchak v. Meese*, 11 F.L.R. 1687 at 1636-37 (C.A. 7th Circ., 1985); see also *In re Polovchak*, 454 N.E. 2d 258 (Ill. S.C., 1983). The boy in fact originally sought asylum when he was 12, but the ultimate judicial resolution of the case did not come until he was 17, which appeared to influence the court's assessment of his capacity.

There has been a considerable amount of constitutionally based litigation in the United States concerning the rights of children to participate in health care decisions affecting their lives. Courts have considered whether parents should decide such questions as whether their child will have an abortion,[94] or access to contraceptives[95] or be committed "voluntarily" (that is, by the parents) to mental health facilities.[96] Clearly the resolution of these issues requires a careful balancing of the rights of parent, child and state and will depend on the nature of the proposed treatment and the maturity of the child. It does not seem adequate, however, to deny a child all right to participate in a decision about such matters solely on the basis of age.

Parents generally make decisions about what schools and churches their children will attend. In Canada and the United States[97] courts have upheld the parental right to send a child to a religious school rather than a public school as an aspect of religious freedom. These cases arose in the context of quasi-criminal charges brought *by the state against the parents* for violating school attendance laws. It can be argued that a mature child should have the right, as against his parents and the state, to decide such issues as what church to attend and whether to attend a religious school or to engage in religious practices at a public school.[98] Is a mature child not entitled to "freedom of conscience and religion" as guaranteed by s. 2 of the Charter of Rights?

The constitutional aspects of the parent-child relationship must also be considered in light of s. 15 of the Charter which prohibits any person from being denied "equal protection and equal benefit of the law without discrimination . . . and in particular without discrimination on the basis of . . . age". It is

---

94 *Planned Parenthood of Central Missouri v. Danforth*, 428 U.S. 52 (1976); *Bellotti v. Baird*, 428 U.S. 132 (1976); *Bellotti v. Baird*, 443 U.S. 622 (1979); and *Akron v. Akron Centre for Reproductive Health*, 103 S. Ct. (1983).

95 *Carey v. Population Services Int.*, 431 U.S. 678 (1977).

96 *Parham v. J.R.*, 442 U.S. 584 (1979). See also *Bartley v. Kremens*, 402 F. Supp. 1039, vacated and remanded for consideration 431 U.S. 119 (1977).

97 *R. v. Wiebe*, [1978] 3 W.W.R. 36 (Alta. Prov. Ct.) (education law violates religious freedom guarantees of the Alberta Bill of Rights). In the United States, see, e.g., *Wisconsin v. Yoder*, 406 U.S. 205 (1972); in a dissenting judgment, Justice Douglas raised the question of the child's rights to make this sort of decision. See also the discussion of s. 2(*a*) of the Charter, *supra*.

98 See, Comment, "Adjudicating What *Yoder* Left Unresolved: Religious Rights for Minor Children after *Danforth* and *Carey*" (1978), 126 U. Penn. L. Rev. 1135; also "The Constitution and the Family" (1980), 93 Harv. L. Rev. 1156 at 1377-83. In a recent incident in Manitoba, a 17-year-old student at a public high school refused to stand for the Lord's Prayer. School officials were only prepared to excuse him from this religious exercise if his parents requested it, and they did not do so. The threat of litigation invoking ss. 2(*a*), 7 and 15 of the Charter apparently forced the school officials to relent. The case received substantial attention in the Canadian media, and focused attention on the rights of adolescents: see, e.g., "Student raises uproar over refusal to stand for prayer", *Kingston Whig Standard*, 11th January 1986.

clearly discriminatory if a 15-year-old girl is denied the opportunity to make decisions about health care questions or school attendance. The only question is whether provisions such as s. 1 of the Charter can be invoked to justify such restraints on the rights and freedoms of young persons. This is another area where claims under ss. 7 and 15 of the Charter may overlap and be mutually reinforcing.

4. State versus Parent

The state has the right, and indeed the duty, to protect children from harm and promote their welfare. This will inevitably involve some infringement or curtailment of parental rights, though doubtless much state action in this regard can be justified under s. 1 of the Charter as "reasonable limits . . . demonstrably justified in a free and democratic society".

The state may enact laws which uniformly curtail the rights of all parents. For example, compulsory school attendance laws require all parents to send their children to a school. A parent cannot decide that his 10-year-old child should join the labour force rather than attend school. Other laws may have a specific focus. For example, child protection legislation allows the state to intervene to protect children when "the level of care . . . falls below that which no child in this country should be subject to".[99]

A difficult issue is whether a child's constitutional rights can be used to justify a governmental limitation of parental rights. In *Re T.L.W.; Re Application by Children's Aid Society of York*, parents challenged the admissibility of evidence in a protection proceeding as being obtained illegally and hence in violation of their right under s. 8 of the Charter to be free from "unreasonable search". In holding that the search was "reasonable", Nevins Prov. J. declared:

> The case we have . . . is totally different in that the statute [Ontario's Child Welfare Act] under which the search was ostensibly conducted deals not only with the authority of representatives of the state, namely the Children's Aid Society, but more importantly deals with the *rights* of a class of persons who are unable to protect themselves, namely children. As against the *child's right* of course is the right of the adult parties, usually the parents, to be afforded the protections guaranteed by the Charter of Rights.
>
> In this context, I feel that one must not only consider the question of whether or not the search was technically authorized by statute, but one must also consider the nature and purpose of the entire statute under which the case is proceeding and the particular facts and circumstances of the case. In addition one must consider whether there would be a possible violation of another person's *rights*, namely, the *right of a child to have life and security of the person*.

---

99 *Re Brown* (1975), 9 O.R. (2d) 185 at 189 (Co. Ct.).

> . . . before the court decides whether a search, albeit "illegal" was "unreasonable", the court must bear in mind the broad purposes of the statute and also *the rights of the child or children* which may in a given set of circumstances be in conflict with those of the parents.[100]

The approach of Nevins Prov. J. justifies a violation of parental constitutional rights, to be free from "unreasonable search", by balancing them against the supposed constitutional rights of the child, to life and security of the person.

It is submitted that while the state may be justified in limiting parental rights, it is wrong to conceive of a child protection case as a situation where the court or state is somehow protecting the *constitutional rights* of the child. Rather, this should be viewed as a situation in which the state limits the constitutional rights of parents, and incidentally those of a child, in order to promote the welfare of the child. As argued above, there may be situations in which a *child* may himself assert constitutional rights against the state or a parent. If the approach of Nevins Prov. J. is followed, it might be difficult to justify such state intervention with the family as compulsory school attendance laws, where the state infringes parental rights to promote the *welfare* of children but clearly without protecting the constitutional *rights* of children. Conceptual difficulties may arise if the child himself becomes involved in protection proceedings and argues that despite allegations or abuse or neglect, he wishes to exercise *his* rights to liberty and security of the person by returning to his family. Further, if the approach of Nevins Prov. J. is adopted, one could argue that in a criminal context, constitutional rights of the accused must in some way be abridged to protect the constitutional rights of actual or potential victims whose "life . . . and security of the person" have been infringed. Perhaps more fundamentally, it seems inappropriate to allow a state agency to invoke the provisions of the Charter of Rights to limit the rights of a citizen. The Charter is intended to protect individuals from the state, not to justify interference by the state or its agencies.

While the outcome in *Re T.L.W.* may be correct, it is better to view this as a situation in which the limitations on parental rights can be demonstrably justified as "reasonable limits . . . in a free and democratic society". This appropriately places the onus under s. 1 of the Charter upon those who seek to restrain parental rights to justify their actions.[101] It is better to consider that individuals, including children, have constitutional rights which the state may limit, if justified, rather than to conceive of the state as exercising constitutional rights on behalf of children against their parents.

---

100 [1983] W.D.F.L. 009 (Ont. Prov. Ct.), at 16-17 of unreported judgment. Emphasis added.

101 See the discussion of s. 1 of the Charter, *supra*. The decision in *Re T.L.W.* may be in some doubt in light of *Hunter v. Southam Inc.* (1984), 11 D.L.R. (4th) 641 (S.C.C.), the leading decision on the interpretation of s. 8 of the Charter. See also *R. v. Carrière* (1983), 32 C.R. (3d) 117 (Ont. Prov. Ct.), on the unreasonableness of an illegal search.

Another decision which presents a somewhat confused discussion of some of the constitutional issues which arise in this situation is *Shingoose v. Minister of Social Services of Saskatchewan*. A parent was challenging a permanent wardship order made in regard to her children, *inter alia*, on the grounds that the initial proceeding violated s. 7 of the Charter because the children did not participate in the original proceeding. Halvorson J. rejected the challenge stating:

> The *right of the child* to be heard is adequately covered by the fact that the *interests of the child* are advanced by the Minister [responsible for child welfare].[102]

It is not clear from the reported decision what were the ages of the children involved and whether they were capable of expressing wishes or instructing counsel. If, however, the children were capable of expressing a preference about how their lives should be led, it is our view that they should be recognized as having an independent s. 7 right to participate in proceedings which affect their "liberty" and "security of the person". It is wrong to confound the child's *interests* (or welfare) with any *constitutional rights* he may have.

The state clearly has a demonstrably justified interest in promoting the welfare of children, and may in the process infringe upon the constitutional rights of parents and children. The basis for state intervention to promote the welfare of a child was articulated by Justice Rehnquist of the U.S. Supreme Court:

> A stable, loving homelife is essential to a child's physical, emotional and spiritual well-being. . . .
>
>   In addition to the child's interest in a normal homelife, "the State has an urgent interest in the welfare of the child. . . . Few could doubt that the most valuable resource of a self-governing society is its population of children who will one day become adults and themselves assume the responsibility of self-governance. "A democratic society rests, for its continuance, upon the healthy well-rounded growth of young people into full maturity as citizens, with all that implies . . .". Thus "the whole community" has an interest "that children be both safeguarded from abuses and given opportunities for growth into free and well-developed citizens."[103]

---

102 (1983), 26 Sask. R. 235 at 238 (Q.B.). Emphasis added.

103 Dissenting in *Santosky v. Kramer*, 102 S. Ct. 1388, 8 F.L.R. 3023 at 3034-3035. See also the discussion in nn. 121-123 *infra*, and accompanying text. In this regard, reference should also be made to *T.T. v. Catholic C.A.S. of Metro. Toronto* (1984), 39 R.F.L. (2d) 279 (Ont. Prov. Ct.), where Thomson Prov. J. observes, at 294:

    "1. The parent is not the only person protected by s. 7. The child as well may have individual rights which are safeguarded by the section. . . . Whether one is acknowledging the possible priority of these as a reasonable limitation under s. 1 of the Charter. . . or is recognizing that application of s. 7 requires in some cases an obvious balancing of protected but competing rights, the point is that the issue is not fully resolved once one recognizes that the security or

In a Canadian context, the issue which must always be resolved is whether limitations on the constitutional rights of parents and children are "reasonable", and whether deprivations of "liberty" and "security of the person" occur in accordance with the "principles of fundamental justice". Clearly an important factor in determining whether s. 1 may be invoked is a consideration of the child's welfare, though this must be balanced against other important interests.[104]

In summary, it is our view that the state has a strong social interest in promoting the welfare of children, if necessary protecting them from their parents or themselves. This interest may be conceived of as a very important "social right" which a child has to grow up in a safe, healthy and nurturing environment. It is wrong, however, to conceive of a child protection proceeding as a situation where the state is acting to protect the constitutional rights of a child. The limitation of parental constitutional rights for the sake of promoting a child's "social rights" involves a difficult balancing of interests in order to determine what constitutes a "reasonable limit" upon the rights of parents, and sometimes upon the constitutional rights of children as well.

For illustrative purposes, brief consideration will be given to some situations in which the state's intervention in the family to promote the welfare of a child may raise issues under the Charter of Rights.

(a) Vagueness of Legislation

In *Alsager v. District Court of Polk County, Iowa* an American court ruled "unconstitutionally vague" a state statute which allowed termination of parental rights if the parents refused to give their child "necessary parental care and protection" or if there was parental conduct "detrimental to the physical or mental health or morals of the child". Hanson C.J. stated:

> The initial danger present in a vague statute is the absence of fair warning. Citizens should be able to guide their conduct by the literal meaning of phrases expressed on the face of statutes. . . .

---

liberty interests of the parent have been affected. Another, more problematic way of acknowledging the possible competing interests is by referring to the 'state's right to safeguard the health and welfare of children'."

104 See, e.g., *Re L.D.K.* (1985), 48 R.F.L. (2d) 164 (Ont. Prov. Ct.), *per* Main Prov. J. where a child welfare authority sought a protection order so that a 12-year-old girl suffering from acute leukemia could receive chemotherapy and blood transfusions. The girl and her parents were Jehovah's Witnesses and were refusing treatment, although the weight of medical opinion was that this represented the child's only chance for survival. The parents and child preferred a less intrusive mega-vitamin therapy. The court dismissed the application, ruling that giving her a transfusion would infringe her security of the person and violate her rights under ss. 2(*a*) and 15 of the Charter. Under the circumstances the court did not consider that s. 1 could be invoked to override her constitutional rights.

The second danger present in a vague statute is the impermissible delegation of discretion from the state legislature to the state law enforcement body. . . .

The Alsagers were not given fair warning of what was and was not prohibited by the Iowa law. The petition which instituted the termination proceeding against them merely alleged the conclusory language of the state: "refused to give their children necessary parental care and protection" and "conduct detrimental to the physical or mental health or morals of their children". A reading of the petition and the termination statute would not give the Alsagers notice of what they were doing wrong. They were not given a factual basis from which to predict how they should modify their past conduct, their "parenting", to avoid termination.[105]

It can be argued that child protection legislation, such as Nova Scotia's Children's Services Act which, for example, allows a child to be made a temporary or permanent ward of the state if the child is "living in circumstances that are unfit or improper", is unconstitutionally vague.[106] Similarly, legislation like Saskatchewan's Family Services Act which allows a court to dispense with a parent's consent to adoption, thereby irrevocably severing a parent's connection to his child, if this is in the "best interests"[107] of the child, may be unconstitutionally vague. It may be argued that in these situations individuals may be deprived of a cherished aspect of their "liberty and security of the person", namely a parent-child relationship, under a standard which seems arbitrary or undefined.

The possibility of challenging legislative or administrative action as being unconstitutional on the grounds of statutory vagueness received a boost from a number of recent decisions under the Charter of Rights. In *Luscher v. Deputy Minister, Revenue Canada, Customs and Excise* the appellant challenged the rights of government officials, acting under the Customs Act, to impound magazines classified as "immoral or indecent"; the initial decision was subject to court review. The Federal Court of Appeal held that the action in question was a violation of s. 2(*b*) of the Charter — freedom of thought and expression — and in view of the vague nature of the government power could not fall within s. 1 of the Charter. Justice Hugessen stated:

. . . one of the first characteristics of a reasonable limit prescribed by law is that it should be expressed in terms sufficiently clear to permit a determination of where and what the limit is. A limit which is vague, ambiguous, uncertain, or subject to discretionary determination is, by that fact alone, an unreasonable limit. If a citizen cannot know with tolerable certainty the extent to which the exercise of a guaranteed freedom may be restrained, he is likely to be deterred from conduct which is, in fact, lawful and not prohibited. Uncertainty and vagueness

---

105 406 F. Supp. 10 at 18-20, affirmed on other grounds 545 F. 2d 1137 (C.A. 8th Circ., 1976). See also *In re Crooks*, 262 N.W. 2d 786 (Iowa, 1976); *Davis v. Smith*, 5 F.L.R. 2749 (Ark., 1979); *Custody of a Minor*, 389 N.E. 2d 68 (Mass., 1979); *Roe v. Conn*, 417 F. Supp. 768 (Ala. Dist. Ct., 1976); and *Linn v. Linn*, 286 N.W. 2d 765 (Neb., 1980).

106 Children's Services Act, s. 2(*m*)(ii).

107 S. 53.

are constitutional vices when they are used to restrain constitutionally protected rights and freedoms. While there can never be absolute certainty, a limitation of a guaranteed right must be such as to allow a very high degree of predictability of the legal consequences.[108]

The finding that a statute "riddled with vagueness" is incapable of serving as a "reasonable limit" has also been applied by the Ontario Court of Appeal and the British Columbia Court of Appeal.[109] The present Canadian approach to vagueness seems to be based more on s. 1 than on s. 7 of the Charter, though the American courts have treated the vagueness doctrine as an aspect of procedural due process. The two approaches are clearly closely related.

The concern expressed in American decisions like *Alsager* and Canadian cases like *Luscher* may at least prompt those seeking judicial severance of the parent-child link to more fully set out the nature of their case in pleadings or other pre-hearing notices, or face constitutionally based requests for fuller particulars and adjournments.[110] Though it may be impossible to legislatively specify in precise terms exactly what kind of parental conduct will render the family subject to protection proceedings, it may be difficult to justify a failure to give parents adequate notice of the case they are expected to meet. In two Nova Scotia cases, *Re M.B.*,[111] involving an unmanageability complaint for a 14-year-old ward, and *Re B.M.*,[112] involving a 13-year-old boy facing truancy charges, applications to bring children into state care were dismissed on the basis of s. 7 of the Charter. The notices served did not give the children involved adequate information about the case they had to meet, and hence they were deprived of liberty in a manner not in accordance with the principles of fundamental justice.

(b) Right to Challenge Evidence

In cases involving the welfare of children there is often a tendency to relax the rules of evidence, and this is generally acceptable, at least from a constitutional point of view. It would seem, however, that if this goes so far as to violate

---

108 (1985), 17 D.L.R. (4th) 503 at 506 (Fed. C.A.); Customs Act, R.S.C. 1970, c. C-40.

109 *Ont. Film & Video Appreciation Soc. v. Ont. Bd. of Censors* (1983), 41 O.R. 583, affirmed 45 O.R. (2d) 80 (C.A.) (power of Censor Board to censor in absence of statute guidelines not a "reasonable limit"); and *R. v. Robson* (1985), 19 D.L.R. (4th) 112 (B.C.C.A.) (provision of provincial motor vehicle law allowing police officer to suspend temporarily a driver's licence when officer has "reason to suspect that the driver . . . has consumed alcohol" struck down).

110 See *In re Jay Edward R.*, 10 F.L.R. 1177 (Cal. C.A. 3rd Circ., 1983), which allowed an appeal in a stepparent adoption case on the grounds, *inter alia*, that the notice of the application which the natural father received failed to contain specific factual allegations supporting the petition.

111 (1984), 65 N.S.R. (2d) 181 (Fam. Ct.).

112 N.S. Fam. Ct., Roscoe Fam. Ct. J., 19th March 1985 (not yet reported).

"the fundamental principles of justice", for example by denying the right of an affected party to cross-examine or challenge evidence, then there may be a violation of s. 7 of the Charter of Rights.

For example, in custody and child protection cases it is the practice of some judges to interview a child alone in chambers. It may be asked whether in some circumstances such a practice would violate constitutional rights of parents. In *Re Maricopa County Juvenile Action*, a judge in a dependency (protection) proceeding based on alleged sexual abuse of a 10-year-old girl interviewed the child alone in his chambers. The Arizona Supreme Court upheld a challenge to this procedure based on a violation of the procedural due process rights of the parents.

> Considering the nature of the interests involved in this case, it is essential under the adversary system that parents be given the opportunity to challenge the testimony of their children when such testimony is essential to establishing the parental misconduct alleged in the petition. Without the opportunity to test the reliability of a child's statements, the adversary process is subverted and made meaningless. . . . there may be instances in which the court may wish to limit the conditions under which children are examined by providing that only counsel for the parties be present. Testimony which is traumatic in nature would merit an examination in chambers, and the presence of counsel alone would be justified where a party's presence is potentially inhibiting.[113]

This "due process" issue has also arisen in the context of American custody disputes between parents, where it has been held that an individual also faces a potential loss of a "liberty interest". In a number of cases courts have ruled that in such disputes there is a constitutional right to cross-examine a person who prepared a social assessment.[114] In one case it was held that despite a statutory grant of testimonial privilege, a marriage counsellor could be constitutionally compelled to disclose the contents of communications from the parents.[115] It is possible that this reasoning could be used in Canada, for example, to challenge the statutory privileges of s. 10 of the Divorce Act, 1985 (marriage counsellor appointed by court) or s. 31(7) of Ontario's Children's Law Reform Act (closed mediation), or the common law mediator's privilege which courts have been developing.[116]

---

113 8 F.L.R. 2175 at 2176, 638 P. 2d 692 (Ariz. S. C., 1981); see also *Re Stanley F.*, 152 Cal. Rptr. 5 (C.A., 1978). For a similar approach, see *Re R.C.*, Ont. Prov. Ct., Karswick J., 8th January 1980 (unreported), reproduced in Bala, Lilles and Thomson, *Canadian Children's Law: Cases, Notes and Materials*, at 178.

114 *Duro v. Duro*, 10 F.L.R. 1605 (Mass. S. C., 1984); *Landers v. Landers*, 9 F.L.R. 2337 (Fla. C.A., 1983).

115 *M. v. K.*, 9 F.L.R. 2135 (N.J. S.C., 1982).

116 Divorce Act, 1985, S.C. 1986, c. 4, s. 10; Children's Law Reform Act, s. 31(7) [en. 1982, c. 20, s. 1]; and see, e.g., *Cronkwright v. Cronkwright*, [1970] 3 O.R. 784 (H.C.).

(c) Onus and Standard of Proof in Protection Proceedings

A recent decision of the U.S. Supreme Court closely examined the issue of due process and parental rights. In *Santosky v. Kramer*[117] the court considered the constitutionality of a New York law which allowed for the termination of parental rights "on a fair preponderance of the evidence". The court stated that the right to the care, custody and upbringing of one's children was an extremely important one and that the threatened intervention by the state would permanently deprive the parents of this right. The Supreme Court held that the private interest of the parents was "a commanding one"[118] and weighed heavily against the ordinary civil "preponderance standard" that the state law set out; such a significant termination of rights required a higher standard of proof.

The Supreme Court was also concerned that a termination proceeding had many of the *indicia* of a criminal trial and was oriented towards the state's position.[119] That is to say that the state, with all its human and financial resources, is pitted directly against the parents. This imbalance, coupled with a "preponderance of the evidence" standard of proof, created a significant prospect of erroneous termination of parental rights. Lastly, the court held that the state's interests in promoting the welfare of the child and in reducing the costs of the proceedings were not inconsistent with a higher standard of proof than a "preponderance of the evidence". The Supreme Court concluded that a "clear and convincing evidence" standard of proof would strike a fair balance between the parents' rights and the state's legitimate concerns, and that any lower standard of proof would be unconstitutional. The "clear and convincing evidence" standard requires that parental misconduct be proved by the state to a degree higher than on the mere balance of probabilities, the usual civil standard, but it falls somewhere short of "beyond a reasonable doubt", the ordinary criminal test.[120]

It is notable that the court in *Santosky* did *not* conceive of a termination case as one in which the interests of parents and children were antithetical. The court rejected the theory which assumes that "termination of the natural parents' rights invariably will benefit the child".[121] The contest was between the parents and the state, with the state presenting its case on the basis of the views of its agencies as to what would best promote the welfare of the child.

---

117 102 S. Ct. 1388 at 1388 (1982).

118 *Ibid.*, at 3026.

119 *Ibid.*, at 3027.

120 For a fuller discussion of the significance of this standard, see Helen Sigmond, "Involuntary Termination of Parental Rights: The Need for Clear and Convincing Evidence" (1980), 29 Am. U.L. Rev. 771; and Charles Daskow "Standard of Proof in Parental Termination Proceedings" (1982), 6 J. Juv. L. 27.

121 *Supra*, n. 117 at 3028.

> The factfinding . . . is not intended to balance the child's interest in a normal family home against the parents' interest in raising the child. . . . Rather the . . . hearing pits the state directly against the parents. . . .

> At the factfinding, the State cannot presume that a child and his parents are adversaries . . . until the State proves parental unfitness, the child and his parents share a vital interest in preventing erroneous termination of their natural relationship. Thus, at the factfinding, the interests of the child and his natural parents coincide to favour use of error-reducing procedures.[122]

The *Santosky* decision marks a judicial recognition of the importance of parental rights and indicates that when a final balance is struck, these rights may take primacy over competing interests. Though the court was perhaps influenced by American notions of "substantive due process", the court's emphasis was clearly on providing parents with adequate procedural safeguards before the state could terminate the parent-child relationship.

In Canada, questions of standard and onus of proof in protection proceedings have not been the subject of specific legislative direction, and the courts have been somewhat inconsistent in their approach.

For example, in *Re S.*, Main Prov. J. seemed to suggest that, at least in abuse cases, the ultimate onus of persuasion might be upon the parents:

> If the court is satisfied that on the balance of probabilities there has been "abuse", then it should be quick to act to protect the child. If the balance does not tip either way, then the resulting doubt should be determined in favour of the safety of the child [and, if the circumstances warrant, the child permanently removed from his family].[123]

On the other hand, in other cases judges have recognized that the onus must rest on the state protection agency, and have even suggested that the standard of proof may be higher than that in any ordinary civil case, particularly if a child is to be permanently removed from his family. For example, in *D. v. Children's Aid Society of Kent*, Clements Co. Ct. J. stated:

> The power given to the children's aid society under the Act is to impose an agency of the government on behalf of society into the home when necessary. The contest, it must be remembered, is between the society and the natural parents in most instances. . . .

> There is a civil onus on the children's aid society on the application of this nature but not the usual onus as stated in *Re Chrysler* [per Karswick Prov. J] . . . :

---

122 *Ibid.*, at 3027. This approach offers further support for the argument made above that the analysis offered by Nevins Prov. J. in *Re T.L.W.*; *Re Application by C.A.S. of York*, [1983] W.D.F. L. 009 (Ont. Prov. Ct.), is unsound.

123 (1979), 10 R.F.L. (2d) 341 at 350 (Ont. Prov. Ct.). Emphasis added; see also *In re Linda C.*, 8 F.L.R. 2436, 451 N.Y.S. (2d) 268 (App. Div., 1982), which held that despite *Santosky*, it was appropriate to have a lower standard of proof in a child protection case based on sexual or physical abuse.

"The authorities are clear that although the onus is of a civil nature where the contest over custody is between the mother and a children's aid society the onus is still *very demanding* and it must be *clearly demonstrated* that the child's best interests are served by removing her from the natural parents and placing her into the custody of the state in the agency of the children's aid society." . . .

The standard of proof, therefore, is not that of the balance of probabilities per se; nor is there a test akin to the onus in criminal matters. No magic formula need be devised other than the *heavy onus* on the director of the children's aid society to satisfy the court the allegations necessary to intervene are met and clearly met without reference or deference to the second issue after a finding is made, i.e., the finding that the child is in need of protection, as to the appropriate placement under s. 30 of the Act. As has been said by the court in *Re Brown* . . .:

"Society's interference in the natural family is only justified when the level of care of the child falls below that which no child in this country should be subjected to."[124]

Ultimately, Canadian courts, or legislatures, will have to resolve the question of the onus and standard of proof in a protection proceeding. In addressing the issue, it will be necessary to keep in mind that parents may have constitutionally recognized rights. If it is accepted that the concept of "liberty and security of the person" in s. 7 of the Charter includes a parental right to enjoy a relationship with their children, the approach of *Santosky v. Kramer* would suggest that a state agency must satisfy a heavy onus before removing a child from his family, particularly if this removal is to be permanent.[125] Arguably, many Canadian judges, following the approach of *D. v. Children's Aid Society of Kent*, have already recognized the importance of the parent-child relationship and have effectively afforded the family this protection.[126] In a recent decision of the Nova Scotia Court of Appeal, the court reviewed the issue of onus, including much of the Canadian and American jurisprudence set out

---

124 (1980), 18 R.F.L. (2d) 223 at 226-27 (Ont. Co. Ct.). Emphasis added; see also *C.A.S. of Winnipeg v. M.* (1980), 15 R.F.L. (2d) 185 at 189 (Man. C.A.).

125 It should be noted that in New York State, as in other American jurisdictions, a child may be found to be neglected and removed from his home without a full termination of parental rights. *Santosky* only deals with the issue of the nature of onus on the state at a termination hearing. It may be that when only a temporary removal of a child from his family is sought, the onus upon the state is not as high; see *In re Linda C.*, *supra*, n. 123. This would correspond with the view of some Canadian judges about the nature of the onus in a child protection case. For example, in *C.A.S. of Kingston v. Neilson*, Ont. Prov. Ct., 15th June 1972 (unreported), Thomson Prov. J. stated:

". . . the court should always keep in mind the nature of the order which is being sought by the applicant [state agency]. It is true that only one set of grounds can be found in the Act to justify all three of the orders possible under the Act [supervision in the home, temporary removal and permanent separation of parent and child], but it would seem to me that the court should require much clearer and cogent evidence to be presented to it when a permanent separation of the children is being sought rather than a temporary separation."

126 See *Re Protection of Children Act; Re S.V.'s Infant* (1963), 43 W.W.R. 374 (B.C. Co. Ct.), *per* Harvey Co. Ct. J.

here, and apparently accepted that the standard of proof in a protection is higher than in an ordinary civil case. The court did not rule on the s. 7 argument, however, being content to rest on the "common law" of protection hearings.[127]

(d) Statutory Preclusion of Hearing

In *Re J.; Catholic Children's Aid Society of Metropolitan Toronto v. S.*[128] a child protection agency sought termination of access by natural parents to their two children. The children had previously been made permanent state wards, and their foster parents planned to adopt them. Judge Nasmith indicated that while adoption ultimately appeared to be in the best interests of the children, so too was a continuation of access, though it was not clear that this was possible under the Ontario legislation. In refusing the agency request to terminate access, the judge discussed the applicability of the Charter:

> Surely the association among family members including parents and children comes under s. 2(*d*) [freedom of association]. . . .
>
> It is also fitting, I think to consider legislation that restricts the disclosure of accurate birth information to adopted children or that restricts their right to see birth parents as profoundly affecting their rights to liberty and security of the person under s. 7.
>
> And insofar as adopted children are discriminated against in this regard, we have the application of s. 15.
>
> We do not, in my view, have any question here about whether the [constitutional] rights of adopted children are very profoundly affected. . . .[129]

The judge proceeded to consider whether s. 1 of the Charter could be invoked. He observed that frequently in adoptions it was advantageous to maintain secrecy and confidentiality. In this case, however, the biological parents already knew the identity of the prospective adoptive parents and the children had maintained contact with their biological parents while in the care of the prospective adoptive parents. During the period in the care of the foster parents it was demonstrated that termination of access was not in the best interests of the children. The judge observed that under the legislative scheme, court records of adoption proceedings were to be sealed, unless otherwise ordered by the court,[130] and commented:

---

127 *J.L. v. C.A.S. of Halifax* (1985), 44 R.F.L. (2d) 437 (N.S.C.A.).

128 (1985), 48 R.F.L. (2d) 371 (Ont. Prov. Ct.).

129 *Ibid.*, at 385.

130 In *Ferguson v. Dir. of Child Welfare* (1983), 44 O.R. (2d) 78 (C.A.), the Ontario Court of Appeal rejected challenges based on ss. 2, 7 and 12 of the Charter to legislative provisions sealing adoption records except by court order. In a similar vein, see *In re Roger B.*, 418 N.E. 2d 751 (Ill., 1981).

I think that the situation is very different if we are dealing with blanket prohibitions. Ultimately, someone will have to decide whether blanket prohibitions are justifiable under s. 1 of the Charter if they cut off the child care choices that may otherwise be found on evidence to be in the best interests of children.

> On this point it is very helpful for me to look at . . . *Re Southam Inc. and R.* (1983), 41 O.R. (2d) 113 (C.A.). . . . As I understand the decision, it was precisely because of the blanket nature of the prohibition against attending Juvenile Court that the [Ontario] Court of Appeal declared [s. 12 of the Juvenile Delinquents Act] . . . to be unconstitutional. It seems to me that the issue in this case is closely analogous. . . . The more reasonable approach (as found in the *Southam* case) would be to leave the option open and make decisions based on the evidence in the individual cases.[131]

As with a number of other decisions in this area, ss. 7 and 15 of the Charter interact and are mutually reinforcing. Section 7 offers procedural protection: can the state justify depriving parents and children of vital aspects of their liberty and security of the person without the opportunity for an individualized hearing and determination that this is necessary to promote the child's interests? Section 15 approaches essentially the same question from a different angle: is an absolute statutory bar on contact between biological parents and their children justifiable for children who are adopted, when other children are not treated in this fashion? The general approach of *Re J.* might be applied in other circumstances where parents, children or other individuals face loss of familial ties without the opportunity for a hearing.

X SEARCH AND DETENTION: SECTIONS 8-10

> 8. Everyone has the right to be secure against unreasonable search or seizure.
>
> 9. Everyone has the right not to be arbitrarily detained or imprisoned.
>
> 10. Everyone has the right on arrest or detention
>
> (*a*) to be informed promptly of the reasons therefor;
>
> (*b*) to retain and instruct counsel without delay and to be informed of that right; and
>
> (*c*) to have the validity of the detention determined by way of *habeas corpus*. . . .

It can be argued that these provisions may be invoked in situations where the child welfare authorities have exercised their broad police-like power to apprehend a child. Even before the Charter, the courts recognized the potential for the "abuse of the supernormal powers" of search and apprehension given to children's aid societies for the protection of children.[132] Since the Charter, in

---

131 *Supra*, n. 128 at 387.

132 For an example of a case in which such powers were abused, see *Ex parte D.*, [1971] 1 O.R. 311 (H.C.).

T.T. v. Catholic Children's Aid Society of Metropolitan Toronto,[133] Thomson Prov. J. accepted that s. 8 of the Charter applied to seizures of persons, as well as of property, and appeared to accept that in appropriate circumstances s. 8 could be applied in situations where a child welfare authority apprehended a child. This interpretation seems particularly plausible in light of *Hunter v. Southam Inc.*[134] where the Supreme Court of Canada specifically recognized that s. 8 is intended to protect the right of "individual privacy", and used s. 8 to find unconstitutional warrantless searches under the Combines Investigation Act, though acknowledging that there might be circumstances in which such searches might be reasonable.

In *Shingoose v. Minister of Social Services of Saskatchewan*[135] a parent challenged an apprehension of her child under provincial child protection legislation as being in violation of ss. 9 and 10 of the Charter. Halvorson J. dismissed this challenge, saying that a child was not subject to "detention" under child protection legislation, and hence ss. 9 and 10 had no application. The judge also indicated that even if s. 9 were applicable, the detention was not "arbitrary" as there was a legislative right to an interim care hearing within 30 days of the apprehension. It is, however, submitted that if a child is apprehended by a child protection authority, this may well involve "search", "seizure" and "detention". "Detention", for example, even on a narrow definition has been considered to include "some form of compulsory restraint".[136] All provinces have legislation which allows child protection authorities to "search for", "apprehend" and "detain" a child believed to be in need of protection.[137] This does not mean that such searches and detention necessarily are unconstitutional. It does, however, mean that searches are to be "reasonable" (that is, presumably at least allowed by legislation)[138] and detention is not to be "arbitrary". Section

---

133 (1984), 46 O.R. (2d) 347 (Prov. Ct.). It should be noted that it has been held that ss. 7 and 8 of the Charter are not violated by the provisions of Ontario's Children's Law Reform Act allowing leave permitting a court to give leave to the parties to a paternity proceeding to have blood tests: *Re N. and D.* (1985), 49 O.R. (2d) 491 (Prov. Ct.).

134 [1984] 2 S.C.R. 145. See, however, *R. v. Parton* (1983), 9 C.C.C. (3d) 295 (Alta. Q.B.).

135 (1983), 149 D.L.R. (3d) 400 (Sask. Q.B.). See also *Re Martin and Dept. of Social Services* (1980), 108 D.L.R. (3d) 765 (Sask. C.A.).

136 See *R. v. Therens* (1985), 18 D.L.R. (4th) 655 (S.C.C.). It is clear that "detention" is broader than "arrest", and, for example, s. 10(*c*), allowing application for a writ of *habeas corpus* in cases of "detention", can be used in regard to an involuntary committal of a mental patient; *Ref. re Procedures and the Mental Health Act* (1984), 5 D.L.R. (4th) 577 (P.E.I. C.A.). See also *Re D.L.D.; D.L.D. v. Fam. & Children's Services of London & Middlesex*, [1986] W.D.F.L. 1108 (Ont. Prov. Ct.), which ruled the placement of a child in a locked psychiatric ward by a children's aid society violated ss. 7 and 10 of the Charter.

137 See, e.g., Ontario's Child and Family Services Act, s. 40, which uses terms like "apprehend", "detain", "search for" and "remove".

138 See *Hunter v. Southam Inc.*, *supra*, n. 134, which holds that s. 8 generally protects a "right to privacy", and discusses the concept of "unreasonable search".

10 may guarantee a child who has been apprehended certain rights, though presumably s. 1 of the Charter would permit a legislature to deny some of these rights to children who lack the capacity to exercise them. On the other hand, for an older child, it might well be constitutionally necessary to inform the child of the reasons for apprehension and of his right to counsel. Further, the child or his parents have a right to release by a writ of *habeas corpus* if the detention is not lawful.[139]

It is also interesting to note that there have been cases in which the courts have used the Charter essentially to protect young persons from apparent police harassment. In *R. v. D.E.M.*[140] a 15-year-old girl was reported as "missing" by her mother; police officers located her and were apparently going to have her taken home when they searched her purse and found some marijuana. The court ruled her detention "unlawful" and dismissed a charge under the Narcotic Control Act on the ground of a violation of s. 8 of the Charter.[141] In *R. v. I.C.V.*[142] the police questioned a 15-year-old female who was "loitering" around a shopping mall and, upon conducting a routine computer check, discovered that her parents had reported her as missing. She was "arrested" under child welfare legislation as a child apparently in need of protection, and a scuffle ensued. The court dismissed a charge of assaulting a police officer on the ground that the police had violated ss. 7, 8, 9 and 10(*b*) of the Charter of Rights.

A final young offenders issue under s. 10(*b*) of the Charter is the question of whether minors charged under the Young Offenders Act can retain counsel without the intervention of a *guardian ad litem*. In *R. v. W.W.W.*[143] the Manitoba Court of Appeal ruled that an accused young person could only retain counsel through an adult representative — a *guardian ad litem*. This decision does not appear to have been followed in other jurisdictions in Canada, and it has been severely criticized as being inconsistent with established criminal procedures.[144] The decision can also be considered to be contrary to the principles of accountability and responsibility articulated in the Young Offenders Act and to the legal representation scheme embodied in that Act.[145] It also seems contrary

---

139 See *Roe v. Conn.*, 417 F. Supp. 769 (Ala. Dist. Ct., 1976), which held that in some circumstances a child in a neglect proceeding was entitled to procedural due process, including the right to state appointed counsel.

140 (1984), 13 W.C.B. 397 (Ont. Prov. Ct.), *per* Nasmith Prov. J.

141 Narcotic Control Act, R.S.C. 1970, c. N-1.

142 [1985] W.D.F.L. 2087 (Ont. Prov. Ct.), *per* Main Prov. J.

143 [1984] 6 W.W.R. 477 (Man. C.A.).

144 See R. Komar, "Annotation: Litigation Guidelines in Youth Court" (1984), Y.O.S. 3305 to 3305-8; see also a vigorous dissent in *R. v. W.W.*, [1985] 5 W.W.R. 147 (Man. C.A.), *per* Matas J.A. Bill C-106, 2nd Session, 33rd Parliament, third reading 17th June 1986, will amend s. 11 of the Young Offenders Act to reverse this decision.

145 Ss. 3 and 11 of the Young Offenders Act.

to ss. 10(*b*) and 15 of the Charter to require a young person to have a guardian to retain counsel. At the very least there should be an onus to establish that such obvious discrimination is "demonstrably justified". Unfortunately these Charter issues are not discussed by the majority of the Manitoba Court of Appeal in its decision in *R. v. W.W.W.*

XI PROCEEDINGS IN CRIMINAL AND PENAL MATTERS: SECTION 11

11. Any person charged with an offence has the right

(*a*) to be informed without unreasonable delay of the specific offence;

(*b*) to be tried within a reasonable time;

(*c*) not to be compelled to be a witness in proceedings against that person in respect of the offence;

(*d*) to be presumed innocent until proven guilty according to law in a fair and public hearing by an independent and impartial tribunal;

(*e*) not to be denied reasonable bail without just cause;

(*f*) except in the case of an offence under military law tried before a military tribunal, to the benefit of trial by jury where the maximum punishment for the offence is imprisonment for five years or a more severe punishment;

(*g*) not to be found guilty on account of any act or omission unless, at the time of the act or omission, it constituted an offence under Canadian or international law or was criminal according to the general principles of law recognized by the community of nations;

(*h*) if finally acquitted of the offence, not to be tried for it again and, if finally found guilty and punished for the offence, not to be tried or punished for it again; and

(*i*) if found guilty of the offence and if the punishment for the offence has been varied between the time of commission and the time of sentencing, to the benefit of the lesser punishment.

This section applies only to a person "charged with an offence", and therefore is only relevant for young persons (aged 12-17 inclusive) charged under the Young Offenders Act or provincial offence legislation. It is not applicable to those children or adolescents who may suffer a loss of "liberty" or "security of the person" without facing criminal charges, for example in a child protection proceeding. These provisions have been successfully invoked in a number of criminal trials of young persons,[146] just as many adults have used them to obtain acquittals or otherwise secure protection for their rights.

---

146 See the cases cited *supra*, n. 9; and Bala and Lilles, *Young Offenders Service*, "Charter of Rights" section.

XII CRUEL AND UNUSUAL TREATMENT: SECTION 12

> 12. Everyone has the right not to be subjected to any cruel and unusual treatment or punishment.

One of the leading cases under s. 12 is *Re Mitchell and R.* where the court invoked the Charter to require the release of an inmate after 12 years in custody for an indeterminate disposition. The inmate had a record of petty property offences and did not pose a threat to society. Justice Linden wrote:

> . . . the standard to be applied in determining whether treatment or punishment is cruel and unusual is whether the treatment or punishment is so excessive as to outrage standards of decency and surpass all rational bounds of treatment or punishment. The test, thus, is one of disproportionality: is this treatment or punishment disproportionate to the offence and the offender? Evidence that the treatment or punishment is unusually severe, and excessive in the sense of not serving a valid penal purpose more effectively than a less severe treatment or punishment, will suffice to satisfy the test of disproportionality. . . . I agree with Chief Justice Laskin that public opinion should not play a part in the determination.[147]

This approach was followed in *R. v. B.M.* to dismiss a truancy charge against a 13-year-old boy. The consequence of a conviction under the provincial legislation in question was indefinite committal to a reform school. The court noted that: "The sentence is too severe in light of the 'crime' ".[148]

In *Shingoose v. Minister of Social Services of Saskatchewan*[149] the mother of children who had been made permanent wards under child protection legislation argued that this constituted "cruel and unusual treatment". While recognizing that the removal of the children from their mother's care was "no doubt agonizing to the mother and possibly the children", Halvorson J. determined that it was not cruel in that it did not "shock the conscience" or "offend contemporary standards of decency". Further, the court noted that the treatment must be both "cruel *and* unusual", and the removal of the children from an unfit mother was not unusual, but a common practice in all provinces. Though the court's test for "cruel and unusual" may be questioned,[150] it will probably be difficult to argue that substantive custody or access decisions are "cruel and unusual" if they have been made in the "best interests of a child". In any event, s. 1 of the Charter of Rights will probably be invoked to justify any such action as necessary to promote the welfare of the children involved.

It would seem, however, that in some circumstances s. 12 of the Charter may be invoked by those who represent children who have been confined to

---

147 (1983), 42 O.R. (2d) 481 at 505-506 (H.C.).

148 N.S. Fam. Ct., Roscoe Fam. Ct. J., 19th March 1985 (not yet reported), at 14.

149 (1983), 149 D.L.R. (3d) 400 (Sask. Q.B.).

150 See *Re Mitchell and R.*, *supra*, n. 147.

various facilities in order to obtain a declaratory judgment or a prerogative writ to regulate the conduct of juvenile custodians. See, for example, the American case of *Nelson v. Heyne*[151] where it was held that certain practices in regard to corporal punishment and drug treatment for institutionalized juveniles were "cruel and unusual" punishment. Further confinement of juveniles under the pretext of providing treatment was itself "cruel and unusual" when the state failed to provide "minimal rehabilitative treatment".

It should be noted that s. 12 applies not only to punishment, though most of the litigation has been in the criminal context, but also to treatment, for example, in group homes, mental health facilities and other child care institutions.

XIII SELF-INCRIMINATION: SECTION 13

> 13. A witness who testifies in any proceedings has the right not to have any incriminating evidence so given used to incriminate that witness in any other proceedings, except in a prosecution for perjury or for the giving of contradictory evidence.

Section 13 does not create a broad privilege against self-incrimination and, for example, does not prohibit the compulsory taking of breath samples.[152] It does not provide that a witness cannot be compelled to answer a question (see s. 11(c) of the Charter), it only prevents subsequent use of incriminating answers that a witness may be compelled to give. Further, it only limits subsequent use in proceedings used to "incriminate" the person, that is, criminal prosecutions or other proceedings which impose a "penalty".[153] Thus, for example, in a child protection case based on allegations of physical abuse, a parent could be compelled to testify, but no statements the parent made could be used against the parent in a later criminal prosecution of that parent (whether under the Criminal Code or child welfare legislation).[154] Further, if a person made a statement in a

---

151 471 F. 2d 352 (C.A. 7th Circ., 1974); see also *Morales v. Trueman*, 383 F. Supp. 53, reversed on other grounds 535 F. 2d 865 (C.A. 5th Circ., 1976). See also *Lunney v. M.H.*, [1985] 2 W.W.R. 444 (Alta. Q.B.) (fingerprinting young person might in "unusual" case violate s. 12); and *R. v. R.E.F.* (1985), Y.O.S. 85-075 (Ont. H.C.) (detention of young person in adult segregation unit after Young Offenders Act, s. 16 transfer order violated s. 12, though detention in usual adult facility did not violate Charter.)

152 *R. v. Altseimer* (1982), 38 O.R. (2d) 783 (C.A.).

153 *Caisse Populaire Laurier d'Ottawa Ltée v. Guertin; Caisse Populaire Laurier d'Ottawa Ltée v. Simard* (1983), 150 D.L.R. (3d) 541 (Ont. H.C.).

154 See *Re Donald and Law Soc. of B.C.* (1983), 7 C.R.R. 305 (B.C.C.A.), for a discussion of "incriminate"; there it was held that s. 13 of the Charter precluded use of testimony from a prior civil trial (defamation) in a later disciplinary proceeding under the Barristers and Solicitors Act, R.S.B.C. 1979, c. 26 (professional discipline). It would seem difficult to argue that subsequent child protection proceedings are proceedings which "incriminate" a parent, though a parent would probably view the potential consequences as a punishment or penalty.

criminal prosecution, this would ordinarily be admissible in a subsequent civil proceeding, such as a child protection proceeding.

XIV INTERPRETER: SECTION 14

14. A party or witness in any proceedings who does not understand or speak the language in which the proceedings are conducted or who is deaf has the right to the assistance of an interpreter.

Section 14 clearly applies to all kinds of proceedings, not simply criminal prosecutions.

XV EQUALITY RIGHTS: SECTION 15

15.(1) Every individual is equal before and under the law and has the right to the equal protection and equal benefit of the law without discrimination and, in particular, without discrimination based on race, national or ethnic origin, colour, religion, sex, age or mental or physical disability.

(2) Subsection (1) does not preclude any law, program or activity that has as its object the amelioration of conditions of disadvantaged individuals or groups including those that are disadvantaged because of race, national or ethnic origin, colour, religion, sex, age or mental or physical disability.

While the rest of the Charter of Rights came into effect on 17th April 1982, by virtue of s. 32(2) of the Charter s. 15 did not come into effect until 17th April 1985. The purpose of the delay was to provide the federal and provincial governments with sufficient time to review and amend their legislation and programs to bring them into conformity with s. 15, though it seems that relatively little was done in this regard during these three years.

Section 15 is probably the most complex and potentially significant provision of the Charter. The full impact of this provision will depend very much on how it is interpreted by the courts. In this chapter only a few very general and tentative remarks will be made.

First, it is clear that the equality provisions of the Charter are going to have a much greater impact than the corresponding portions of the Bill of Rights. Section 1(*b*) of the Bill guaranteed individuals "equality before the law and the protection of the law" without discrimination by reason of "race, national origin, colour, religion or sex" and the Bill of Rights was invoked, for example, to strike down a law which made it an offence only for Indians to be publicly intoxicated.[155] It did not, however, guarantee an Indian woman the same rights upon marrying a white man as those afforded an Indian man marrying a white woman, as Indian women were merely being denied a "benefit" under the

---

155 *R. v. Drybones*, [1970] S.C.R. 282.

law.[156] The Charter is clearly written in a much broader fashion, ensuring that individuals are equal *"before* and *under* the law" and have the right to the "equal *protection* and equal *benefit* of the law."

In one case under the Bill of Rights, *R. v. Burnshine*,[157] it was held that legislation which provided for longer sentences of incarceration for offenders under the age of 22 did not violate the Bill of Rights because the *intent* of Parliament was not to punish, but to provide further opportunities for rehabilitation. Such an approach would not seem possible under the Charter because individuals are equal *"under"* the law. Further, as noted earlier, in determining the constitutionality of laws under the Charter,[158] courts should consider both the legislative purpose and its actual effect. This does not, however, mean that all individuals will necessarily be treated identically. Sections 15(2) and 1 of the Charter will undoubtedly play a role, and if the experience in the United States is accepted, will result in courts upholding the constitutional validity of many laws such as child protection legislation, compulsory school attendance laws, and juvenile justice statutes, which treat children and adolescents differently from adults.

In *MacKay v. R.*, in discussing s.1(*b*) of the Bill of Rights, McIntyre J. offered examples of "acceptable distinctions recognized in law":

> If we are to have safety on the highways, the blind or those with deficient sight must be forbidden to drive. If young people and children are to be protected and their welfare fostered in youth, we have long recognized that special legislative provisions must be made for them imposing restrictions and limitations upon their freedom more stringent than upon adults. In matters of criminology, differences which have been considered conductive [sic] to the welfare of society and to young offenders have been considered permissible. . . . There are many such cases where the needs of society and the welfare of its members dictate inequality for the achievement of socially desirable purposes. . . . I would be of the opinion . . . that as a minimum it would be necessary to inquire whether any inequality . . . has been created rationally in the sense that it is not arbitrary or capricious and not based upon any ulterior motive or motives offensive to the provisions of the *Canadian Bill of Rights*, and whether it is a necessary departure from the general principle of universal application of the law for the attainment of some necessary and desirable social objective. Inequalities created for such purposes may well be acceptable under the *Canadian Bill of Rights*.[159]

While it is clear that some kinds of statutory distinctions, whether based on age, sex or other criteria, will be considered to be constitutionally acceptable, there is disagreement as to whether the issue of justification is to be resolved primarily under s. 1 or s. 15(1) (or in appropriate cases under s. 15(2)). Some

---

156 *A.G. Can. v. Lavell; Isaac v. Bedard*, [1974] S.C.R. 1349.

157 [1975] 1 S.C.R. 693.

158 See, e.g., *R. v. Big M Drug Mart Ltd.* (1985), 18 D.L.R. (4th) 321 (S.C.C.), discussed, *supra*, nn. 9-11 and accompanying text.

159 [1980] 2 S.C.R. 370 at 406-407.

have argued that any kind of distinction, based on age, sex or other grounds, is "discrimination" and a violation of s. 15(1); on this view, such discrimination must be shown to be "demonstrably justified" as a "reasonable limit" under s. 1 of the Charter. This approach places a s. 1 onus on a party to uphold a particular distinction. Another analysis suggests that s. 15(1) of the Charter itself incorporates a balancing test. This approach was recently adopted by the British Columbia Court of Appeal, in *Andrews v. Law Society of British Columbia*. McLaughlin J. wrote:

> "Discrimination" is treated as a synonym of "unreasonable classification" or "unjustifiable differentiation". . . . s. 15 incorporates principles of justification and reasonableness independently of those found within s. 1.[160]

Adopting this second approach, even "unjustified discrimination" may be constitutionally upheld, for example in situations of war or national emergency. On either view, some forms of discrimination will be constitutionally acceptable. The primary difference between the two approaches is a question of which party bears the onus of establishing constitutional acceptability. The Supreme Court of Canada will doubtless have to resolve this disagreement.

It seems certain that some kinds of discrimination are inherently more likely to be subject to judicial scrutiny under the Charter. Thus, a law denying 10-year-olds the right to vote would easily be constitutionally justified, but one denying blacks or women this right would not. In the United States, the courts have developed three levels or intensities of judicial scrutiny for discrimination: strict, intermediate and minimal. The "strict scrutiny" test is applied to such "inherently suspect" classifications as race, religion and ethnic origin, and requires proof that a particular classification is necessary to achieve "an overriding state interest" which cannot be achieved in any less prejudicial manner. The "minimal scrutiny" test merely requires that the state establish that the classification has a "rational relationship" to a valid state interest, and, for example, classifications based on economic criteria fall into this category. The "intermediate" scrutiny test requires that a classification must "serve important governmental objectives and that it is substantially related to the achievement of those objectives". In the United States gender is a classification which warrants "intermediate scrutiny". In Canada, particularly in light of s. 28 of the Charter (see discussion, *infra*), it may well be argued that gender classifications require the equivalent of "strict scrutiny".

On the other hand, it has been suggested that some of the other classifications in the Charter "such as age and mental or physical disability, are clearly

---

160 [1986] 4 W.W.R. 242 (B.C.C.A.). This decision contains a quite extensive review of the literature on the nature of the relationship between ss. 15(1) and 1 of the Charter.

subject to *bona fide* qualifications or requirements [and] a less stringent test may come to be applied to these, such as the American one of intermediate scrutiny".[161]

1. Age Discrimination

Clearly, the issue in most cases involving age discrimination is going to be whether this is constitutionally "unjustified discrimination". Mere assertions that a particular form of age discrimination is necessary for the "best interests" of the child or society should be subject to rigorous scrutiny.[162]

Advocates for minors will doubtless wish to consider challenges to various legislative schemes which deny youths the "benefit and protection" of the law. For example, is it "reasonably justified" to make it more difficult for a 17-year-old to obtain welfare than an 18-year-old? In Quebec, persons under 30 have generally received lower welfare payments than those over this age; this is surely subject to challenge under s. 15 of the Charter. Are prohibitions based on age regarding certain kinds of employment "reasonable limits"? Might s. 43 of the Criminal Code, which allows parents and other adults to assault a child under some circumstances, provided only "reasonable force" is used for the purposes of correction, be challenged under s. 15? Is it demonstrably justified that teachers should be able to use corporal punishment to discipline their students?

In many parts of Canada, in order to obtain an abortion females under a stipulated age require parental consent in addition to the usual requirement of the approval of a therapeutic abortion committee pursuant to s. 251 of the Criminal Code.[163] Cannot a mature 15-year-old argue that she is being subject to unjustified discrimination on the basis of age? Why, for example, in Ontario does a 15-year-old require parental consent, but not a 16-year-old?[164]

---

161 See Tarnopolsky, "The Equality Rights" in Beaudoin and Tarnopolsky (eds.), *Canadian Charter of Rights and Freedoms: Commentary* (1982), at 395 and especially at 400-407 and 422.

162 In this regard, the comments of the Supreme Court of Canada in interpreting the Ontario Human Rights Code, S.O. 1981, c. 53, and its provisions prohibiting age discrimination are of interest. In *Ont. Human Rights Comm. v. Etobicoke* (1982), 132 D.L.R. (3d) 14 at 20 (S.C.C.), it was stated:
"We all age chronologically at the same rate, but aging in what has been termed the functional sense proceeds at widely varying rates and is largely unpredictable. In cases where concern for the employee's capacity is largely economic, that is where the employer's concern is one of productivity, and the circumstances of employment require no special skills that may diminish significantly with aging, or involve any unusual dangers to employees or the public that may be compounded by aging, it may be difficult, if not impossible, to demonstrate that a mandatory retirement at a fixed age, without regard to individual capacity, may be validly imposed under the Code."

163 Criminal Code, s. 251 [am. 1974-75-76, c. 93, s. 22.1].

164 See, e.g., Ontario, regulations under the Public Hospitals Act, R.S.O. 1980, c. 40, R.R.O.

In a recent decision, *R. v. L.A.L.*,[165] a young male was charged with the offence of buggery (anal intercourse) under s. 155 of the Criminal Code. Under s. 158(1) of the Code, if two men over the age of 21 voluntarily participate in such acts, they cannot be charged. The Crown argued that this age discrimination was constitutionally justified as it would protect children from sexual abuse. Karswick Prov. J. noted that the effect of s. 158(1) is to give a person over 21 the defence of consent, while denying this to a younger person. The court invoked s. 15 of the Charter to allow the youth to raise the defence of consent, concluding that s. 158 of the Code "does not focus on the protection of a victim, but rather it focuses on the creation of a defence". The denial of the defence of consent on the basis of age was not constitutionally justified.

One complex and fundamental question which the courts will have to resolve is when it is permissible to impose uniform restrictions based on age, and when individualized decision making is necessary. Thus, it might be justified to have a law that all young persons under a stipulated age are to be denied the right to vote. It may not be necessary to afford a particularly bright 17-year-old an individualized hearing to demonstrate his ability to participate in the democratic process. On the other hand, it seems impermissible to deny all persons below a specified age the right to participate in certain kinds of legal proceedings which vitally affect their interests; surely a mature 15-year-old can claim status to participate in a child protection proceeding. Presumably in deciding whether individualized decision making is necessary the courts will consider the nature and significance of the issue, as well as the administrative difficulties associated with individualized decision making.[166]

1980, Reg. 865, ss. 50-51, effectively requiring parental consent for an abortion performed on a female under 16. See more generally, Dickens, *Medico-Legal Aspects of Family Law* (1979), at 50-54 for a discussion of Canadian law and practice regarding abortions for minors. For a discussion of this and other issues, see J. Wilson, "Children and Equality Rights", in Bayefsky and Eberts (eds.), *Equality Rights and the Canadian Charter of Rights and Freedoms* (1985).

165 Ont. Fam. Ct., Karswick Prov. J., 28th May 1986 (not yet reported).

166 See *Moe v. Dinkins*, 533 F. Supp. 623 (N.Y., 1981), where the court held that age based restrictions on marriage without parental consent did not require individualized findings of immaturity. The court distinguished this from a situation where a minor sought an abortion (which in the U.S.A. generally requires an individualized determination) on the ground that the child's own decision about marriage was only being postponed, whereas a decision about abortion could not be postponed.

2. Sex Discrimination

Clearly s. 15 of the Charter can be used to challenge legislation which unjustifiably discriminates on the basis of sex. It has already been invoked in a number of provinces to strike down legislation requiring married parents to register their children under the name of the father.[167]

As discussed above under s. 7 of the Charter, there are many circumstances in which unwed fathers are the subject of discriminatory treatment in adoption and child protection legislation. Any denial of a right of participation in such proceedings must be "demonstrably justified". As noted, the claims of unwed fathers in these cases should be strengthened if it can be shown that they are asserting rights under s. 7 of the Charter, in particular rights of "liberty" and "security of the person", that is the right to enjoy a parent-child relationship.

Affiliation proceedings, which provide a legal process for identifying the unwed father of a child and requiring him to pay maintenance, present a *prima facie* case of sex discrimination. In *Shewchuk v. Ricard*, a British Columbia Provincial Judge found that the province's Child Paternity and Support Act violated the father's s. 15(1) right to equal protection and equal benefit of the law.[168] Auxier Prov. J. also found that the onus under s. 1 of the Charter to justify such discrimination had not been satisfied. On appeal, the British Columbia Supreme Court reversed the trial judgment and upheld the constitutional validity of the Act on the basis that the legislation was saved by s. 15(2) of the Charter. It was held to be a statute to ameliorate the conditions of a disadvantaged group of children who might otherwise not receive the father's maintenance, and thus fell within s. 15(2)[169]. On a further appeal, the British Columbia Court of Appeal upheld the legislation, though a three-judge panel split on whether it was valid because of s. 15(1), s. 15(2) or s. 1.[170] The case fails to address the sex-based discrimination against *the father* by raising the interests of another "disadvantaged group" — children born out of wedlock. It is the authors' submission that s. 15(2) can be used to protect only the interests directly at stake in the legislation — the alleged sex discrimination against men — not the interests of a third party. The child's interests are best considered in a balancing test. It is not clear why the interests of children cannot be protected in legislation which imposes support obligations upon both parents.

---

167 See E. Rosenfeld, "Ontario Infants can Receive Mother's Surname", *The Globe and Mail*, 10th December 1985, at 1. The jurisdictions include Alberta, British Columbia, Saskatchewan, Manitoba, Ontario, Quebec and the Northwest Territories.

168 [1985] 6 W.W.R. 427, 17 C.R.R. 117 (B.C. Prov. Ct.), Child Paternity and Support Act, R.S.B.C. 1979, c. 49.

169 [1985] 6 W.W.R. 436, 66 B.C.L.R. 107 (S.C.), *per* Locke J.

170 [1986], 4 W.W.R. 289 (B.C.C.A.).

Even if legislation is not discriminatory on its face, it may be possible to challenge individual judicial decisions under s. 15 of the Charter. For example, in the Alabama case of *Ex parte Devine*, it was held that application of the judicially created "tender years doctrine" violated the equal protection clause of the Fourteenth Amendment of the American Constitution:

> We conclude that the tender years presumption represents an unconstitutional gender-based classification which discriminates between fathers and mothers in child custody proceedings solely on the basis of sex. . . . The tender years presumption . . . imposes legal burdens upon individuals according to the "inherent characteristics" of sex. By requiring fathers to carry the difficult burden of affirmatively proving the unfitness of the mother, the presumption may have the effect of depriving some loving fathers of the custody of their children. . . .[171]

It has been suggested by some commentators that a "disparate impact" argument can be made under s. 15 in regard to some family law legislation. For example, a husband ordered to pay spousal support might argue that although support legislation appears to be sexually neutral, in fact the way the legislation is applied discriminates against men, as the vast majority of payor spouses are men. The American courts, however, have been reluctant to accept "statistical arguments" concerning "disproportionate" or "disparate impact" of legislation which is on its face neutral in the absence of evidence of an impermissible discriminatory intent or purpose on the part of the legislature.[172]

Claims of sex discrimination may in some circumstances be buttressed by relying on s. 28 of the Charter, the Sexual Equality provision, which provides:

> 28. Notwithstanding anything in this Charter, the rights and freedoms referred to in it are guaranteed equally to male and female persons.

Section 28 stipulates that all the rights referred to in the Charter are guaranteed equally to men and women. It falls short of requiring the equal treatment of male and female persons; that objective is obtained through the Equality Rights provision of s. 15 of the Charter. Section 28 only requires that the provisions of the Charter be applied without discrimination between the sexes.

---

171 398 So. 2d 686 at 695-96 (Ala. S.C., 1981).

172 See, e.g., "A Monograph on Family Law and the Charter of Rights" (1983), 6 F.L.R.R. 51-52, for a discussion of this argument. For American case law, see, e.g., *Washington v. Davis*, 426 U.S. 229 (1976). For an example of a case where a court did accept the "disparate impact" argument see *Griggs v. Duke Power*, 401 U.S. 849 (1971). There it was held that an employer's requirement that job applicants have a high school education, where this requirement was not significantly related to job functions, violated the anti-discrimination provisions of the Civil Rights Act when it had the effect of disqualifying black applicants at a substantially higher rate than whites.

Within its relatively narrow sphere, however, s. 28 provides stronger protections than s. 15. Section 28 does not appear subject to legislative override by s. 33 of the Charter, under which Parliament or a legislature may enact laws which will operate notwithstanding s. 2 or ss. 7 to 15 of the Charter. It also seems that in light of the opening words of s. 28 — "Notwithstanding anything in this Charter" — the section was not restricted by the general limitation of s. 1 of the Charter. Section 28 may in some cases be used to buttress arguments founded on ss. 7 and 15 against sexual discrimination.

3. Unenumerated Grounds of Discrimination

It should be noted that the Charter has a general guarantee of equality, with s. 15(1) declaring that "Every individual is equal . . . without discrimination and *in particular*, without discrimination based on race, national or ethnic origin, colour, religion, sex, age, or merit or physical disability". The specified types of discrimination are only examples of the kind of discrimination that could produce inequality. While the majority of cases will doubtless focus on the enumerated forms of discrimination, other challenges are possible. It may, for example, be argued that adoption laws which destroy the opportunity of one class of individuals — adoptees — to learn the identity of their biological parents unjustifiably discriminate against this group.[173]

XVI ENFORCEMENT: SECTION 24

24.(1) Anyone whose rights or freedoms, as guaranteed by this Charter, have been infringed or denied may apply to a court of competent jurisdiction to obtain such remedy as the court considers appropriate and just in the circumstances.

(2) Where, in proceedings under subsection (1), a court concludes that evidence was obtained in a manner that infringed or denied any rights or freedoms guaranteed by this Charter, the evidence shall be excluded if it is established that, having regard to all the circumstances, the admission of it in the proceeding would bring the administration of justice into disrepute.

The remedies section is critical to the effectiveness of the Charter. It gives a court broad powers, including the authority to: declare a particular statute unconstitutional; order that a child be returned to a parent; dismiss a proceeding; or add an individual as a party to a proceeding despite the absence of statutory authority. There may be situations where the statute itself is not found

---

173 Such an argument was rejected in regard to adoptees in *In re Roger B.*, 418 N.E. 2d 751 (Ill., 1981). For a case in which a Canadian court invoked s. 15 of the Charter to strike down a statute on an "unenumerated ground", see *Andrews v. Law Soc. of B.C.*, [1986] 4 W.W.R. 242 (C.A.). The court ruled that a legislative requirement that a person be a Canadian citizen violated s. 15 of the Charter.

unconstitutional, but a Charter right has been breached in the application of the law; in such cases a s. 24 remedy might include dismissal of proceedings, return of the child to parental care, or exclusion of particular evidence subject to s. 24(2).

Section 7 of the Charter, as outlined earlier, could be the basis for a "right to privacy" in the family. When a child welfare worker investigates a complaint of abuse or neglect, it may involve an interview with the parents at which admissions of ill-treatment are made. Although the parents may not realize it, those admissions may later be evidenced against them in a child welfare hearing. To date, such "confessions" have not attracted the same legal protections seen in the field of criminal law. There is no uniform practice by child welfare workers of warning the parents about the potential use of the statement.[174] Indeed, some workers may give the parents the impression that the worker may be confided in and accepted as a friend and not as a "person in authority". Will these practices, if continued, violate the "family privacy" right because statements are taken without regard to "the principles of fundamental justice"?

First, one could allege that the parent's right to "liberty" and "security of the person" under s. 7 had been infringed. Again, there is the problem whether the right of the child, not the parent, has been violated. As noted above, the U.S. concept of "family privacy" has been broad enough to cover both.

Second, one could argue that the "principles of fundamental justice" require that whenever a statement is taken: (1) an investigative child welfare worker must clearly identify himself as someone who can remove a child and give evidence in court; (2) the worker must first give a warning to the parents that they have the right to remain silent and to retain a lawyer; and (3) that any statement must be "voluntary" in line with the criminal law cases.

Third, s. 24(1) of the Charter could be invoked to seek exclusion of any statement made without the above cautions. For a result favourable to the parents, it would have to be shown that, under s. 24(2), the admission of the statement would "bring the administration of justice into disrepute". Because of the central theme of child protection in the child welfare statutes, this test may be difficult to meet. It may be argued that only in the cases of outright deception, such as those suggested in *Rothman v. R.*[175] (in a criminal context), will the courts exclude statements in the early development of the Charter.

---

174 Alberta, *Child Welfare Programs* (1982), at 15: in this policy manual, it states that families have a "right to family privacy", but no instructions are given on a warning prior to taking statements; at the same time, the investigating worker is expected to "maintain a role of helper rather than adversary" (at 16) and to obtain information on the "nature of the neglecting behaviour and the knowledge . . . the other parent has of the neglect" (at 27).

175 (1981), 59 C.C.C. (2d) 30 at 74 (S.C.C.).

A bolder approach to the questions of cautions and voluntariness surrounding statements, would be a challenge to any statutory apprehensions undertaken with key evidence from statements. This would be an invitation to the courts to "read down" the statutory power to apprehend and hold children in care to circumstances where cautioned, voluntary statements have been taken or there is adequate independent evidence.

Finally, rather than attack the statute, it could be argued that the absence of a caution or of voluntariness would vitiate an individual apprehension altogether. This follows from the line of reasoning set forth by Justices Laskin and Hall in *Brownridge v. R*.[176] In that case, in a separate judgment for the majority, they held that the denial of the right to counsel in a criminal matter would vitiate the conviction. The statutory offence (refusal of breathalyzer sample) remained constitutionally intact.

It should also be noted that a court lacks authority to provide a remedy which it is not "competent" to award. So, for example, a family court dealing with a child protection or adoption case will generally not be able to award monetary damages if a Charter right is violated. It would be necessary to proceed through the ordinary civil courts for such a remedy.

XVII SECTIONS 25-27

25. The guarantee in this Charter of certain rights and freedoms shall not be construed so as to abrogate or derogate from any aboriginal, treaty or other rights or freedoms that pertain to the aboriginal peoples of Canada including

(a) any rights or freedoms that have been recognized by the Royal Proclamation of October 7, 1763; and

(b) any rights or freedoms that now exist by way of land claims agreements or may be so acquired.

26. The guarantee in this Charter of certain rights and freedoms shall not be construed as denying the existence of any other rights or freedoms that exist in Canada.

27. This Charter shall be interpreted in a manner consistent with the preservation and enhancement of the multicultural heritage of Canadians.

Arguably ss. 25 and 27 might be applicable in some child protection or adoption cases where arguments could be raised about the desirability of a child being raised in the cultural or religious environment of his biological family.

---

176 [1972] S.C.R. 926. See also *Clarkson v. R.* (1986), O.L.W. 603-035 (S.C.C.), where, in a murder case, a statement by the accused to the police was ruled inadmissible because of the failure of the police to adequately afford her the right to consult with counsel, as guaranteed by s. 10(b) of the Charter. Madam Justice Wilson described it as a "blatant violation" of Charter rights, and invoked s. 24(2) to exclude the statement "Otherwise, s. 10(b) would cease to have any meaningful context. . . ."

XVIII CONCLUSIONS

It is not the intention of this chapter to exhaustively examine all of the implications that the Canadian Charter of Rights and Freedoms may have for families and children. Rather, an attempt has been made to discuss present Canadian jurisprudence, to raise certain issues not yet resolved by the courts, and to offer suggestions as to how the Charter might be employed to assist in the resolution of these issues. By drawing analogies to American and pre-Charter Canadian jurisprudence, it was shown that the rights of parents and children should be considered fundamental rights, and should be subject to constitutional protection. Clearly, the Canadian courts have taken the first steps to constitutionally protect these rights.

Few questions have been definitively answered here, but it is hoped that the discussion will stimulate others to consider whether Charter rights of individuals are being violated in various situations. Also, the Charter may be relevant to issues not raised in this chapter, such as the right of children to standing in custody proceedings. A constitutional document like the Charter has the potential to be a guarantor of the rights of all Canadians and as such should be considered in a broad range of situations affecting the fundamental rights of children and families.

3

THE RIGHTS OF MINORS TO CONSENT TO TREATMENT AND TO RESIDENTIAL CARE

Barbara Landau

I INTRODUCTION

Traditionally, discussions of the balance of power between parents, the state and the child have not included serious consideration of the rights of children separate from their adult caretakers. Children were presumed to lack the cognitive ability and maturity of judgment necessary to make independent decisions. It was assumed that parents were best able to understand and articulate their children's needs and that they would act in their children's best interests.[1] Parents were seen as the natural advocates for children and any suggestion that the child should participate in the decision-making process was generally dismissed as unnecessary or likely to undermine parental authority.[2] As a safeguard for children whose parents abused their parental rights, the state would intervene to supervise and if necessary remove the child from their care.[3]

---

1 For a discussion of the balance of power between parents, the state and the child see Andrew Kleinfeld, "The Balance of Power Among Infants, Their Parents and the State" (1970), 4 Fam. L.Q. 319; "Parental Power" (1970), 4 Fam. L.Q. 409; "The Relation to the State" (1971), 5 Fam. L.Q. 63. Also see John Wilson, *The Rights of Adolescents in the Mental Health System* (1978), at 194, and Jack Westman, *Child Advocacy* (1979), at 257.

2 Joseph Goldstein, "Psychoanalysis and a Jurisprudence of Child Placement, with Special Emphasis on the Role of Legal Counsel for Children" (1978), 1 Int. J.L. & Psych. 109 at 110-14. Joseph Goldstein, Anna Freud and Albert Solnit, *Before the Best Interests of the Child* (1979).

3 Bernard Dickens, "Legal Responses to Child Abuse in Canada" (1978), 1 Can. J. Fam. L. 87 at 90. Kleinfeld, "The Relation to the State", *supra*, n. 1, at 66.

At no point in the process did children have an automatic right to be consulted or separately represented to ensure that the arrangements made reflected their wishes.[4]

Today there are increasing demands to change this situation and to recognize certain rights of children separate from both their parents and the state. At the outset it is important to clarify the use of the term "children's rights" for the purpose of this paper. Michael Wald, in his paper "Children's Rights: A Framework for Analysis",[5] suggests that rights can be considered in terms of four different categories, namely:

> (1) generalized claims against the world, for example, the right of freedom from discrimination and poverty; (2) the right to greater protection from abuse, neglect or exploitation by adults; (3) the right to be treated in the same manner as an adult, with the same constitutional protections, in relationship to state actions [for example, the right to vote, marry, drive]; (4) the right to act independently of parental control and/or guidance [for example, the right to consent to medical care].[6]

The first category includes claims that are not restricted to benefitting children, but in fact are aimed at improving the condition of the world in general. Such claims or "rights" are really ideal, not legally enforceable, demands that could be made by a child in a court of law. In fact these "rights" are more appropriately designated as "protections" that serve to highlight the inferior status of children, rather than rights that would enhance the position of the child vis-à-vis adults.

The second category of rights is similar in that it also deals with protections rather than separate rights and it emphasizes the dependence of children on adult care and guidance. What this category recognizes is that children are not helpless chattels subject to the complete discretion of their parents. The state insists on certain minimal standards of parenting and sets certain requirements. If these standards are not met, the state will intervene to limit parental discretion. In this category, as in the first, the legal status of the child has not really been altered and in most cases the protections are ordered whether or not the child wishes the state to intervene.

The third category, namely full adult legal status, draws attention to the difference in status of children and adults. For example, because of their age children are not permitted to vote, marry, drink alcohol, or drive a car. In

---

4 Katherine Catton, "Models of Procedure and the Juvenile Courts" (1976), 18 Cr. L.Q. 181; Packer, "Two Models of the Criminal Process" (1964), 113 U. Pa. L. Rev. 1; and Jeffrey Leon, "Recent Developments in the Legal Representation of Children — A Growing Concern with the Concept of Capacity" (1978), 1 Can. J. Fam. L. 375.

5 See Chapter 1 of this text, *supra*, at 3. Also published in (1979), 12 U.C. D.L. Rev. 255.

6 *Ibid.*, at 7.

addition children are not granted the same procedural protections as adults appearing in court or before administrative tribunals. Minors may not be bound by contractual obligations and they cannot be drafted into the armed forces. All of these legal differences are premised on the assumption that children lack the judgment, maturity and conceptual powers necessary for full adult privileges and responsibilities. However, different jurisdictions have selected different ages for obtaining privileges or imposing obligations. Since there is no consistency or clear rationale for choosing a particular age at which various legal rights are entrenched, the choice is open to challenge on the basis that it is arbitrary and not founded on actual developmental differences in capacity.

The fourth category is in some ways similar to the third. However, rather than dealing with general rights enjoyed by adults, this category involves the right of children to act independently of their parents prior to the age of majority. The types of issues covered by this category range from everyday decisions such as hair length, bedtime and choice of clothing, to very serious matters that could have long-term consequences such as choice of religion, decisions about medical care and decisions about psychiatric treatment. While it is sometimes difficult to draw the line as to which matters should be left to parental discretion and which should require participation or even a final decision by a child, or which matters should be resolved within the family and which should be referred to an external body in cases of dispute, I will take the position in this paper that family autonomy is to be protected from external interference in all but the most serious decisions. That is, matters of everyday living should be left to parental discretion, especially while children are living at home. It would be terribly disruptive to family life and would place an enormous burden on the legal system if every child had an enforceable right to complain to a court or a tribunal about relatively minor everyday matters.

The more difficult issues involve decisions that are likely to have a serious effect on the child's present and future life. These matters tend to involve questions such as should children have the right to make decisions about medical care or mental health treatment without parental consent or even in opposition to their parents' wishes? For example, should a child be able to decide to: use contraceptives, have or refuse to have an operation or abortion, enter or be released from residential care, or seek counselling services? If a child can be shown to have the necessary capacity to make such decisions, should parents be permitted to consent to medical or psychiatric care contrary to their child's wishes? If the child lacks the capacity to give a valid consent, what protections if any are needed to ensure that parental decisions are in fact in the child's best interests? Should parents be permitted to consent to non-therapeutic, non-essential medical procedures or refuse therapeutic treatment when the child lacks capacity?

The issues raised by Wald's last two categories of rights, namely adult status rights and rights independent of parents, are the most complex and generate the most emotionally charged responses. Particularly the last category raises serious questions about the balance between maintaining family autonomy and recognizing the rights of an individual. Wald suggests five factors that should be considered in determining whether to give children increased power to make or participate in significant decisions, namely:

> . . . (a) whether the child can make such decisions adequately; (b) if not, whether other decision makers, or decision-making processes, are likely to arrive at better decisions than the parents; (c) whether the state can really remove the decision-making power from the parents; (d) the costs of removing the decision from the parents in terms of family autonomy and family privacy (both valued goals in our society); (e) the costs of *not* giving the decision to the child. For some specific issues, it also must be considered whether there are parental interests . . . which may equal or exceed the child's interest in autonomy.[7]

This chapter will attempt to explore the issues of admission to residential care and consent to medical treatment as examples of serious matters where children's rights should be extended. The discussion will focus on the balance of interests involved in making such decisions and on recommendations for increased rights for children in keeping with their developmental abilities.

II ADMISSION TO RESIDENTIAL CARE: THE RIGHTS OF MINORS, PARENTS AND THE STATE

I will begin with a discussion of the issue of voluntary commitment to mental hospitals or to other forms of residential care. The cases on this topic clearly exemplify the potential conflict of interest between parents and children because in most jurisdictions in Canada and the United States, parents are free to make decisions on medical care, placement in mental hospitals, institutions for the retarded and group homes with no requirement that the child even be consulted.[8] In these cases there is a clear liberty interest in the child that is not protected by adequate due process safeguards. In fact, the only check on parental discretion in seeking placement, is the requirement that the attending physician approve the commital.[9] This problem was clearly described by one

---

7 *Ibid.*, at 17.

8 James Ellis, "Volunteering Children — Parental Commitment of Minors to Mental Institutions" (1974), 62 Cal. L. Rev. 840 at 840-41; Richard Gosse, "Consent to Medical Treatment: A Minor Digression" (1974), 9 U.B.C.L. Rev. 56 at 58-64; The Law Reform Commission of Canada, *Study Paper on Consent to Medical Care* (1979), at 71-72; Lee Teitelbaum and James Ellis, "The Liberty Interest of Children: Due Process Rights and their Application" (1978), 12 Fam. L.Q. 153 at 179.

9 Barbara Landau, "Barriers to Consent to Treatment: The Rights of Minors in the Provision of Mental Health Services" (1979), 2 Can. J. Fam. L. 245.

American commentator and his description accurately reflects the present status of minors under most provincial statutes:

> In most states, parents may commit their children to mental institutions without a hearing or any other form of judicial scrutiny. If a parent wants a child committed, and a hospital will accept the child as a patient, no legal authority will hear the child's protest. Moreover the child-patient has no standing to petition for release from the institution until he or she reaches the statutory age of majority. Until that time, any request for discharge must be made by the parent. Thus the minor admitted to a mental hospital on the application of a parent is denied access to virtually all procedural protections — notice, hearing, appellate review, and habeas corpus — rights afforded all other patients institutionalized against their will.[10]

What is paradoxical is that if the child met the criteria for involuntary admission, he/she would in fact have greater procedural protection than a child who was diagnosed as not presenting a danger to himself/herself or to the community. Not only can the "volunteered" minor be deprived of his/her liberty without provision for a hearing or legal representation in most provinces, but also there is no legal basis for the minor to refuse treatment or to prevent disclosure of his/her clinical records once the parents have consented.[11]

In order to understand the present situation, it is necessary to examine the underlying policies and assumptions on which it is based. To the extent that these assumptions are not in fact valid, the present law or practice may not be justified. The underlying assumptions appear to be that:

1. Parents are the natural advocates for their children and are motivated primarily by considerations of their children's best interests.

---

10 Ellis, *supra*, n. 8, at 840. See the Child and Family Services Act, S.O. 1984, c. 55, which has addressed and attempted to resolve some of these issues, discussed later in this chapter at Part III. 3.

11 It is possible to argue that this is not in fact an accurate description of the present situation. That is, it could be argued that in fact institutions and other types of residential placements do not have the power to admit or detain a child who has reached the common law age of discretion or discernment (for boys this was 14 years and for girls 16 years) or to treat a child who had the cognitive ability to understand the nature and consequences of the treatment being offered.

In relation to the power to determine where a child will reside and to detain the child, if parents no longer have these powers once the child attains the age of discretion, it would follow that the parents cannot delegate these powers to anyone else. Therefore residential facilities that are operating *in loco parentis* or on the basis of parental consent, may be acting beyond their powers if they admit, detain or retain a child who has reached the age of discretion against the child's wishes: see Michael Code, "The Existing State of the Law in Ontario with Respect to Consent to Medical Treatment", paper prepared for the Interministerial Committee Regarding Medical Consents and Custody for Mental Incompetents (1979), at 11-12; *Ex parte Barford* (1860), 8 Cox C.C. 405, 121 E.R. 467 (sub nom. *R. v. Howes); In re Agar -Ellis* (1833), 24 Ch. D. 317 at 326. Also see the Child and Family Services Act, discussed later in this chapter at Part III. 3.

2. Children and parents have such similar interests that independent representation of children is unnecessary.

3. The goal of ensuring family privacy and autonomy takes priority over introducing the state as an arbitrator of family disagreements.

4. Minors lack the capacity to make reasonable judgments as to their needs, so it is desirable to let the parents, who have more mature judgment, speak for them.

5. The provision of health care is a desirable service aimed at preventing future, more serious social problems and at improving the present quality of life for the child and family. Therefore, it is better to err on the side of ensuring that treatment is obtained rather than encouraging reluctant patients to withdraw from its potential benefits. This is consistent with the state's interest in the general welfare of its citizens.

6. Mental health professionals are in the best position to offer the necessary protection, namely, that people are not admitted without proper justification. This matter is outside the expertise of the courts. In addition, it is undesirable to put a child through the emotional trauma of an adversarial court hearing in order to determine his/her treatment needs.

Before analyzing the existing case law and statutes on this subject, it is important to challenge the presumptions listed above. The principal issue that needs to be considered is whether, or to what extent, children have interests that need to be protected, independent of any state or parental interests. Also, if there are competing interests, under what circumstances should the interests of the child outweigh the competing considerations? Several of the points noted above will be addressed in the following discussion.

While it is true that parents are the natural advocates for their children and are under a legal duty to care for and supervise them, the justification for state support of parents loses much of its force if children are not living at home. For children living in institutions or residential care, the day-to-day care and control by parents is replaced by custody and treatment by strangers. While it can be presumed (unless proven otherwise) that parents love their children and will exercise their decision making in a way that will reflect an understanding of their child's unique needs and sensitivities, the same cannot be presumed for strangers, no matter how professionally trained and well motivated they may be. In any case, while state support of parental decision making for children is justified in many circumstances, this justification disappears when parents seek to give up their custodial obligations.

Teitelbaum and Ellis, in their article entitled "The Liberty Interest of Children: Due Process Rights and Their Application", recommend that when parents seek to remove a child from their home, either by charging the child as incorrigible or by volunteering the child for placement in an institution, due process protections should be provided, regardless of the motives of the parent. It is the consequence of the decision for the child, not the parents' intention, that calls for third party scrutiny in situations where children have been given over to some public authority or agency for care. While Teitelbaum and Ellis were writing specifically about retarded children in institutions, their words are equally applicable to any child placed in long-term residential care, that is:

> Parental commitment of children to public institutions for the mentally retarded seems to stand on the same basis (as parental commitment of children to institutions for delinquents). The conditions which justify or even demand deference to parental choice are absent when removal from the home for an indefinite period is sought. Again, motives may be the best or not; their characterization is unimportant. In the case of commitment, as with incorrigibility (or delinquency) cases, the family has reached the conclusion that the child has a problem which cannot or can no longer be managed (treated) in the home. When that conclusion is reached, the same liberty interest ought to be involved, whatever the nature of the proceeding.[12]

Even if the parents are coping well with the stress of a disturbed or severely handicapped child and sincerely wish to do what is best, the most important question for the parents and the child should be: is institutional placement (or the particular medical decision) the most appropriate choice to meet the child's needs? Parents may not be very sophisticated or knowledgeable about the range of resources available to give them relief and to assist their child. By requiring procedural protections in which an impartial decision maker reviews the situation, the child's interest in the least restrictive type of service would be protected.

The assumption that parents and children have identical interests also needs to be questioned. While children and parents may have similar interests in many situations, this is no longer the case once a decision is made that will greatly alter the child's life-style. When children are placed in institutional care, the most significant interest the children have that sets them apart from their parents is their liberty interest.

Whether or not it is for a positive purpose, placement in an institution is a deprivation of liberty. In fact, Teitelbaum and Ellis note that civil commitment of children is seen as a "massive curtailment of liberty" by the U.S. Supreme Court.[13]

As they point out, there are many similarities between confinement in an institution for treatment and confinement in a state institution for delinquents. Both are intended to have a rehabilitative effect but both involve a very serious

---

12 Teitelbaum and Ellis, *supra*, n. 8, at 173.

13 *Humphrey v. Cady*, 405 U.S. 504 at 509 (1972); see *O'Connor v. Donaldson*, 422 U.S. 563 (1975).

change from the child's normal life. They cite *In re Gault* as highlighting the differences between living at home and the deprivation of liberty in an institution:

> A boy is charged with misconduct. The boy is committed to an institution where he may be restrained of liberty for years. . . . His world becomes "a building with whitewashed walls, regimented routine and institutional hours. . . ." Instead of mother and father and sisters and brothers and friends and classmates, his world is peopled by guards, custodians, state employees and "delinquents". . . .[14]

The above concerns about parental decision making in relation to admission to residential care would seem to invite greater state involvement in these matters. On the theory that the state is under an obligation to exercise its *parens patriae* power to protect those citizens who are incapable of protecting their own interests,[15] it would seem that the response to unfettered parental discretion would be greater state surveillance.

Such an inference would follow from the assumption that minors lack the capacity to make reasonable judgments about their lives. However, presumptions about the ability of minors to make reasonable decisions have received a great deal of attention from psychologists, particularly in recent years. Several psychologists have attempted to determine whether children have the requisite capacity.[16]

Piaget and other researchers surveyed have found that children of 15 years of age appear to have the necessary conceptual skills to give a valid consent. In the age range of 11 to 14 years, children appear to be in a state of transition in their cognitive and social development. Children below the age of 11 years do not appear to have adequate conceptual ability to make final decisions as to their treatment needs. However, according to one survey,[17] the children's linguistic, intellectual and cognitive abilities are adequate for them to have some role in decisions affecting their lives. Certainly children below the age of 11 can understand sufficiently to express opinions, even if there are limitations on their ability to fully appreciate consequences or to resist pressures to conform with adult views.

---

14 *In re Gault*, 387 U.S. 1 at 27 (1967).

15 *Eyre v. Countess of Shaftsbury* (1722), 2 P. Wms. 103, 24 E. R. 659 (Ch. D.); *Wellesley v. Wellesley* (1828), 11 Bligh N.S. 124, 4 E. R. 1078 (H.L.). Also see Kleinfeld, "The Relation to the State," *supra*, n. 1, at 66.

16 Jean Piaget and B. Inhelder, "Diagnosis of Mental Operations and Theory of Intelligence" (1947), 51. Am. J. Ment. Defic. 401. See also J.H. Flavell, *The Developmental Psychology of Jean Piaget* (1963); Jerome Kagan, "A Conception of Early Adolescence" (1971), 100 Daedalus 997; Thomas Grisso and Linda Vierling, "Minor's Consent to Treatment — A Developmental Perspective" (1979), 9 Professional Psychology 412.

17 Leon, *supra*, n. 4, at 433, and Katherine Catton, "Who are the Children?" unpublished manuscript for the Child and the City Programme, University of Toronto (1978), at 2.9 - 2.15.

A third interest that needs to be addressed is the state's interest. The state, in its *parens patriae* role as a protector of the welfare of children and other vulnerable citizens, has an interest in ensuring that medical or psychiatric treatment is offered as early as possible to prevent future, more serious difficulties. For this reason, the state has been reluctant to introduce lengthy, expensive procedures that could delay treatment or deter parents from seeking necessary care. Rather, the preference has been to support parental decision making and to rely on medical or other mental health expertise for screening out those individuals who would not benefit from treatment.[18]

In addition, the state has an interest in maintaining family unity and avoiding potentially disruptive, adversarial procedures that could lead to families abandoning their children to the care of the state.[19] Also, many mental health professionals would argue that due process provisions, such as judicial or administrative hearings, would be counter-therapeutic for both the child and other family members, would be cumbersome and inefficient and that the fears of wrongful commitment are grossly exaggerated.[20] Their position is that legalistic measures interfere with the child's right to treatment and that the trend towards giving children an increasing voice in these matters will mean that many who would benefit from treatment will not be able to be helped.[21]

On the other hand, it can be argued that due process protections are justified because of the high risk of error in the diagnosis of emotionally disturbed and mentally retarded persons. Numerous studies and articles have called into question the reliability and predictive validity of diagnoses.[22] If mental health professionals have difficulty in judging who is emotionally disturbed or mentally retarded or who is likely to show dangerous behaviour in the future, then it can be argued that additional checks should be required to

---

18 *Parham v. J. R.*, 99 S. Ct. 2493 at 2495 (1979). This case will be discussed in greater detail later in this chapter. Also see *Mathews v. Eldridge*, 424 U.S. 319 at 335 (1976).

19 Ellis, *supra*, n. 8, at 891-92. See *In re Lee,* Cook County Cir. Ct. — Juvenile Division, No. 68 - 1362, 24th August 1972 (unreported).

20 Ellis, *supra*, n. 8, at 843; Kadish, "A Case Study in the Signification of Procedural Due Process — Institutionalizing the Mentally Ill" (1956), 9 W. Pol. 93 at 96, 103; "Analysis of Legal and Medical Considerations in Commitment of the Mentally Ill" (1947), 56 Yale L.J. 1178 at 1192.

21 Letter from Robert W. Taylor, Ph.D., to the editor, 7 *Psychology Today*, December 1973, at 145.

22 Ennis and Litwack, "Psychiatry and the Presumption of Expertise: Flipping Coins in the Courtroom" (1974), 62 Cal. L. Rev. 693. For a similar analysis in the case of mentally retarded children see Teitelbaum and Ellis, *supra*, n. 8, at 186-90. Also see Vernon Quincey, "Assessments of the Dangerousness of Mental Patients Held in Maximum Security" (1979), 2 Int. J. L. & Psych. 389-406.

avoid the possibility of misdiagnosis and therefore unnecessary commitment to residential care.[23] As John Panneton points out very forcefully in his article entitled, "Children, Commitment and Consent: A Constitutional Crisis":

> One of the glaring deficiencies in the behavioral sciences which accentuates the need for legal formalities is the elasticity given to the concept of mental illness. It has been claimed by respected medical authorities that the diagnostician has the ability to shoehorn into the mentally disabled class virtually any person he wishes and for whatever reasons. Moreover, because there is little absolute knowledge about the child development process, a minor's behavioral and personality traits are particularly susceptible to misdiagnosis. Although it is not suggested that doctors institutionalize children maliciously, very few safeguards exist to assure against an honest error either by the doctor or by the person applying for admission. Nor is there any need for medical authorities to articulate reasons for their decisions in the voluntary admissions process. No accountability has been built into the system, since the patient or one acting on his behalf has allegedly made the decision to enter the institution freely. Because of these weaknesses, grave consequences may ensue when a person applies for admission to a mental facility.[24]

A second source of error arises from the ability of mental health professionals to determine what type of treatment is necessary, even if the diagnosis is correct and the child does require treatment. A number of studies have found that psychiatrists tend to err on the side of caution,[25] particularly with children,[26] and therefore hospitalize children when other less restrictive alternatives would be preferable.[27]

Since less restrictive community based programs are usually cheaper than institutional care, and tend to encourage greater independence and self-help than programs in institutions, avoiding unnecessary placements in institutions or long-term residential programs may mean considerable savings in the government health budget.[28]

An important question that should be addressed is: will the introduction of procedural safeguards decrease the likelihood of error in either diagnosis or

---

23 *O'Connor v. Donaldson, supra,* n. 13, at 578, 584, 587 (Burger C.J. concurring); Rosenhan, *On Being Sane in Insane Places* (1973), 179 Science 250, reprinted in (1973), Santa Clara L.J. at 179. This study found that once an individual had been committed to a facility it was difficult for staff to distinguish normal from abnormal behaviour. This study indicates the importance of avoiding incorrect placements, rather than relying on post-placement reviews to discover those who have been incorrectly admitted.

24 (1977), 10 Fam L.Q. 295 at 312.

25 Teitelbaum and Ellis, *supra,* n. 8, at 186-87.

26 Thomas Szasz, *The Manufacture of Madness* (1970), at 35. Also see *Parham v. J.R., supra,* n. 18, at 2577.

27 T. Scheff, *Being Mentally Ill: A Sociological Theory* (1966). Also see Ennis and Litwack, *supra,* n. 22, and Ellis, *supra,* n. 8 at 864-66.

28 National Institute of Mental Health, Statistical Note 115, *Children and State Mental Hospitals 4* (April 1975), at 200. Also see *Parham v. J.R., supra,* n. 18, at 2578.

placement? In answer to this question, while there is no clear data on this point as yet, it is expected that the principal value of a hearing or third party review (by a judge or administrative tribunal) would be to decrease the risk of error by increasing the extent to which professionals are held accountable for their judgments. As Teitelbaum and Ellis acknowledge:

> Since procedural safeguards have not been traditionally required before a child is institutionalized, we have no data from which to measure the effectiveness of such procedures in reducing errors. But the traditional purposes of procedural safeguards seem relevant to these cases. The availability of an adversarial due process hearing would put the professionals proposing the commitment to their proof. Subjecting their reasons for proposing the placement to impartial examination will tend to reduce errors much in the same way as delinquency proceedings or criminal trials; by forcing careful evaluation of the relevant evidence.[29]

What is not clear is whether the parents' interest in preserving their decision-making role and in obtaining relief from the serious physical and emotional strain of living with a disturbed or retarded child would be met by increased procedural safeguards. It is likely that a hearing would be an added strain and would be upsetting for parents. However, in an increasing number of cases, parents are indicating that institutional care is not their placement of choice, but it is the placement that is often recommended by professionals (especially for retarded children)[30] or it is chosen at a time of extreme tension when the parent is emotionally unable to explore alternatives.[31] In these cases, the presence of a knowledgeable reviewing body could assist parents to identify less restrictive options that might better meet their needs, as well as the child's needs.

Earlier in this chapter it was indicated that many children who are younger than 18 years of age have the capacity to express opinions and at some point to make decisions about their treatment. One issue that should be raised is: do children who do not have the capacity to consent or even to participate, require additional procedural protections or should these children be admitted to long-term residential care under the present procedure, that is, on the basis of agreement between the parents and the facility? While a strong argument in favour of a hearing for older, competent children is that they should have a right to participate in decisions that will seriously affect their lives, an equally strong rationale is that the hearing will serve as a means of testing out the appropriateness of the choice of placement. As Teitelbaum and Ellis argue, if competence were a prerequisite to a hearing, then

---

29 Teitelbaum and Ellis, "The Liberty Interests of Children: Due Process Rights and their Application" (1978), 12 Fam. L.Q. 153 at 198.

30 *Ibid.*, at 195; Centerwall and Centerwall, "A Study of Children With Mongolism Reared in the Home Compared to Those Reared Away from the Home" (1960), 25 Pediatrics 678 at 678.

31 Ellis, "Volunteering Children — Parental Commitment of Minors to Mental Institutions" (1974), 62 Cal. L. Rev. 840 at 851.

. . . the only prospective adult mental patients who would be entitled to a civil commitment hearing would be those competent enough to participate in the proceedings — the others could be summarily confined for an indefinite period. And in the case of mentally retarded minors the age differentiation would itself lose meaning. Many of the older minors will have such limited abilities (restricted by their retardation rather than by their chronological immaturity) that they too would be unable to meet the competence requirements for obtaining a hearing. The unsatisfactory results obtained in these examples should indicate the impracticality of making capacity to participate in a hearing a doctrinal limitation on recognition of liberty interests.

Moreover, provision of a hearing serves functions other than allowing the subject a forum. The major purpose of a commitment hearing for juveniles of any age must be to determine the necessity and appropriateness of the proposed placement in an institution. This issue is no less important when a minor is incapacitated either by age or by mental condition.[32]

In recent years, the issues and assumptions raised above have received increasing critical analysis by commentators and have emerged as significant issues, particularly in the United States. For the purpose of this paper, the principal concern in examining the case law on children's rights is to determine what type of procedural protections should be available to children who are being admitted to residential care.[33]

---

32 Teitelbaum and Ellis, *supra*, n. 29, at 185.

33 In most cases referred to, the children are in institutional placements, not group homes, foster care or other smaller residential settings. It can be argued that there are significant differences between the institutional and other residential settings such that more elaborate safeguards are required for those entering institutions. For example, institutions are more likely to have a non-normalized environment, a severely disabled population and patients who stay indefinitely and therefore presumably are the most affected, but least able to care for their own needs. However, other forms of residential care, while more normalized in some respects, still represent a major alteration in the child's basic life-style and therefore perhaps deserve the same or very similar procedural protections. That is, the child is living with strangers, possibly far from his/her home (especially if he/she is in a rural placement), in a new school, with unfamiliar peers, usually for a fairly lengthy period of time (1-2 years) and often does not return home after having been separated so long. Also, most residental settings constrict the child's liberty and require adherence to rules and procedures that are different from a home. For example there may be rules concerning home visits, use of phone, control of mail, control of friendships, daily scheduling of required activities, tighter curfew, etc. Since the admission to such a setting often means a major disruption to the child's life, additional procedural protections should be available, especially if the child objects to the placement or if the child lacks the capacity to question the admission.

While such a requirement would mean a large number of hearings, particularly in heavily resourced areas such as Toronto, the cost to the child and the public of using a more expensive, more restrictive resource than necessary is also a cost that needs to be considered. If the estimate that ⅓ - ½ of the children studied could have been treated in less restrictive alternatives is correct, then a screening device, such as a hearing, will probably pay for itself.

In addition, s. 15 of the Canadian Charter of Rights and Freedoms, protects children from discrimination on the basis of age. If children are not granted the same procedural safeguards as adults, a challenge under the Charter is likely.

The landmark case for establishing procedural protections for juvenile delinquents is *In re Gault*.[34] In the *Gault* case, Gerald Gault, a 15-year-old boy, was found guilty of making lewd telephone calls and was incarcerated for an indeterminate sentence in an industrial school. A writ of *habeas corpus* was brought, seeking the release of Gerald on grounds that the Arizona Juvenile Code was unconstitutional because it allegedly denied juveniles certain due process guarantees. The Supreme Court held that the denial of these due process safeguards violated the Fourteenth Amendment and granted a writ of *habeas corpus*. As a result of *Gault*, there is now a right to counsel, to adequate notice, to confront and cross-examine witnesses, to remain silent and to appeal, and the proceedings must now be transcribed.

The question of the extent to which procedural safeguards can be invoked for the child, separate from his/her parents has been tested in cases of civil commitment. In *Melville v. Sabbatino*[35] the courts were faced with the issue of the right of emancipated 16 to 18-year-olds to seek release from hospital. Since relevant mental health legislation in Connecticut did permit adolescents of this age to sign themselves into care, the courts held that they should also be allowed to sign themselves out, even if they had been admitted by their parents.[36] While this finding is somewhat limited, the court did state in *obiter* that the due process requirements of *Gault* would apply to the commitment of younger children by their parents.

In *Saville v. Treadway*[37] a Tennessee statute authorizing parents to commit their mentally retarded children to an institution was struck down. The court held that the voluntary admission procedure lacked essential safeguards and thus violated the constitutional due process rights of the children. The court established an independent review board staffed with three individuals who had expertise in mental retardation. The court required a hearing in which the child had independent representation, a right to notice, an opportunity to be heard and the right to a judicial review of the decision of the admissions board.

Perhaps the two most significant cases are *Bartley v. Kremens*[38] and *J. L. v. Parham*,[39] both decided on the same day by the United States Supreme Court. In both of these cases the lower court decisions were reversed on appeal. However, since the lower court decisions had a definite impact on statutory reform[40] and

---

34 387 U.S. 1 (1967).

35 *Melville v. Sabbatino*, 30 Conn. Supp. 320, 42 U.S. L.W. 2242 (Sup. Ct., 1973).

36 *Ibid.*, at 325.

37 *Saville v. Treadway*, 404 F. Supp. 430 (Tenn. Dist. Ct., 1974).

38 402 F. Supp. 1039 (1975), vacated and remanded for reconsideration 431 U.S. 119 (1977).

39 412 F. Supp. 112 at 139 (Ga. Dist. Ct., 1976).

40 The Mental Health Procedures Act, Pa. Stat. Ann. tit. 50., 7101-7503 (Purdon, 9th July, 1976), repealed the Mental Health and Mental Retardation Act, 1966, Pa. Stat. Ann., tit. 50,

on the general recognition of the rights of children, both judgments will be discussed.

In *Bartley,* a class action was launched on behalf of all persons 18 years of age or younger who had been, or might be, admitted to mental health facilities in the Commonwealth of Pennsylvania. The plaintiffs sought to secure a declaration that the admission and commitment procedures set out in Pennsylvania's relevant legislation[41] were unconstitutional with respect to minors. Essentially, their complaint was that existing legislation denied them equal protection under the law and failed to provide the required due process safeguards. Using arguments reminiscent of *Gault,* they claimed that they had been denied the right to notice and a pre-commitment hearing before a judicial officer, that they were denied the right to present evidence on their own behalf by calling witnesses and subpoenaing records, that they were denied the right to adequate representation, that they were denied the opportunity to confront and cross-examine witnesses against them, and that they were denied assurance that they could only be institutionalized on the basis of a high standard of proof that they indeed needed custodial care.[42]

The majority of the United States District Court held that the due process requirements of the Constitution were applicable to the institutionalization of minors. Citing an earlier authority, one of the judges endorsed the important principle that:

> "It matters not whether the proceedings be labelled 'civil' or 'criminal' or whether the subject matter be mental instability or juvenile delinquency. It is the likelihood of involuntary incarceration — whether for punishment as an adult for a crime, rehabilitation as a juvenile for delinquency, or treatment and training as a feeble-minded or mental incompetent — which commands observance of the constitutional safeguards of due process.[43]

In both *Bartley v. Kremens*[44] and subsequently in the very similar case of *Parham v. J.R.,*[45] when the majority of the District Court Judges struck down the relevant state statutes as unconstitutional, they were endorsing certain policy objectives over others. In the first place, the majority recognized that by

---

4101-4704 (Purdon, 1969 and Supp. 1976) that was found to be unconstitutional in *Bartley v. Kremens, supra,* n. 38. Also see New Mexico: *Voluntary Residential Treatment of Minors* (43-1-16, N.M.S.A., 1979).

41 The Pennsylvania Mental Health and Mental Retardation Act, 1966, 50 P.S. Pa., 4401, *et seq.*

42 *In re Winship,* 397 U.S. 358 (1970).

43 *Supra,* n. 38, at 1046, quoting from *Heryford v. Parker,* 396 F. 2d 393 at 396 (C.A. 10th Circ., 1968).

44 *Secretary of Pub. Welfare of Pennysylvania v. Institutionalized Juveniles (Bartley v. Kremens),* 99 S. Ct. 2523 (1979).

45 *Parham v. J.R.,* 99 S. Ct. 2493 (1979).

extending additional rights to children it was expanding the role of the state in monitoring parental decisions. This is the way the court in *Bartley* characterized the issue:

> The question is both difficult and unique. Viewing the issue as whether or not a parent may effectively waive personal rights of a child when the child objects to the waiver creates a confrontation between a liberty interest of plaintiffs we find constitutionally protected and the consistently recognized authority of parents to direct the rearing of their children.[46]

In weighing these competing interests, the court favoured additional protection for the children. Implicit in this preference is the recognition that parental motives for hospitalizing children may not reflect their best interests and that psychiatric diagnoses are sufficiently inaccurate to justify more elaborate procedures, both prior to commitment and post-commitment. Specifically, the court held that the children were entitled to: a post commitment hearing, written notice of the hearing, representation by counsel and the right to be present at hearings. A standard of clear and convincing proof had to be met before admission could be granted.[47]

At the Supreme Court level, the decisions in both *Bartley* and *Parham* were reversed. The court seems to have fallen back from the momentum of *Gault* and appears to be seeking an intermediate position that balances the rights of parents and children against an underlying concern about extending state intervention. These cases reflect the difficulty the courts have in deciding matters that involve conflict between parents and their children. In *Parham*, Chief Justice Burger, writing for the majority, held that:

> Notwithstanding a child's liberty interest in not being confined unnecessarily for medical treatment, and assuming that a person has a protectable interest in not being erroneously labelled as mentally ill, parents — who have traditional interests in and responsibility for the upbringing of their child — retain a substantial, if not the dominant, role in the decision, absent a finding of neglect or abuse. However, the child's rights and the nature of the commitment decision are such that parents do not always have absolute discretion to institutionalize a child; they retain plenary authority to seek such care for their children, subject to an independent medical judgment.[48]

In addition the majority indicated the state had an interest in not discouraging families from seeking out needed treatment. The state also had an interest in keeping health care costs down by ensuring that only those who genuinely

---

46 *Bartley v. Kremens, supra*, n. 38, at 1047.

47 It should be noted that this standard of proof is less demanding than the criminal standard of "beyond a reasonable doubt" required in *In re Winship, supra*, n. 42, but is higher than the "balance of probabilities" standard used in civil cases.

48 *Parham, supra*, n. 45, at 2496.

needed care were admitted and in making sure that clinicians were not diverted from their primary task of patient care by involvement in time-consuming pre-admission procedures.

The interests of the parents and of the state would seem to support the exercise of parental discretion. However, the court recognized that there was a significant risk of error in relying on parental decisions to commit children and therefore decided that (as summarized by the Reporter of Decisions):

> . . . some kind of inquiry should be made by a "neutral factfinder" to determine whether the statutory requirements for admission are satisfied.[49]

Not only is there a high risk of error in parental decisions, but, as has already been noted, there is a high risk of error among mental health profession-als. However, despite the court's recognition of the fallibility of psychiatric diagnoses in *O'Connor v. Donaldson*,[50] it decided to rely on a medical inquiry rather than requiring a judicial or administrative hearing. The court expressed the opinion that the combination of an independent medical opinion at the time of admission, followed by periodic reviews of the child's condition would provide adequate safeguards to ensure that children were not "dumped" inap-propriately into institutions. In addition the court reasoned that doctors were far better qualified to make medical decisions than were judges or administrative officers. It did not feel that it could reduce the error in medical decision making by shifting the onus to a judicial body. This reliance on medical authority has been criticized by a number of commentators[51] as overlooking the following difficulties, namely that:

(a) mental health professionals tend to over-institutionalize children;

---

49 *Parham, ibid.*, at 2496.

50 *O'Connor v. Donaldson*, 422 U.S. 563 (1975).

51 See *Parham, supra*, n. 45, at 2509, where Chief Justice Burger states:
"In general, we are satisfied that an independent medical decisionmaking process, which includes the thorough psychiatric investigation described earlier, followed by additional periodic review of a child's condition, will protect children who should not be admitted; we do not believe the risks of error in that process would be significantly reduced by a more formal, judicial-type hearing."
Also see *Parham*, at 2507 for a similar statement; Ellis, "Volunterring Children — Parental Commitment of Minors to Mental Institutions" (1974), 62 Cal. L. Rev. 840, at 867; Landau, "Barriers to Consent to Treatment: The Rights of Minors in the Provision of Mental Health Services" (1979), 2 Can. J. Fam. L. 245 at 251; Gunnar Dybwad, Mental Health Law Project, "Case Comment on Parham v. J.L. and J.R.", at 5; Teitelbaum and Ellis, "The Liberty Interests of Children: Due Process Rights and their Application" (1978), 12 Fam. L.Q. 153 at 186-90 and 198-99; Ennis and Litwack, "Psychiatry and the Presumption of Expertise: Flipping Coins in the Courtroom" (1974), 62 Cal. L. Rev. 693, and Quincey, "Assessments of the Dangerousness of Mental Patients Held in Maximum Security" (1979), 2 Int. J.L. & Psych. 389.

(b) admission decisions are often made without adequate knowledge of alternative community resources and without adequate information about the child's special needs; and

(c) institutional psychiatrists and other mental health professionals lack the objectivity and independence to serve as neutral factfinders.[52]

The court falls back on the argument that a formal fact-finding hearing would cause a significant intrusion into the parent-child relationship. However, at the point where parents are seeking hospitalization it is very likely that the parent-child relationship is already seriously disturbed and, from the child's point of view, the "volunteered" treatment may be seen as incarceration and rejection.[53]

It should also be noted that the dissents in *Parham* and *Bartley* were limited in scope. In both cases, the dissenting judges agreed that pre-admission hearings were unnecessary (except in the case of state wards). Despite the recognition that the child's liberty interests were at stake and despite the belief that

> . . . a child who has been ousted from his family has even greater need for an independent advocate.

> Additional considerations counsel against allowing parents unfettered power to institutionalize their children without cause or without any hearing to ascertain that cause. The presumption that parents act in their children's best interests, while applicable to most child-rearing decisions, is not applicable in the commitment context. Numerous studies reveal that parental decisions to institutionalize their children often are the result of dislocation in the family unrelated to the children's mental condition. . . . In these circumstances, I respectfully suggest, it ignores reality to assume blindly that parents act in their children's best interests when making commitment decisions and when waiving their children's due process rights.[54]

Nevertheless, the dissenting judges recommended fewer protections for children than would be offered to adults. When it is considered that the population of children in question is limited to those who are supposedly "voluntary", that is, non-emergency cases, and who are not in imminent danger to themselves or others, the risk associated with a short delay for a hearing would seem minimal. Particularly when the risks are balanced against the serious interference in the child's life and the wasted expenditure of public funds for unnecessary commitment, the limited protections are difficult to justify.

---

52 Ellis, *ibid.*, at 863-68; Dybwad, *ibid.*, at 5; Panneton, "Children, Commitment and Consent: A Constitutional Crisis" (1977), 10 Fam. L.Q. 295 at 332-33.

53 Panneton, *ibid.*, at 300-305. See also *Parham, supra*, n. 45, at 2576 for the concern by the dissent that civil commitment entails a "massive curtailment of liberty", *Humphrey v. Cady*, 405 U.S. 504 at 509 (1972).

54 *Parham, supra*, n. 45, at 2519.

In the first place, post-commitment hearings are far more likely to rubber stamp the *fait accompli*. Unless great care is taken, the onus would be on the child to prove why he/she was wrongfully committed and should be released, rather than on the parents or guardians and medical authorities to establish why the child requires and will benefit from the particular program under consideration.

Second, the argument that post-admission hearings would have the advantage of not interfering with the commencement of needed treatment presumes that treatment is needed. Yet the opinions and statistical studies cited by the dissenting judges in *Parham* are contrary to this presumption. They indicate that a high percentage (⅓ - ½) of the institutionalized children could have been treated without admission to care.[55]

Third, if the primary interest of the state lies in maintaining and supporting the family as an intact unit, this would argue strongly in favour of a policy of exhausting all possible community alternatives before permitting hospitalization.

However, the judges preferred a post-admission hearing because they believed that in this way the adversarial role would shift away from the parents onto the hospital staff.

While acknowledging that there may be some advantage to a post-admission hearing in that it allows staff to observe the child's behaviour as a basis for judging the need for continued care, if this were a strong reason for post-admission hearings, it should apply to adults as well. On the contrary, it can hardly be therapeutic to arrange the situation so that the child views the staff, who are now acting *in loco parentis*, as his/her adversaries, or better still jailors. Also it is not therapeutic to shift the focus away from family relationships onto the child who has been isolated and labelled as the "identified patient".[56]

Finally, while due process procedures always involve *some* adversarial components, it would seem that a pre-admission hearing would be seen by the child as a fairer, more objective proceeding that ran less risk of creating negative feelings. In fact, the minority argue that if children perceived the hearing as fair, they would be more likely to accept the legitimacy of the need for treatment. This argument is far more persuasive when applied to a pre rather than a post-admission hearing.

In summary, the cases reviewed in this chapter indicate some willingness to give the child an independent voice in decisions affecting him/her and a movement towards increased procedural protections, especially when the child's interests conflict with the exercise of state power. In cases involving

---

55 *Parham, supra*, n. 45, at 2517.

56 Virginia Satir, *Conjoint Family Therapy* (1967).

challenges to parental decision making, the courts have understandably been far more reluctant to intervene. However, there does seem to be a growing recognition that children's interests and parents' interests are not always identical and that admission to long-term residential care represents a major disruption of the child's life and restricts the child's basic liberty. The risk that the child will be placed in a setting involving a greater loss of liberty than is necessary is high because errors in diagnosis are not uncommon and less restrictive alternatives are often overlooked. As a result, there is a growing consensus that the persons who make such serious decisions should be held accountable for demonstrating that:

(a) the child in fact has a serious mental disorder or developmental handicap, such that residential placement is warranted;

(b) no less restrictive alternative is feasible;

(c) the facility being considered has a program available that would be appropriate for the type of mental disorder or developmental disability suffered by the child;

(d) the program has been demonstrated to be effective for similar problems; and

(e) there is a substantial likelihood that the child will benefit from the program offered.[57]

Accountability for the services provided is an important issue; equally important is the issue of who has the legal right to consent to or refuse treatment.

III CONSENT TO TREATMENT: THE RIGHTS OF MINORS, PARENTS AND THE STATE

At present, a good deal of confusion exists as to the child's ability to consent to treatment. So far the issue has been: can the child be coerced into treatment the parents perceive as necessary? The other side of the coin is: can a child elect treatment where the parents refuse? On a policy level the confusion is related to the ongoing difficulty of sorting out the balance of power, or perhaps the balance of responsibilities among parents, the state and minors. On a more practical level, doctors are concerned about their legal liability if they accept the consent of minors.

The rule at common law is that doctors must obtain the patient's informed consent prior to providing treatment. If the doctor fails to obtain a valid consent, he/she could be exposed to both civil liability in a tort action for assault and battery (that is, for damages as a result of any unauthorized touching or

---

57 See the Child and Family Services Act.

interference with the patient) or to a criminal charge of assault.[58] The question that arises in relation to children and incompetent adults is: are they capable of giving an informed consent, and if not, who can consent for them?

It is important to understand the requirements of a valid consent in order to evaluate the rights of the child in this matter. Four crucial elements must be present for a valid consent. The patient must have the capacity to give his/her consent; the consent must be *voluntarily given*; it must be an *informed* consent; and the consent must be directed toward a *specific act* or set of acts. In essence, the patient must have the capacity to understand the nature and consequences of the treatment, including potential risks and benefits, and be able to arrive at a reasoned decision whether to accept or reject the proposed treatment.[59]

In the case of adults of normal intelligence, it is presumed that they have the requisite capacity to consent.[60] The most frequent legal question that arises for the patients is did the doctor give them sufficient information on which to base an informed decision. However, for children and incompetent adults, the question is more basic; that is, does the individual have the cognitive capacity to make such a decision? Since the law does not specify a particular age or intelligence quotient above which the doctors can safely rely on the patient's consent, in practice the doctors tend to err on the side of caution and require the consent of parents or guardians for minors and incompetent adults.[61]

Justification for the parents' decision-making power on health matters is usually tied to the parents' common law and statutory duty to provide necessaries of life, including medical treatment for their children. At common law, a corollary to the parents' (actually the father's) right to custody of the child was the legal obligation to ensure adequate medical care. When the child's health suffered, the parents could be charged with an offence. Since few charges were ever laid against parents for failure to meet this requirement, the common law proved to be an inadequate tool for protecting the child's interests.[62]

While the common law offered little protection, the Courts of Chancery could intervene by exercising their *parens patriae* jurisdiction to protect the welfare of children and others who were unable to care for themselves. In cases

---

58 Ruth Jane Zuckerman, "Legal Barriers to Services for Adolescents", unpublished paper prepared for the Bi-Regional Institute on Adolescence, Denver, Colorado (April 1978), at 3.

59 Corinne Sklar, "Legal Consent and the Nurse" (1978), 74(3) Can. Nurse 34 at 35; see also by the same author, "Minors in the Health Care System" (1978), 74(8) Can. Nurse 18. Also see Landau, *supra*, n. 51, at 256.

60 In fact, for everyday medical matters, doctors do not bother with the formal consent requirements. Rather, most health care is administered on the basis of "implied consent" by the adult.

61 Gosse, "Consent to Medical Treatment: A Minor Digression" (1974), 9 U.B.C.L. Rev. 56 at 60-62.

62 Barbara Tomkins, "Health Care for Minors — The Right to Consent" (1975), 40 Sask. L. Rev. 41 at 41-44.

where the child's safety was endangered by parental action or failure to act, the court could intervene by removing the child from the parents' custody and providing medical care. Such a solution was a drastic measure used only in extreme cases, and again this intervention by the state did not require the participation or consent of the child.

In practice children are rarely consulted on matters of their health care and except in cases of emergency, medical practice in general has been to require parental consent for minors.[63] One argument that is sometimes raised to justify the failure to obtain the child's consent is that children lack legal capacity; that is, that they are not *sui juris*. If this position were correct, then it would follow that children in Canada would not have the status of persons separate from their parents, at least not in the eyes of the law. I submit that such a position is incorrect on legal grounds[64] and unacceptable on a public policy basis.

There are many instances in English and Canadian law where infants are either deemed to be competent or are held accountable in ways that are inconsistent with the position that children are not *sui juris*.[65] For example, in areas such as liability for harm to others or to the community — that is tort and criminal liability — the child is considered to be responsible at a very young age. In criminal matters, the child is held criminally responsible once he/she has the capacity to form a criminal intent. According to the *doli incapax* rule, below the age of 7, infants have absolute immunity; between 7 and 14 there is a rebuttable presumption of incapacity and beyond 14 the child is presumed to have the same mental capacity in criminal matters as an adult.[66]

In tort cases, there is no arbitrary age below which children will not be held liable.[67] In these cases the test for liability is based entirely on the ability of the individual child to understand and intend his/her particular actions.[68]

However, in contract cases, as in cases involving personal property, the general rule has been that the individual must have reached the age of majority (with certain exceptions). The policy basis for this difference is that in contract cases, the concern is to protect the minor from being taken advantage of by others. However, in tort or criminal cases the concern has been primarily for the injured party or public interest,[69] hence the younger age for liability.

---

63 Zuckerman, *supra*, n. 58, at 6-8.

64 For a most informative analysis of the concept of *sui juris* in Roman and American law, see Roman Komar, *A Submission to the Professional Conduct Sub-Committee of the Law Society of Upper Canada on the Legal Representation of Infants* (1981).

65 Alexander Cairns (ed.), *Eversley's Law of Domestic Relations* (1926), at 252-64. Also see W. Blackstone, *Commentaries on the Laws of England*, (1976-79), Book 1, at 463.

66 Wayne La Fave and Austin Scott Jr., *Criminal Law* (1972), at 351.

67 *Sheasgreen v. Morgan*, [1952] 1 D.L.R. 48 at 61-62 (B.C.S.C.).

68 *Tillander v. Gosselin* (1966), 60 D.L.R. (2d) 18 (Ont. H.C.).

69 Prosser, *Law of Torts*, 4th ed. (1971), at 102-103.

While minors are protected from contracts that may put the child at a disadvantage, the law makes an exception for contracts that meet the dual test of being both necessary and on the whole for the benefit of the child.[70] Included in this category are contracts for medical treatment. That is, to ensure that adults will be willing to offer such necessary and beneficial services, the law will hold minors (or their parents) liable to pay for the reasonable cost of care.[71]

In order to clarify the common law position with respect to consent to treatment several questions will be addressed, namely:

1. *If the child has the capacity to consent to treatment, can his/her parents veto such a consent?*

In *Booth v. Toronto General Hospital*,[72] a 19-year-old consented to the removal of a thyroid gland (at that time the common law age of majority was 21 years). The physician did not obtain parental consent and the question was, could this minor consent to his own treatment? Chief Justice Falconbridge held that:

> The act charged is one of the nature of trespass or assault, but it has been proved beyond doubt that the plaintiff's consent had been gained. He is not of the highest intelligence, but it appears that he was nineteen years of age and capable of taking care of himself. . . .

> The only question of law involved was whether the boy's parents should have been consulted, but that was effectively answered, and it has been shewn that he is capable of doing a man's work.[73]

The judge in this case noted that Booth was living on his own, holding a job and was self-supporting and these factors seem to have had considerable weight in assessing his ability to make other personal decisions, such as in relation to health care.

In the case of *Johnston v. Wellesley Hospital*,[74] a 20-year-old man consented to a cosmetic facial operation. The physician did not consult Johnston's parents and an action was brought against the hospital alleging assault on the basis that Johnston, who had not reached the common law age of majority — 21 — was unable to consent to the operation. The Ontario High Court had no difficulty in dismissing this action with the following explanation:

---

70 D. Percy, "The Present Law of Infants' Contracts" (1975), 53 Can. Bar Rev. 1 at 2-4; also G.H. Treitel, *The Law of Contract*, 3rd ed. (1970), at 468-72; G.C. Cheshire and C. Fifoot, *The Law of Contract*, 8th ed. (1972), at 389-96.

71 *Ibid*. Also see *Dale v. Copping* (1610), 1 Bulst. 39, 80 E.R. 743; *Huggins v. Wiseman* (1690), Carth. 110, 90 E.R. 669. See also Wilson, *The Rights of Adolescents in the Mental Health System* (1978), at 29; Law Reform Commission of Canada, *Study Paper on Consent to Medical Care* (1979), at 71-75. Also see Percy, *ibid*., at 6-9.

72 *Booth v. Toronto General Hosp.*, [1910], 17 O.W.R. 118 (K.B.).

73 *Ibid*., at 120.

74 *Johnston v. Wellesley Hosp.*, [1971] 2 O.R. 103 (H.C.).

Although the common law imposes very strict limitations on the capacity of persons under 21 years of age to hold, or rather to divest themselves of, property or to enter into contracts concerning matters other than necessities, it would be ridiculous in this day and age, where the voting age is being reduced generally to 18 years, to state that a person of 20 years of age who is obviously intelligent and as fully capable of understanding the possible consequences of a medical or surgical procedure as an adult, would, at law, be incapable of consenting thereto.[75]

A more recent case, *Gillick v. West Norfolk and Wisbech Area Health Authority*,[76] is a decision of the House of Lords dealing with the question of whether a doctor can offer medical advice, in this case with respect to contraception, to a minor under the age of 16 without her parents' consent. A majority of two out of three judges reversed the unanimous decision of the English Court of Appeal and reinstated the decision of the trial judge when it held that a doctor could offer such medical advice on the consent of the minor without her parents' consent or even knowledge if the doctor reached the following conclusions:

. . . (1) that the girl (although under 16 years of age) will understand his advice; (2) that he cannot persuade her to inform her parents or to allow him to inform the parents that she is seeking contraceptive advice; (3) that she is very likely to begin or to continue having sexual intercourse with or without contraceptive treatment; (4) that unless she receives contraceptive advice or treatment her physical or mental health or both are likely to suffer; (5) that her best interests require him to give her contraceptive advice, treatment or both without the parental consent.[77]

Lord Fraser of Tullybelton indicated that the basis of his judgment centered on his respect for medical discretion as indicated in the following statement:

That result ought not to be regarded as a licence for doctors to disregard the wishes of parents on this matter whenever they find it convenient to do so. . . . The medical profession have in modern times come to be entrusted with very wide discretionary powers going beyond the strict limits of clinical judgment and, in my opinion, there is nothing strange about entrusting them with this further responsibility which they alone are in a position to discharge satisfactorily.[78]

In a concurring judgment, Lord Scarman endorsed the grounds cited by Lord Fraser and in addition indicated that he accepted the mature minor doctrine. He specifically stated that:

I would hold that as a matter of law the parental right to determine whether or not their minor child below the age of 16 will have medical treatment terminates if and when the child

---

75 *Ibid.*, at 108.

76 [1985] 3 All E.R. 402.

77 *Ibid.*, at 413.

78 *Ibid.*

achieves a sufficient understanding and intelligence to enable him or her to understand fully what is proposed. It will be a question of fact whether a child seeking advice has sufficient understanding of what is involved to give a consent valid in law. Until the child achieves the capacity to consent, the parental right to make the decision continues save only in exceptional circumstances.[79]

In arriving at his conclusion, Lord Scarman cited with approval the judgment of Addy J. of the Ontario High Court in *Johnston v. Wellesley Hospital*. This case also adopted a mature minor doctrine, that is that when a minor is capable of understanding the nature and consequences of the particular treatment, then the minor is capable of giving a valid consent.

It is important to recognize that where an informed consent is obtained, there is no requirement at common law to obtain any other consent. Also, if the individual is capable of consenting, the doctor would be liable if he/she did not obtain the minor's consent, even if the parent or guardian approved of a particular treatment.[80] Despite this situation, doctors are still more concerned with suits initiated by irate parents than with the possibility that a minor would bring a suit because the doctor insisted on consulting the parents — either in addition to or even instead of the child. In practice, in the absence of clear statutory guidelines, there have only been three exceptions to the general practice of presuming a minor incapable of consenting. These exceptions are the "emergency care" rule, the "mature minor" rule and, in the United States, the "emancipated minor" rule.[81]

Both *Booth* and *Johnston* could be interpreted as fitting the exception to the emancipated minor rule. If this were the case then the courts could adopt a narrow view such that non-emancipated children, even if they had the ability to understand, would be denied a voice in deciding their health needs.

In the United States, it appears that the U.S. Supreme Court has taken a broader view of the problem. In the cases of *Planned Parenthood of Central Missouri v. Danforth*[82] and *Bellotti v. Baird*,[83] the U.S. Supreme Court struck down legislation requiring parental consent as a prerequisite for a minor's abortion on the grounds that it violated a constitutionally protected right of privacy and self-determination with respect to abortion decisions. The court seemed to presume that minors who were pregnant and who understood the nature and consequences of an abortion could be seen as mature minors, irrespective of their chronological age or whether they were living at home or

---

79 *Ibid.*, at 423-24.

80 Bernard Dickens, "Use of Children in Medical Experimentation" (1975), 43 Medico-Legal Journal 166.

81 Sharpe, "Consent to Medical Treatment" (1974), 22 Chitty's L.J. 319, n. 9.

82 428 U.S. 52 (1976).

83 428 U.S. 132 (1976).

were financially dependent. The court, in balancing the interests of the child, parents and state in abortion decisions, found that the child's interest was paramount. Despite a strong argument that a parental veto was essential in order to maintain parental authority and family solidarity, the court held that:

> It is difficult, however, to conclude that providing a parent with absolute power to overrule a determination, made by the physician and his minor patient, to terminate the patient's pregnancy will serve to strengthen the family unit. Neither is it likely that such veto power will enhance parental authority or control where the minor and the nonconsenting parent are so fundamentally in conflict and the very existence of the pregnancy already has fractured the family structure. Any independent interest the parent may have in the termination of the minor daughter's pregnancy is no more weighty than the right of privacy of the competent minor mature enough to have become pregnant.[84]

The case of *Clark v. Clark*[85] involves an adult; however it is relevant to the issue of minor's consent because it addresses the issue of whether a parent can veto a decision made by an individual who has the capacity to consent. Justin Clark was a 19-year-old mentally retarded, cerebral palsied youth who had been placed by his parents at the age of 2 in the Rideau Regional Centre, an institution for retarded persons. Justin Clark hoped to be placed in a group home located in the community and to be discharged from the institution. His father opposed this plan and applied for a declaration that Justin was a mentally incompetent person. At the hearing, His Honour Judge Matheson found that Justin, despite his physical and intellectual limitations, was not mentally incompetent and was entitled to consent to the placement in opposition to his parents' wishes. This case reinforces the common law rule that where an individual does have the competence to consent, no one can veto that consent or substitute a contrary decision. Justin Clark was not competent to make complex decisions or to provide for his financial needs, however where Justin did have the capacity to make decisions, namely with respect to where he wished to live, his parents could not veto his decision.

Arguably, if Justin had been less than 18 years of age and had the requisite capacity, he should have been able to make the same decision. That is, at common law, the relevant factor is the capacity to make an informed decision, not the attainment of any particular age. Similarly, if Justin had been found to lack the capacity to decide where to live, age would not have been relevant. That is, if Justin had been 50 years of age and had lacked capacity, he would not have been able to consent to a discharge from the Rideau Regional Centre or to a placement in a community group home.

2. *If a child has the capacity to consent to treatment, does the child also have the right to refuse treatment?*

---

84 *Planned Parenthood of Central Missouri v. Danforth, supra,* n. 82, at 75.

85 *Clark v. Clark* (1982), 40 O.R. (2d) 383 (Co. Ct.).

That is, can parents force a child to accept treatment against the child's wishes? Before examining whether existing legislation in Ontario or other provinces assists in clarifying the position of children, I will briefly address the question of whether children who have the capacity to request treatment, also have the capacity to refuse treatment initiated by another person.

It follows logically from the basic common law requirements for consent that if the child is competent, his/her consent must be obtained. Failure to obtain consent would raise the possibility of a court action. Therefore, if a child who had capacity refused treatment, the doctor would have no authority to proceed, because where the individual is capable of giving a valid consent, no other person can consent for him/her.

The case of *In re Smith*[86] was a decision upholding the right of a 15-year-old girl to refuse an abortion even though this was contrary to her parents' wishes. Her parents did not have the right to consent to this medical procedure because once she was competent to decide, no one could offer substitute consent. In this case the court upheld the privacy right of the child to make this important decision involving her future. Had the doctor proceeded and performed the abortion against the wishes of the child, the doctor would probably have been found guilty of assault and battery for performing such a procedure without a proper consent.

3. If the child lacks capacity, what are the limits on the parents' right to offer substitute consent?

According to Fleming, the rule can be stated as follows:

> Minors, it appears, can give an effective consent if they fully comprehend the nature and consequences of whatever is proposed. . . . But for children who are too young, parents can give the necessary consent at any rate *to procedures which are in the (best) interest of the child*, perhaps even *to any procedure to which a "reasonable parent" would consent.*[87]

Fleming's statement incorporates the two tests of substitute consent that appear in the case law, that is, the narrow test that only "therapeutic" procedures that are "beneficial", in the sense that they would lead to a cure for some condition, can be authorized by parents or guardians, and the broader test that a procedure could be consented to if it were "reasonable in the circumstances", even if it were non-therapeutic.[88] In looking at the case law, the English and

---

86 *In re Smith*, 295 A. 2d 238 (Md. C.A., 1972).

87 J.G. Fleming, *The Law of Torts*, 5th ed. (1977), at 77. Emphasis added.

88 It should be noted that the terms "therapeutic", "beneficial" and "reasonable in the circumstances" are imprecise terms and can lead to differences in opinion. However, the principal focus in this part is on procedures that are non-therapeutic, that is, highly intrusive, irreversible and not required to cure any condition of the patient. For example, contraceptive sterilization would fall into this category.

American decisions tend to show that where the procedure is clearly therapeutic, no cases have challenged the parents' right to decide. Where cases involved procedures that are non-therapeutic, the courts tend to allow the parents to consent if the procedures involve minimal risk and intrusion.[89] For example, many of the English cases permitted parents to consent to blood tests of children where the question of paternity was raised. While the blood test was of no medical benefit, it involved minimal risk of harm and arguably could lead to a financial and social benefit for the child. For this reason parents can usually consent to such procedures as blood tests and X-rays.

However, where highly intrusive, irreversible procedures are involved, such as contraceptive sterilization, the courts in the past have tended to adopt a much narrower "best interest" interpretation of substitute consent. For example, in the case of *Re D.*,[90] the court refused to allow the parents to consent to the sterilization of their 11-year-old, mildly retarded daughter on the grounds that the procedure could not be shown to be in her best interest. It should be noted that the English court did not rule out the possibility that under some set of facts it might authorize parental consent. What this case stands for is that where the procedure is non-therapeutic, neither the parents nor the doctor have an absolute discretion to authorize treatment.

The American cases take an even firmer position. For example, in the case of *Wade v. Bethesda Hospital*[91] a girl charged the physicians, the local child welfare authority and the Probate Court Judge with battery. The girl had been sterilized when she was incompetent and the child welfare agency had been authorized to consent by the judge. The court held that the facts of the case were irrelevant as there were "no set of circumstances or conditions" under which a court could authorize a non-therapeutic sterilization. This case demonstrates that the American courts adhere to a narrow "best interest" test when the procedures are highly intrusive or irreversible, or when there is a serious risk of harm to the child.

Until very recently there was no Canadian case law on this issue. However, several factors suggest the position that would be expected from the Canadian courts on the issue of third party consent to non-therapeutic procedures, such as sterilization. In the first place, English and American case law strongly indicates that substitute consent would not be permitted by the courts, except in the most exceptional circumstances. In addition, the absence of any statutory provisions permitting sterilization of incompetents demonstrates that legislatures do not approve of such procedures. Finally, the fact that Alberta and British Columbia

---

89 *S.v. S.; W. v. Official Solicitor*, [1972] A.C. 24. Also see *supra*, n. 87.

90 *Re D. (A Minor) (Wardship: Sterilization)*, [1976] Fam. 185.

91 337 F. Supp. 671 at 673-74 (Ohio Dist. Ct., 1971).

repealed their legislation that had permitted sterilization under limited circumstances is a further reinforcement for the position that the Canadian attitude would likely be against sterilization.

However, in the first case on this point, *Re Eve*,[92] the Prince Edward Island Supreme Court reversed a lower court ruling and held that the court had the authority and the jurisdiction to authorize the non-therapeutic sterilization of a 24-year-old retarded, aphasic woman. In this case, the girl's mother had brought an application to be appointed committee of the person and the estate of her daughter and at the same time had requested that she be permitted to consent to the sterilization of her daughter, solely on contraceptive grounds. The court granted the mother's request. This case will likely have very significant ramifications for the power of the courts and the parent or guardian to consent to a variety of highly intrusive non-therapeutic measures for incompetent persons. The case is presently under appeal to the Supreme Court of Canada which has reserved judgment on this matter.

Writing for the majority in the *Eve* case, Campbell J. applied a "best interests" test in a manner that greatly enhanced the discretion of the mother and the court to make decisions that were non-therapeutic, irreversible and highly intrusive even under circumstances where there is no urgent need for such a procedure.

Campbell J. found that the court had an unlimited *parens patriae* jurisdiction to act on behalf of children and others who were not capable of protecting themselves. According to Campbell J. there are three limitations on the exercise of the court's *parens patriae* powers, namely:

1. *It must be shown that the real, the genuine, object is to protect the child. . . .*

2. *There must be no overriding interest the other way. . . .*

3. *There must be a likelihood of substantial injury to the child.*[93]

In this case, Campbell J. held that the purpose of sterilization would be to protect Eve from pregnancy. However, in considering whether the first test was met, there was no mention in Campbell J.'s judgment that Eve's pregnancy would in fact present a danger to her or even to the child, although she would probably be incapable of caring for the child independently. Second, there was no mention made of trying to use any less intrusive, alternative methods of contraception. Third, there was no mention of any imminent risk of pregnancy and no mention of any physical risks or serious psychological harm associated with pregnancy. In addition, there was no mention of any risk of retardation for

---

92 (1980), 115 D.L.R. (3d) 283 (P.E.I. C.A.).
93 *Ibid.*, at 318-19.

the child based on the mother's condition. In fact, other than the judge's concern that Eve would not understand the implications of intercourse, pregnancy or birth, there was no other basis for concluding that Eve needed to be protected from pregnancy by an irreversible procedure.

Campbell J., in assessing the second criterion, namely, whether there was any overriding interest against sterilization, completely avoided any of the moral or ethical questions that would appear to be raised by this case. Instead he set up an absurd comparison to justify the sterilization. He said that some *competent* women *elect* to be sterilized as a means of contraception (usually those who have had several children):

In justice, can we refuse them their substituted right to choose? I think not.[94]

It is difficult to follow this reasoning. How can the substituted consent of the state and the parent be viewed as "patient autonomy"? How can the conscious choice of a competent woman (or man) to limit family size be treated as analogous to the sterilization of an incompetent person that is aimed at preventing any choice about a family? Under the guise of "patient autonomy" would the court uphold a substituted right to choose a lobotomy? Or euthanasia? Or extraordinary life saving measures (that prolong pain and suffering in terminally ill patients)? What is the limit of what the parent or guardian can consent to — and what the court will authorize?

With regard to the third criterion, there was no likelihood of substantial injury to Eve resulting from a pregnancy. However, by using a very broad definition that included social, mental, physical and economic factors, Campbell J. found that unless Eve were sterilized her movement in the community would be restricted. However, again no less drastic alternative was explored and no explanation was offered as to why, after 24 years, there was suddenly this special need to restrict Eve's freedom. Since she supposedly had reached puberty several years earlier and had not exhibited any sexually promiscuous behaviour, it is difficult to understand the judge's concern.

The dissenting judgment accepted the majority's view that the court has the authority and jurisdiction to authorize a non-therapeutic sterilization of a mentally retarded person. However, MacDonald J. limited this power to exceptional circumstances, which he did not feel were present on the facts of this case.

MacDonald J. pointed out that in the absence of statutory provisions to act as guidelines, the court should be very cautious in finding that the rights of a mentally incompetent person could be violated. In examining the case law, MacDonald J. noted that the *parens patriae* power of the court was intended to

---

94 *Ibid.*, at 319.

protect the child from harm. When a therapeutic treatment was being proposed, the parent or guardian could consent and in fact, if they failed to take action, the court could intervene to protect the child.

MacDonald J. concluded his opinion by citing with approval the Law Reform Commission's views regarding the dangers on moral, ethical and social policy grounds for committing such intrusions into a person's life:

> . . . whatever benefit might be achieved by permitting the operation cannot compare with the harm that conceivably might occur if other applications for sterilization were made. . . . In the circumstances the operation cannot be classified as anything more than a possible social convenience to Eve, and I foresee the convenience aspect as possibly relating to persons other than Eve.[95]

The case of *K. v. Public Trustee*[96] appears at first consideration to follow the decision reached in *Re Eve* by the Prince Edward Island Supreme Court. That is, the British Columbia Court of Appeal did grant the parents of a 10-year-old, severely retarded girl the right to give substitute consent to a hysterectomy despite the fact that the procedure was irreversible and sterilization for contraceptive purposes has usually been considered non-therapeutic. The parents had applied to the court for permission to proceed with the surgery for their severely retarded child in order to prevent the onset of puberty. The reasons for the parents' request were that the child suffered a phobic aversion to blood and, in addition, would be incapable of managing the hygenic aspects of menstruation.

At the trial level, Mr. Justice Wood rejected the parents' application on the basis that this was a case involving the rights of mentally retarded persons generally and this child specifically with respect to the question of substitute consent for a non-therapeutic sterilization. In balancing the competing interests of the child and mentally retarded people generally as opposed to the parents' right to give a substitute consent, he concluded that

> . . . a person seeking to give "substituted" consent to a non-therapeutic sterilization has the onus of demonstrating that the procedure is "in the best interests of the incompetent" because society "regards the right to security of the person to be of such fundamental importance to the well-being of all its members that the law must necessarily raise it as a presumption against anyone who would seek to give substituted authority for non-therapeutic medical treatment or surgery".[97]

The trial judge required the parents to establish by a clear and convincing standard that the surgery was in the child's best interest and he applied the

---

95 *Ibid.*, at 310.

96 (1985), 19 D.L.R. (4th) 255 (B.C.C.A.).

97 *Ibid.*, at 268.

objective criteria, set out in Working Paper 24 of the Law Reform Commission of Canada entitled "Sterilization", which he concluded must be met before a non-therapeutic sterilization would be approved.[98]

In reversing his judgment, the British Columbia Court of Appeal in a unanimous judgment held that Wood J. erred in several fundamental ways. The reasons given would clearly distinguish this case from *Eve*. Mr. Justice Anderson, in his reasons for judgment, stated that the learned trial judge erred because

> [He] approached this case as though it were a case involving the sterilization of a mentally disabled person for purely contraceptive purposes. Accordingly he applied rigid objective standards which were clearly inapplicable. In this case, the fact of sterilization was irrelevant. It was conceded that for infant K pregnancy would be a disaster. The loss of the right to reproduce was, therefore, not a matter open for consideration.[99]

The learned justice went on to say

> . . . this case cannot and must not be regarded as a precedent to be followed in cases involving sterilization of mentally disabled persons for contraceptive purposes. This case did not involve the loss of legal rights and the issue to be determined here was as follows: "Having regard solely to the welfare of Infant K, including a consideration of all relevant factors, should the proposed operation proceed?" Put in another way the question might have been posed as follows: "Is it in the best interests of Infant K to undergo major surgery in order to avoid the risk of suffering by Infant K which may result if the operation is not performed?"[100]

In response to the trial judge's concern that this was a case of a non-therapeutic procedure, Anderson J.A. responded as follows:

> In my view, the proposed operation was purely therapeutic in nature. The whole purpose of the operation was to protect infant K from the risk that if the operation were not performed she would be subject to increased trauma and, moreover, there was a risk that her ability to progress in other areas would be affected.[101]

Finally, Craig J.A. expressed the view that Wood J. had made a significant error in that he had placed too great a focus on the rights of mentally disabled people generally rather than on the best interest of this particular child, although the judge did appear to recognize that his sole concern should be the best interests of the infant K.

The case of *K. v. Public Trustee* cannot be seen as a change in judicial policy with respect to substitute consent for non-therapeutic procedures in cases of sterilization. This case can clearly be distinguished from *Eve* in that the

---

98 Law Reform Commission of Canada, Working Paper 24, "Sterilization" (1979), at 234-35.

99 *Supra*, n. 96, at 274.

100 *Ibid.*, at 275.

101 *Ibid.*

British Columbia Court of Appeal took the position that the operation was therapeutic and that the hysterectomy was not for the purpose of contraception, but rather to meet other health care needs of the child.

4. *If a child lacks capacity, what are the limits on the parents' right to refuse necessary medical care?*

Under normal circumstances, parents of children who lack capacity have the duty to provide necessary medical care and to make decisions as to proper treatment on behalf of their children. This is particularly true where the proposed treatment is considered to be beneficial, therapeutic and necessary to a child's survival. If parents fail to obtain necessary medical care, the state has the duty to intervene and either charge the parents criminally or initiate child welfare proceedings and take over the parental role in order to safeguard the child's best interests.

Two cases raise the issue of to what extent case law and statute law offer equal protection to children who are mentally or physically handicapped. In both of the cases, the parents refused medical care that would almost certainly be offered to a normal child.

Phillip Becker[102] was an 11-year-old mentally retarded boy who had been placed at birth in an institution in California by his parents because he suffered from Down's syndrome. Phillip required remedial heart surgery to prevent a degenerative heart condition that would greatly reduce his life expectancy. Without the surgery he could expect to die between the ages of 20 and 30, and the doctors predicted that his final years would be spent in considerable pain and suffering as his health deteriorated. His parents, who rarely visited the institution, refused to consent to the medical care on the grounds that the quality of his life was such that it should not be prolonged. The state of California initiated child protection proceedings claiming the parents were neglecting their son because they refused to consent to the surgery. The lower court and the Court of Appeal upheld the parents' right to withhold their consent and the U.S. Supreme Court refused to hear an appeal. A couple who acted as volunteers at the institution applied for guardianship of Phillip so that they could consent to the treatment for him. The court granted this request and the decision was upheld by the state Court of Appeal, over the parents' objection. However, by this time Phillip was 16 years of age and surgery had been delayed beyond the time that it could be safely conducted. Had Phillip been of normal intelligence this matter probably would not have come to court because Phillip's parents would likely have authorized the treatment.

The case of Stephen Dawson[103] is in many ways a close parallel to that of Phillip Becker. Stephen was severely retarded from the effects of meningitis

---

102 *Re Phillip B.*, 156 Cal. Rptr. 48, cert. denied 100 S. Ct. 1597 (1980).

103 *Re Supt. of Fam. and Child Services and Dawson* (1983), 145 D.L.R. (3d) 610 (B.C.S.C.).

which he suffered shortly after birth. At age 6 he required a routine shunt operation to relieve pressure on his brain caused by the build up of cerebro-spinal fluid. His parents refused to consent to the surgery and argued that their child should be allowed to die in dignity rather than endure a life of suffering. The lower court found in favour of the parents. The British Columbia Supreme Court reversed the decision maintaining that despite his severe handicaps, Stephen was a happy child who responded to others and smiled and laughed. Also, if the shunt operation was not performed, Stephen would not necessarily die, but might lead a life of progressive deterioration filled with pain.

Mr. Justice McKenzie, in his reasons for judgment, held that Stephen should be declared a child in need of protection, removed from his parents' care and given the operation because, in his words, refusing the operation "would mean regarding the life of a handicapped child as not only less valuable than the life of a normal child, but so much less valuable that it is not worth preserving. I tremble at contemplating the consequences if the lives of disabled persons are dependent upon such judgments".[104]

In addition, the judge held that in this case, the child's future was not so certain that if the operation were not performed the child would definitely die. Rather, refusing the surgery might mean prolonged pain for the child and therefore to withhold the treatment meant that the child might be exposed to further pain.

This case demonstrates that there are limits on the parents' right to make or refuse to make medical decisions with respect to their children. Again, if Stephen had been a normal child, it is unlikely that the parents would ever have considered refusing the operation. Where the child is not able to consent, the court must balance the parents' right to make decisions against the state's duty to protect those citizens who cannot care for themselves.

A number of statutes will now be examined to determine what the statutory position is with respect to a minor's right to consent to treatment.

IV STATUTORY REQUIREMENTS RELATING TO CONSENT

In this part a number of statutes, from Ontario and other jurisdictions, will be examined in order to determine: whether there are limitations imposed by statute on the ability of minors to consent, whether statute law has removed or clarified any of the common law disabilities and finally whether statutes have by and large ignored the issue of the minor's right to consent to or refuse treatment.

---

104 *Ibid.*, at 623.

1. Ontario Mental Health Act[105]

Under the Mental Health Act, no provision is made for minors, that is those under 18 years of age, to consent to or refuse admission to hospital or treatment. With regard to consent to an informal or voluntary admission, the Act is silent on the rights of minors. That is, s. 8 reads as follows:

> Any person who is believed to be in need of the observation, care and treatment provided in a psychiatric facility may be admitted thereto as an informal patient upon the recommendation of a physician.

It could be argued that since there is no mention of any age requirements for a "person" applying for admission, this provision in no way disqualifies minors who have the requisite capacity seeking admission on their own. Additional support for this position could be found in s. 2 which states:

> Nothing in this Act shall be deemed to affect the rights or privileges of any person except as specifically set out in this Act.

The same position could be taken with respect to discharge of voluntary patients as no mention is made of any age requirements, either in the Act or in the accompanying regulations.

In the interpretation section of the Act, neither the definition of "patient" nor "mentally competent" precludes application to children. For example the definition of "mentally competent" in s. 1(g) follows the common law requirements:

> "Mentally competent" means having the ability to understand the subject-matter in respect of which consent is requested and able to appreciate the consequences of giving or withholding consent.

Since there is no mention of age in these definitions, it is submitted that if a child meets the common law standard codified in s. 1(g), he/she is competent to make the necessary decisions outlined in this Act without regard to minority status.

In contrast, s. 29(3) and (9), regarding disclosure of clinical records, and s. 35(2), regarding consent to treatment for involuntary patients, specifically require the consent of the nearest relative where the patient has not attained the age of majority. It could be argued that s. 29(3) and (9) is consistent with other legislative attempts, such as that in the Young Offenders Act,[106] ss. 38 and 39, to protect the young person from adverse publicity; however, this section in no way limits the ability of the minor to consent to or refuse admission. If anything, the

---

105 R.S.O. 1980, c. 262.
106 S.C. 1980-81-82-83, c. 110.

fact that this section has a specific reference to the age of majority, whereas s. 8 has no age reference, is supportive of the common law position for all matters that do not explicitly require a particular age. Also, it could be argued that s. 29(3) and (9) does not prevent the minor from refusing to allow his/her records to be disclosed. In fact, it would seem that where the minor was competent to make such a decision, the hospital should be under a duty to seek his/her consent before releasing documents.

In addition, s. 35(2) specifically requires the consent of the nearest relative of a minor before psychiatric treatment is administered. Since there is no parallel section for consent to treatment for *voluntary* or informal patients, there is no statutory requirement that minors attain the age of majority prior to exercising their capacity to consent.

According to the rules of statutory construction, a common law right of action cannot be abrogated except by explicit statutory language. For example, this rule was applied in *Lawson v. Wellesley Hospital* where Dubin J.A. held that:

> It is, I think, fundamental that no common law action can be taken away without express language.[107]

This statute offers a good example of a law that does not prevent the minor from having a say, and in fact the conclusive say in admission, discharge and treatment decisions, if he/she is competent. Yet prevailing practice is to presume that decisions on health care are the exclusive right of the parents. Since the state has a strong interest in ensuring treatment for disturbed individuals, both so that society is protected, and so they are helped to be productive, it would seem to be in the state's interest not to discourage a child from seeking assistance under the Act.

A report of the Ontario Council of Health entitled *Committee on Mental Health Services in Ontario, Legal Task Force, Part I: Civil Rights and the Mentally Ill* (1979), considered the issue of consent to treatment by voluntary minor patients. The Task Force made the following recommendation:

> Rec. 38 "That the provincial age of majority for psychiatric (and other) consents be sixteen years. Minors below sixteen, if considered competent by two physicians, should be able to give autonomous consent."

This recommendation of a particular age was intended to be consistent with the Public Hospitals Act, Reg. 865, s. 50,[108] which establishes 16 as the age for

---

107 *Lawson v. Wellesley Hosp.* (1975), 9 O.R. (2d) 677 at 685 (C.A.). See also Sir Peter Maxwell, *On the Interpretation of Statutes,* 5th ed. (1912).

108 R.S.O. 1980, c. 410, Hospital Management Regulation, R.R.O. 1980, Reg. 865.

medical consent, including consent to surgery. Also this is consistent with the recommendation of the Uniform Law Conference of Canada, 1975, namely that at 16 the minor would be presumed to be competent, although a lower age could be determined on an individual basis.

A further justification given for the age of 16 by the Task Force was that under the existing child welfare legislation,[109] parental responsibility ended at 16. As noted earlier, the law is hesitant to encroach on parental decision making while the parents are expected to fulfil certain obligations.

There are definite advantages to setting a specific age at which the minor is presumed to have capacity, for example, doctors will be able to treat those minors without fear that they will be held liable for assault because they relied on the minors' consent. Hopefully the greater willingness of doctors to treat these minors in confidence would increase the probability that minors would seek assistance for problems they were reluctant to share with their parents (for instance, venereal disease, contraception, drug abuse, emotional disorder and abortion). However, it is important that whatever age is chosen there still be the flexibility of permitting younger children to consent if they have the capacity. One disadvantage of adopting a specific age is that this age quickly becomes the norm and doctors will either worry about or not seriously consider the possibility that younger children may be competent.

The proposed law reform paper entitled "Options on Medical Consent — Part 2," which was withdrawn due to public response,[110] also advocated a presumption of capacity for persons 16 years of age or older[111] and a rebuttable presumption of incapacity below age 16.[112] Where the patient had competence, the proposed Act clearly stated that the patient had the authority to give or withhold consent.[113] Thus none of the Acts or proposals reviewed thus far, eliminate the child's right to consent.

---

109 Child Welfare Act, R.S.O. 1980, c. 66 [repealed by the Child and Family Services Act, S.O. 1984, c. 55, s. 108]. See discussion, *infra*.

110 As an example, Right to Life groups were apparently concerned that by permitting competent minors to consent to medical care, young people would have easier access to abortions without parental involvement. Of course the fact that a minor had the capacity to consent would not mean they could in any way by-pass the Criminal Code, R.S.C. 1970, c.C-34, requirements that the mother's life or safety was endangered by the pregnancy (s. 251(4)(*c*)) or that a hospital committee had to approve the request (s. 251(4)(*b*)). What would change is that those minors with capacity could initiate a request for an abortion without parental consent.

111 S. 5.

112 S. 6.

113 S. 8.

2. Ontario Public Hospitals Act

Sections 50 and 51 of Reg. 865 under the Public Hospitals Act appear to be relevant to the ability of minors to consent to treatment. These sections state:

50. No surgical operation shall be performed on a patient or an out-patient unless a consent in writing for the performance of the operation has been signed by,

(a) the patient or out-patient, as the case may be, where the patient or out-patient is,

(i) sixteen years of age or over, or

(ii) married;

(b) a parent, guardian or next-of-kin of the patient or out-patient, as the case may be, where the patient, or out-patient is unmarried and under sixteen years of age; or

(c) the spouse or a parent, guardian or next-of-kin of the patient, or out-patient as the case may be, where the patient or out-patient is unable to consent in writing by reason of mental or physical disability, but where the surgeon believes that delay caused by obtaining the consent would endanger the life or a limb or vital organ of the patient or out-patient, as the case may be,

(d) the consent is not necessary; and

(e) the surgeon shall write and sign a statement that a delay would endanger the life or a limb or vital organ, as the case may be, of the patient or out-patient.

51. Where the attending physician or the administrator is of the opinion that a consent in writing should be obtained before a diagnostic test or a medical treatment procedure is performed on a patient or an out-patient, such consent shall be signed by,

(a) the patient or out-patient, as the case may be, where the patient or out-patient is,

(i) sixteen years of age or over, or

(ii) married;

(b) a parent, guardian or next-of-kin of the patient or out-patient, as the case may be, where the patient or out-patient is unmarried and under sixteen years of age; or

(c) the spouse or a parent, guardian or next-of-kin of the patient or out-patient, as the case may be, where the patient or out-patient is unable to consent in writing by reason of mental or physical disability.

As mentioned in relation to the Ontario Council of Health report on mental health services in Ontario, this Act purports to change the common law position by establishing a specific age — 16 — as the prerequisite for consenting to medical treatment and surgery. At common law, the ability to understand the nature and consequences of the treatment, not the attainment of a particular age, is the significant requirement. In addition, at common law, once it is determined that the individual has the requisite capacity, no one else has to or even can offer a substitute consent.[114] However, under s. 50(*b*) and s. 51(*b*) a parent or next-of-kin would be expected to give consent in writing despite the fact that a 14 or 15--year-old (or possibly younger) could meet the common law standard. Not only does the regulation suggest that the parents' consent is essential, it appears to make the consent of those under 16 irrelevant.

On closer examination it is this writer's opinion that this regulation does not in fact abrogate the common law rights of minors. In the first place, it is clear that the regulation is limited in its effect to public hospitals. It does not establish the necessary consent requirements for patients being treated as out-patients, in the physician's office, in their home or in a private hospital.

Second, a number of commentators[115] have taken the position that the Public Hospitals Act and regulations thereto are intended to establish the administrative rules for "hospitals", while a separate statute, the Health Disciplines Act,[116] governs the conduct of doctors. The purpose of the Acts is fundamentally different; the former sets administrative standards for the effective management of public hospitals and the latter sets ethical standards for the professional relationship between a doctor and his/her patient. Such a position is supported by the words of s. 29(1) of the Public Hospitals Act which limit the scope of the Public Hospitals Act to regulations pertaining to hospitals, not to doctors:

> Subject to the approval of the Lieutenant Governor in Council, the Minister may make such regulations *with respect to hospitals* as are considered necessary.[117]

In his article entitled, "Minors and Consent for Medical Treatment," Krever discusses the impact of ss. 50 and 51, Reg. 865, and warns doctors that the common law rules still apply in their dealings with minors:

> The application to out-patients cannot overcome the reality that the regulation is concerned with hospital management. My fear is that this new amendment has given the impression and, perhaps, a false sense of security, to members of the medical profession that a consent of a child over 16 is full authority to the physician, and that a child under 16 may, in no circumstances other than an emergency, be treated without parental consent. My own view is, as I have indicated, that the amendment accomplishes no such result . . . if the new regulation purports to legislate with relation to the liability and rights of physicians *generally* (and not

---

114 B. Dickens, "Use of Children in Medical Experimentation" (1975), 43 Medico-Legal J. 166.

115 Horace Krever, "Minors and Consent for Medical Treatment", lecture delivered to the University of Toronto (1974), at 19-20, reprinted in B. Dickens, *Materials in Medical Jurisprudence* (1979). See also Michael Code, "The Existing State of the Law in Ontario with Respect to Consent to Medical Treatment", paper prepared for the Interministerial Committee Regarding Medical Consents and Custody for Mental Incompetents (1979), at 61-63.

116 R.S.O. 1980, c. 196.

117 Emphasis added.

simply with relation to hospital management) it is, once more in my opinion, *ultra vires* because it is not so authorized by the parent statute, the Public Hospitals Act. To repeat, the Act empowers the Minister to make regulations in respect of public hospitals, *not* physicians and surgeons, so that, at most, O. Reg. 100/74 [now Reg. 865] affects hospitals in their practice of requiring consents, since it can only validly regulate hospital management.[118]

There is another basis for the position that the regulation has only a limited effect. In the analysis of the Mental Health Act, it was argued that a common law right of action could only be abrogated by very explicit statutory provisions.[119] The same principle applies in this situation. If the legislature intended to replace the common law criteria for consent, with "age" as the most significant variable, the consequence would be to deprive a child under 16, who had capacity of his/her cause of action for assault or battery against the hospital or doctors. That is, at common law, if the doctor carried out some medical procedure on a person under 16 with the consent of the parents, but failed to obtain the consent of the patient (or if the patient objected to the procedure) and the patient was competent to give or withhold consent, then the doctor would be civilly and criminally liable. While there is no case law on point in Canada, it could be predicted that if the procedure was essential or clearly in the child's best interests and the child was still under the parents' care and control, the doctor would be protected if he/she acted in good faith in reliance on the parents' consent. However, if the doctor acted on the parents' instructions and the procedure in question was not essential or therapeutic, or in the child's best interests, and in fact was highly intrusive or had irreversible consequences (for example, sterilization), then it is this writer's opinion that both the doctor and the parents could be liable.

As Michael Code noted in his review of this Act:

> In the first place the words are not permissive; they do not expressly permit the physician and hospital to proceed without the competent patient's consent. . . . Similarly they do not expressly state that the consent of the parent is sufficient to relieve the physician and hospital from liability, they merely require the parents' consent. Furthermore, the provisions merely require a consent "in writing", they do not purport to regulate the law of consent generally. . . .[120]

In summary, it appears that the common law test of capacity still stands. Certainly the Public Hospitals Act has no effect on the majority of physician-client contacts as these take place outside public hospitals. Even where in-patients in public hospitals are involved, it has been argued that the regulation does not alter the relationship between the doctor and his/her patient with respect to consent.

---

118 Krever, *supra*, n. 115.

119 Maxwell, *supra*, n. 107.

120 *Supra*, n. 115, at 28.

3. The Child and Family Services Act

An Ontario Act, the Child and Family Services Act, is significant in that it deals directly with the question of consent to services and agreements by both children and parents for services and programs funded by the Ministry of Community and Social Services. The Act includes voluntary community based services as well as admission to residential and institutional settings. It also includes services offered by the children's aid society and programs offered to those young offenders who are subject to provincial legislation. In addition, the Act sets regulations that are relevant to the issue of minor's consent to intrusive treatment procedures, psychotropic drugs and access to records. While the Act deals with mental health services, including residential care, it does not deal with the issue of consent to medical treatment.

By way of overview, the Act essentially codifies the common law, with certain notable exceptions. What is particularly important about this Act is that it provides a statutory definition of consent and specific guidelines as to the criteria and procedures to be followed by service providers and mental health professionals for each of the services, programs and agreements covered by the Act. In addition, it includes a preamble or "Declaration of Principles" that sets out the philosophy that is to be applied whenever decisions are made under the Act.

(a) Section 1 — Declaration of Principles

The paramount objective of the Act is to promote the best interests, protection and well-being of children. The Act recognizes that many parents need assistance in caring for their children and this assistance should be provided in such a way as to support the autonomy and integrity of the family unit. Also the assistance should be provided on the basis of mutual consent whenever possible.

(b) Section 2 — Duties of Service Providers

To ensure that the intent of the Declaration of Principles is carried out, s. 2 of the Act places a positive duty on service providers to ensure that children and parents have an opportunity to express their views and preferences where appropriate and to be represented by a person of their choice when decisions are being made that will affect their lives and welfare. In addition, service providers have an obligation to ensure that both children and families have an opportunity to express their concerns about the services they are receiving. The Act sets a clear standard for professional accountability; namely, the service provider shall ensure that decisions affecting children and parents are made according to clear, consistent criteria and are subject to procedural safeguards.[121] A failure to fulfil these duties could cast doubt on the voluntariness of the consent to a service or agreement.

(c) Section 4 — Statutory Definition of Consent

Section 4 of the Act sets out the definition of capacity and the criteria for obtaining a valid consent as follows:

> 4. (1) . . .
>
> (*a*) "capacity" means the capacity to understand and appreciate the nature of a consent or agreement and the consequences of giving, withholding, or revoking the consent or making, not making or terminating the agreement.
>
> (2) A person's consent or revocation of a consent or participation in or termination of an agreement under this Act is valid if, at the time the consent is given or revoked or the agreement is made or terminated, the person,
>
> (*a*) has capacity;
>
> (*b*) is reasonably informed as to the nature and consequences of the consent or agreement, and of alternatives to it;
>
> (*c*) gives or revokes the consent or executes the agreement or notice of termination voluntarily, without coercion or undue influence; and
>
> (*d*) has had a reasonable opportunity to obtain independent advice.

It should be recognized that the definition of capacity and the elements for a valid consent represent a codification of the common law position, with the addition of the requirement that children and parents be given an opportunity to obtain independent advice.

(d) Sections 27 and 28 — Application of Consent under Part II of the Act

Sections 27 and 28 of the Child and Family Services Act set out whose consent is required for various types of services namely:

(i) Consent to Counselling Services

A person who is 12 years of age or older:

That person's consent.

NOTE: If the child is between 12 and 15 years of age, the service provider has a duty to discuss with the child at the earliest appropriate opportunity the desirability of involving the child's parent.[122]

---

121 S. 2(2)(*b*).
122 S. 28.

A person who is less than 12 years of age:	That person's consent if the person meets the criteria set out in s. 4(2), or the child's parent if the child does not meet the criteria in s. 4(2). That is, s. 4(2) states that a valid consent may be given by a person if at the time the consent is given the person: (a) has capacity (b) is *reasonably informed* (c) gives the consent *voluntarily* and (d) has had an opportunity to obtain *independent advice*.

(ii) Consent to Non-Residential Services

(Other than counselling services, a community support service such as an activity group.)

A person who is 16 years of age or older:	That person's consent.
A person who is less than 16 years of age:	That person's consent if the person meets the criteria set out in s. 4(2) or the child's parent if the child does not meet the criteria in s. 4(2).

(iii) Consent to Residential Services

A person who is 16 years of age or older:	That person's consent, unless the court orders otherwise.[123]
A person who is less than 16 years of age:	Consent of the child's parent or alternatively, if the child is in the care of the children's aid society, the consent of the society.[124] NOTE: The consent of the child's parent is not sufficient by itself. The Act requires that the service provider take the child's wishes into account, if they can be reasonably ascertained.[125]

---

123 S. 27(1).
124 S. 27(2).
125 S. 27(6).

(e) Sections 29 and 30 — Application of Consent under Part II of the Act.

Sections 29 and 30 set out the requirements for consent to Temporary Care Agreements with the children's aid society and for consent to Special Needs Agreements with either the children's aid society or the Ministry of Community and Social Services, namely:

(i) Consent to Temporary Care Agreements

A person who is between 12 years of age and 15 years of age:	That person's consent.[126]
	NOTE: The child must be a party to a temporary care agreement if he/she is 12 years of age or older, unless the child has been found, on the basis of an assessment that is not more than one year old, to lack the capacity to participate in a Temporary Care Agreement because of a developmental handicap. In this case, the child's consent would not be required.[127]

(ii) Consent to Special Needs Agreements

A person who is 16 years of age or older:	That person's consent if he/she is not in the care of his/her parent and has a special need.[128]
A person who is less than 16 years of age:	Consent of the child's parent. Alternatively, if the child is in the care of the children's aid society, the consent of the society.[129]

The above information summarizes whose consent is required for various types of services offered under Part II of the Act. It should be noted that even where the consent of a child under 16 years of age is not required, the Act requires that the child have an opportunity to express his/her views and to be represented when decisions affecting the child's interests are being made or when the child has concerns about the services that he/she is receiving.[130]

For more serious decisions, such as admission to residential services or placement with the children's aid society under a Temporary Care Agreement,

---

126 S. 29(2).

127 S. 29(3).

128 S. 31(1), (2).

129 S. 30.

130 Ss. 2(2)(*a*) and 27(6).

there are specific provisions permitting the child to request a review of the decision by an impartial body. In the case of residential services, if a child who is between the ages of 12 and 15 objects to a placement, he/she can initiate a mandatory review by the Residential Placement Advisory Committee.[131] In addition, service providers and mental health professionals must inform the child that he/she has a right to object to the placement. If the child does object it is not necessary that this objection be put in writing. If a child of any age conveys an oral or written objection to a service provider or mental health professional, there is a duty to advise the Residential Placement Advisory Committee. If the child is 12 years of age or older and objects at the outset to the residential placement, the Residential Placement Advisory Committee must hold a review during the third week of the child's placement. While the placement continues, the Residential Placement Advisory Committee must conduct follow-up reviews every nine months during the placement.[132]

The Residential Placement Advisory Committee may at any time, on its own initiative or at the request of any person, conduct a review of an existing or a proposed residential placement of a child. That is, a child of any age may request a review of a placement and this request may be made prior to or at any time during a stay in residential care.[133]

The Residential Placement Advisory Committee must also review all residential placements of children in an institution where the placement is intended to last or actually does last 90 days or more. These review procedures are intended to offer additional protection to children who are less than 16 years of age in cases where their parents have the right to place the children in residential care.

It should be noted that the Residential Placement Advisory Committee is not a decision-making body. That is, the Advisory Committee may make a recommendation, but this recommendation is not binding on the parents of children who are younger than 16 or on the service provider. If the child is unhappy about the recommendation of the Residential Placement Advisory Committee or if the Residential Placement Advisory Committee's recommendation is not followed, the Act provides additional protection for the child. That is, the child may apply to the Children's Services Review Board for a decision as to where he/she should remain or be placed.[134] The Children's Services Review Board has more procedural protections and decision-making power than the Residential Placement Advisory Committee. It may conduct its review by

---

131 S. 34(6).

132 S. 34(6)(*b*).

133 S. 34(*a*).

134 S. 36(1).

holding a hearing. The child would have the right to independent advice and to be represented at this review. The Children's Services Review Board may make one of three decisions, namely:

(a) order that the child be transferred to another residential placement;

(b) order that the child be discharged from the present residential placement; or

(c) confirm the existing placement.

(f) Part V — Rights of Children

(i) Rights of Children in Care

Part V of the Child and Family Services Act sets out the rights of children who are in residential care under this Act, including children who are in the care of a foster parent, or who are placed in temporary detention following a charge under the Young Offenders Act or Part IV (Young Offenders) of the Child and Family Services Act.

The rights of the child are outlined in ss. 96 through 104 and do not require the child's consent, but rather set out the expectations on service providers with respect to the care of children and the children's participation in decisions while living in a residential facility. Specifically, s. 103 encourages the child's participation and involvement whenever significant decisions are made with respect to medical treatment, education, religion, discharge, or transfer of a child to another residential placement. The Act places a duty on service providers to consult with the child and obtain his/her views, to the extent that it is practical given the child's level of understanding, whenever significant decisions affecting the child are made. This section does not require that the child be any particular age or have any particular level of capacity before being consulted.

Section 104 sets out the duty on service providers to inform children as to their rights while in care. That is, all children, regardless of age or capacity have a right to be informed, in language suitable to each child's level of understanding, of such matters as:

(a) children's rights under Part V of the Act;

(b) the procedure to be followed when a child wishes to make an internal complaint alleging violation of his/her rights;

(c) the fact that there is an Office of Child and Family Service Advocacy to assist children and families;

(d) the review procedures available to children who are 12 years of age or older who have been placed in residential care;

(e) the review procedures available to children who have been placed in temporary detention or in secure or open custody under the Young Offenders Act or held in a place of open custody under Part IV (Young Offenders) of the Child and Family Services Act;

(f) children's responsibilities in residential placement; and

(g) the daily rules in effect in the particular residential placement, including disciplinary procedures.

When a child is concerned that his/her rights have been violated and is not satisfied with the results of an internal review, the child, the child's parent or another person representing the child has a right to request in writing that the Minister appoint an independent person to conduct a further review. The person who is appointed to conduct the review may conduct a hearing into the matter and in any event must report within 30 days to the individual who made the complaint, the service provider and the Minister.[135] The Minister may then take appropriate action upon receiving the report.[136]

(g) Part VI — Extraordinary Measures

(i) Secure Treatment

Section 110 of the Act requires that any admission to a secure treatment facility, that is a locked treatment facility, with the exception of an emergency admission, must happen as a result of a court hearing. In this case, there are a number of procedural safeguards available to the child, such as legal representation, or a right to a hearing before a judge, and objective criteria that must be met before placement can be authorized.

If a child is less than 16 years of age, the child's parents, may, with the written consent of the Administrator of the Secure Treatment Program, apply to the court for an order committing the child to a secure treatment program. For children 16 years of age or older, if the Administrator gives written consent, the child may apply or the child may consent to the parents applying for admission. The decision as to admission in both cases is made by a judge upon presentation of sufficient evidence demonstrating that the criteria for admission set out in s. 113(1) of the Act have been met. These criteria include:

> (a) the child has a mental disorder;
>
> (b) the child has, as a result of the mental disorder, within the forty-five days immediately preceding . . . caused or attempted to cause serious bodily harm to himself, herself, or another person;

---

135 S. 106.
136 S. 107.

(*c*) the child has

(i) within the twelve months immediately preceding . . . caused, attempted to cause or by words or conduct made a substantial threat to cause serious bodily harm to himself, herself or another person, or

(ii) [as a result of a mental disorder has] caused or attempted to cause a person's death;

(*d*) the secure treatment program would be effective to prevent the child from causing or attempting to cause serious bodily harm to himself, herself or another person;

(*e*) treatment appropriate for the child's mental disorder is available at the place of secure treatment . . .

(*f*) no less restrictive method of providing treatment appropriate for the child's mental disorder is appropriate in the circumstances.

There are special protections with respect to admission of children who are less than 12 years of age. In this case the court is not permitted to order a child into a secure treatment program unless the Minister consents to the child's commitment.

The admission to a secure treatment facility involves a serious restriction on the liberty of the child. For this reason, it is important that the child retain and instruct counsel prior to the hearing and that the child be encouraged to exercise his/her right to attend at the hearing. There are two exceptions to the child's attendance at the hearing. These are:

(a) the court believes that the child's presence at the hearing will cause the child emotional harm; or

(b) if the child, after obtaining legal advice, consents in writing not to be present and to permit the hearing to continue in his/her absence.[137]

Again, because of the seriousness of the consequences of a secure treatment hearing, oral evidence may be presented as to the reasons for the application for secure treatment as well as alternative proposals. The parties have the opportunity to cross-examine witnesses and the judge has an opportunity to evaluate the credibility of the witnesses in a way that is not possible when hearings are restricted to affidavit evidence. The child may waive the right to have oral evidence presented at the hearing, but again only after the child has obtained legal advice and given his/her consent in writing.[138] This is considered to be such a serious matter that the judge may overrule the child's waiver and hear oral evidence and the Act does not permit a parent to give substitute consent to waiving this right.

The Child and Family Services Act provides for emergency admissions to secure treatment under the following circumstances:

---

137 S. 110(7)(*a*), (*b*) (to be proclaimed).
138 S. 111(1) (to be proclaimed).

(a) a parent of a child who is less than 16 years of age consents; or

(b) a child who is 16 years of age or older consents.

In addition, the Administrator must believe on reasonable grounds that:

> (*a*) the child has a mental disorder;
>
> (*b*) the child has, as a result of the mental disorder, during the seven days immediately preceding the day of the application, caused or attempted to cause serious bodily harm to himself, herself or another person;
>
> (*c*) the secure treatment program would be effective to prevent the child from causing or attempting to cause serious bodily harm to himself, herself or another person;
>
> (*d*) treatment appropriate for the child's mental disorder is available at the place of secure treatment to which the application relates; and
>
> (*e*) no less restrictive method of providing treatment appropriate for the child's mental disorder is appropriate in the circumstances.[139]

Additional protections are set out in the Act for children who are less than 12 years of age. For children under the age of 12, the Minister must consent to the child's emergency admission. That is, the consent of a child and or parents is not sufficient for admission. For children who are between the age of 12 and 16, it is possible to be admitted on an emergency basis, if after obtaining legal advice, the child consents to his/her admission. In this case, parental consent is not required for an emergency admission.

The Act sets a clear time limit on emergency admissions; that is, that within five days of admission, the child must either be released or an application must be made to the court for a hearing with respect to commitment to a secure treatment program.[140]

(ii) Intrusive Procedures

The Child and Family Services Act provides special procedural safeguards with respect to the use of intrusive procedures. An intrusive procedure is defined in the Act as:

> (i) a mechanical means of controlling behaviour,
>
> (ii) an aversive stimulation technique, or
>
> (iii) any other procedure,
>
> that is prescribed as an intrusive procedure.[141]

---

139 S. 118(2)(*a*)-(*e*) (to be proclaimed).

140 S. 118 (to be proclaimed).

141 S. 108(*b*).

Intrusive procedures can only be used in the specific circumstances outlined in s. 125(3) of the Act. That is, an intrusive procedure can be used only:

(a) if the intrusive procedure is specifically approved by the Minister for use by that particular service provider;

(b) in keeping with any condition or limitation specified by the Minister;

(c) if approval is obtained from the service provider's review team, not more than 30 days in advance of the use of the intrusive procedure.

Every service provider is required to appoint a review team which includes persons employed by the service provider and at least one person who is not employed by the service provider and who is approved by the Minister. In addition, a medical doctor may be part of the review team. At least three members of the review team are required to approve or reject any proposed use of an intrusive procedure.[142]

The Act sets out certain criteria or guidelines that must be followed by the review team in deciding whether or not to approve the use of an intrusive procedure in a particular case. The criteria are:

(a) the child's behaviour justifies its use;

(b) at least one less intrusive alternative has been tried and has not improved the child's behaviour;

(c) no other less intrusive alternative is practical; or

(d) there are reasonable grounds for believing that the intrusive procedure would improve the child's behaviour.[143]

In addition to the criteria set out above, the review team is not permitted to authorize an intrusive procedure unless it first obtains the consent of a parent or the children's aid society (where the child is in the care of the children's aid society) for children less than 16 years of age, or the consent of the child if the child is 16 years of age or older. In the case of children less than 16 years of age, or for children who lack capacity, the review team is required to first consider the child's views and preferences, where they can be reasonably ascertained, before approving the use of an intrusive procedure.[144]

As a general rule, the service provider must obtain the approval of a specially appointed review team before using intrusive procedures. There are certain limited exceptions which permit a service provider to use intrusive procedures on an emergency basis for a limited period of time. In the case of an emergency, intrusive procedures are only permitted where:

---

142 S. 123(3).

143 S. 125(4) (to be proclaimed).

144 S. 125(5) (to be proclaimed).

(a) a delay would cause the child or another person serious mental or physical harm;

(b) the intrusive procedure is specified in the Minister's approval;

(c) the child is 16 years of age or more and consents to the use of the intrusive procedure or apparently does not have capacity;

(d) the child is less than 16 years of age and the child's parent, or where the child is in the custody of the children's aid society, the society either:

(i) consents to the intrusive procedure, or

(ii) is not immediately available.

Under these circumstances, the service provider may use the intrusive procedure for a period not exceeding 72 hours without the approval of the review team. After 72 hours, the approval of the review team must be obtained or else the service provider must discontinue its use.[145]

(iii) Psychotropic Drugs

As with intrusive procedures, the Child and Family Services Act has very specific criteria for who may consent to the administration of a psychotropic drug and under what circumstances these drugs may be administered. The provisions of the Act with respect to consent to psychotropic drugs are as follows:

(a) if the child is 16 years of age or older the child must consent;

(b) if the child is less than 16 years of age the child's parents, or if the child is in the custody of the children's aid society, the society must consent;

(c) if a child is less than 16 years of age or any age and lacks capacity within the meaning of s. 4 of the Act, the service provider must consider the child's views and preferences, where they can be reasonably ascertained, prior to administering the drug. The only exception to this requirement is in the case of an emergency.[146]

The Child and Family Services Act sets out very clear criteria that must be met before a valid consent can be given. The service provider must ensure that the following information is explained to the child and the parent:

(a) the identity of the particular psychotropic drug;

(b) the condition that the psychotropic drug is intended to alleviate;

(c) the range of intended dosages;

(d) any risks and possible side effects;

---

145 *Ibid.*

146 S. 126 (to be proclaimed).

(e) how the risks and side effects vary with different dosages;

(f) the frequency of administering the drug; and

(g) the length of time during which the psychotropic drug is to be administered.[147]

It should be noted that the service provider must explain all of the above to the child and the parents because even when a child is less than 16 years of age or lacks capacity, the child's views and preferences must be considered if they can be reasonably ascertained.

(h) Part VIII — Confidentiality of and Access to Records

(i) Confidentiality of Records

The Child and Family Services Act sets out specific guidelines with respect to which records may be disclosed and to whom. The Act states that:

(a) if the child is under the age of 16 years, the service provider must obtain the written consent of the child's parents or the society, where the child is in the custody of the society, unless there is an exception to requiring this consent;

(b) one exception is that a child's counselling record may only be released with the written consent of the child. This would include children age 12 and over who have consented to counselling services;

(c) if the child is 16 years of age or older, the service provider must obtain the child's written consent before his/her record can be released, unless there is an exception to requiring this consent.[148]

In order to offer better protection with respect to disclosure of records, the Child and Family Services Act sets out guidelines as to what information must be clarified with the consenting individual before disclosure is permitted. This includes:

(a) the specific information to be disclosed;

(b) the purpose of the disclosure;

(c) the person to whom the records may be disclosed;

(d) whether further disclosure of the records is permitted and if so, to whom and for what purpose; and

(e) the period of time during which the consent remains in effect, unless it is revoked.[149]

---

147 S. 126(2) (to be proclaimed).

148 S. 165 (to be proclaimed).

149 S. 165(4) (to be proclaimed).

The consent is revoked when the service provider receives notice in writing to this effect or when the service provider otherwise obtains actual notice of the consent being revoked.[150]

(ii) Access to Records

With certain exceptions, a child who is 12 years of age or older has the right to, and must be given, access to his/her own records upon request.[151] The Act specifies that the consent of the child's parent is not required for the child to have access to his/her own records if the child is 12 years of age or older.

The Child and Family Services Act starts from the premise that individuals have a right to know and correct information contained in their files. This basic rule is subject to certain specific exceptions that take into account the possible harm to a third party from disclosure and the possible harmful effects of disclosure of sensitive information to the client. The exceptions reflect an attempt to balance open disclosure to individuals of records affecting them with a concern for the interest of other parties, such as parents, informants, external assessors and others who may also be directly affected by the disclosure. The Child and Family Services Act uses the test of physical or emotional harm to either the child or another person as a reason for refusing disclosure. This is a very narrow test because it is limited to situations where access to all or part of the record would directly cause the child or a third party physical or emotional harm. The fact that the child is already emotionally disturbed is not a sufficient reason to refuse access. Rather, the onus is on the individual who is attempting to restrict access to establish a casual relationship between the particular information and the possibility of physical or emotional harm as a result of disclosure.

On the other hand, the Child and Family Services Act recognizes that information is required by individuals in order to make informed decisions, such as whether to transfer to another program, whether to request a discharge, whether to continue in a treatment program, whether to agree to release information to another agency or individual, or as the basis for preparing for a review. In addition, the Act recognizes that it is important to ensure that records are accurate. An open policy with respect to access to records permits individuals to correct erroneous information contained in the file and encourages more accurate and more specific record keeping. It is particularly important where the records may be released to another agency or tribunal, or used to make decisions about the individual's present or future care.

---

150 S. 165(5) (to be proclaimed).
151 S. 165 (to be proclaimed).

The Child and Family Services Act is a considerable step forward in the direction of increasing the rights of children to participate in significant decisions affecting their welfare and life-style. In a number of areas the Act still maintains a somewhat paternalistic approach and falls short of the desired safeguards for children, particularly when serious decisions are being made. For example, the Act does not provide for pre-placement reviews of children who are referred for residential care. Rather, the onus is on the child, who is 12 years of age or older, to initiate a complaint following admission if he/she objects to the placement.

Because residential care represents such a serious disruption to the child and a considerable expense to the government, it would be preferable to hold pre-placement reviews except in emergency cases. Additional support for this position comes from the research literature which suggests that many unnecessary residential placements could be avoided if pre-placement reviews were held.

The Act also fails to prohibit certain highly intrusive procedures such as electric convulsive therapy, psychosurgery, non-therapeutic sterilization and non-therapeutic medical or chemical experimentation.

Given the abuses that have occurred in the past, and the fact that these procedures have not been found to be particularly beneficial for children, it would have been desirable for the Act to have abolished their use with children.

A further concern is that the time limits for children remaining in secure treatment programs are far too long. Although the initial decision is made after a court hearing, which does provide procedural safeguards, the court order can last for 180 days and can then be renewed again for 180 days, meaning that a child could be held in a locked treatment facility for up to one year. This type of program represents a tremendous restriction on the child's liberty and a dramatic change in the child's living arrangements and therefore reviews should be held at frequent intervals to determine that a secure treatment environment is still required.

Finally, the Act is inconsistent with respect to the age at which a child can make decisions. At common law, a child of any age who has the necessary cognitive capacity, may consent to decisions affecting his/her welfare. By setting specific age limits under the Act, the Act appears in some instances to limit common law rights and therefore may prevent some young, but highly mature children from making decisions affecting their lives.

Despite these concerns, the Act represents a tremendous improvement both in philosophy and in the specific provisions dealing with consent. It is hoped that this Act will serve as a catalyst for similar legislative reform in other provinces.

4. Statutory Provisions re Consent in Other Jurisdictions

A brief survey of legislation in other provinces and countries offers little in the way of guidance for formulating a consistent policy in relation to consent by minors. In Quebec,[152] children 14 years of age can give a valid consent with the stipulation that parents be notified if the minor is hospitalized for more than 12 hours or if treatment is prolonged. The Quebec statute is limited in its application to health care by physicians in institutions.[153]

In British Columbia, the Infants Act[154] was amended to allow a minor of 16 years of age to give a valid consent to any surgical, medical, mental or dental treatment. Nevertheless, the physician or dentist is first required to make a reasonable effort to get parental consent or, failing that, a written opinion from another physician or doctor is required.[155]

In British Columbia the mental health legislation permits an infant of age 16 years or older, who is capable of expressing his/her own wishes, to be admitted and detained as a voluntary patient, solely on his/her own request.[156] As mentioned earlier, in Ontario a regulation enacted under the Public Hospitals Act[157] allows a 16-year-old to give a valid consent for diagnostic and surgical procedures that take place in a public hospital.

In 1975, the Conference of Commissioners on Uniformity of Legislation in Canada[158] adopted several recommendations that would fix the age of consent at 16 years for medical, surgical, psychiatric and dental advice and treatment. Because of their controversial nature, the Conference suggested that a jurisdiction might want to opt out of allowing a 16-year-old child to consent to contraception, sterilization or an abortion. While such legislation would offer some improvement for doctors who are unwilling to allow minors (up to age 18) to consent, nevertheless it avoids several of the more sensitive areas where adolescents are deterred from seeking treatment because their confidentiality is not protected. Clearly, there is still no agreement on the age of consent and there appears to be little effort to codify what this author believes to be the common law position, that is, to base consent on the cognitive capacity of the child.

---

152 Public Health Protection Act, R.S.Q. 1977, c. P-35, s. 42.

153 See Tomkins "Health Care for Minors — the Right to Consent" (1975), 40 Sask. L. Rev. 41 at 59.

154 R.S.B.C. 1979, c. 196, s. 16.

155 *Ibid.*, s. 16(4)(*a*),(*b*). See also the Medical Consent of Minors Act, S.N.B. 1976, c. M-6.1.

156 The Mental Health Act, R.S.B.C. 1979, c. 25, s. 19(2).

157 Hospital Management Regulation, ss. 50, 51.

158 Proceedings of the Fifty-Seventh Annual Meeting of the Uniform Law Conference of Canada, Halifax (1975), at 162-63, where a proposed draft of a model Medical Consent of Minors Act is set out.

In other countries the same inconsistency is apparent. For example, at least one state in Australia allows 14-year-olds to consent to "care and treatment required by (his/her) state of health. . . ."[159] In England the statutory age for consent to treatment is 16.[160] In the United States, the individual states have adopted a variety of different ages for consent. Generally, the tendency has been to lower the age below the age of majority, at least for certain specific types of problems. For example, some states allow minors to consent to contraception but exclude sterilization. Others allow minors 12 or older to consent to "care and counselling" related to the diagnosis and treatment of drug use and venereal disease while others set 16 or older as the age of consent for those with a mental or emotional disorder who wish treatment.[161]

This variety of positions reveals the underlying uncertainty of legislators towards encroaching on an area that has traditionally been the parents' prerogative. It has only been recently that children have challenged parental controls in relation to treatment in the courts, and it has only been for the past few years that the state has been concerned about the possibility that minors who are not permitted to consent in confidence will not be treated at all for venereal disease, drug abuse, mental health problems (especially those with suicidal tendencies) and contraception. What is needed is a complete rethinking of all legislation in relation to the treatment of children.

V PROPOSALS FOR LEGISLATIVE CHANGE

Throughout this chapter concerns have been raised about the lack of procedural and substantive protections for children entering residential care or receiving medical or mental health treatment. For example, it has been pointed out that under most provincial legislation and/or practice, those under 18 years of age are admitted as "voluntary" patients to mental hospitals, institutions for the retarded and group homes on the basis of parental consent and the agreement of the attending physician. There are no objective criteria to meet to qualify for admission, no review procedures to ensure that admission is really necessary and no requirement to explore less restrictive or alternative settings that might offer more suitable programs. Usually there are no requirements that the child's views be obtained and if the child does express a preference, there are no guidelines to suggest the weight that should be given to these views.

Even when a child wishes treatment or admission, the law is very unclear about the child's rights to seek treatment without parental consent. The practice

---

159 New South Wales, Minor Property and Contracts Act, 1970 (N.S.W.), Act 60, s. 49.

160 Family Law Reform Act, 1969 (U.K.) c. 46, s. 8.

161 Zuckerman, "Legal Barriers to services for Adolescents", unpublished paper prepared for the Bi-Regional Institute on Adolescence, Denver, Colorado (1978), at 45.

for both medical and psychiatric treatment has generally been to require parental consent until the patient reaches 18 even where the child is capable of understanding the nature and consequences of the decision and the doctor is convinced that treatment would be desirable.

Once the child has been admitted, there are no legislative provisions governing consent to treatment. That is, even if the child has the requisite cognitive capacity, there is no requirement that his/her consent or even opinion be ascertained prior to administering treatment. In most provinces, if a child strongly objects to a treatment procedure or wishes to raise a serious complaint about his/her treatment program, there is no procedure set out in law for doing this. Also, just as the decision to admit requires parental consent, similarly the decision to discharge cannot be initiated by the child, but requires either parental consent or a decision to discharge by the facility.

Once the child is in the program, most provinces have no legal provisions requiring either internal reviews (that is, by the facility's own staff) or external reviews (that is by persons not employed in the facility) to evaluate such matters as: whether treatment goals have been established, whether the child is making satisfactory progress towards these goals, whether the program being offered is adequate or should be changed, whether continued in-patient treatment is required, or whether a less restrictive setting should be considered. Similarly, although some institutions, notably those for the retarded, have voluntarily adopted certain internal review procedures when highly or even moderately intrusive treatment measures are being considered, such as electro-shock, psychosurgery or aversive conditioning, many facilities for the emotionally disturbed do not follow such procedures. In any case, there are no legal requirements, or sanctions governing the administration of such intrusive, potentially harmful treatment procedures.

Finally, while some provinces have made progress in establishing legislative standards for children in care, these standards usually do not have the force of "rights". As a result children would have a difficult time bringing a complaint against a facility that failed to meet a particular standard.

These are some of the numerous problems that I feel should be addressed in future legislation on the subject of minors consenting to treatment and to residential care. These issues are not easily legislated and once in legislation will be difficult to enforce. That is, any legislation will have to consider seriously the competing interests of parents, children and the state.

As a note of caution, there is a tendency to place too high expectations on any piece of law reform. Changing the legal requirements cannot ensure high quality programming, prevent parental rejection, create resources that are presently missing or eliminate faulty diagnosis. Economic and time constraints will make some provisions that appear desirable from the viewpoint of children's rights, less desirable when looked at from the viewpoint of crowded court-rooms, lengthy delays, bureaucratic confusion and the cost of additional personnel.

The Ontario Child and Family Services Act represents a start in dealing with these complex issues. Although it only applies to a limited range of services, this Act can serve as a model with respect to its philosophy and the procedural protections it offers to ensure that children have a voice in serious decisions that affect their lives.

part II

THE CHILD, THE FAMILY AND THE STATE

4

CUSTODY LAW REFORM IN ONTARIO: THE CHILDREN'S LAW REFORM ACT*

Allan Q. Shipley

I REFORM OF CHILD CUSTODY LAW

1. Background

By 1982, when the Children's Law Reform Amendment Act, 1982[1] came into effect, comprehensive legislative reform of child custody law in Ontario was long overdue. The Infants Act — renamed the Minors Act[2] — had been in force without major amendments for more than half a century. It did not even refer to the best interests of the child. Although the "welfare of the child" was mentioned, it had no greater importance in the statute than the conduct of the parents and the parents' wishes.

In 1973 the Ontario Law Reform Commission published a report on children as Part III of its Report on Family Law.[3] However, the research on which

---

*The views expressed in this paper are those of the author, not the Ontario Ministry of the Attorney General. Portions of this paper have been revised from presentations made for the Canadian Bar Association — Ontario Conference "All in the Family", 26th September 1981, and the Law Society of Upper Canada Conference "Children's Law Reform Act", 19th February 1983.

1 S.O. 1982, c. 20.

2 R.S.O. 1980, c. 292.

3 Ontario Law Reform Commission, *Report on Family Law*, Pt. III "Children" (1973).

the report was based had been completed in 1968, long before many of the innovative developments in child custody law. Accordingly, the Ontario Law Reform Commission report did not recommend major changes in the Infants Act. Nevertheless, the commission's report made a major contribution in recommending abolition of the legal concept of illegitimacy[4] and sparked a review of child custody law as part of the family law reform program of the Ministry of the Attorney General.

The mid-1970s was a period of unprecedented interest in reform of family and children's law. One breakthrough was the publication of *Beyond the Best Interests of the Child.*[5] Then, in 1975, the Children Act, 1975[6] was enacted in the United Kingdom, the Family Law Act[7] was enacted in Australia, and the British Columbia Royal Commission on Family and Children's Law reported on custody, access and guardianship.[8]

By 1978, when the Ontario Family Law Reform Act[9] rewrote the law on family property and support, development of proposals for child custody reform were just beginning. Consequently, the Family Law Reform Act, 1978 contained only a single provision dealing with custody. In anticipation of the reforms that would be following, the Act proclaimed that a court could "order that either parent or any person have custody of or access to a child in accordance with the best interests of the child".[10] The "best interests of the child" was for the first time recognized in Ontario legislation as the sole consideration in the determination of custody and access.

Finally, in December 1979, as the International Year of the Child drew to a close, Bill 205, the Children's Law Reform Amendment Act, 1979, was given first reading in the Ontario legislature and marked the next major step in reform of child custody law in Ontario.[11]

---

4 With the Children's Law Reform Act, 1977, S.O. 1977, c. 41, Ontario became the first Canadian province to declare the equal status of children, whether born within or outside marriage: see now, Children's Law Reform Act, R.S.O. 1980, c. 68, s. 1.

5 J. Goldstein, A. Freud and A.J. Solnit (1973).

6 1975 (U.K.), c. 72.

7 1975 (Australia), No. 53 (Cth).

8 *Fifth Report*, Pt. VI "Custody, Access and Guardianship" (1975).

9 S.O. 1978, c. 2.

10 *Ibid.*, s. 35(1) [re-en. 1982, c. 20, s. 3(3)]

11 Bill 205, introduced for consultation purposes only, died on the Order Paper at the end of 1979. Bill 140 was introduced in 1980, but before it could be enacted the 1981 election was called. Bill 125 was introduced in June 1981, carried over by special resolution to 1982, enacted, and proclaimed in force on 1st October 1982.

2. Goals

Major law reform is never a simple undertaking, and family law reform is particularly difficult because the responsibility for making the right decisions is so great. It is hard to imagine what legal rules are more important than the legal rules by which we provide for and protect the future care and guidance of a child. A poor choice of rules could have an effect on family life for years to come. For these reasons it is especially important that family law reform be built upon a consensus. It is not an area for bold social experimentation. It must fit with the needs and views of as much of society as possible. Accordingly, every effort must be made to strike the chord that will provide the greatest social harmony.

A major goal of family law reform is to assist families in understanding their legal rights and responsibilities and to inform them of the powers that society has to make authoritative judgments about those rights and responsibilities. The clearer the law and the legal process, the better the parties can assess their position and their options. In discussing divorce, including custody, Professor Robert Mnookin, a leading exponent of this view, has written,

> We see the primary function of contemporary divorce law not as imposing order from above, but rather as providing a framework within which divorcing couples can themselves determine their post dissolution rights and responsibilities.[12]

This function of family law was also identified by the Attorney General responsible for introducing the legislation. Mr. McMurtry, speaking about the Children's Law Reform Act to a meeting of family law practitioners stated,

> The fact that the legislation sets out the courts' powers in custody disputes does not mean that custody must or should generally be resolved in the courts but it does recognize that we will always need the authority and independence of the courts to resolve at least some disputes.
>
> Certainly, legislation does not exist solely or even primarily to guide courts in their decision making. Its most important function is to lay down the rules under which we are expected to conduct our social relations. Therefore, it is important to spell out as clearly as possible for the general public the kinds of factors they need to take into account in dealing with matters of custody and access. For example, it is important to inform the parents that they are expected to consider the views and preferences of their child.
>
> The more predictable the court process is made by the legislation the better the position of the parties to evaluate their options and in particular the benefit of going to court. Presumably the more predictable the court process is, the more likely it will be that the parties will reach their own agreement.[13]

---

12 R.H. Mnookin and L. Kornhauser, "Bargaining in the Shadow of the Law: the Case of Divorce" (1978-79), 88 Yale L.J. 950.

13 Hon. R. Roy McMurtry, Address to the Canadian Bar Association — Ontario, Family Law Section, Toronto, 9th November 1982.

Similar views were expressed by Mr. Justice Estey in his dissenting judgment in *Leatherdale v. Leatherdale* where he wrote,

> Family law, more than any other branch of the law, must provide, where it is possible, simple and clear rules which readily lend themselves to expeditious application in the trial courts. Litigation over family matters is never economic, always a heavy expense and a painful experience. The simpler the rules, the easier their application by the courts; and even more importantly, the more readily applied by the legal advisers to the members of the family who must always strive to settle family differences without recourse to the delays, expense and pain of court proceedings.[14]

Undoubtedly, given the individuality of each child, there is less scope for creating certainty in custody cases than there is in, for example, matrimonial property cases. There must also always be sufficient flexibility and discretion to protect the unique interests of each individual. However, there are many areas of child custody law where the high degree of uncertainty can be reduced. The tension between the quest for predictability of law and the reality of the indeterminacy of human nature provides the energy for continuing law reform.

(a) Best Interests of the Child

Obviously any reform of child custody law must focus on the best interests of the child. Full commitment to the best interests of children in custody matters means using the best interests of the child as the standard for all aspects of the proceedings. It is not enough to require that the merits of the case be decided in the best interests of the child. Both the proceedings leading up to the decision and the provisions for enforcing the decision must be aimed at protecting the best interests of the child.[15] For example, it may be in the best interests of the child to be in the custody of a relative with whom he or she has been living. Therefore, it is important not to place arbitrary restrictions on the status of persons who may apply for custody. If the child has developed a strong relationship with his mother's "common law" partner, then it is not in the best interests of the child to statute-bar the "common law step-parent" from making an application.[16] The potential benefits to children of permitting any person to apply for custody greatly outweigh the possibility of harm arising from frivolous applications.

Of course, it is in the best interests of the children that custody orders, once made, should be obeyed. This matter is discussed in detail below. But the need to

---

14 [1982] 2 S.C.R. 743 at 772-73.

15 Compare E. Bayda, "Procedure in Child Custody Adjudication: A Study in the Importance of Adjective Law" (1980), 3 Can. J. Fam. L. 57, especially at 64-67.

16 *Re Moores and Feldstein*, [1973] 3 O.R. 921 (C.A.); *Smith v. Hunter (Sears)* (1979), 15 R.F.L. (2d) 203 (Ont. H.C.)., and see *Gow v. Woolley* (1984), 28 A.C.W.S. (2d) 349 (Ont. Prov. Ct).

consider the best interests of the child after the custody order can arise even on such an apparently technical point as the effect of an appeal on the original custody order. The normal rule with respect to civil orders is that an appeal will stay the original order. So, the loser in the custody dispute could avoid the effect of the custody order by commencing an appeal. However, in custody cases it is recognized that appeals are usually unsuccessful. Therefore, in most cases the appeal would simply have prolonged the period of legal uncertainty for the child. Consequently, having regard to the best interests of the child, s. 77 of the Children's Law Reform Act[17] provides that in custody cases an appeal not stay the order unless the appeal court orders otherwise. The order made by the original court should go into effect immediately and give the child the legal stability and certainty he or she requires. Because the appeal court will confirm the original custody order in a vast majority of cases there is little likelihood that the child will be further disrupted.

As these examples demonstrate, the best interests of children will be fully served only if we focus on the needs of the child at every stage of the proceedings.

II THE CHILDREN'S LAW REFORM ACT: SOME PRINCIPAL FEATURES

1. The Meaning of Custody

One of the first problems in reforming child custody law is to determine the legal meaning of "custody". Historically, custody was considered to be an element or incident of guardianship. However, over a long period of time custody came to be understood as equivalent to guardianship.[18] Consequently, in the public mind and usually in the judicial mind as well, custody was equated with guardianship of the person.[19] For example, Mr. Justice Thorson of the Ontario Court of Appeal stated in *Kruger v. Kruger*:

> In my view, to award one parent the exclusive custody of a child is to clothe that parent, for whatever period he or she is awarded the custody, with full parental control over, and ultimate parental responsibility for, the care, upbringing and education of the child, generally to the exclusion of the right of the other parent to interfere in the decisions that are made in exercising that control or in carrying out that responsibility.[20]

---

17 En. 1982, c. 20, s. 1.

18 See *Hewer v. Bryant*, [1970] 1 Q.B. 357 at 373 (C.A.), *per* Sachs L.J.

19 Ontario Law Reform Commission, *Report on Family Law*, Pt. III, "Children" (1973), at 88, 93; Saskatchewan Law Reform Commission, *Proposals on Custody, Parental Guardianship, and Civil Rights of the Minor* (1981), at 27ff.

20 (1979), 25 O.R. (2d) 673 at 677 (C.A.); see also *Pierce v. Pierce*, [1977] 5 W.W.R. 572 (B.C.S.C.).

Nevertheless, both the terms "custody" and "guardianship" continued to be used and the procedures for obtaining guardianship were different from the procedures for obtaining custody.[21] This created an anomalous situation in Ontario. Guardianship orders, which embraced all parental rights and responsibilities, were being made where the only purpose of the application was to establish legal authority for a specific, limited purpose, such as meeting residency requirements for waiver of school fees.[22] Parents, in consenting to a guardianship order, surrendered virtually all of their parental rights and responsibilities, usually "through the simple process of paying a $2 fee to the Surrogate Court Registrar and having him complete a form application for the applicant's signature".[23] In contrast, a parent who wished exclusive rights and responsibilities over the person of the child and who submitted to a full hearing and inquiry into the best interests of the child would usually obtain a custody order that still carried with it some legal doubt as to whether it did confer exclusive parental rights and responsibilities.

Another problem arising from the term "guardianship" was that it could refer to guardianship of the person of the child, guardianship of the property of the child, or both. Although parents as natural guardians were entitled to guardianship of the person, despite popular belief, they were not guardians of their children's property.[24] So, for example, where a child won a prize in a lottery or was given a legacy in a will, a parent could not give a valid receipt or discharge on behalf of the child unless a court had appointed the parent guardian of the property of the child.[25]

In an attempt to clarify this confusion, s. 20(2) of the Children's Law Reform Act declares,

> A person entitled to custody of a child has the rights and responsibilities of a parent in respect of the person of the child. . . .

And s. 48 of the Act reserves the concept of guardian for guardianship of the property of a child. Since the Act came into force on 1st October 1982, there has been no statutory provision in Ontario under which to apply to be appointed guardian of the person of the child.[26]

---

21 Guardianship was exclusively a matter for the Surrogate Court under the Minors Act, s. 12. Custody could be granted in the Surrogate Court or Supreme Court under the Minors Act, s. 1 or in the Family Court, County Court or Supreme Court under the Family Law Reform Act, s. 35.

22 *Re Liau*, [1971] 2 O.R. 616 (Surr. Ct.); *Re Novin-Kashany* (1980), 28 O.R. (2d) 757 (Surr. Ct.).

23 *Re Liau*, *ibid.*, at 619.

24 Compare *Huggins v. Law* (1887), 14 O.A.R. 383; *Re Clason*, [1931] 2 D.L.R. 530 (Sask. C.A.). See now, Law Commission (U.K.), Working Paper 91, *Family Law — Review of Child Law: Guardianship* (1985), at 59ff.

25 Compare *Re Salmond*, Ont. S.C., 4th July 1984 (not yet reported) *per* endorsement of Holland J. (guardians appointed where minor won cash lottery prize).

26 The Minors Act was repealed by the Children's Law Reform Amendment Act, 1982, S.O. 1982,

The intention to eliminate guardianship of the person and replace it by custody can be seen further in s. 78,[27] which provides that any reference in any statute or document with respect to the person of the child shall be construed to refer to custody of the child.

The success of this attempt to distinguish between personal rights and property rights in relation to the child remains to be seen.[28]

Obviously the question of the rights and responsibilities of a parent in respect of the person of a child is left open. Reference must be made to the common law and statute law to compile a catalogue of rights and responsibilities.[29] Interestingly, Part III of the Children's Law Reform Act when first introduced[30] did refer to care and control along with education, moral and religious training as elements included in the rights and responsibilities of a parent. However, in the legislative committee reviewing the Bill there was no agreement about what should be included and what should be omitted.[31] Consequently, when the Bill was re-introduced in the following session, the references to specific rights and responsibilities were dropped completely.

Certainly, the right to care and control, the right to direct education and religious training, the right to discipline and the right to consent to medical treatment are among the rights and responsibilities of a parent. At least the task of a person who has been awarded custody under a court order in determining his rights and responsibilities is no greater than that of a parent who has custody naturally. Moreover, the Ontario Act makes a clearer statement about parental rights and responsibilities than the Family Relations Act, enacted in British Columbia in 1978, which states:

> Subject to this Act, a guardian of the person of a child has all the powers over the person of the child as a guardian appointed by will or otherwise had on May 19, 1917 in England under Acts 12, Charles the Second, chapter 24, and 49 and 50 Victoria, chapter 27, section 4.[32]

---

c. 20, s 4.

27 En. 1982, c. 20, s. 1.

28 A similar distinction in the Children Act, 1975 (U.K.), c. 72, ss. 85, 86, has drawn some criticism: see, S. Maidment, "The Fragmentation of Parental Rights" (1981), 40 Cambridge L.J. 135.

29 See, e.g., J. Eekelaar, "What are Parental Rights?" (1973), 89 L. Q. Rev. 210; Law Commission (U.K.), *supra.*, n. 24, at 52ff.

30 See, e.g., Bill 125, An Act to Amend the Children's Law Reform Act 1977, 1st reading, 19th June 1981.

31 Ontario Legislative Assembly, *Proceedings of the Standing Committee on Administration of Justice*, 15th January 1982.

32 R.S.B.C. 1979, c. 121, s. 25.

2. Joint Custody

A concept that has received much attention in family law in the past few years is the concept of joint custody. The adversarial system has conditioned us to think that in every dispute there will be a winner and a loser. Thus, although the law declared decades ago that parents enjoyed joint custody of their children,[33] only very recently did the courts begin to make orders that recognized the continued joint custodial rights of the parents following separation.

No fixed rules developed for the form of joint custody. Because the parents were living separate and apart the structure of the order recognizing joint rights was often varied to reflect the parents' living arrangements. Sometimes the child was placed in the care and control of one parent with the other parent having visiting rights and both parents having the rest of the rights jointly in relation to the person of the child. Or, one parent had legal custody and the other parent had only care and control.[34] In still other cases the child lived half the time with one parent and half the time with the other parent.[35] The variation in the types of joint custody orders resulted in new terms like "divided custody" and "split custody".

For the purpose of legislative reform it is more important to capture the essential legal principle than to incorporate all the permutations of the principle. Accordingly, s. 28 of the Children's Law Reform Act states very simply that the court may grant custody of the child to "one or more persons".[36] This provides a legislative basis upon which a wide variety of joint custody orders can be made to fit the circumstances and the best interests of the child.

The attractiveness of joint custody is that where both parents are loving and capable each can remain significantly involved in the upbringing of the child, jointly making decisions on such questions as education, religious upbringing, and cultural development. Under a joint custody order a parent who fully recognizes that leaving the child in the matrimonial home is in the child's best interests need not bear the stigma and guilt of losing custodial rights. The child need not experience feelings of desertion and abandonment.[37]

If joint custody might benefit both the child and the parents, except where one of the parents is clearly unfit, then it seems reasonable to ask why our

---

33 Infants Amendment Act, 1923, S.O. 1923, c. 33, s. 3.

34 See, e.g., *Huber v. Huber* (1975), 18 R.F.L. 378 (Sask. Q.B.).

35 Compare *Allen v. Allen* (1983), 20 A.C.W.S. (2d) 537 (Ont. Prov. Ct.), where an original order for alternating custody was subsequently varied; *Fontaine v. Fontaine* (1980), 18 R.F.L. (2d) 235 (Man. C.A.), where the Manitoba Court of Appeal upheld an order for alternating custody.

36 En. 1982, c. 20, s. 1. Compare The Saskatchewan Infants Act, R.S.S. 1978, c. I-9, s. 3(6) [re-en 1978, c. 32 (Supp.), s. 3]; Divorce Act, 1985, S.C. 1986, c. 4, s. 16(4).

37 M. Roman and W. Haddad, *The Disposable Parent: The Case for Joint Custody* (1978).

legislation should not establish a presumption in favour of joint custody, so that the courts would be required to make a joint custody order unless joint custody were proven to be inappropriate. California appeared to take such a move in 1979.[38] Section 4600.5 of the California Civil Code now provides:

> (a) There shall be a presumption, affecting the burden of proof, that joint custody is in the best interests of a minor child where the parents have agreed to an award of joint custody or so agree in open court. . .
>
> If the court declines to enter an order awarding joint custody pursuant to this subdivision, the court shall state in its decision the reasons for denial of an award of joint custody.

The words of this section contain an important clue to a major problem of joint custody; that is, the agreement of the parents. No matter how desirable joint custody may be from an objective standpoint, if one of the parents refuses to co-operate with the other parent, joint custody can easily be sabotaged and the child thrust into the turmoil of interspousal bickering and bad feelings. Consequently, the courts in many jurisdictions have declined to make joint custody orders where it appears that there is no reasonable prospect of co-operation between the parties.

In the Ontario Court of Appeal, Mr. Justice Thorson stated,

> . . . any Court that is considering the making of an award of joint custody, should be guided by the following precepts: if the Court has before it the right combination of thoughtful and mature parents who understand what is involved in such an arrangement and are willing to try it, the Court should feel encouraged to go ahead with it; but if they are not evidently willing, the Court should not seek to impose it on them, because it is then not likely to work, and because the price to be paid if it does not work is likely to be altogether too high to warrant taking the risk that is then present of trying it.[39]

In 1980 the President of the Family Division of the High Court in the United Kingdom issued a Practice Direction recommending that the courts not make orders inconsistent with requests by both parties for joint custody. Where only one party requests joint custody the court should not make an order for joint custody except with the agreement of the parties or after giving the parties an opportunity to be heard.[40]

Thus, insofar as the presumption in favour of joint custody arises only where the parties have agreed, the California legislation does not seem to differ

---

38 See now, California Civil Code, ss. 4600 and 4600.5, in effect 1st January 1980.

39 *Kruger v. Kruger* (1979), 25 O.R. (2d) 673 at 681 (C.A.). Compare *Parsons v. Parsons* (1985), 48 R.F.L. (2d) 85 (Nfld. U.F.C.), where the court having regard to the experience of 3 years of joint custody under a separation agreement and to the wishes of the children, ordered joint custody despite the request of each parent for sole custody.

40 [1980] 1 All E.R. 784.

substantially from the approach taken by the courts in Canada and the United Kingdom. Although it is now reported[41] that some American states have established a presumption that joint custody is in the best interests of the child whether or not the parents agree, most American states with joint custody legislation seem to follow the California approach.

Section 4600(b) of the California Civil Code provides,

> Custody should be awarded in the following order of preference according to the best interests of the child:
>
> (1) To both parents jointly pursuant to section 4600.5 or to either parent.

It is noteworthy that at the time the California legislation was being drafted, attempts to give preference to joint custody over sole parental custody were unsuccessful, so that the section was enacted with equal preference for joint and sole custody.[42]

The view of the majority of courts and legislators appears to be that as desirable as the goals of joint custody may be, until the means of achieving these goals are clearer it is more prudent to maintain flexibility in the law and to avoid establishing broad presumptions.[43]

There lies within the provisions of the Children's Law Reform Act the opportunity for an innovative approach to some of the legal problems of joint custody. Reflecting the view that custody is a "bundle of rights"[44] s. 21 of the Act permits a parent to apply for an order "determining any aspect of the incidents of custody of the child".[45] In the first place this power may avoid custody contests in some instances. Traditionally, if the parent wished to exercise exclusive control over one aspect of the incidents of custody, such as religious upbringing, the parent would have applied for custody. By winning all the incidents of custody the parent would have had the one incident, religious upbringing, most desired. The Children's Law Reform Act, by clearly permit-

---

41 J. Folberg, "Joint Custody Law — the Second Wave" (1984-85), 23 J. Fam. L. 1 at 3.

42 J.A. Cook, "Joint Custody, Sole Custody: A New Statute Reflects a New Perspective" (1980), 18 Conciliation Courts Rev. 1 at 4.

43 Just as joint custody seemed to be gaining widespread support some concerns began to be expressed: see, e.g., J. Shulman and V. Pitt, "Second Thoughts on Joint Custody: Analysis of Legislation and its Implications for Women and Children" (1982), 12 Golden Gate U.L. Rev. 538. A resolution in favour of a presumption of joint custody failed to pass the Family Law Section of the Canadian Bar Association — Ontario in the spring of 1985. The addition of a presumption in favour of joint custody in the Divorce Act, 1985 was opposed by the Canadian Advisory Council on the Status of Women.

44 *Hewer v. Bryant*, [1970] 1 Q.B. 357, and text accompanying n. 18, *supra*.

45 Compare Guardianship Act, 1973 (U.K.), c. 29, s. 1(3) and Children's Law Reform Act, s. 21 [en. 1982, c. 20, s. 1].

ting a parent to apply for a determination of an incident of custody, allows a parent to obtain control of one aspect of custody without engaging in an all-or-nothing contest for full custody. The equal entitlement to custody conferred by s. 20[46] of the Act remains in effect, subject only to the sole right given to the one parent with respect to, for example, religious upbringing.

The other side of this power can be exercised where the court would make a joint custody order but for a fundamental disagreement over one of the incidents of custody.[47] Under s. 28 the court could grant joint custody over all those incidents of custody in respect of which there was likely to be agreement, thus creating a form of limited joint custody. For example, one parent may be granted care and control and the right to determine cultural upbringing, while both parents would have joint rights with respect to the child's schooling and medical treatment.[48]

3. The Best Interests Guidelines

One of the purposes of the Children's Law Reform Act, declared in s. 19,[49] is to ensure that applications to the courts in respect of custody are to be determined on the basis of the best interests of the child. Accordingly, s. 24[50] of the Children's Law Reform Act affirms that the merits of an application in respect of custody shall be determined on the basis of the best interests of the child. Although for many years that principle had been taken for granted in practice, it is important as a statutory expression of government policy. An interesting feature of s. 24 is that it lists a number of factors that the court is to consider in determining the best interests of the child. The use of guidelines has been recommended by a number of law reform studies,[51] and guidelines were enacted by British Columbia[52] and Saskatchewan[53] and by Ontario in the Child Welfare Act.[54]

---

46 En. 1982, c. 20, s. 1.

47 See, e.g., *Chouinard v. Chouinard* (1982), 31 R.F.L. (2d) 6 (Sask. Q.B.) (disagreement over religion and education).

48 Compare *Donald v. Donald* (1980), 3 Sask. R. 202 (Q.B.), where in fact joint custody was ordered but the father was given responsibility for education and religious training: s. 28 [en. 1982, c. 20, s. 1].

49 En. 1982, c. 20, s. 1.

50 En. 1982, c. 20, s. 1.

51 Law Reform Commission of Canada, *Family Law* (1976); National Conference of Commissioners on Uniform State Laws (U.S.A.), Uniform Marriage and Divorce Act (1970), s. 402; Royal Commission on Family and Children's Law, *Fifth Report*, Pt. V, "Custody, Access and Guardianship" (1975).

52 Family Relations Act, s. 24.

53 The Infants Act, s. 3(3) [re-en. 1978, c. 32 (Supp.), s. 3].

54 R.S.O. 1980, c. 66 [repealed and substituted by the Child and Family Services Act, 1984, S.O. 1984, c. 55] s. 1 [now s. 37(3)].

While it is appropriate that "the best interests of the child" should be the sole principle for determining custody, the principle is not easily definable. Because each case involves an individual determination of its merits, there is a risk that "best interests", instead of being an objective standard, could become a justification for subjective, idiosyncratic decision making. "Best interests" would mean what the court wanted it to mean. In the context of considering custody on divorce, then Professor Gosse and Professor Payne wrote,

> A strong argument can be made that several hundred judges across Canada exercising custody jurisdiction on divorce require, or are at least entitled to, specific statutory direction. If there were specific guidelines, Parliament would have spelled out social policy for the courts to apply and the courts would then know in concrete terms what they are supposed to do. Lawyers and others would have these guidelines as a basis for negotiation in settling custody disputes and drawing separation agreements.[55]

The guidelines included in s. 24(2) of the Act are as follows:

(*a*) the love, affection and emotional ties between the child and,

(i) each person entitled to or claiming custody of or access to the child,

(ii) other members of the child's family who reside with the child, and

(iii) persons involved in the care and upbringing of the child;

(*b*) the views and preferences of the child, where such views and preferences can reasonably be ascertained;

(*c*) the length of time the child has lived in a stable home environment;

(*d*) the ability and willingness of each person applying for custody of the child to provide the child with guidance and education, the necessaries of life and any special needs of the child;

(*e*) any plans proposed for the care and upbringing of the child;

(*f*) the permanence and stability of the family unit with which it is proposed that the child will live; and

(*g*) the relationship by blood or through an adoption order between the child and each person who is a party to the application.

The list in s. 24 is not exhaustive. The court must consider all the needs and circumstances of the child. Room must be left for consideration of the needs of the particular child and for recognition of new factors found to be relevant to the needs of children in general. However, the list does include the essential elements generally acknowledged as important in weighing the best interests of the child.[56]

---

55 R. Gosse and J.D. Payne, "Children of Divorcing Spouses: Proposals for Reform", in Law Reform Commission of Canada, *Studies on Divorce* (1975), at 174.

56 Some indication of the usefulness of guidelines may be found in the fact that these guidelines

Although there are differences between the formulation of these guidelines and guidelines in other jurisdictions, one of the common features is consideration of the child from the point of view of present social, emotional and psychological relationships, the stability of those relationships in the past, and the likelihood that those relationships will continue in the future.

The needs of the child and the ability and willingness of the proposed custodians to meet these needs are obvious factors.

An interesting element of the Children's Law Reform Act guidelines is the recognition given to natural and adoptive parents. It was quite clear in Ontario law that natural parentage did not confer a presumptive right to custody of a child; the best interests of the child is the sole factor.[57] However, it does not follow that natural and adoptive parentage are totally irrelevant to the best interests of children. Rather, it seems reasonable that natural and adoptive relationships between the child and the applicants should be one of the many factors the court ought to consider in determining the best interests of the child.

In some respects the most important factor contained in the guidelines is the views and preferences of the child. Without guidelines the courts would surely consider the needs of the child and the suitability of the parents. But it cannot be taken for granted that the courts or even the parents would always try to ascertain the views and preferences of the child. Inclusion of this factor in the guidelines requires both the court and the parties to focus on the child. No custody order can be made without consideration of the child's position. The child need not always give evidence[58] and young children will not be able to. But in requiring the court and the parties to direct themselves to the issue in every case, the guidelines give unprecedented recognition of the rights of children in custody proceedings.

4. Conduct

One area of child custody law that has been affected by the supremacy of the best interests principle is the issue of the conduct of the parent. While the Infants Act was the major custody statute in Ontario, the court was specifically directed to consider the conduct of the parent in determining an application for custody.[59] However, the importance of parental conduct was challenged by the

---

were referred to even before they became law: *B. v. R.* (1982), 28 R.F.L. (2d) 150 (Ont. U.F.C.), and have been used in deciding custody corollary to divorce: *Marples v. Marples*, Ont. S.C., Carnwath L.J.S.C., 12th May 1983 (unreported).

57 *Re Moores and Feldstein*, [1973] 3 O.R. 921 (C.A.); *K.K. v. G.L.*, [1985] 1 S.C.R. 87.

58 See *infra*, "Judicial Interviews".

59 See also, Divorce Act, R.S.C. 1970, c. D-8, s. 11. But now see Divorce Act, 1985, s. 16 (9).

Supreme Court of Canada in *Talsky v. Talsky*,[60] where it was found that a wife "well nigh impossible" as a wife might nevertheless be a wonderful mother. The point of the *Talsky* case was that parental conduct that did not affect the person's ability to be a parent was not relevant to a determination of custody. In particular the conduct of one parent towards the other parent would usually be of little importance. Adultery would not, in itself, be significant in a custody case. Only if the adulterous conduct resulted in neglect of the needs of the children would it have a bearing on the custody case.

Although the courts often followed the lead of the *Talsky* case so that, for example, homosexuality was not seen as a bar to custody, nevertheless there continued to be cases in which parental conduct seemed to be a factor, even if not expressly so stated.[61] For example, courts seemed to be particularly troubled if disregard of parental conduct resulted in "rewarding" the parent who broke up the family.[62]

The Children's Law Reform Act addresses this issue and sharpens the focus on the interests of the child by specifically declaring, in s. 24(3), that past conduct is not relevant in an application for custody unless it is relevant to the ability of the person to act as a parent.[63] Stated positively, an applicant's conduct is relevant only where it has a bearing on parenting ability. On the one hand it aims to remove the opportunity to expose sordid details of alleged matrimonial misconduct unrelated to parenting capacity, while on the other hand, it remains broad enough to include conduct towards children other than the child who is the subject of the application.

From a strictly legal point of view it may be meaningless to make the obvious statement that "conduct is not relevant unless it is relevant". Nevertheless, having regard to the educative purpose of law, such a statement may be quite useful.

5. Time Limitations

One of the great contributions of *Beyond the Best Interests of the Child*[64] was to remind us of the importance of a child's sense of time. In our adult lives,

---

60 [1976] 2 S.C.R. 292.

61 *Bezaire v. Bezaire* (1980), 20 R.F.L. (2d) 358 (Ont. C.A.) (where homosexuality was not a bar to custody, but a breach of conditions of a previous court order seemed to concern the court).

62 *Re L.*, [1962] 3 All E.R. 1 (C.A.); *K.J.C. v. C.C.* (1983), 34 R.F.L. (2d) 306 (Sask. Q.B.).

63 Compare National Conference of Commissioners on Uniform State Laws (U.S.A.), Uniform Marriage and Divorce Act, 1970, s. 402; Guardianship Act, 1968 (N.Z.) No. 63, s. 23; Saskatchewan Law Reform Commission, *Proposals on Custody, Parental Guardianship and Civil Rights of Minors* (1981), at 3-4. See also Divorce Act, 1985, s. 16(9).

64 J. Goldstein, A. Freud, A.J. Solnit (1973).

where we never seem to have enough time to do the things we want to do, it is easy to forget that for children time seems to drag on endlessly. When we were young the wait for Christmas, summer holidays or the next birthday was always interminable. Now, if we are truly to concern ourselves about the best interests of the child in a custody dispute, we must be prepared to recognize the significance of the child's sense of time. A 5-year-old child who has to wait a year for the final determination of a custody dispute has spent 20 per cent of his or her life in a state of conflict and uncertainty. The psychological impact of such a disruption can have serious repercussions for the child's emotional well being.[65] The time that is wasted by the parties in tactical battles and legal manoeuvring is precious time taken away from the child in which he or she could be strengthening important psychological and social relationships.

This concern about the child's sense of time has given rise to s. 26,[66] which provides that where a custody application has not been heard within six months after the commencement of proceedings, a "show cause" hearing will be held. The parties will be required to justify to the court why the case should not proceed at the earliest date "compatible with a just disposition of the application". The court will then fix a suitable date and give directions for completion of the proceedings. This power to summons the parties before the court to explain the delay gives the court the authority to supervise the proceedings in the best interests of the child. It also provides an opportunity for the party who is eager to proceed to expose the delaying tactics of the other party.

There may be some concern that placing a time limit on custody proceedings will interfere with mediation and settlement negotiations. However, if the attempts to settle the case without trial are *bona fide* and agreed to by both parties then the court may extend the time. Furthermore, in cases where there is no emergency involved, the parties should be encouraged to exhaust the alternatives to legal proceedings before launching a formal court application for custody. Legal proceedings should not be started simply to obtain some imagined tactical advantage in negotiating a settlement. For the child, the commencement of legal proceedings likely means the end of hope.

Although such a provision may occasionally create inconveniences for the parties and their counsel, and even the courts, the best interests of the child would seem to demand such measures. Making a young child the subject of legal proceedings is a serious intervention in his or her life; every reasonable effort must be made to minimize the disruption.

---

65 *Ibid.*, at 40ff; K. Weiler and G. Berman, "Re Moores and Feldstein" (1974), 12 Osgoode Hall L.J. 207 at 217-18.

66 En. 1982, c. 20, s. 1.

6. Assessments

The pre-eminence now given to the best interests of the child has meant that we must develop better ways of determining what the interests of the child really are. The better the information about the child, the better the determination can be.[67] One of the most popular methods of obtaining information about the child's best interests is to engage an expert to prepare an assessment of the child and the family. Although in many cases in the past the parties did make use of expert assessments, problems arose, particularly where one of the parties would not consent. The usual practice of the courts in Ontario was to require the consent of the parties before making an order. By coincidence, during the period of time between the first introduction of the Children's Law Reform Act in 1979 and its final passage in 1982, it was held that the Ontario Supreme Court had inherent jurisdiction "to order a family clinic assessment of the parties, where that assessment appears reasonably necessary to arrive at a just and proper decision in the best interest and welfare of the children".[68] Nevertheless no such power existed in the district courts and the powers of the family courts were not fully spelled out.[69]

Section 30 of the Act[70] aims to answer some of the questions that surround the issue of assessments.[71] First, it makes clear that the court now has the right to order an assessment without the consent of a party. As mentioned earlier, the fact that the court has the power to order an assessment without consent may in fact induce more parties to agree to an assessment without an order. Most parties will see the wisdom of recognizing the inevitable.

Many problems can arise if the court chooses the expert. For example, there is a danger that the court will give too much weight to a report prepared by an expert of its own choosing. Furthermore, the parties must have confidence in the expert, both to ensure co-operation in conducting the investigation and to respect the result. Also, because the parties will be responsible for paying the

---

67 Compare *Gordon v. Gordon* (1980), 23 R.F.L. (2d) 266 (Ont. C.A.), and see R.S. Abella, "Procedural Aspects of Arrangements for Children upon Divorce in Canada" (1983), 61 Can. Bar Rev. 434 at 458ff.

68 *Cillis v. Cillis* (1981), 23 R.F.L. (2d) 76 (Ont. Div. Ct.).

69 The power to appoint experts has been recommended by, among others, the Ontario Law Reform Commission, *Report on Evidence* (1976), and the Law Reform Commission of Canada, *Evidence* (1975), and *Family Law* (1976). Also see, e.g., Family Relations Act, R.S.B.C. 1979, c. 121, s. 15.

70 En. 1982, c. 20, s. 1. This section borrowed considerably from the Alberta Rules of Court, Pt. 15, R. 218.

71 See S. Borins, "Family Assessments in Custody and Access Disputes under the Children's Law Reform Act" (1982), 24 R.F.L. (2d) 90. The Honourable Judge Borins' article comments on an earlier draft Bill in which the section numbers were different. See also J. McLeod, "Annotation" (1986), 49 R.F.L. (2d) 47.

expert, they should have an opportunity to make the selection. Accordingly, the court is required, if possible, to appoint a person chosen by the parties unless the parties cannot agree.

On the other side, the assessor must consent. In deciding whether to consent the assessor can raise with the parties the arrangements to be made for payment of the fees. Also, because of the six-month time factor, the assessor will also consider whether the investigation can be carried out in a reasonable time.

The Act does not specify who may be appointed, other than to require that the person have "technical or professional skill". The needs of children are so varied that it is unsafe to legislate qualifications for the assessors. A practical problem is that in a province as large as Ontario there is also great variation in the resources available among communities. While psychiatrists and psychologists will probably be sought most often, social workers, child care workers, family counsellors and mental retardation workers are examples of other persons who may have skills in assessing the needs of a particular child.

If the purpose of the assessment is to provide information for the court, then the court must have broad powers to obtain information about all persons who have had or are likely to have a significant role in the care and the upbringing of the child. For example, where a party is remarrying it may be important to include the prospective stepparent in the assessment.[72] Section 30(5) permits the court to require such persons, on notice, to attend for the assessment.

One of the most difficult issues regarding assessments is how to deal with the party who refuses to co-operate. Contempt proceedings may be used to compel[73] the person to attend, but they are not likely to create the co-operative spirit necessary to permit the assessor to make a useful evaluation. Therefore, the Children's Law Reform Act followed a similar provision first enacted in the Ontario Child Welfare Act.[74] The Act provides that where a person refuses to attend or undergo an assessment the court may draw such inferences in respect of the ability and willingness of the person to satisfy the needs of the child as the court considers appropriate.

The form of the report is not dictated by the legislation. However, under s. 30(11) the court may give such directions in respect of the assessment as the court considers appropriate.[75] The report is not confidential since the purpose of

---

72 See, e.g., *Reid v. Reid* (1975), 11 O.R. (2d) 622 (Div. Ct.), where the court expressed strong concern about the fact that there was no information before the court in respect of the potential "step-father". In that case the court appointed legal counsel for the child.

73 Contempt proceedings were found not to be available in *Cillis v. Cillis, supra*, n. 68.

74 S. 29, now Child and Family Services Act, 1984, s. 50.

75 See G. Awad, "Basic Principles in Custody Assessments" (1978), 23 Can. Psychiatric Assoc. J. 441, for a useful guide.

the assessment is to obtain information for the court and not to engage in treatment.[76]

A continuing concern about the use of experts is that the testimony of the expert will be given undue weight in arriving at the decision of the court. Indeed, there may be an over-reliance by the parties themselves on the opinion of experts.[77] To the extent that this concern can be met by legislation, the Act provides that the assessor may be called as a witness at the hearing and that the parties may submit their own expert evidence. However, problems could arise if the party who wishes to dispute the assessment is compelled to require the assessor to attend. Normally a party cannot cross-examine his or her own witness. Presumably practical solutions will be found if such a problem does develop.

7. Mediation

The expense, both financial and emotional, of resolving custody disputes in the courtroom has generated much interest in finding ways to minimize the use of the court process in custody cases. Furthermore, it seems likely that a child's interests will be better served by a custody arrangement that is worked out by the parties than by an order imposed upon them by a court.[78] As a result, there have been a number of initiatives in Ontario aimed at reducing the need for protracted and damaging custody trials. These different methods of dispute resolution share the general goal of resolving issues using a non-adversarial approach. Thus, we have pre-trial conferences, conciliation projects and mediation services available in various jurisdictions to assist the parties.

A pre-trial conference is held in every contested Supreme Court case in Toronto. After the case has been set over for trial the parties and their lawyers meet with a judge or a quasi-judicial official, called a Family Law Commissioner, either to settle the issues between the parties or to narrow the issues in dispute.[79] The rules of the Provincial Court (Family Division) also provide for pre-trial conferences before a judge.[80]

---

76 *Ibid.*, at 442.

77 See, e.g., Saskatchewan Law Reform Commission, *Tentative Proposals for Custody Law Reform* Pt. II, "Procedures and Support Services" (1980), at 25ff.

78 R.H. Mnookin and L. Kornhauser, "Bargaining in the Shadow of the Law: The Case of Divorce" (1978-79), 88 Yale L.J. 950 at 957.

79 See R.S. Abella, "Procedural Aspects of Arrangements for Children upon Divorce in Canada" (1983), 61 Can. Bar Rev. 434 at 453ff; A.H. Lieff, "Pre-Trial of Family Law in the Supreme Court of Ontario: Simplify and Expedite" (1976), 10 Gazette 300 (Law Society of Upper Canada). See also D.R. Timms, "Who Are These Family Law Commissioners Anyway, and What do They do?" (1984-85), 5 Advocate's Quarterly 149.

80 Rules of the Provincial Court (Family Division), R.R.O. 1980, Reg. 810, RR. 21-23.

In the conciliation project at the Provincial Court (Family Division)[81] in Toronto parties who commenced legal proceedings were asked if they wished to be referred to the conciliation service. Referrals were made by Family Court Judges, lawyers and Supreme Court officers. The conciliation service differs from the pre-trial conference in that the conciliator is a trained social worker, not a judge or judicial officer and the parties are usually not seen with their lawyers present during the interview. The conciliator generally meets with the parties, individually and together on more than one occasion and then files a report with the court. Long term counselling needs are referred to outside agencies.

More recently, a non-governmental family mediation service has been established in the Ontario Supreme Court building in Toronto. This is essentially a referral service through which lawyers can obtain the private services of experienced family mediators. In addition, there are a growing number of mediators offering private mediation services to persons with family law problems.

While these services are encouraging parties to reach out-of-court settlements, there is still much to be learned in this area about the most appropriate ways to develop and fund them. For example, should these services be considered "court" services (that is, part of the administration of justice) or "social" services (that is, a counselling service for families)? Should they be publicly or privately funded? What are the minimum qualifications for being a mediator? How should cost effectiveness be measured? How can the services be provided on a province-wide basis? Consequently, the Children's Law Reform Act takes a cautious but permissive approach. First, it chooses the somewhat neutral term "mediation". Then, in s. 31(3)[82] it sets out as generally as possible the goal of mediation by requiring the mediators "to confer with the parties and endeavour to obtain an agreement". Without expressly encouraging or discouraging mediation, the Act continues with some procedural guidelines in respect of mediation ordered by the court.

A significant policy choice is that mediation is entirely voluntary. It is not mandatory and it cannot be ordered by the court, except upon request by the parties.[83] In view of the breadth of meaning that could be given to the term "mediation", it does seem wiser at this stage to let the parties choose their own definition and request the court to make a general order for mediation. There is no limitation in the Act of the issues that could be submitted to mediation and in

---

81 Ontario Ministry of the Attorney General, *Final Report of the Conciliation Project* (1980).

82 En. 1982, c. 20, s. 1.

83 New Brunswick Child and Family Services and Family Relations Act, S.N.B. 1980, c. C-2.1, s. 131, permits the court to order the Minister of Social Services to make conciliation services available to the parties.

fact the Family Law Act of Ontario[84] and the Divorce Act, 1985 encourage mediation of all issues in dispute, namely custody, access, support and even the division of property.

Before entering into mediation, the parties are required to choose either "open" mediation, where the mediator will file a full report on all relevant matters, or "closed" mediation, where the mediator sets out only the terms of the agreement reached or the fact that there is no agreement. Open mediation can be helpful in some cases in eliminating the need for an assessment.

If the parties do choose closed mediation, then the Act clearly provides that "evidence of anything said or of any . . . communication made in the course of the mediation is not admissible in any proceeding except with the consent of all parties. . . ."[85] While confidentiality has been recognized in respect of discussions to assist divorcing spouses to reconcile,[86] the law has not been so clear in relation to discussions to effect settlement of issues where reconciliation is not possible.[87] In many cases the guarantee of confidentiality will enable the parties to make the same full and frank disclosure to the mediator that they make to their own lawyers.

With respect to payment of the mediator, the Act incorporates a standard provision of private mediation agreements, requiring the parties to bear the responsibility for the fees and expenses of the mediator. If one of the parties is unwilling to assume the expense of a mediator, then the party could refuse to consent to the appointment of the mediator. However, the Ontario Legal Aid Plan will in some cases give special consideration to payment of disbursements for a mediator and is considering the role of the plan in assisting persons who wish to obtain mediation services.

8. Judicial Interviews

In following the guidelines in s. 24 for determining the best interests of the child, the court must consider "the views and preferences of the child, where such views and preferences can reasonably be ascertained".[88] Obviously there are many ways that the court might ascertain the views and preferences of the child. One way is to let the child express his or her own views and preferences.

---

84 In *Simpson v. Simpson* (1980), 30 O.R. (2d) 497 (H.C.), the parties agreed to use a psychologist to mediate access disputes.

85 S. 31(7).

86 Divorce Act, s. 21, see now Divorce Act, 1985, s. 10(4), (5); *Shakotko v. Shakotko* (1976), 27 R.F.L. 1 (Ont. H.C.).

87 See now, *Porter v. Porter* (1983), 40 O.R. (2d) 417 (Ont. U.F.C.).

88 S. 24(2)(*b*).

The sense of injustice felt by children who are not given an opportunity to be heard is evident in this excerpt from a letter written to an Ontario Supreme Court Judge following a custody hearing:

> We wish to speak our minds about the judge's decision. I feel this judgment was poorly made and is unfair to my brother, my sister and myself. I feel all three of us have suffered and will continue to suffer until something is done about where we are living now. We all feel as if we are being held against our own will. . . . Either the judge was blind or some of this information was not made available. [My sister] and I can hardly see the need for sending a social worker if we cannot speak more in detail about our true feelings and our [custodial parent].[89]

The purpose of s. 65[90] is to ensure that the child has an opportunity to express his or her views and preferences to the court where the child wishes to do so and to require the court to take into consideration the views and preferences to the extent the child is able to express them.

In some cases the child may not feel comfortable expressing views in open court or in front of the parents. Accordingly, s. 65(2) provides that the judge may interview the child. However, the Act also requires that the interview be recorded. This would seem to imply that a transcript could be obtained by the parents, for example, if an appeal were being considered.[91]

The issue of judicial interviews is a sensitive one.[92] Some judges feel that there is no point in interviewing the child unless complete confidentiality can be guaranteed. Others feel that interviews should never be conducted. Perhaps it is not surprising that the Act permits interviews, but requires them to be recorded.[93] On balance, judicial opinion in cases in the United States, England and Australia[94] suggests that interviews should not be conducted on the basis of complete confidentiality, without some access to the information for the purposes of an appeal or a new application. Although there is precedent for having a

---

89 Mr. Justice Galligan, "Separate Representation of the Child", in Department of Continuing Education, Law Society of Upper Canada, *Family Law Week* (1976), at D-12.

90 En. 1982, c. 20, s. 1.

91 *H. v. H.*, [1974] 1 All E.R. 1145 (C.A.).

92 R.S. Abella, "Procedural Aspects of Arrangements for Children upon Divorce in Canada" (1983), 61 Can. Bar Rev. 434; D.M. MacDougall, "The Child as a Participant in Divorce Proceedings" (1980), 3 Can. J. Fam. L. 141 at 152ff.

93 National Conference of Commissioners on Uniform State Laws (U.S.A.), Uniform Marriage and Divorce Act (1970), s. 404.

94 *Coleman v. Brown*, 300 N.E. 2d 269 (Ill. Sup. Ct., 1973); *Duncan v. Duncan*, 528 S.W. 2d 806 (Mo. C.A., 1975); *Re Ryan* (1976), 27 F.L.R. 327 (Aus. Fam. Ct.); *H. v. H*, *supra*, n. 91. And see now, *Jandrisch v. Jandrisch* (1980), 16 R.F.L. (2d) 239 (Man. C.A.), especially *per* Huband J.A., at 249.

court reporter present,[95] the Act would not seem to preclude the use of unobtrusive mechanical recording equipment from which a transcript could be prepared.

The judicial interview should be used for the benefit of the child to permit the expression of views in a free and relaxed manner. It is not meant to be used as an investigative tool to pry out of a reluctant child personal feelings and preferences. Judicial interviews should not be used as a substitute for psychological assessments of the child.[96] Such assessments are provided for elsewhere in the Act and should be used where the court is interested in the expert opinion that they can provide. Certainly the judge must not allow the wishes of the child to be the sole basis for the decision[97] or to go beyond ascertaining the wishes of the child.[98]

9. Enforcement of Custody Orders

No matter how far we develop our laws and procedures for protecting the best interests of the child in the initial determination of custody, the wisest, best-founded, most informed judicial decision is meaningless if one of the parties does not abide by the order. Accordingly, protection of the best interests of the child means not only that the appropriate award of custody is made by the court but also that the custody order is obeyed.[99] The most serious breach of a custody order is an abduction of the child by the other parent.

Recent concerns about child abduction probably arise not so much from an increase in abduction, for which there are no accurate measures, as from an increase in awareness of the trauma experienced by children who are suddenly uprooted from their familiar surroundings or deprived of their relationship with the other parent.

Just as law cannot completely eliminate any crime, law cannot eliminate child kidnapping. Probably at best law can serve as a deterrent and make abduction a less attractive alternative. In this regard, the Children's Law Reform Act has taken major steps to deter child abduction and to strengthen the powers

---

95 *Guy v. Guy* (1975), 22 R.F.L. 294 at 295 (Ont. H.C.).

96 B. Chisholm, "Obtaining and Weighing the Children's Wishes" (1976), 23 R.F.L. 1.

97 *Saxon v. Saxon*, [1974] 6 W.W.R. 731 (B.C.S.C.); *Jespersen v. Jespersen* (1985), 48 R.F.L. (2d) 193 (B.C.C.A.).

98 *Jandrisch v. Jandrisch, supra*, n. 94.

99 See now, Support and Custody Orders Enforcement Act, 1985, S.O. 1985, c. 6. This Act establishes a provincial Director of Support and Custody Enforcement, with the duty to enforce custody orders filed with the director. The procedures available to the director, however, will largely be those that exist under the Children's Law Reform Act and other existing applicable law.

to enforce custody orders. The importance attached to these goals is reflected in s. 19, which sets out the purposes of Part III of the Act. Accordingly, close attention should be given to s. 19. Three of the four purpose clauses relate to child abduction and enforcement of custody orders. These clauses declare that the purposes of Part III are:

> 19. . . .
>
> (*b*) . . . to make provision so that the courts of Ontario . . . will refrain from exercising . . . jurisdiction in cases where it is more appropriate for the matter to be determined by a tribunal having jurisdiction in another place with which the child has a closer connection;
>
> (*c*) to discourage the abduction of children . . . and
>
> (*d*) to provide for the more effective enforcement of custody and access orders and . . . for the recognition and enforcement of custody and access orders made outside Ontario.

For the most part the provisions contained in the Children's Law Reform Act are not unique. They have been taken from a wide variety of sources and adapted and moulded together into a comprehensive scheme. Among the influences on Part III were the Hague Convention on Civil Aspects of International Child Abduction,[100] the Canadian Uniform Extra-provincial Custody Orders Enforcement Act,[101] the American Uniform Child Custody Jurisdiction Act[102] and specific provisions in legislation in other jurisdictions, such as British Columbia[103] and Australia.[104]

(a) Relationship of the Hague Convention and the Children's Law Reform Act

Although the Hague Convention[105] presents a potentially effective approach to the problem of child abduction, it is not without its limitations. First, because it is based on reciprocity, it will not be operative in relation to abductions between Canada and non-member states. If Iran does not ratify the convention, the convention will not apply to abductions between Canada and

---

100 See now, Children's Law Reform Act, s. 47 [en. 1982, c. 20, s. 1], adopting the Hague Convention as part of the law of Ontario.

101 Uniform Law Conference of Canada, *Proceedings* (1974), at 108, 114. In 1981, this Uniform Act was replaced by the Uniform Custody Jurisdiction and Enforcement Act, which was based largely on a 1981 draft of the Children's Law Reform Act: see *Proceedings* (1981), at 91.

102 National Conference of Commissioners on Uniform State Laws (U.S.A.), Uniform Child Custody Jurisdiction Act (1968).

103 E.g., British Columbia's Family Relations Act, ss. 36, 37.

104 Family Law Act, 1975 (Australia), No. 53 (Cth), s. 70. While Pt. III of the Children's Law Reform Act was in preparation officials in the Ontario Ministry of the Attorney General were also major contributors to the development of the Hague Convention and the new Canadian Uniform Custody Jurisdiction and Enforcement Act, *supra*, n. 101.

105 See H.A. Leal, chapter 6, *infra*.

Iran. Second, the convention is not intended to be binding between territorial units within a federal state (Art. 33).[106] For example, it will not be binding between Ontario and New Brunswick, both of which have adopted the convention. Third, the convention, of course, does not apply to abductions within Ontario. Finally, the convention does not contain a mechanism for *enforcing* orders. Therefore, in order to deal with child abduction as broadly as possible, the Children's Law Reform Act contains a further series of provisions on child abduction. These provisions sometimes parallel and sometimes complement the Hague Convention. Indeed, some of the provisions, such as address disclosure and apprehension orders, will be important adjuncts in Hague Convention cases.

(b) Jurisdiction under the Children's Law Reform Act

The underlying principle of the Hague Convention is that custody disputes should be determined in the place the child habitually resides, and not in the place to which the child has been abducted. The most effective way to carry out this principle is through rules regarding the authority of courts to make custody orders. This approach has been adopted in the Children's Law Reform Act.

The starting point for any custody case is s. 22,[107] which states that

> A court shall only exercise its jurisdiction to make an order for custody of or access to a child where,
>
> (a) the child is habitually resident in Ontario . . .

Thus s. 22 expresses in a positive statement the Hague principle that courts should not exercise jurisdiction over children who are habitually resident in another territory or state. Although courts in recent years have increasingly declined to exercise jurisdiction over children resident in another state[108] there was no rule against the exercise of jurisdiction.[109] Now there is no jurisdiction in Ontario courts to grant custody of a child who has been abducted into Ontario, except in very limited circumstances.[110]

---

106 British Columbia has specifically excluded interprovincial application: Family Relations Act, s. 42.1(5) [en. 1982, c. 8, s. 1]. But Quebec has proposed that the essential elements of the convention apply interprovincially, based upon the Act Respecting the Civil Aspects of International and Interprovincial Child Abduction, S.Q. 1984, c. 12: see Uniform Law Conference of Canada, *Proceedings* (1985), at 236.

107 En. 1982, c. 20, s. 1.

108 *Re Ridderstroem and Ridderstroem*, [1972] 2 O.R. 113 (C.A.); *Re Loughran*, [1973] 1 O.R. 109 (C.A.).

109 Compare *Charmasson v. Charmasson* (1981), 34 O.R. (2d) 498 (C.A.); *Stalder v. Wood* (1975), 20 R.F.L. 214 (Man. C.A.).

110 *T. v. T* (1983), 33 R.F.L. (2d) 97 (Ont. Co. Ct.); *Gilbert v. Gilbert* (1985), 47 R.F.L. (2d) 199 (Ont. U.F.C.).

At least for determining whether a child is habitually resident in Ontario, s. 22(2) provides some guidance as to the meaning of habitual residence, particularly where the child might otherwise be habitually resident in two jurisdictions.[111]

There are at least three instances in which the court may deal with a child who is not habitually resident in Ontario. First, s. 22(1)(*b*) permits a court to exercise jurisdiction where, among other things, the child has a real and substantial connection with Ontario and, on the balance of convenience, it is appropriate for jurisdiction to be exercised here.[112] Second, under s. 23[113] an Ontario court may exercise jurisdiction if the court is satisfied that the child would suffer serious harm. This provision was based on s. 4 of the Canadian Uniform Extra-provincial Custody Orders Enforcement Act,[114] and a similar provision is contained in Art. 13 of the Hague Convention. The "serious harm" test should be strictly construed.[115] A strict test is all the more important in light of the Hague Convention and its "grave risk" standard. The more easily our courts find "serious harm" as a means of assuming jurisdiction over out-of-province children, the more easily other territories will find it to assume jurisdiction over children kidnapped from Ontario. We must insist on strict standards here in order to protect our own children elsewhere.

A third instance in which an Ontario court may make an order in respect of a non-resident child is set out in s. 41,[116] which gives the court power to make an interim order. If the court does not have jurisdiction to make a custody order because the child is not habitually resident in Ontario, it must still have some powers to deal with children. Otherwise, the kidnapper could choose to stay here indefinitely with his *de facto* custody. Under s. 41 a court has the power: (1) to

---

111 The courts may also refer to the Hague Convention for assistance in interpreting "habitual residence", although "habitual residence" is not defined in the Convention on Child Abduction, probably intentionally so. However, it is a common concept in many other Hague conventions. See *Cruse v. Chittum*, [1974] 2 All E.R. 940 (Fam. Div.). M.L. Parry, "Comment [on Cruse v. Chittum]" (1975), 53 Can. Bar. Rev. 135. See also Dicey and Morris, *The Conflict of Laws*, 10th ed. (1980), at 144-45; and the Law Commission (U.K.), *Working Paper 68* and the Scottish Law Commission, Memorandum 23, *Custody of Children — Jurisdiction and Enforcement within the United Kingdom* (1976).

112 In *Wickham v. Wickham* (1983), 35 R.F.L. (2d) 448 (Ont. C.A.), the court applied s. 22(2)(*b*); *Obregon v. Obregon* (1984), 39 R.F.L. (2d) 164 (Ont. U.F.C.).

113 En. 1982, c. 20, s. 1.

114 Uniform Law Conference of Canada, *Proceedings* (1974), at 114.

115 See *T. v. T*, *supra*, n. 110, where a claim under s. 23 was denied. See also, *Husband v. Husband* (1984), 39 R.F.L. (2d) 104 (Sask. Q.B.). But see *Clement v. Clement* (1982), 29 R.F.L. (2d) 29 (Man. C.A.), where the court adjourned to permit further submissions under s. 4 of the Extra-provincial Custody Orders Enforcement Act, 1975 (Man.), c. 4. [repealed 1982, c. 27, s. 20].

116 En. 1982, c. 20, s. 1.

make an interim order[117] (2) to stay an application on the condition that an application be brought in an appropriate extra-provincial jurisdiction,[118] or (3) order the return of the child to an appropriate jurisdiction[119] and order payment of the cost of reasonable travel and other expenses of the child and any parties or witnesses.[120]

This is an important parallel provision to the Hague Convention, where Art. 8 requires the court to order return of a child who has been wrongfully removed. However, this provision differs in the options it provides for the applicant. It also gives the court a better opportunity to safeguard the interest of the child on an interim basis.

(c) Jurisdiction within Ontario

In a province as large as Ontario, where the distance from Rainy River to Renfrew is greater than the distance in Europe from London to Lisbon, abductions within the province are as serious as many international kidnappings.

Therefore, in an attempt to deter abduction from one part of Ontario to another, the Rules Committees of the Supreme Court and the Family Court have made rules that require proceedings for custody to be commenced in the court that has jurisdiction where the child ordinarily resides.[121] Within Ontario jurisdiction is based on ordinary residence rather than habitual residence. Presumably, ordinary residence is not as strict a test as habitual residence. It seems desirable to strive for some distinction between the jurisdictional test that should apply between countries on the one hand and counties or judicial districts on the other hand. In any event, ordinary residence is a significant standard that has been frequently adopted in Canada in child abduction cases.[122] The courts have held that ordinary residence cannot be established by abduction unless the other party has acquiesced.[123] These new provisions in the rules can assist considerably in deterring "forum shopping" in child abduction cases within the province.

---

117 *Maybury v. Campbell* (1982), 32 R.F.L. (2d) 348 (Ont. Master). *Logothetis v. Logothetis* (1985), 43 R.F.L. (2d) 448, reversed 46 R.F.L. (2d) 20 (Man. C.A.).

118 Compare *Re D.J.C. and W.C.* (1975), 8 O.R. (2d) 310 (C.A.); *Logothetis v. Logothetis, ibid.*; *Lavitch v. Lavitch* (1985), 46 R.F.L. (2d) 310 (Man. Q.B.).

119 *Maybury v. Campbell, supra*, n. 117.

120 Compare *Cant v. Cant* (1984), 43 R.F.L. (2d) 305 (Ont. Co. Ct.), where the court awarded actual damages for expenses to recover an abducted child.

121 Rules of Civil Procedure, O.Reg. 560/84, R. 71.05; Rules of the Provincial Court (Family Division), R.R.O. 1980, Reg. 810, R. 38(2).

122 See, e.g., *Nielsen v. Nielsen*, [1971] 1 O.R. 541 (H.C.).

123 *Ibid.*, at 546-47.

(d) Enforcement of Extra-provincial Orders[124]

The Hague Convention does not differentiate between cases in which a valid custody order has been made and cases where the custody rights arise by operation of law or legal agreement. All breaches are treated alike and the only remedy for a breach is the return of the child. However, in some cases, especially within Canada, we may wish to draw distinctions. For example, if a child is habitually resident in Alberta and there is no custody order, we may agree that Ontario law should follow the principles of the Hague Convention and order return of the child to Alberta; nevertheless, where there is a valid court order in Alberta, Ontario should be able to give full force and effect in Ontario to the order of another province. Under Hague Convention principles, Ontario would not have the power to enforce the Alberta order. Certainly within Canada there has been a strong desire to enforce custody orders made in other provinces. That was the basis for the Uniform Extra-provincial Custody Orders Enforcement Act, 1974.[125] Accordingly, the Children's Law Reform Act makes special provision for enforcing extra-provincial custody and access orders. The fact that the enforcement provisions also apply to access orders should not be overlooked. Access rights have equal status with custody rights in almost every section of the Act.

Section 42[126] provides that a court in Ontario shall recognize a custody or access order of an extra-provincial tribunal unless the respondent is able to satisfy the court that one of the criteria set out in subs. (1) is not met by the order. This provision in effect establishes a rebuttable presumption in favour of extra-provincial orders.

Extra-provincial orders are not restricted to orders made in Canada; they include orders of all extra-provincial tribunals, from Albania to Zambia.[127]

---

124 See generally, C. Davies, "Interprovincial Custody" (1978), 56 Can. Bar Rev. 17; "Uniform Legislation: the Interstate and Interprovincial Child" (1979), 29 U. T. L.J. 138; Uniform Law Conference of Canada, "Extra-provincial Custody Orders Enforcement: Ontario Report", in *Proceedings* (1978), at 143ff; "International Conventions on Private International Law", in *Proceedings* (1979), at 133ff. K. Weiler, "The Exercise of Jurisdiction in Custody Disputes" (1980), 3 Can. J. Fam. L. 281.

125 Uniform Law Conference of Canada, *Proceedings* (1974), at 108, 114. A major weakness of this Act was that if no custody order had been made, a province was not required to decline jurisdiction over a child habitually resident in another province. See *Proceedings* (1979), *supra*, n. 124, at 133ff and Uniform Law Conference of Canada, "Uniform Custody Jurisdiction and Enforcement Act", in *Proceedings* (1981), s. 3.

126 En. 1982, c. 20, s. 1.

127 S. 18(1)(*b*): " 'extra-provincial order' means an order, or that part of an order, of an extra-provincial tribunal that grants to a person custody of or access to a child"; s. 18(1)(*c*): " 'extra-provincial tribunal' means a court or tribunal outside Ontario that has jurisdiction to grant to a person custody of or access to a child."

Therefore, some of the grounds for avoiding enforcement may not appear very relevant to Canadian orders. To avoid enforcement of the extra-provincial order the respondent must satisfy the court on one of the following grounds:

  (a) he was not given reasonable notice of the proceedings in which the order was made;

  (b) he was not given an opportunity to be heard;

  (c) the law of the place did not require the courts to consider the best interests of the child. (This is clearly not intended to permit a review of the merits of the case. It is simply a question of the applicable law. Nor need the law declare that the best interests of the child is the sole or even paramount consideration. It is sufficient if the law requires the tribunal *to have regard for* the best interests of the child.)

  (d) the order is contrary to public policy in Ontario. (This is similar to Art. 20 of the Hague Convention, according to which a state need not return a child if it would not be permitted by the fundamental principles relating to the protection of human rights and fundamental freedoms.)

  (e) the extra-provincial court would not have had jurisdiction if it were a court in Ontario, applying the provisions of s. 22. (This ensures that a parent does not abduct the child from Ontario, obtain an order in a kidnapping haven, and then apply to enforce the order in Ontario.)

As with Art. 13 of the Hague Convention the success of this provision will depend in part upon the courts taking a narrow view of these exceptions.

Where the person opposing recognition of an extra-provincial order alleges that the child would suffer serious harm, s. 23, discussed *supra*,[128] may be invoked or an application under s. 44, discussed *infra*, may be heard.

Certainly for the applicant the benefits of obtaining recognition of the foreign order are very great. Section 42(2) provides that an extra-provincial order that is recognized by an Ontario court shall be deemed to be an order of the court and enforceable as such. This will trigger a number of enforcement mechanisms, which will be discussed below.

The right to make an application in respect of an extra-provincial order is not dependent upon reciprocity with the extra-provincial jurisdiction. Ontario will enforce an order from Timbuctoo, regardless of whether Timbuctoo will

---

128 See text accompanying n. 115.

enforce an Ontario order. That is the principle that was adopted in the Canadian Uniform Extra-provincial Custody Orders Enforcement Act, on the ground that our courts should not be inhibited in acting in the best interests of a foreign child just because the foreign state has not entered into a reciprocal agreement with Ontario.[129]

In any event, the question of reciprocity is of lesser importance within Canada. Every province, except Quebec, has adopted the Canadian Uniform Extra-provincial Custody Orders Enforcement Act or the Uniform Custody Jurisdiction and Enforcement Act.[130] Accordingly, in almost any province an application can be brought to enforce an order from another province. Quebec's interprovincial child abduction legislation is based on reciprocity.[131]

In summary, if a custody or access order, including an interim order, has been made in Ontario and the child is abducted to a province other than Quebec, an agent may be retained in the other province to make an application under the relevant legislation for enforcement of the Ontario order in the other province. If a child is kidnapped to Quebec it is possible to make an application for *habeas corpus* under the Code of Civil Procedure.[132]

(e) Superseding an Extra-provincial Order

A continuing concern in Canada has been the power of the courts of one province to vary a custody order made in another province or in another country.[133] The problem is a familiar one created by our mobile society: the custody order is made in Nova Scotia but now all the parties are resident in Ontario. Instead of speaking of varying the orders of another country or province, s. 43[134] talks of superseding an extra-provincial order, which is, in effect, the power to make a new order. However, in order to maintain respect for foreign orders whenever appropriate, strong restrictions are placed on the

---

129 Uniform Law Conference of Canada, *Proceedings* (1974), at 108.

130 Alberta, Extra-provincial Enforcement of Custody Orders Act, R.S.A. 1980, c. E-17; British Columbia, Family Relations Act, s. 38ff; Manitoba, Child Custody Enforcement Act, S.M. 1982, c. 27; New Brunswick, Child and Family Services and Family Relations Act, s. 130 [re-en. 1982, c. 13, s. 7]; Newfoundland, Custody Jurisdiction and Enforcement Act, S.N. 1983, c. 30; Nova Scotia, Reciprocal Enforcement of Custody Orders Act, S.N.S. 1976, c. 15 (although Nova Scotia has made reciprocity a condition for enforcing extra-provincial orders, Ontario has been designated a reciprocating province.); Prince Edward Island, Custody Jurisdiction and Enforcement Act, S.P.E.I. 1984, c. 17; Saskatchewan, The Extra-Provincial Custody Orders Enforcement Act, R.S.S. 1978, c. E-18 (Supp.).

131 An Act Respecting the Civil Aspects of International and Interprovincial Child Abduction, S.Q. 1984, c. 12.

132 R.S.Q. 1977, c. C-25, ss. 851-59 [am. 1982, c. 32, s. 52], 860, 861.

133 Uniform Extra-provincial Custody Orders Enforcement Act, *supra*, n. 125, s. 3.

134 En. 1982, c. 20, s. 1.

jurisdiction of the court to supersede an extra-provincial order. It must be shown *both* that there has been a material change in circumstances that affects or is likely to affect the best interest of the child, *and* that either the child is now habitually resident in Ontario or at least no longer has a real and substantial connection with the place where the extra-provincial order was made.[135] The criteria listed in s. 43(1)(*b*) are almost the same as the criteria in s. 22(1)(*b*). Therefore, the jurisdiction to supersede will exist only in cases where it is clear that no purpose would be served in returning the child or enforcing a stale order. Where there is any doubt, under s. 43(2) the court may decline jurisdiction.

Just as the court has jurisdiction under s. 23 to deal with a child who is not habitually resident if it is likely that he will suffer serious harm, so too the court under s. 44[136] is able to supersede an extra-provincial order if satisfied that the child would suffer harm if the extra-provincial order were enforced.

(f) Ancillary Provisions

The Children's Law Reform Act contains a number of highly important ancillary powers to assist in discouraging abductions and in enforcing orders. The sections are needed to deal with enforcement problems within Ontario, to complement the Hague Convention, and to carry out enforcement of extra-provincial orders.[137]

First of all, the Children's Law Reform Act adopts with some modification the following powers originally contained in the Ontario Family Law Reform Act:[138]

(a) the power to make an order restraining any person from molesting, annoying or harrassing the applicant or a child in the lawful custody of the applicant;[139]

(b) the power to punish for any wilful contempt of the process or orders of a family court in respect of custody of or access to a child;[140]

---

135 Compare *Hayes v. Hayes* (1981), 23 R.F.L. (2d) 214 (Sask. U.F.C.); *Nielsen v. Pierce* (1983), 35 R.F.L. (2d) 409 (Alta. Q.B.).

136 En. 1982, c. 20, s. 1.

137 S. 42(2) of the Act provides that an extra-provincial order that is recognized by a court in Ontario shall be deemed to be an order of the court and enforceable as such.

138 R.S.O. 1980, c. 152.

139 Family Law Reform Act [repealed by the Family Law Act, 1986, 1986, c. 4] s. 34 [see now s. 46]; Children's Law Reform Act, s. 36. An order can be made to protect only the applicant and the applicant's children, not relatives or third parties: *Layton v. Layton* (1982), 28 R.F.L. (2d) 85 (Ont. H.C.). It is an offence, for which the police may arrest without warrant, to contravene a restraining order: Children's Law Reform Amendment Act, 1986, S.O. 1986, c. 8, s. 4.

140 Family Law Reform Act, s. 37 [see now Family Law Act, 1986, s. 49]; Children's Law Reform Act, s. 39. See, e.g., *Martinez v. Martinez* (1984), 40 R.F.L. (2d) 325 (Ont. Prov. Ct.).

(c) the power to order disclosure of the particulars of the address for the purpose of enforcing an order for custody or access.[141]

Section 35[142] of the Children's Law Reform Act also recognizes orders for supervised access, which can sometimes help to deter kidnapping.[143] An order shall not be made without the consent of the proposed supervisor.[144] Thus, the supervisor is given an opportunity to negotiate the conditions under which he will be paid.

Perhaps the most eagerly awaited enforcement power was the power of any court in custody matters, including family court, to direct the sheriff or the police or both to locate, apprehend and deliver the child to a person named in the order.[145] According to s. 37[146] this power may be exercised where the court has reasonable and probable grounds for believing,

(a) that the child has been unlawfully withheld,[147] or

(b) that the child is likely to be removed from Ontario in contravention of a custody order or separation agreement.

The sheriff and police are given some powers to enter and search, but in general they are required only to take reasonable steps — not all possible steps — to locate and apprehend the child.

This provision was not intended to alter the traditional role and responsibility of the sheriff in enforcing civil orders. The sheriff's duty to enforce orders continues.[148] Where no emergency is involved, for example where access rights are being withheld, the sheriff will often be able to enforce the

---

141 Family Law Reform Act, s. 26 [am. 1982, c. 20, s. 3]; Children's Law Reform Act, s. 40. See *Glover v. Glover* (1980), 18 R.F.L. (2d) 126 (Ont. C.A.) and *Robertson v. Robertson* (1982), 36 O.R. (2d) 658 (C.A.), for discussion of s. 26 of the Family Law Reform Act. Compare Support and Custody Orders Enforcement Act, 1985, S.O. 1985, c. 6, s. 6.

142 En. 1982, c. 20, s. 1.

143 *Re Dulong v. Klaus* (1980), 3 A.C.W.S. (2d) 87 (B.C.S.C.).

144 Compare *Leveque v. Leveque* (1982), 18 A.C.W.S. (2d) 477 (B.C.S.C.).

145 In the absence of a specific statutory provision there may be doubt about the jurisdiction of the court to direct the police to enforce a custody order: see *Leponiemi v. Leponiemi* (1982), 35 O.R. (2d) 440 (C.A.).

146 En. 1982, c. 20, s. 1.

147 An order will not be made if the applicant has only *de facto* custody, despite failure of custodian to exercise legal custody: *Fich v. Fich*, Walmsley Prov. J., Ont. Prov. Ct., 9th February 1984 (not yet reported).

148 In *Re Hooey and Hooey* (1983), 19 A.C.W.S. (2d) 461 (Ont. Prov. Ct.), an order had been directed to the sheriff.

order. Where a breach of the peace is anticipated, the police are available to assist the sheriff. However, they are concerned that needless involvement of the police in enforcing custody and access orders will interfere with their other law enforcement duties. If the situation develops such that the police are subject to unreasonable demands, consideration may have to be given to building restrictions into the legislation.

When seeking orders directed to the police, regard should be had for the legitimate needs and concerns of the police. For example, because police will not usually be familiar with the form of civil order, orders should contain sufficient detail to inform the police as to the scope of their authority. The scope of the order could be a major issue in criminal proceedings for assault of a police officer in the execution of his duty.

No provision is made in the legislation for the sheriff or the police to transport children throughout the province or from province to province. Therefore, attention must be given to making arrangements for delivering the child into the control of the proper person. Someone other than the applicant may be named in the order to receive the child on behalf of the applicant.

In each judicial district a liaison network can be established among the bench, the bar, the sheriff's office and the police to develop mutually acceptable procedures for implementing orders made under s. 37.

Under s. 37(1) a private person, such as a private detective, relative, teacher, social worker and so on, can be authorized to apprehend a child, but these persons cannot be ordered to do so by the court and do not have the power to enter and search.

A number of powers can also be exercised under s. 38[149] to protect access and custody rights where there is a possibility that the child will be wrongfully removed from Ontario or wrongfully detained outside Ontario. Upon application the court may require any one or more of the following:

(a) that specific property be transferred to a trustee to secure return of the child;

(b) that child support payments be made to a trustee;

(c) that a bond be posted;[150] or

---

149 En. 1982, c. 20, s. 1.

150 Compare *Pang v. Pang* (1980), 4 A.C.W.S. (2d) 467 (Ont. H.C.); *Vogel v. Vogel* (1981), 10 A.C.W.S. (2d) 223 (B.C.S.C.).

(d) that the passport be delivered to the court or other trustee.[151]

Of these powers the passport power is likely to be most popular, although its limitations are readily admitted. For example, no passport is required to enter the United States. Nevertheless, where an order is made in relation to a Canadian passport the person obtaining the order should notify the passport office in the Department of External Affairs. The passport office maintains a control list which it uses to review all applications for new passports. When a foreign passport is involved, notice should be given also to the relevant foreign embassy or consulate, even though not all countries will respect court orders made in Canada. The order should state what arrangements will be made to permit the respondent to use the passport when the children are not in the respondent's care and control. If there are travel documents other than passports they should be included in the order as well.

Child abduction is a desperate act committed by a desperate parent. Although the law cannot eliminate desperation, the Children's Law Reform Act makes a strong statement of public concern against the lawlessness of the child kidnapper. The specific provisions of the Act aim both to discourage kidnapping and to provide remedies for abduction. A large measure of responsibility will fall on the legal profession to use these statutory tools carefully, creatively, and — always — in the best interests of the child.

---

151 Referred to in *Ishaky v. Ishaky* (1978), 7 R.F.L. (2d) 138 (Ont. C.A.); *West v. West* (1980), 4 A.C.W.S. (2d) 198 (B.C.S.C.).

5

JOINT CUSTODY IN CANADA: TIME FOR A SECOND LOOK*

Judith P. Ryan

It has now been ten years since the great debate over joint custody began. Since that time, a majority of the American states have enacted statutes expressly providing for joint custody as an option in contested cases, expressing a preference for joint custody as the option of choice, or even making joint custody the legal presumption in all cases where parents of dependent children separate and divorce. In Canada, two early decisions of the Ontario Court of Appeal, followed by courts in other provinces, have effectively precluded joint custody as an option in all cases of contested custody.

Taking its cues from the Court of Appeal, the legal profession has tended not to encourage and even to discourage joint custody by agreement, especially where other matters, such as support, possession of the matrimonial home and division of property are in issue. Such opposition by the bar is frequently made in ignorance of the significant social science research which documents the importance to the child of the continued involvement of both parents following separation and divorce. In many cases the lawyer's personal beliefs and prejudices may foreclose the consideration of a viable option which is in the best interests of the child in favour of an alternative which is in the best interests of one or other of the parents.[1]

This paper will examine the basis for judicial and legal opposition to the concept of joint custody, in light of the existing empirical data from social science research. The research itself will be subjected to critical analysis and future directions for both the law and social science research will be proposed.

---

*Winning paper for the Seventh Annual Lieff Family Law Essay Competition.

1   Anita D. Fineberg, "Joint Custody of Infants: Breakthrough or Fad?" (1979), 2 Can. J. Fam. L. 417.

I THE LAW AND JOINT CUSTODY

1. Historical Context

Custody law has long been characterized by rules that favoured one parent over the other for sole custody of their children. Under the English common law (carried over from Greco-Roman law), children were regarded as the property of their father and their custody, where disputed, was awarded arbitrarily to him.[2] In the early 19th century, industrialization drew increasing numbers of fathers out of the home as the work-place and left mothers as the primary nurturers and caretakers of their children. At the same time, society began to place a higher value on maternal care in accordance with evolving theories of child development. As a result, the long-standing preference for fathers was replaced by a preference for mothers as custodians, particularly of young children. The "tender years" doctrine, as developed over the first half of the 20th century, became the primary rule in custody disputes, literally dictating maternal custody unless the mother was found to be unfit.[3] This presumption was eventually supplanted in the mid-1970s by the sexually more neutral "best interests" standard.[4] In theory, this meant that both parents had an equal opportunity to obtain custody of their children upon the marriage breakdown. In practice, however, there was still an underlying preference for maternal sole custody to "fit" mothers.[5] Even under the "best interests" test, mothers obtain custody in 85 to 90 per cent of all cases, and fathers rarely.[6]

But times are changing. Today there are a number of significant social trends that should cause us to re-examine the traditional practice of awarding sole custody to mothers. The women's movement, for one, with its emphasis on equality of the sexes, has meant that more women are pursuing careers outside the home, while men are participating to a far greater extent in child rearing and household maintenance functions. As one writer puts it:

---

2 H.H. Foster and D.J. Freed, "Life with Father: 1978" (1978), 11 Fam. L.Q. 321. See also Derdeyn, "Child Custody Contests in Historical Perspective" (1978), 12 Am. J. Psych. 133.

3 The "tender years" doctrine is said to have originated with the passage of Talfourds Act by the English Parliament in 1839 permitting Chancery to award custody to the mother if the child was less than 7 years of age: See Mnookin, "Child Custody Adjudication: Judicial Functions in the Face of Indeterminacy" (1975), 39 L. & Contemp. Prob. 226 at 233.

4 The "best interests" test can be traced back to an 1881 decision of a Kansas court in which custody of a 5-year-old girl was awarded to a grandmother who had raised her rather than her natural father. The paramount consideration was said to be the welfare of the child: see *Chapsky v. Wood*, 26 Kan. 650 (1881).

5 Elizabeth Scott and Andre Derdeyn, "Rethinking Joint Custody" (1984), 45 Ohio St. L.J. 455 at 468; see *infra*, n. 61.

6 Statistics Canada, *Divorce: Law and the Family in Canada* (1983), at 207.

> The sole custody concept is a product of a world that no longer exists. It is based on the premise that mother is the nurturer, father is the breadwinner, and schools, church and extended family are there to offer support. . . . Sixy per-cent of women with children now work. Fathers nurture. Parenting has become more complicated and the social supporting infrastructure is not what it was.[7]

Moreover, child development research which, in the past, focused almost exclusively on the role of the mother, has recently emphasized the importance of fathers in the healthy development of children.[8]

At the same time as fathers are participating more and gaining more recognition for their role, families are splitting up at an unprecedented rate. Since the federal Divorce Act[9] was amended in 1968, the divorce rate has more than doubled, increasing from 124.2 per 100,000 population to 251.3 in 1979.[10] Some 40 per cent of all Canadian marriages now end in divorce and this number is rising. Statistics Canada estimates that in excess of 1 per cent of all existing families have been dissolved in each year since the mid-1970s, a figure which "likely represents only the tip of the family and marriage dissolution ice-berg".[11] Over half a million dependent children have been affected by divorce during the past decade — more than the entire population of the city of Vancouver.[12]

Given the above trends, it is not surprising that increasing numbers of fathers desire to remain involved with their children in a significant way following marriage breakdown and that many of them are seeking custody of their children.

2. Joint Custody in the United States

Changing family structures and new theories of child development have led many American states to re-examine traditional custody preferences and to enact legislation which provides for some form of joint custody or shared parenting on marriage breakdown.[13] In 1979 only 5 states had so-called "joint

---

7   Sheila F.G. Schwartz, "Toward a Presumption of Joint Custody" (1984), 18 Fam. L.Q. 225 at 233.

8   See Roth, "The Tender Years Presumption in Child Custody Disputes" (1975), 15 J. Fam. L. 423.

9   R.S.C. 1970, c. D-8.

10   *Supra*, n. 6 at 81.

11   *Ibid.*, at 60.

12   *Ibid.*, at 96.

13   There is at this time no generally accepted legal definition of the term "joint custody". As used here, "joint custody" is synonymous with "shared parenting", and describes a custodial arrangement in which both parents continue to enjoy joint legal responsibility and authority for the care and control of the child after the separation and divorce.

custody" laws.[14] Today, some 32 states have such legislation, running the gamut from simple recognition of the legality of joint custody as an option available to co-operative parents to the creation of a strong presumption for joint custody as *the* custodial arrangement preferred by law.[15]

Initially, in the absence of specific legislation, some U.S. courts questioned their authority to make orders for joint custody.[16] One appellate court even went so far as to create the legal presumption that joint custody is contrary to the child's best interests.[17] Early joint custody legislation therefore was directed towards clarifying the judge's authority to allow and to order joint custody as an option in custody disputes.

Judicial reluctance to utilize this option, however, led in 1979 to the passage in California of joint custody legislation which has since served as the model for legislation in other states across the United States. The California legislation, amended in 1983, expressly states that "it is the public policy of the state to assure minor children of frequent and continuing contact with both parents after the parents have separated or dissolved their marriage".[18] Accordingly, where both parents agree, there is a statutory presumption that joint custody is in the best interests of a minor child.[19] Where parents do not agree, the statute establishes joint custody as a co-equal preference with sole custody.[20] However, if the court declines to order joint custody, it *must* specifically state in its decision the reasons for such denial.[21] Moreover, in awarding sole custody to either parent, the court *must* consider which of the two parents is more likely to allow the child frequent and continuing contact with the other parent — the so-called "friendly parent" provision.[22]

Other states have gone further in making joint custody a clear first preference[23] or in making the presumption that joint custody is in the best interests of the child, whether or not the parents agree.[24] For example, the Florida statute requires the court to order shared parenting unless this would be detrimental to

---

14   Jay Folberg, "Issues and Trends in the Law of Joint Custody", in Jay Folberg (ed.), *Joint Custody and Shared Parenting*, Association of Family and Conciliation Courts (1984), at 159.

15   For a summary of American joint custody statutes and judicial interpretations as of 1st January 1984, see Folberg, *ibid.*, App. "A", at 265.

16   *See Re Pergament*, 28 Or. App. 459 (1977).

17   *Lumbra v. Lumbra*, 136 Vt. 529 (S.C., 1978).

18   California Civil Code, s. 4600(*a*).

19   *Ibid.*, s. 4600.5(*a*).

20   *Ibid.*, s. 4600.(*b*)(1).

21   *Ibid.*, s. 4600.5(*a*).

22   *Ibid.*, s. 4600.(*b*)(1).

23   See, for example, the statutes of Kansas, Kentucky, Montana and New Mexico.

24   See the statutes of Florida, Idaho and New Hampshire.

the child.[25] Similarly, in Idaho a denial of joint custody must be based on a preponderance of the evidence.[26] On the other hand, Colorado requires a finding that joint custody would be advantageous to the child before it can be ordered.[27] Today, in the United States all but a handful of joint custody laws authorize, implicitly or explicitly, court-ordered joint custody in the absence of parental agreement.[28] Some judges remain reluctant to order joint "physical" custody in such cases, but will compel joint "legal" custody when requested by one parent or even on the court's own motion.[29] In order to promote agreement in custody disputes, some states encourage and others require that the parties attend at state-supported counselling and mediation services.[30] Yet another approach has been to label joint custody orders "provisional" in order that they can be implemented on a trial basis.[31] Thus, while there is still much variation in law from state to state, it is obvious that the concept of joint custody has received significant recognition and acceptance in the child custody laws of the United States. Let us now turn to the Canadian scene.

3. Joint Custody in Canada

In contrast to the United States, no Canadian province has yet enacted legislation specifically making joint custody a preference in child custody arrangements or authorizing joint custody in the face of opposition by one or both parents. The law in this area appears to be governed by two cases of the Ontario Court of Appeal which were decided early in the debate over joint custody (1979), and which have since been followed elsewhere in Canada.[32]

The *Baker* case was the first decision of a Canadian superior court on joint custody. In her trial judgment, dated 25th April 1978, Boland J. wrote:

> "Courts must be responsive to the winds of change. In today's society, the breakdown of the traditional family is increasingly common, and new ways of defining post-divorce family structures are desparately needed. It is apparent that the traditional award of custody to the mother and access to the father is the cause of many of the problems and most of the tensions

---

25   Florida Stat. s. 61. 13(2)(6)(2)(1982, Supp.).

26   Idaho Code, s. 32-717 B(4) (1982).

27   Col. Rev. Stat., s. 1410-124(4) (1983).

28   See Scott and Derdeyn, "Rethinking Joint Custody" (1984), 45 Ohio St. L.J. 455 at 456, and Folberg, *supra*, n. 14, App. "A".

29   See *Re Levin*, 102 C.A. 3d 981 (1980); *Re Wood*, 141 C. A. 3d 671 (1983); *Weidner v. Weidner*, 338 N.W. 2d 351 (Iowa S.C., 1983); and *Beck v. Beck*, 84 N.J. 451 (Sup. Ct., 1981).

30   See, for example, the statutes of California, Connecticut and Florida.

31   Ohio Rev. Code Ann. s. 3109. 04(A).

32   See *Baker v. Baker* (1979), 8 R.F.L. (2d) 236 (Ont. C.A.); and *Kruger v. Kruger* (1979), 11 R.F.L. (2d) 52 (Ont. C.A.).

between parents and children and between the parents themselves. Our courts see many cases in which the father has been deprived of access. Gradually he loses interest or finds he cannot afford to continue his court battles, and as a result the child is deprived of the love, influence and financial support of its father. Joint custody would seem to be the ideal solution to present challenges and past experiences."[33]

Unfortunately, even the strongest advocates of joint custody would probably agree that *Baker* was not an appropriate case for joint custody. Neither party in this bitter court battle requested or wanted joint custody; both had demonstrated an inability to co-operate in matters concerning the child. On the facts, then, it is not surprising that the Court of Appeal overturned the trial judgment. One writer, however, says that the appellate court went far beyond this to condemn joint custody as an alternative to the "traditional concept of custody and access" and to create a presumption in favour of sole custody in contested custody proceedings.[34]

In its judgment, the Court of Appeal criticized the trial judge for not making any reference to the "legal literature" in her reference to "experts in the field of child study".[35] In *Baker*, however, Boland J. may have been slightly ahead of her time. As we shall see below, although there was considerable popular interest in joint custody at this time, there was little, if any, actual published social science research to substantiate her claims for this novel approach. Moreover, the appellate judgment suffers from the same deficiencies as the trial judgment. It makes reference to only one article by a Toronto psychiatrist without any analysis of its merits,[36] and draws on two reported decisions of New York State courts,[37] where joint custody was refused because the parties were "so severely antagonized and embattled that joint custody could only enhance family chaos". Not stopping here, the court went even further to adopt the value-laden and highly subjective words of a colleague speaking on "divided custody":

> *"My judgment here is based on the very strong feeling that divided custody is inherently a bad thing.* A child must know where its home is and to whom it must look for guidance and admonition and the person having custody and having that responsibility must have the opportunity to exercise it without any feeling by the infant that it can look elsewhere. It may be an unfortunate thing for the spouse who does not have custody that he or she does lose a great

---

33 *Ibid.*, at 243. The trial judgment is reported at (1978), 3 R.F.L. (2d) 193.

34 Julien D. Payne and Patrick J. Boyle, "The Canadian Law and Joint Custody, Co-Parenting versus Sole Custody: A Question of Presumptions", in *Joint Custody and Shared Parenting*, Jay Folberg (ed.), Association of Family and Conciliation Courts (1984), at 245.

35 *Baker, supra*, n. 32, at 244.

36 Edward J. Rosen, "Joint Custody: In the Best Interests of the Child and Parents" (1978), 1 R.F.L. (2d) 116.

37 *Braiman v. Braiman*, 407 N.Y.S. 2d 449 (C.A., 1978); and *Dodd v. Dodd*, 403 N.Y.S. 2d 401 (S.C., 1978).

deal of the authority and indeed to some extent the love and affection of the child that might otherwise be gained, but this is one of the things which is inherent in separation and divorce. The parents cannot have it both ways."[38]

This was hardly a firm foundation upon which to limit joint custody "to the exceptional circumstances which are rarely, if ever, present in cases of disputed custody"![39]

Five months later, a judge of the Ontario Provincial Court (Family Division) attempted to narrow *Baker* to the proposition that joint custody is inappropriate "where parents are unable or unwilling to cooperate sufficiently to make the shared responsibility work properly".[40] Nasmith Prov. J. adopted the approach of the English Courts to joint custody[41], and asked himself the question:

> Has it been established on the balance of probabilities that it is in the best interests of the children to have the custodial rights of one parent abrogated? If not, what order, if any, does the evidence indicate *would* be in their best interests?[42]

Nasmith Prov. J. answered the central question in the negative and awarded joint custody even though this had not been requested by either parent. In so doing, he relied upon expert testimony which indicated that the children had coped well with the shared custody arrangement subsisting since the separation, in the absence of marked parental conflicts. Although no social science research was cited, Nasmith Prov. J. asked in his judgment:

> . . . how the judicial and health professionals came to the conclusion that it was better for a child to have only one parent particularly *in the face of studies* which indicate that the severing of the strong bonds that can exist between the child and parents may produce serious emotional trauma for the child.[43]

Within two months the Court of Appeal had occasion to review its position on joint custody. In *Kruger v. Kruger* the highest court of Ontario once again declined to award joint custody in the absence of the agreement of both parties. In this case, however, unlike *Baker*, the parents had co-operated in a *de facto* shared parenting arrangement prior to trial and the father had requested an order for joint custody in appealing an award of sole custody to the mother. A majority

---

38   *Baker, supra*, n. 32, at 246. Emphasis added.

39   *Ibid.*

40   *Compeau v. Compeau* (1979), 2 Fam. L. Rev. 284 (Ont Prov. Ct.).

41   *Jussa v. Jussa*, [1972] 1 W.L.R. 881 (Fam. Div.).

42   *Compeau, supra*, n. 40, at 287.

43   *Ibid.* Emphasis added.

of the court held that the fact there was no "agreement" between the parties on the subject of joint custody was a major consideration in deciding whether to order it. The majority stated:

> The fact remains that in this case there is no agreement between the parties on the issue of joint custody. That fact, in my opinion, *makes all the difference* to the approach which should be taken by this court to the question whether it should now seek to impose an order for joint custody. . . .[44]

In this case, lack of agreement seemed to be equated with the contesting of legal proceedings, from which the court inferred an unwillingness or inability of the parents to co-operate in child rearing. In fact, the only evidence of the wife's views on joint custody came indirectly through her counsel, on the appeal. When asked whether the wife would agree to or accept an order for joint custody, her counsel replied merely that his instructions were to support the trial judgment.[45] From this, the court assumed that, "she is not agreeable to such an order and is not prepared to accept it of her own will".[46]

Moreover, the court refused to assume that the two parties, who had been able to get along together as parents under the interim custody arrangement in effect before the trial, would continue to do so in future. The majority concluded that:

> . . . any court that is considering the making of an award of joint custody, should be guided by the following precepts: if the court has before it the right combination of thoughtful and mature parents who understand what is involved in such an arrangement and are willing to try it, the court should feel encouraged to go ahead with it; but if they are not evidently willing, the court should not seek to impose it on them, because it is then not likely to work, and because the price to be paid if it does not work is likely to be altogether too high to warrant taking the risk that is then present of trying it.[47]

Once again, the court considered in its reasoning the negative judgment of a New York court in *Dodd v. Dodd*, while ignoring an earlier decision of that same court, supportive of joint custody.[48] And once again, no reference was made by the majority to the burgeoning joint custody literature or the emerging social science research on the effects of divorce on children and families. Clearly, the majority did not wish to encourage joint custody as a judicial option, except on the consent of the parties — the very circumstances in which such an order would be unnecessary!

---

44 *Kruger, supra*, n. 32, at 80. Emphasis added.

45 One wonders whether the option was ever put to her directly for consideration.

46 *Kruger, supra*, n. 32, at 79.

47 *Ibid.*, at 82.

48 *Perotti v. Perotti*, 78 Misc. 2d 131 (S.C., 1974).

In a strong dissent, Wilson J.A. urges that:

> It is perhaps timely for courts in Canada to shed their "healthy cynicism" and reflect in their orders a greater appreciation of the hurt inflicted upon a child by the severance of its relationship with one of its parents. While purporting to award custody on the basis of the child's best interests, our courts have tended to overlook that in some circumstances it may be in the child's best interests not to choose between the parents but to do everything possible to maintain the child's relationship with both parents.[49]

In support of her opinion, she quotes the Law Reform Commission of Canada, in its Report on Family Law:

> "The law should be made more flexible, making custody less an all-or-nothing proposition; a judicial determination that one parent will assume primary responsibility for raising and caring for a child should not necessarily exclude the other from the legal right to participate as a parent in many other significant areas of the child's life."[50]

In her view,

> . . . that participation should only be terminated if the state of the husband and wife relationship is such as to make it necessary or desirable to do so. It certainly should not be done without due consideration being given to the full range of options open to the court.[51]

Wilson J.A. then canvasses the various options open to the court, including joint custody, and expresses the opinion that "the appropriate option in any given case will be the one which best serves the needs of the child or children". Showing a keen awareness of the impact of divorce on all members of the family, she then goes on to say:

> These developments in the approach of the courts to custody matters all reflect a new awareness that in the mind of a child authority and love are inter-related and that the transformation of a mother or father into a "visitor" is a traumatic experience for a child frequently attended by feelings of rejection and guilt. And in many cases it is wholly unnecessary. Most mature adults, after the initial trauma has worn off, are able to overcome the hostility attendant on the dissolution of their marriages or at the very least are capable of subserving it to the interests of their children. This is particularly so now that the social stigma attending divorce has all but disappeared and men and women are picking themselves up and putting their lives together again. Indeed, the so-called "friendly divorce" is one of the phenomena of our time. It is in this social milieu that more imaginative and, if I may say so, more humane custody orders find their place.

> And what if occasional resort has to be made to the courts when the parents cannot agree on a major matter affecting the child? Is this to be the determinative consideration? It seems to me to be a modest price to pay in order to preserve a child's confidence in the love of his parents and with it his own sense of security and self-esteem.[52]

---

49   *Kruger, supra*, n. 32, at 69.

50   *Ibid.*, at 70.

51   *Ibid.*

52   *Ibid.*, at 73.

In the instant case, Wilson J.A. would have awarded joint (legal) custody to both parents with care and control of the children to the mother and liberal access to the father.[53]

The decisions in *Baker* and *Kruger* did not sound the death knell for joint custody in Canada.[54] Most likely, however, they slowed the acceptance of this custody option, particularly among the legal profession. As a result the full range of custody options envisaged by Wilson J.A. may not have been considered in all custody disputes and some Canadian children (and their families) may thereby have been deprived of an arrangement which would best serve their short and long-term interests. This writer argues that it is time to take a second look at joint custody as a viable custody option for separating and divorcing families in Canada. The second half of this paper will re-examine the cautious approach of Canadian courts to this alternative and consider whether this caution can now safely be relaxed, in light of research findings which are currently available from the social sciences.

II THE LITERATURE

1. The General Literature

The first articles on the subject of joint custody appeared in the popular press and magazines in or about the year 1974. Generally, these were anecdotal reports describing personal experiences with a shared parenting arrangement. Three references to joint custody appeared in the legal literature in 1975 and three more in the psychological literature the following year.[55] Since 1977, about 15 to 20 books have been written each year on custody, many of these on joint custody.

The first major book on joint custody, *The Disposable Parent*, by Roman and Haddad, was published in 1978.[56] In it, the authors challenge the traditional practices of courts in awarding child custody in divorce, and criticize the views expressed by Goldstein, Freud and Solnit in their controversial book *Beyond the*

---

53 Some writers and statutes distinguish between joint "legal" and joint "physical" custody. The former refers to an arrangement whereby the child resides primarily with one parent who has responsibility for the day-to-day care of the child, with both parents sharing equal rights and responsibilities for major decisions affecting the child's life. Joint "physical" custody includes sharing the residential care of the child as well as decision making.

54 Julien E. Payne, "Co-Parenting Revisited" (1979), 2 Fam. L. Rev. 243.

55 Philip M. Stahl, "A Review of Joint and Shared Parenting Literature", in Jay Folberg (ed.), *Joint Custody and Shared Parenting*. Association of Family and Conciliation Courts (1984), at 26.

56 M. Roman and W. Haddad, *The Disposable Parent* (1978).

Best Interests of the Child.[57] This influential little volume, co-authored in 1973 by the daughter of the founder of psychoanalysis, asserts that "children have difficulty in relating positively to, profiting from, and maintaining contact with two psychological parents who are not in positive contact with each other".[58] Assuming that divorced parents cannot be in "positive contact", the authors recommend that custody be expeditiously and permanently awarded to the parent most likely to be the "psychological parent" and, further, that the non-custodial parent have no legally enforceable rights to visit the child, all such contact to be solely within the discretion and control of the custodial parent. Although the authors' conclusions are wholly unsupported by empirical evidence, they have been widely accepted by the courts and quoted in reported child custody cases.[59] This is often in striking contrast to the courts' non-use of empirical data supporting joint custody, and may be explained in part on the basis that the views of Goldstein, Freud and Solnit lend support to the courts' traditional practices in custody matters.

Other critics argue that, "rather than fostering co-operation between the parents, the guidelines developed in *Beyond the Best Interests of the Child* promote a situation where parents are pitted against each other in a 'winner take all' battle".[60] Schwartz says:

> The notion of winner takes all causes the parents to take adversary positions regarding custody. It forces exaggeration and mistruth. It discourages the parents from focusing on what is really in the best interests of any individual child. It discourages mature compromise and encourages competition for control and struggles for power.[61]

Although there has been much written on the subject of joint custody in the past decade, as yet there have been few formal research projects to study this alternative and its possible effects. We turn next to consider the empirical research.

2. The Empirical Research: Critique and Overview

The empirical literature presently consists of 14 research studies.[62] Taken

---

57   J. Goldstein, A. Freud and A.J. Solnit, *Beyond the Best Interests of the Child* (1973).

58   *Ibid.*, at 38.

59   Jay Folberg, and Marva Graham, "Joint Custody of Children Following Divorce" (1979), 12 U.C. D.L. Rev. 523; see *supra*, nn. 16 and 22 at 526 and 559 respectively.

60   *Ibid.*, at 558.

61   Schwartz, "Toward a Presumption of Joint Custody" (1984), 18 Fam. L.Q. 225 at 231.

62   The studies in chronological order are:
      1. H.F. Keshet and K.M. Rosenthal, "Fathering after Marital Separation" (1978), 23(1) Soc. Wk. 11-18.
      2. K.E. Gersick, "Fathers by Choice: Divorced Men who Receive Custody of their Children", in G. Levinger and O.C. Mole (eds.), *Divorce and Separation: Contexts, Causes, and*

individually, no single study can be said to demonstrate with any certainty the superiority of joint over sole custody. All 14 are characterized to a greater or lesser degree by sampling and methodological deficiencies which cast doubt upon their individual findings. These deficiencies could be successfully exploited in cross-examination by counsel opposed to joint custody.

Typically, the samples are extremely small in size, and biased as a result of non-random selection. Almost all the subjects are white, middle class parents who voluntarily chose joint custody and who made themselves available for the purposes of the research. Hardly any include families with court-ordered joint custody or with custody agreements reached "in the shadow of coercive laws".[63] This seriously limits the possibilities of generalizing from the results. On the other hand, the intensive study of small numbers of joint custody families can be very useful in generating theories and hypotheses for future testing. The existing studies rarely state any explicit theoretical basis or hypotheses to be tested, and do not clearly identify dependent and independent variables.

Moreover, the designs of the various research studies are quite heterogeneous, making comparisons between them difficult. Virtually all suffer from a serious absence of control groups. Ideally, two kinds of controls should be built into the research design:

Consequences (1979).

3. A. Abarbanel, "Shared Parenting after Separation and Divorce: A Study of Joint Custody" (1979), 49 Am. J. Orthopsychiat. 320-29.

4. J. B. Grief, "Fathers, Children, and Joint Custody" (1979), 49 Am. J. Orthopsychiat. 311-19.

5. N. M. Nehls and M. Morgenbesser, "Joint Custody: An Exploration of the Issues" (1980), 19 Fam. Process 117-25.

6. C.R. Ahrons, "The Continuing Coparental Relationship between Divorced Spouses" (1981), 51 Am. J. Orthopsychiat. 415-28.

7. Susan Steinman, "The Experience of Children in a Joint Custody Arrangement: A Report of a Study", [1981] Am. J. Ortho. 403-414.

8. M.A. Watson, "Custody Alternatives: Defining the Best Interests of the Children" (1981), 30 Fam. Rel. 474-79.

9. S.W. White and B.C. Bloom, "Factors Related to the Adjustment of Divorcing Men" (1981), 30 Fam. Rel. 349-60.

10. F.W. Ilfeld Jr., H.Z. Ilfeld, J.R. Alexander, "Does Joint Custody Work? A First Look at Outcome Data of Relitigation" (1982), 139(1) Am. J. Psychiat. 62-66.

11. B. Rothberg, "Joint Custody: Parental Problems and Satisfaction" (1983), 22 Fam. Process 43-52.

12. G.A. Awad, "Joint Custody: Preliminary Impressions" (1983), 28 Can. J. Psychiat. 41-44.

13. Howard H. Irving, Michael Benjamin, and Nicolas Trocme, "Shared Parenting: An Empirical Analysis Utilizing a Large Canadian Data Base", in Folberg (ed.), *Joint Custody and Shared Parenting* (1984).

14. W.P.C. Phear, J.C. Beck, B.B. Hauser, S.C. Clark, and R.A. Whitney, "An Empirical Study of Custody Agreements: Joint Versus Sole Legal Custody", in Folberg (ed.), *Joint Custody and Shared Parenting* (1984).

63   Scott and Derdeyn, "Rethinking Joint Custody" (1984), 45 Ohio St. L.J. 455 at 485.

(a) a systematic comparison of joint and sole custody families, matched on specific characteristics, such as family size, income, social class, number and ages of children; and

(b) comparison between different sub-types of joint custody arrangements, such as voluntary court-ordered, physical versus legal custody, and so on.

This would enable us to compare both within and between the two groups and to formulate criteria regarding which types of families are best suited for which types of joint custody arrangements.[64]

Other weaknesses of the existing studies derive from their almost exclusive reliance on the clinical interview as the method of data collection. This introduces the possibility of "interviewer bias" and serves to undermine the reliability of the research findings. Unfortunately, few of the "joint custody" studies attempt to guard against bias by also using independent "objective" measures, such as standard psychological tests, scales, and direct observation.

Moreover, the focus of the clinical interview is on the individual parent as the primary unit of analysis, rather than on the parental relationship or family system. In many studies only one parent is included in the sample, and data about children is almost always obtained through the report of that parent rather than by direct interview of the children themselves. This approach ignores a substantial body of existing research which says that the family as a whole is greater than the sum of its constituent parts. Moreover, it is highly doubtful that individual family members can report accurately on significant interactional processes of which they themselves may be unaware. What is needed are more measures taken of all members of the family, and of the family as a system, using a broader range of data gathering techniques (including direct observation by a neutral third party).[65] Also needed are longitudinal studies which examine changes in family interactions around joint custody over time.

One final comment concerns the surprisingly unsophisticated nature of the data analysis in "joint custody" research, compared with other social science research. Of the 14 studies, only a few use simple percentages, while even fewer employ standard statistical tests (typically, the "chi-square" test). Even here, a failure to report concurrent strength coefficients casts doubt upon the validity of the research findings and may lead to spurious conclusions.[66] Future researchers

---

64   Michael Benjamin and Howard H. Irving, "Research and Shared Parenting: A Critical Review", June 1984 — in press.

65   *Ibid.*

66   *Ibid.*

should adopt multi-operational/multi-dimensional approaches using a variety of statistical measures, including the multi-variate techniques of regression analysis.[67]

Having said that no one study can conclusively demonstrate the superiority of joint over sole custody, looking at the empirical literature as a whole one cannot ignore the overall coherence of the research findings.

One study after another reports few problems of adjustment and high degrees of satisfaction with a joint custody arrangement. The two studies reporting negative outcomes suffer from the most serious methodological deficiencies.[68]

Irving sums it up as follows:

> . . . if similar findings are consistently reported despite variations in sample size, data collection instruments and analytical procedures, then these findings may be given considerable weight. . . . Conclusions drawn from such a data base merit serious attention.[69]

Let us now turn to the substantive findings from the extant empirical research.

3. Joint Custody and Children

The most frequently mentioned research, when speaking about children and divorce, is that of Wallerstein and Kelly. Commencing in 1971, Wallerstein and Kelly conducted a longitudinal clinical study of 60 divorced families in California in which the mother had sole custody of 131 children ranging in age from 3 to 18 years. Clinical interviews with both the parents and children (but no nuclear family control group) were done within 6 months of separation, and again at 18 months and 5 years after separation. The results were reported in a series of journal articles and ultimately a book entitled, *Surviving the Breakup: How Children and Parents Cope with Divorce* (1980), by J. Wallerstein and J. Kelly.

Wallerstein and Kelly report that most children experience feelings of loss following their parents' divorce and further that the effects of their being left in the almost exclusive care of one parent are negative. Among the "sole custody" children, they noted problems of attachment and separation anxiety, loyalty conflicts, strained interaction with parents (especially the non-custodial parent), disturbed cognitive performance and school functioning, and sex role identi-

---

67 W. Glenn Clingempeel, and D. Dickon Reppucci, "Joint Custody after Divorce: Major Issues and Goals for Research", in Folberg (ed.), *Joint Custody and Shared Parenting* (1984), at 109.

68 Benjamin and Irving, *supra*, n. 64.

69 *Ibid.*

fication. Moreover, consistent with other research studies, these problems were more intense and persistent for boys than for girls.[70] Wallerstein and Kelly, however, went on to demonstrate that a significant relationship exists between the amount of parental contact and positive post-divorce adjustment of children — the more contact with the non-custodial parent, the better adjusted the child, academically and socially. They conclude that children adjust much better to divorce if they can maintain a stable and loving relationship with both parents, and recommend joint custody as the custody option of choice.

The Wallerstein and Kelly research is significant for traditional custody policy because it shows:

(a) that traditional sole custody is not without problems and may in fact have serious negative effects on children;

(b) that the traditional visiting pattern of every other weekend is simply not enough for most children and their fathers to maintain a positive relationship over time; and

(c) that the greater incidence of adjustment problems for boys may be a function of a custody policy which places them more often in the sole custody of their mothers.

And what do we learn from the research on "joint custody" children? Although most researchers have not interviewed these children directly (relying instead on parental reports), their findings concerning them are remarkably consistent. Most, although not all, "joint custody" children made a relatively easy adjustment to the demands of living in two households, even where their parents had very different life-styles. Their adjustment was facilitated by co-operation between the parents, the use of transition schedules that were regular and predictable, and by the fact that their parents typically lived in relatively close geographical proximity to one another. Problems occurred in only a minority of cases which tended not to have these characteristics.

Abarbanel, in her in-depth case study of four joint custody families, found that some children experienced disruption in moving between homes, but that all were able to manage. Most of the children she studied felt "at home" in both environments and saw themselves living in two homes. Abarbanel suggests:

> Perhaps the security of an ongoing relationship with two psychological parents helps to provide the means to cope successfully with the uprooting effects of shifting households.[71]

In another study, Steinman looked at 32 joint custody "veterans" ranging in age from 4 to 15 years. Seventy-five per cent of these children had lived in joint custody arrangements for over one half of their lives. Steinman found that joint custody was beneficial for children in three major areas:

---

70   J. Santrok, "Relation of Type and Onset of Father Absence to Cognitive Development" (1972), 43 Child Development 455.

71   Abarbanel, *supra*, n. 62, at 328.

(a) they received the clear message that they were loved and wanted by *both* parents;

(b) they had a sense of importance in their family and the knowledge that their parents made great efforts to jointly care for them, both factors being important to their self-esteem; and

(c) they had physical access to both parents, and the psychological permission to love and be with both parents. This protected them from the crippling loyalty conflicts often seen in children caught in the crossfire of their parents' ongoing battles.[72]

Moreover, Steinman points out:

> These children clearly had two psychological parents to whom they were positively attached and loyal, despite the marital split. This does not support the assumption in Freud, Solnit and Goldstein's *Beyond the Best Interests of the Child* that children cannot relate well to two separated parents who are not in positive relation to one another. We have found that children can relate when parents who cannot relate positively as husband and wife can communicate constructively around the children. In our sample, in which parents generally supported each other as parents and supported the child's relationship with the other parent, the children benefitted from watching their parents go to a great deal of effort to jointly care for them. It gave them a sense of importance in their family.[73]

Steinman goes on to deal with a major concern of those opposing joint custody, that is, whether switching homes generates anxiety and confusion in the child about where he or she belongs. Steinman found that most of the children were impressively able to keep their complex schedules in mind and demonstrated a sense of mastery over switching back and forth between homes. Twenty-five per cent of the children, however, were anxious and insecure, worrying about themselves, their parents and their possessions. These children fell into 2 groups: 4 to 5-year-old girls (2 others of this age group who travelled with sisters were not having trouble) and 7 to 9-year-old boys who felt insecure about their ability to keep track of things and who were having learning problems at school. We do not know whether these children might also have experienced problems in sole custody situations.

The research also indicates that continuity of school life and friendships were very important to the children studied, particularly the latency age and adolescent children. They valued the stability of remaining in one school and used schools as an anchor. Adolescents, however, preferred to reside primarily in only one home, while seeing the other parent on a regular basis. Their parents continued to make decisions jointly.

---

72 Susan Steinman, "Joint Custody: What We Know, What We Have Yet to Learn and the Judicial and Legislative Implications" (1983), 16 U.C. D.L. Rev. 739 at 747.

73 *Ibid.*

The empirical research, therefore, would not appear to lend support to the subjective concerns of the Ontario Court of Appeal expressed by Weatherston J. and adopted in *Baker*.[74] On the contrary, it appears that many children can and do benefit from having two homes on divorce. We should not assume automatically that they need only one.

Let us now turn to the research on joint custody parents.

4. Joint Custody and Parents

Available research on divorcing adults shows that most post-divorce mothers with sole custody feel overburdened and imprisoned by their children. Ultimately, they become emotionally and physically exhausted and socially isolated.[75] Wallerstein and Kelly observed that the mother/child relationship deteriorated seriously within the first year after divorce.

At the same time, divorcing fathers are not sufficiently burdened. In a study of 40 separated or divorced fathers of 63 children, 80 per cent in the sole custody of their mothers and 20 per cent in joint custody, Grief reported that non-custodial fathers experienced stress severe enough to bring on physical problems, depression, and a strong sense of loss.[76] In the usual pattern, fathers had lost wife, home and children, and were left with only visitation rights and support obligations. Some became so overwhelmed by the pain of seeing their children only infrequently that they withdrew and visited even less. Grief reports:

> The greater the father's involvement with his child, the greater his sense of having an ongoing parental role in the child's life after divorce. Most importantly, this becomes self-reinforcing: the more opportunities fathers have to act as fathers, the more they see themselves as fathers and seek to continue that involvement. . . .
>
> On the other hand the less opportunity fathers have to act as fathers, the less they see themselves as fathers and ultimately, the less they are motivated to be with their children. A clear danger of child absence is perceived role loss, leading to further withdrawal from the child.[77]

An analysis of the "joint custody" research reveals that something other than the traditional "all or nothing" approach to custody can benefit both mothers and fathers, as well as children. Although society still tends to be critical of mothers who do not seek sole custody of their children, those who do

---

74 See quote from *Baker v. Baker* (1979), 8 R.F.L. (2d) 236 (Ont. C.A.), *supra*, at 190-91.

75 Folberg and Graham, "Issues and Trends in the Law of Joint Custody", in J. Folberg (ed.), *Joint Custody and Shared Parenting* (1984), at 553.

76 Grief, *supra*, n. 62.

77 *Ibid*.

choose joint custody get to share the responsibilities and burdens of child rearing on an everyday basis.[78] Moreover, there is emerging evidence of a link between a continuing relationship with the child and compliance with child support obligations:

> One of the most positive attributes of joint custody is its potential for avoiding problems of nonsupport arising out of bitterness over the custodial decision. Not only does regular contact with the children create an incentive to provide for their needs, but participating in routine activities of feeding, clothing, housing and caring for children realistically brings home to both parents the escalating expenses of rearing them and promotes more flexible attitudes. Additionally, the likely increased contact between co-parents makes each more aware of the financial capabilities of the other and breeds sensitivity to what each can monetarily contribute. Parents who can rely on each other for more than just economic help are more apt to be understanding of the financial pinches that most sometime encounter.[79]

For fathers, the greatest benefit of joint custody is the alleviation of the sense of loss associated with sole maternal custody.

There is also consensus in the literature that "joint custody" parents adjust much better than their "sole custody" counterparts to the trauma of separation and divorce. The only two studies which do not support this finding are those with the most serious deficiencies from a research point of view.[80] Moreover, some 77 to 84 per cent of joint custody parents reported high levels of satisfaction with the shared parenting arrangement overall, and with parent/child relations in particular. Irving has identified three sub-groups of parents:

(a) those for whom shared parenting was the only custody arrangement considered and who reported nearly instant success;

(b) those who selected shared parenting with initial uncertainty, encountered varying levels of difficulty, but who ultimately found it satisfying; and

(c) those who typically came to shared parenting through court or court services and for whom it never became satisfying.[81]

Steinman, in her study, identified those characteristics of parents which were important in making joint custody work:

> Foremost was the sense of respect for one another as parents, despite the disappointment in each other as marriage partners. Each appreciated the value of the other to the child, and was sensitive to the possible loss of a parent-child relationship. The parents' relationships were characterized by a similarity in basic child-rearing values. There was the capacity to tolerate the minor differences that existed and to distinguish the important from the unimportant ones.

---

78   Nehls, *supra*, n. 62.

79   Folberg and Graham, *supra*, n. 75, at 564.

80   Benjamin and Irving, "Research and Shared Parenting: A Critical Review", June 1984 — in press.

81   *Ibid.*

These parents were able to relinquish control and not interfere in the other parent's relationship with the child. They were personally flexible and able to accommodate to the needs of the arrangement, the child, and even to the other parent. These were not people who were rigid in their thinking or behaviour. There was a capacity to contain their anger and hostility and to divert it away from the children. There was an ability to take responsibility for their part in the break-up and their current life rather than project blame onto their ex-mate. Finally, there was a sense of parity in these co-parental relationships. They accepted the premise that they were equally significant to and capable of caring for the children. This meant not only the genuine valuing of the other as a parent in raising the child but, equally as important it enhanced the parents' own self-confidence. It was important that each parent had a sense of self-esteem as a parent in his or her own right in order to maintain the balance in the co-parental relationship. These parents were able to separate out their roles and feelings as parents from the marital and divorce-engendered conflicts. They had rarely argued about the children during the marriage, and were able to maintain a "conflict free" sphere around the children, which they protected through the divorcing process. This capacity was central to a smooth running co-parental arrangement. These characteristics, together with a strong personal commitment to the idea of joint custody as a fair and moral solution and commitment to their children, allowed these parents to maintain the arrangement over a number of years.[82]

Although not specifically mentioned, the theme of Steinman's profile is parental co-operation.

Several researchers have studied the co-parental relationship in joint custody families. Given that these parents have either separated or divorced, one might expect a significant degree of conflict stimulated by the frequent contacts which are a part of joint custody. This expectation is not confirmed by the empirical data. The majority of joint custody parents report little or no difficulty in co-operating with each other with respect to the children. This was so even where the marriage had failed because of personality conflicts or communication problems, and there had been a high level of interpersonal conflict at the time of separation. Most respondents reported that their relationship with their former spouse was very or moderately friendly and that, over time, it had remained the same or become more positive.[83] Positive relationships continued even when one or both parents remarried or had a new partner.

The explanation given is that joint custody parents share an intense commitment to parenting *per se*, place great importance on the well-being of their children and are able to circumscribe areas of continuing marital conflict. They accomplish the latter by restricting their interaction to "safe" areas, seldom or never talking about matters that do not concern the children. There is increasing evidence that couples are able to co-operate in shared parenting even though they do not like each other. Woolley found that:

---

82   Steinman, *supra*, n. 72, at 745.

83   Irving, *supra*, n. 80, at 132.

Although many sharing parents became friends after they had been sharing for a while, many others did not. . . . It is not necessary to like each other as people even though they trust each other as parents.[84]

This ability of couples to isolate their marital conflicts from their roles as parents is perhaps the most significant finding coming out of the joint custody research. Traditionally, we have assumed that couples who cannot stay married are by nature hostile to one another and therefore incapable of co-operation. Kelly points out that parents choose to divorce because of unmet needs in the marital relationship and rarely for reasons that have anything to do with their children. We know from this, she says, that parents not in dispute regarding their children prior to divorce, are likely to co-operate thereafter concerning child rearing, despite hostilities evoked by the failed marriage. In most cases, this hostility diminishes during the first year after separation.[85]

What are the implications of the research for court-ordered joint custody in the absence of parental agreement?

5. The Courts and Joint Custody

The joint custody debate is most heated around the question of whether a court should order joint custody in the absence of the agreement of one or both parties. Unfortunately, this is also the area where the existing "joint custody" research assists us the least. No studies have yet been completed that compare "court-ordered" and "voluntary" joint custody families, and very few existing studies even contain families who came to joint custody through the courts or court services (Irving, Ilfeld and Phear excepted). Thus, we must take care not to generalize about joint custody families on the basis of data obtained from biased samples — most of those studied to date chose joint custody freely and were highly motivated to make it work.

The Canadian courts have come down fairly heavily on the side against making orders for joint custody unless the parties can come to an "understanding" (that is, agreement) on at least two essential matters:

(a) each of them accepts that the other is a fit parent to have custody of their children on the shared basis to be arranged; and

(b) each of them is persuaded that he or she can co-operate with the other and that the other in turn can co-operate with him or her, on the basis to be arranged.[86]

---

84 Persia Woolley, "Shared Custody" (1978), 1 Fam. Advocate 6 at 9.

85 Joan B. Kelly, "Further Observations on Joint Custody" (1983), 16 U.C. D.L. Rev. 762 at 763.

86 *Kruger v. Kruger* (1979), 11 R.F.L. (2d) 52 (Ont. C.A.).

This leaves it open for only one spouse to question the parties' ability to "co-operate" and so to remove the option from the court's consideration — notwithstanding the other's positive convictions and demonstrable evidence of past cooperation. Kelly has expressed serious concerns about a policy which requires that *both* parents must agree to a joint custody order. She notes that it is usually the father who seeks joint custody and the mother who opposes it. In her view, the mother's position is enhanced by the knowledge that any refusal on her part will preclude a joint custody order regardless of her reasons. Kelly notes:

> Some women legitimately refuse joint physical custody because they have lived with men who have emotionally or physically abused their children. And some seek relief from physical spousal abuse or harassment. Others who refuse, however, are angry and rejected women who seek revenge and a reinstatement of self-esteem by using their children to punish a spouse who has terminated the marriage. There are also women whose identities are so bound up in their role as full time mother that they can not envision sharing the parenting role with the father without undue anxiety and fear for their own well-being. Further, there are emotionally disturbed women who, due to their own pathology, vigorously fight a father's desire to be involved in the children's lives. Some additional women have been advised by friends or parents not to allow the father anything more than traditional every-other-weekend visitation. In these various instances, there may be no legitimate reasons based on the father's capacity to parent for refusing to consider joint custody. Yet the children of such women would be denied more generous access to their father despite the real possibility that increased contact could be more psychologically beneficial. We need to know what percentage of refusals are based on which of these or other reasons. [87]

Although there is yet no definitive research that resolves this particular issue, there is social science research on divorcing families which should cause jurists and lawyers to re-examine their underlying assumptions.

In the first place, the Ontario court in *Baker* assumed that a child needs only one home and one parent. [88] This assumption appears to have been derived from the unproven assertions of *Beyond the Best Interests of the Child*. [89] Available empirical research, however, clearly demonstrates that a child needs the continuing involvement of two parents following divorce and further that the traditional "sole custody to mother/alternate weekend access to father" order benefits no one: mothers are overburdened, fathers are shut out from their children's lives, and children are deprived of a parent's love and attention. We also know from the "joint custody" research that children can cope with the logistics of living in two separate residences and feel at home in each.

Second, the Canadian courts seem to assume that because the parties do not voluntarily agree on joint custody, they cannot or will not co-operate if this

---

87   *Supra*, n. 85, at 769.

88   *Baker v. Baker* (1979), 8 R.F.L. (2d) 236 at 246 (Ont. C.A.).

89   Weatherston J.'s judgment was written in 1974, shortly after the publication of *Beyond the Best Interests of the Child* (1973).

option is imposed on them by the court. Underlying this assumption may lie the common but unfounded belief that people who divorce are necessarily hostile and unable to co-operate about anything, including their parenting. While this may be true of some marriages, it is not true of all. In fact, the research indicates that there are substantial numbers of divorced persons who can continue to parent co-operatively even though they remain hostile to one another. Courts should not assume that the hostility which they observe at the time of litigation continues thereafter at the same intensity. There is empirical evidence that the anger between most divorcing spouses diminishes within the first year of separation (and after litigation) and that only a small percentage (15 per cent) remain intensely or pathologically angry after two years.[90] Judges must bear in mind that they see people at their worst and they should assess divorcing parents as having the potential to co-operate. Otherwise, unwarranted pessimism may preclude a co-operative parenting option in cases where it is viable.

Finally, there is no reason to assume that an order for sole custody will result in any less hostile an environment for children than an order for joint custody imposed by the courts. On the contrary, an award of sole custody to one of two parents competitively seeking custody may perpetuate hostilities and provoke further litigation between them, that is, for variation, contempt or non-support. On the other hand, an award of joint custody may create an incentive for parental co-operation, because any breakdown of the arrangement may result in an award of sole custody to the parent who did not perpetuate the failure.

If re-litigation rates are indicative of post-divorce parental conflict, then the research of Ilfeld *et al.* is significant. In a study of 414 consecutive custody cases in a Los Angeles court over a two-year period, Ilfeld found that joint custody families were involved in only half as many re-litigations on a percentage basis (16 per cent) as sole custody families (32 per cent). Even in cases when joint custody was court-ordered, without the consent of both parents, their re-litigation rate was no different than sole custody families.[91]

On the basis of what we now know, a leading proponent of joint custody concludes:

> Though court ordered joint custody may be more likely to fail than when parents agree, court ordered joint custody is not necessarily more prone to failure than an order of sole custody following a divisive court contest. The potential benefit to the child is greater because a court ordered joint custody decree may help parents discover their potential for shared parenting and require them to do more for their children rather than less.[92]

---

90 Folberg, *supra*, n. 75, at 43.

91 Ilfeld, Ilfeld and Alexander "Does Joint Custody Work? A First Look at Outcome Data of Relitigation" (1982), 139(1) Am. J. Psychiat. 66 at 139.

92 Folberg and Graham, *supra*, n. 75, at 579.

III FUTURE DIRECTIONS FOR JOINT CUSTODY IN CANADA

Despite its limitations, there is now overwhelming evidence that the continued involvement of both parents post-separation and divorce is in the best interests of children and, further, that joint custody is one way to effectively ensure such involvement. Nonetheless, proponents of joint custody acknowledge that this arrangement is not a panacea for all problems created by divorce, nor is it appropriate for all divorcing families. Joint custody should not be used indiscriminately as a judicial "cop-out" or as a means to avoid hurting one parent.

But joint custody can be a viable option for many more Canadian families than is presently thought possible. Too often this option is foreclosed to them by the preconceived ideas and personal prejudices of professionals who are there to help them with the divorcing process. And too often these ideas and prejudices are unsubstantiated or even contradicted by available empirical research.

Joint custody can no longer be ignored or dismissed as a passing fad by members of the Canadian judiciary and legal profession. The evidence is now in. It is time to extend the full range of custody options to all divorcing Canadian families, in contested as well as uncontested matters. How this might be achieved is the subject of the remainder of this paper.

In the first place, all lawyers and judges dealing with divorcing families should be made aware of the existing empirical research on joint custody, either through publications in legal journals or continuing education programs. Lawyers will then be able to inform their clients of this positive alternative to sole custody and consider it more objectively with them. Lawyers, in turn, can educate judges by calling expert witnesses to testify at custody trials with respect to the research findings. A Brandeis type brief, containing the research reports, might be prepared for an appeal.

At the same time, more research needs to be done in several areas, using more varied and sophisticated research techniques. Specifically, future research should control for as many relevant variables as possible and use multi-variate rather than univariate procedures of data analysis. At present, our knowledge of joint custody is limited almost exclusively (except Irving) to studies of middle class families who chose joint custody extra-judicially and who were highly motivated to make it work. We need more data on the outcome of joint custody reached involuntarily as the result of legal and judicial intervention and the effectiveness of this arrangement in different social classes and ethnic groups. What is the impact, for example, of financial constraints in maintaining two separate residences for a child of low income parents? We need to know more about the development of children who alternate between parental homes, and what specific combinations of age, family composition, geographical proximity and patterns of alternation result in the best psychological outcomes for them.

We need to know more about how joint custody works over time and how changes in the lives of children and parents, such as the remarriage of one or both spouses, affect the arrangement. We also need to know which children make good candidates for joint custody and those for whom the stress of living in two homes outweighs the benefits. And we need to know more about the kinds of parents who can successfully separate marital conflicts from child rearing practices in order to make joint custody work. Finally, we need long-itudinal studies of matched joint and sole custody families, comparing the responses and adjustment of children at different ages and stages of their development. And when this research is completed, we need to ensure that it is made available to all those involved in the divorcing process — professionals and families alike.

Next, more interim and provisional orders should be made for joint custody, pending a final determination of the custody issue. This would be the least disruptive arrangement for the child in that it most closely approximates the situation existing prior to the parents' separation. Moreover, it would afford judges an opportunity to assess the parents' ability to co-operate around the care of their child and allow time for the hostilities attendant upon the initial separation to moderate. This was the approach taken recently by a Master of the Ontario Supreme Court who held that the level of co-operation required to justify an order for joint custody is not the same at the interim and trial stages.[93] In an appropriate case, an interim joint custody order can be made to provide for a trial period during which it can be ascertained whether such an arrangement can work.

Lawyers and judges should also be made aware of the possibilities of enhancing parental co-operation by a referral to mediation or counselling services. In fact, this writer would argue that participation in at least one mediation session, with a clinician trained in mediation skills, should be mandatory for all parents disputing the custody of their children. Extended mediation can produce more than an agreement as to a joint custody "plan". It can also help parents develop the skills necessary to make the plan work effectively. Moreover, joint custody agreements which are reached through the process of mediation have a low "recidivism rate" and rarely come back to the courts for redetermination.[94] Lawyers should consider including in the joint custody agreement itself a provision for mediation of any future custody disputes, prior to either parent seeking relief from the court.

In addition, this author urges that Canada's federal and provincial statutes dealing with the custody of children be amended to make joint custody an

---

93   See *Sood v. Sood*, [1984] W.D.F.L. 682 (Ont. H.C.).

94   S. Gaddis, "Joint Custody of Children: A Divorce Decision Making Alternative" [1978], Conciliation Courts Review 17 at 19.

explicit option in custody cases;[95] and further, that we move in the direction of expressing a statutory presumption or at least a preference for joint custody. Such a presumption would establish joint custody as the rule rather than the exception when parents divorce and would set up an expectation that they continue to be equally responsible for the care and upbringing of their children, even though their marriage has been dissolved. The presumption, of course, could be rebutted by evidence that joint custody would be harmful to the child.

One final solution to the debate over joint custody would be to do away with the use of all traditional custody terms which imply possession and restraint. A more general designation such as "residential and decision making arrangement for children" would be less controversial and would force parents to concentrate on how they are going to get on with the business of continuing to parent their children after separation and divorce, rather than argue over semantics.

---

95   The new Divorce Act, S.C. 1986, c. 4, specifically authorizes courts to make orders granting custody "to any one or more persons" (s. 16(4)). The Act also promotes mediation and conciliation of disputes (ss. 9, 10).

6

INTERNATIONAL CHILD ABDUCTION

H. Allan Leal*

I INTRODUCTION

Reasons are not hard to find for the recent proliferation of cases involving the abduction of children by one parent across international boundaries. In most countries there has been a very substantial increase in the number of broken and dissolved marriages.

One inevitable result is that children of these unions frequently become pawns in the game of inter-spousal recrimination and they are sometimes spirited away out of reach and, therefore, beyond the influence of the other spouse. These nefarious designs are aided and abetted by the ease and speed of modern transportation facilities. They are also more serious for a country like Canada, blessed in many ways by its pluralistic ethnic mix, but in the present context afflicted by the fact that one or both spouses may retain recent and substantial connections with their country of origin. This fact makes it attractive and possible to spirit the children away in the hope of achieving a more friendly familial and judicial climate in which to assert custody rights in their favour when their marriages turn sour.

---

*Mr. Leal was Chief of the Canadian Delegation at The Hague Conference in 1980 when the Child Abduction Convention was formulated.

It must also be added that courts and judges have exacerbated the problem because they have been too eager, even with the best of motives, to assume jurisdiction in custody matters. The presence of the child within the jurisdiction, or less valid reasons, have prompted judges to settle the issue of custody rights in accordance with their own view of the matter which, admittedly, may even include their own perception of what lies in the best interests of the child. This prevalent judicial mind set in these particular circumstances will repeatedly result in the formulation of conflicting custody orders, almost invariably to the detriment of the best interests of the child.

II CRIMINAL SANCTIONS

The sanctions of the criminal law, for a variety of reasons, have proven ineffectual to deal with the problem of the abduction of a child by its parent. In Canada, the provisions of the Criminal Code deal with this issue in a cluster of sections entitled "Kidnapping and Abduction".[1] Included is a section making it a criminal offence for

> Every one who, being the parent, guardian or person having the lawful care or charge of a person under the age of fourteen years, takes, entices away, conceals, detains, receives or harbours that person in contravention of the custody provisions of a custody order in relation to that person made by a court anywhere in Canada with intent to deprive a parent or guardian or any other person who has the lawful care or charge of that person of the possession of that person. . . .[2]

Similarly, s. 250.2 makes it a criminal offence to abduct a child where no custody order has been made, but in these circumstances the consent of the Attorney General is required for prosecution.

Experience has demonstrated that even where the abduction has taken place in the circumstances of an existing custody order it is difficult to motivate police and prosecutors to lay charges — and judges and juries to convict — because of the widespread belief that criminal law is an inappropriate method of resolving what are viewed as essentially domestic disputes of a civil nature. In addition, abduction across international boundaries is attended with very considerable difficulties and obstacles in obtaining extradition of an abducting parent. In sum, the penal sanction has proven woefully inadequate as a deterrent to international child abduction. The crowning disability, of course, is the fact that even if extradition could be achieved and the abducting parent brought

---

1 Criminal Code, R.S.C. 1970, c.C-34, ss. 247 [am. 1985, c. 19, s. 40(2)], and 248-250 [all re-en. 1980-81-82-83, c. 125, s. 20].

2 S. 250.1.

back, there is no guarantee that the abducted child will be returned. The child is the victim and not the perpetrator of the offence, and, *ex hypothesi* has committed no wrong.

The increasing incidence of international child abduction by parents and the commonly shared view that the criminal law process was not adequate to cope with the problem led the Minister of Justice for Canada, the Honourable Ron Basford, Q.C., to present a brief with an outline of the problem and suggestions to control it to the meeting of the Commonwealth Law Ministers held in Winnipeg in August 1977.[3] The final communiqué of that Conference dealt with the matter in these terms:

> One particular problem of immense social importance and requiring concrete early action was that of parental abduction of children from the parent with lawful custody. It was agreed that early examination be given to greater co-operation in the enforcement of custody orders, particularly as criminal proceedings were generally unsuited for use in a family context. The [Ministers] emphasized that their concern was for the welfare of the children and that the existence of a Commonwealth scheme could reduce the number of distressing incidents.[4]

Before any definitive action was taken by the Commonwealth Secretariat, the matter was taken into the work programme of the Hague Conference on Private International Law. This initiative culminated in the Convention on the Civil Aspects of International Child Abduction in 1980 and the provisions of this convention are the subject of review in this chapter.

III COUNCIL OF EUROPE CONVENTION

Before turning to an analysis of the Hague Convention and its relevance for Ontario, reference should be made to the extended work of the Council of Europe in this area. Indeed, it had been suggested in some quarters that a broad adherence by contracting states to the Council of Europe Convention would have obviated the necessity for the Hague Convention on a similar subject matter. With respect, this suggestion is very much wide of the mark and that for a number of reasons. The Council of Europe Convention, signed at Luxembourg on 20th May 1980 and entitled the European Convention on Recognition and Enforcement of Decisions concerning Custody of Children and on Restoration of Custody of Children, in its original conception did not deal with child abduction as such but was restricted to the recognition and enforcement of custody provisions. It was decided eventually to incorporate elements dealing

---

3 *Actes et documents de la quatorzième session de la Conférence de la Haye du droit international privé* (1982), tome III, "Child Abduction", at 45.

4 Communiqué, 26th August 1977, para. 36.

with child abduction into the original convention and this explains the structure of the present Council of Europe Convention.[5] Practitioners may become aware of it in dealing with European states but Canada is not a party to the convention.

IV THE HAGUE CONVENTION ON INTERNATIONAL CHILD ABDUCTION

The genesis of The Hague Convention on Child Abduction was the general agreement on the principle that something had to be fashioned which would ensure the speedy return to his or her habitual residence of a child who had been wrongfully removed, and that the courts or other tribunals in that jurisdiction be called upon to settle the issues in the best interests of the child. Humanity and proper social ordering dictated no less.

It was for these reasons that the proposal was first made by the representative of Canada, T. Bradbrook Smith, Ministry of Justice, Ottawa, at a Special Commission meeting held at The Hague in January 1976 for the purpose of considering subjects to be included on the future work agenda of The Hague following its Thirteenth Session. The subject was formally placed on the agenda of the conference in October 1976.

A comparative and analytical report was prepared by Mr. A. Dyer, First Secretary of the Permanent Bureau of the Conference and submitted to participating states along with a questionnaire. A Special Commission was convened in March 1979 to consider the problem and, after a further meeting of the Special Commission in November 1979, a draft convention was prepared and submitted to participating governments for comment. The draft of the Special Committee and a very helpful comment upon it by Professor E. Perez-Vera of Spain made up the documentation used as a basis for discussion at the Fourteenth Session of the conference in October 1980.

At this session a commission, chaired by Professor A. E. Anton, with Professor E. Perez-Vera as Rapporteur, and including the representatives of 28 states, formulated the Convention on the Civil Aspects of International Child Abduction. On 25th October 1980 the convention was signed on behalf of Canada, France, Greece and Switzerland.

---

5 For a full discussion of the Council of Europe Convention see R. L. Jones, "Council of Europe Convention on Recognition and Enforcement of Decisions Relating to the Custody of Children" (1981), 30 I.C.L.Q. 467, and A. E. Anton, "The Hague Convention on International Child Abduction" (1981), 30 I.C.L.Q. 537. Mr. Jones was a member of the Council of Europe Committee of Experts on the Law Relating to Children and both he and Mr. Anton were members of the U.K. delegation at The Hague Conference at the session dealing with The Hague Convention on Child Abduction. Mr. Anton, a member of the Scottish Law Commission, was chairman of the commission which formulated the Child Abduction Convention.

1. The Process and History of Ratification

Article 40 of The Hague Convention on the Civil Aspects of International Child Abduction (hereinafter referred to as The Hague Convention) contains the provisions of the federal state ratification clause that has characterized The Hague and other international conventions since it was formulated by Canada and the United States and accepted at The Hague Conference in 1972. These provisions will explain the history of the ratification by Canada on behalf of certain provinces, in order to bind them, without requiring the consent of all provinces. The consent of each province is clearly required before a province can be bound since the subject matter of the convention and, therefore, its implementation falls within the classes of matters allotted to the provincial legislatures under the provisions of s. 92 of the Constitution Act, 1867.[6] The provision reads as follows:

Article 40

If a contracting State has two or more territorial units in which different systems of law are applicable in relation to matters dealt with in this Convention, it may at the time of signature, ratification, acceptance, approval or accession declare that this Convention shall extend to all its territorial units or only to one or more of them and may modify this declaration by submitting another declaration at any time.

Any such declaration shall be notified to the Ministry of Foreign Affairs of the Kingdom of The Netherlands and shall state expressly the territorial units to which the Convention applies.

In accordance with these procedures, Canada ratified The Hague Convention on behalf of the provinces of Ontario, New Brunswick, British Columbia and Manitoba on 2nd June 1983. Thus, under the provisions of Article 43, The Hague Convention came into force for Canada (therefore Ontario, New Brunswick, British Columbia and Manitoba), France and Portugal on 1st December 1983. Switzerland became a party by ratification as of 1st January 1984, and Spain as of 7th February 1986.

Subsequently, Canada, by declaration, brought the convention into force with respect to Newfoundland on 1st October 1984; Nova Scotia on 1st May 1984; Quebec on 1st January 1985; the Yukon Territory on 1st February 1985; and Prince Edward Island on 1st May 1986. The non-party provinces and territories in Canada, therefore, are Alberta, Saskatchewan, and the Northwest Territories.

---

6   For a recent and full discussion of federal state clauses in international conventions see H. Allan Leal, "Federal State Clauses and the Conventions of The Hague Conference on Private International Law" (1984), 8 Dalhousie L. J. 257.

2. Implementation

As indicated previously, the subject matter of The Hague Convention lies within the legislative competence of the provincial legislatures. The implementation of its provisions in Ontario was achieved by the passage of s. 47 of the Children's Law Reform Act.[7] Section 47 (2) provides that on and after the date the convention enters into force in respect of Ontario as set out in Article 43 of the convention, the convention is in force in Ontario and the provisions thereof are law in Ontario. The convention itself is made a schedule to s. 47 and is reproduced verbatim. Section 47 (6) provides that the Attorney General request the government of Canada to submit a declaration to the Ministry of Foreign Affairs of the Kingdom of The Netherlands, declaring that the convention extends to Ontario. As indicated previously, this has been done in accordance with the provisions of the second paragraph of Article 40 of the convention. Finally, s. 47 (7) provides that the Attorney General shall publish in the Ontario Gazette the date the convention comes into force in Ontario. This prescription has been fulfilled and the Ontario Gazette for 19th November 1983 contains notice of the coming into force for Ontario as of 1st December 1983. Lest it be thought that federal states may withdraw declarations with respect to constituent units at will, the provisions of Article 44 of the convention make it abundantly clear that constituent units are committed for a term of five years and denunciation on their behalf is subject to the same temporal and notice provisions as would apply to unitary states. Article 44 provides:

> The Convention shall remain in force for five years from the date of its entry into force in accordance with the first paragraph of Article 43. . . . If there be no denunciation, it shall be renewed tacitly every five years.
>
> Any denunciation shall be notified to the Ministry of Foreign Affairs of the Kingdom of the Netherlands at least six months before the expiry of the five year period. It may be limited to certain of the territories or territorial units to which the Convention applies.
>
> The denunciation shall have effect only as regards the State which has notified it. The Convention shall remain in force for the other Contracting States.

We now turn our attention to a detailed analysis of the substantive provisions of the convention.

3. Scope of the Convention

Although the title of chapter 1 of The Hague Convention uses the word "scope", it is meant to be synonymous with "object" and "purpose". The preamble itself affirms the principle that is now generally adopted throughout

---

7   R.S.O. 1980, c. 68, s. 47 [en. 1982, c. 20, s. 1].

the civilized world in the treatment of children generally and frequently enshrined in legislation, as it is at present in Ontario law, that the best interests of children are of paramount importance in matters relating to their custody. The preamble asserts further that the desire to serve these best interests means children ought to be protected internationally from their wrongful removal or retention away from the place of their habitual residence, care and nurturing; and that procedures should exist in the event of such removal which will ensure their prompt return to the state of their habitual residence. The preamble also presages the protection, albeit in a limited way, of the right of access. Access is the obverse side of the coin of custody rights and frequently the award of custody to one spouse is accompanied by an award of a generous right of access to the other. This may, indeed, be the only thing which permits substantial justice to be achieved where the award of joint custody is not feasible. We will deal subsequently with the limitation on access rights in the convention.

The primary purpose of the convention then, as set forth in Article 1(*a*), is "to secure the prompt return of children wrongfully removed to or retained in any Contracting State". Clearly the purpose of the convention is not to deal with recognition or enforcement of custody awards but to restore the *status quo ante* which was disrupted by the abduction and to have the matter of the custody of the child, if it is to be redefined or redetermined, dealt with by the judicial authorities with the assistance of ancillary support services in the state of the habitual residence of the child. In brief, the convention deals with custody rights, not custody decisions.

Implicit in this is the exercise of self-restraint on the part of the judicial tribunals in the requested state who would otherwise be disposed to exercise jurisdiction in making a custody award which would conceivably and usually be in conflict with an existing award in the requesting State, contrary to custody rights arising from operation of laws there, or in conflict with rights established by a recognized agreement of the parties under the law of the requesting state.

It is of special importance for Ontario legal practitioners to be aware that contemporaneously with the enactment of provisions implementing The Hague Convention, the local law of Ontario concerning custody, access and guardianship was revisited and re-enacted to bring it into consonance with the provisions of the convention. In that sense the local law and the conventional rules are complementary and, indeed, the local law contains provisions directed towards filling gaps in The Hague Convention.

For instance, s. 22(1) of the Children's Law Reform Act[8] provides

22.(1) A court shall only exercise its jurisdiction to make an order for custody of or access to a child where,

---

8 En. 1982, c. 20, s. 1.

(*a*) the child is habitually resident in Ontario at the commencement of the application for the order;

(*b*) although the child is not habitually resident in Ontario, the court is satisfied,

(i) that the child is physically present in Ontario at the commencement of the application for the order,

(ii) that substantial evidence concerning the best interests of the child is available in Ontario,

(iii) that no application for custody of or access to the child is pending before an extra-provincial tribunal in another place where the child is habitually resident,

(iv) that no extra-provincial order in respect of custody of or access to the child has been recognized by a court in Ontario,

(v) that the child has a real and substantial connection with Ontario, and

(vi) that, on the balance of convenience, it is appropriate for jurisdiction to be exercised in Ontario.

It is clear from s. 47(9) of the Children's Law Reform Act that where the convention applies and there is a conflict between the conventional rules and any other Ontario enactment, the conventional rules govern. However, because of this recent legislation in Ontario, even in situations where the convention does not apply, the local rules are similar to the conventional rules and accordingly similarity of treatment with respect to extra-provincial orders will result.[9]

The integrated approach of the Ontario legislation adopted at the time of The Hague Convention is apparent from the legislated statement of purposes in the provisions of s. 19 of the Ontario Act which reads as follows:[10]

19. The purposes of this Part are,

(*a*) to ensure that applications to the courts in respect of custody of, incidents of custody of, access to and guardianship for children will be determined on the basis of the best interests of the children;

(*b*) to recognize that the concurrent exercise of jurisdiction by judicial tribunals of more than one province, territory or state in respect of the custody of the same child ought to be avoided, and to make provision so that the courts of Ontario will, unless there are exceptional circumstances, refrain from exercising or decline jurisdiction in cases where it is more appropriate for the matter to be determined by a tribunal having jurisdiction in another place with which the child has a closer connection;

(*c*) to discourage the abduction of children as an alternative to the determination of custody rights by due process; and

---

9 For a full treatment of the relationship of The Hague Convention and the local law of Ontario see Allan Q. Shipley, "Custody Law Reform in Ontario: The Children's Law Reform Act", chapter 4, *supra*.

10 Children's Law Reform Act, s. 19 [en. 1982, c. 20, s. 1].

(*d*) to provide for the more effective enforcement of custody and access orders and for the recognition and enforcement of custody and access orders made outside Ontario.

The object of the convention set forth in para. (*b*) of Article 1, being "to ensure that rights of custody and of access under the law of one Contracting State are effectively respected in the other Contracting States", serves the same purpose as that in para. (*a*) of securing the prompt return of children wrongfully removed or wrongfully detained. By respecting custody and access rights given and enforced in accordance with the law of the state of the habitual residence of the child, one is usually respecting and enforcing these rights in the forum having the closest connection with the child and, therefore, one assumes issues will be resolved with information available and on principles most amicable to the best interests of the child. There are, of course, some circumstances in which this would not be true and the convention has identified and dealt with some exceptions. Obviously, this is a serious and difficult exercise since the nature and number of the possible exceptions must be carefully analyzed and limited to avoid stultifying the main thrust of the convention. We will return to this matter subsequently.

4. Application of the Convention.

In accordance with its mission of resolving conflicts of law in the private sector, The Hague Conference has formulated a convention restricted to the civil aspects of child abduction. This is made express in the terms of the title to the convention but is not expressly dealt with in the provisions of the text. The clearly signalled thrust is that of enforcing civil remedies.

That the local authorities may invoke the adjuncts of the criminal justice administration, such as police forces, in matters of establishing the whereabouts of the child and in securing his or her physical protection and return does not detract from the force of the observation that the concern of the treaty is civil and not criminal justice administration.

The local law of Ontario, because of recent legislation in this area, goes some distance in making sheriff and police forces available for the more effective enforcement of custody and access orders and the prevention of abduction provincially, nationally and internationally. For instance, the Children's Law Reform Act provides that where the court is satisfied that there are reasonable and probable grounds for believing that any person is unlawfully withholding a child from a person entitled to custody of or access to the child, the court may direct the sheriff or a police force, or both, in the area to locate, apprehend and deliver the child to a named person.[11] The legislation provides

---

11 S. 37(2)(*a*) [en. 1982, c. 20, s. 1].

further that the sheriff or police force directed to act shall do all things reasonably able to be done to locate, apprehend and deliver the child in accordance with the order of the court.[12] These important ancillary and quasi-criminal remedies are obviously available for purposes of the administration of the provisions of The Hague Convention on International Child Abduction.

The fairly extensive remedial measures available in our local law to prevent removal or ensure return of a child ought to have a very salutary effect on any disposition to engage in any improper self-help in the enforcement of perceived custody rights. For example, s. 38 (3) of the Children's Law Reform Act provides:

> (3) An order mentioned in subsection (1) [application to prevent unlawful removal of child] or (2) [application to ensure return of child] may require a person to do any one or more of the following:
>
> 1. Transfer specific property to a named trustee to be held subject to the terms and conditions specified in the order.
>
> 2. Where payments have been ordered for the support of the child, make the payments to a specified trustee subject to the terms and conditions specified in the order.
>
> 3. Post a bond, with or without sureties, payable to the applicant in such amount as the court considers appropriate.
>
> 4. Deliver the person's passport, the child's passport and any other travel documents of either of them that the court may specify to the court or to an individual or body specified by the court.[13]

It is clear from the express terms of its title, the preamble and the substantive provisions of the convention that the conventional rules apply only to international situations. Article 33 of the convention, for example, prescribes that

> A State within which different territorial units have their own rules of law in respect of custody of children shall not be bound to apply this Convention where a State with a unified system of law would not be bound to do so.

It should be noted, however, that when the local Ontario rules coincide with the conventional rules, the same result would derive, but not because the conventional rules, *per se*, were being enforced.

The territorial reach of The Hague Convention and therefore the application of its principles, are potentially world-wide inasmuch as adherence to the treaty is not limited to ratification by the states which were members of the Hague Conference on Private International Law at the session at which it was

---

12   S. 37(4) [en. 1982, c. 20, s. 1].

13   En. 1982, c. 20, s. 1.

promulgated.[14] Other states may accede to the convention, and thereby become contracting states, but the accession will have effect only as regards relations between the acceding state and such contracting states as will have declared their acceptance of the accession. Such a declaration of acceptance is also required by any member state ratifying, accepting, or approving the convention after an accession. In this sense the convention is a qualified open convention and reciprocal in nature. As of the date of writing, the convention has been signed by the United States and it is pending ratification by the U.S. Senate in accordance with the procedures established by the U.S. Constitution. Obviously, ratification by the United States would be a boon to the cause of eliminating child abduction worldwide, but particularly to Canada and its provinces which have become subject to its provisions.

5. The Return of the Child

As already indicated The Hague Convention is premised on the view that the issue of custody of children should be left to be decided by the tribunals of the state of the habitual residence of the children. The convention is concerned with custody rights rather than custody decisions and accordingly concentrates upon the prompt return of a child who has been removed from his habitual residence in breach of custody rights being effectively exercised under the law.

It matters not that the abductor, at the date of the application for the return of the child, has already procured, in the courts of his own country, an order awarding him the custody of the child. Nor is the court of the requested state to embark on an inquiry into the merits of custody decisions and disputes concerning custody rights between the parties. The function of the requested state is to order and assist in the prompt return of the child to his or her habitual residence. It is expressly stipulated in Article 19 that a decision under the convention concerning the return of the child is not to be taken as a determination on the merits of any custody issue.

Emphasis is placed throughout the provisions of the convention that it is the *prompt* return of the child that is mandated and directed. This appears initially in para. 3 of the preamble; the reference is carried into para. (*a*) of Article 1; the same admonition appears in the provisions of Article 2 where the contracting states are to use the most expeditious procedures available for implementing the objects of the convention; and Article 11 provides that the judicial or administrative authorities of a contracting state shall act expeditiously in proceedings for the return of children.

Unusually, perhaps, in the experience of Canadian courts, para. 2 of Article 11 provides that if the judicial or administrative authority concerned has

---

14   Article 37.

not reached a decision within six weeks from the date of the commencement of the proceedings, the applicant or the central authority of the requested state, shall have the right to request a statement of the reasons for the delay. If a reply is received by the central authority of the requested state, that authority shall transmit the reply to the central authority of the requesting state, or to the applicant, as the case may be. One assumes, if there is no reply, that resort must be had through normal diplomatic channels for action in the manner usually taken with respect to an allegation of non-adherence to international obligations.

Those legal practitioners and other professionals who have had any experience with child abduction in the pre-treaty era will have become aware how helpful the officers of the Canadian Department of External Affairs, at home and abroad, are in the difficult and protracted business of locating abducted children and effecting their return. That they were not always, or even usually, successful, is not to be attributed to fault on their part. Under The Hague Convention, the first resort to federal officials will probably be to the federal central authority, established pursuant to the provisions of the convention as the Ministry of Justice, Ottawa.[15] This, of course, does not preclude the necessity of the eventual intervention, on invitation, by the Department of External Affairs. Those officials in a real sense remain the "court of last resort" just as they were the only recourse available at the international level in pre-treaty days.

Any action by the requested state for the return of the child is predicated on the fact that there has been a wrongful removal of the child. The jurisdictional fact of "wrongful removal" is defined in Article 3 of the convention as follows:

> The removal or the retention of a child is to be considered wrongful where:
>
> (*a*) it is in breach of rights of custody attributed to a person, an institution or any other body, either jointly or alone, under the law of the State in which the child was habitually resident immediately before the removal or retention; and
>
> (*b*) at the time of removal or retention those rights were actually exercised, either jointly or alone, or would have been so exercised but for the removal or retention.
>
> The rights of custody mentioned in subparagraph (*a*) above, may arise in particular by operation of law or by reason of a judicial or administrative decision,[16] or by reason of an agreement having legal effect under the law of that State.

---

15 The establishment and role of central authorities is dealt with *infra*, at 229, *et seq*. The Domestic Legal Services section of the Department of External Affairs is designated as the authority to which applications are to be addressed for transmission to the proper central authority in Canada.

16 Reference throughout the convention is made to "Custody rights arising by judicial or *administrative decision*" because it was stated that in some state jurisdictions these decisions are made by administrative tribunals. With us in Ontario, it would not have been necessary to add "administrative" and it may even obfuscate the point to do so.

It is difficult to visualize custody rights arising from a source other than those stipulated, but the reference to "in particular" seems to acknowledge the possibility of such rights arising and, if so, then such rights would be entitled to recognition.

The Hague Convention adopts a single criterion for determining the applicable law and it is the law of the state in which the child was habitually resident immediately before the removal or retention. Habitual residence rather than domicile is now generally accepted as the criterion for jurisdiction or choice of law where the criterion is to be based on a residential requirement and not nationality. The term "habitual residence" is not defined in this convention nor, for that matter, in any other convention in the private international law field. At least the local law in Ontario attempts to give some guidance in this matter by defining habitual residence in the context of giving the court jurisdiction in custody matters by providing that:

> A child is habitually resident in the place where he resided,
>
> (*a*) with both parents;
>
> (*b*) where the parents are living separate and apart, with one parent under a separation agreement or with the consent, implied consent or acquiescence of the other or under a court order; or
>
> (*c*) with a person other than a parent on a permanent basis for a significant period of time,
>
> whichever last occurred.[17]

The Ontario legislation provides that the removal or withholding of a child without the consent of the person having custody does not alter the habitual residence of the child unless there has been acquiescence or undue delay in commencing the process by the person from whom the child is removed or withheld.[18] The Hague Convention refers to the applicable law as the law of the state in which the child was habitually resident immediately before the removal or retention. Clearly the removal is not effective to change the applicable law.

The Hague Convention does not state in an exhaustive, definitive way what the rights of custody and of access are which are breached by the wrongful removal of the child. Article 5 of the convention does prescribe, however, that "rights of custody" shall include rights relating to the care of the person of the child and, in particular, the right to determine the child's place of residence. "Rights of access" are also defined in an inclusionary sense, inasmuch as they

---

17 Children's Law Reform Act, s. 22(2) [en. 1982, c. 20, s. 1]. The reference in s. 22(2)(*c*) to the phrase "on a permanent basis for a significant period of time" approximates the meaning of the term used in international law.

18 S. 22(3) [en. 1982, c. 20, s. 1].

shall include the right to take a child for a limited period of time to a place other than the child's habitual residence. Presumably any order made under the law of the state of the habitual residence pursuant to authority to restrict taking a child even for a limited period to a place other than the child's habitual residence would be recognized and a removal taking place in breach of that order would be regarded as a wrongful removal under the convention, notwithstanding the provisions of Article 5(*b*).[19]

6. Limitations on the Return of the Child

The temporal limitations on the applicability of the convention and the exercise of jurisdiction under it are clearly established. In accordance with the provisions of Article 4, the convention, having been applied to a child who was habitually resident in a contracting state immediately before any breach of custody or access rights, will cease to apply when the child attains the age of 16 years.

Where a child has been wrongfully removed and an application is brought before the judicial or administrative authority of the contracting state where the child is within one year from the date of the wrongful removal, the return of the child shall be ordered forthwith.[20] Even where the proceedings are commenced after the expiration of one year following the date of the wrongful removal, the return of the child shall be ordered unless it is demonstrated that the child is now settled in his or her new environment.[21] The extended period under Article 12, para. 2, is to enable relief to be granted even after the one-year period has expired where, for example, the whereabouts of the child are not known to the injured spouse within the year or where the child's residence is revealed in time but the child is again spirited away before proceedings can be taken and the child apprehended. If, however, as a result of residence in one place for an extended period of time, the court is satisfied that the child is settled in his or her new environment, then the best interests of the child will probably be served by refusing to compel its return.

---

19 Children's Law Reform Act, s. 37(2) [en. 1982, c. 20, s. 1] provides that
    "Where a court is satisfied upon application that there are reasonable and probable grounds for believing. . .
    "(*b*) that a person who is prohibited by court order or separation agreement from removing a child from Ontario proposes to remove the child or have the child removed from Ontario. . .
    the court by order may direct the sheriff or a police force, or both, having jurisdiction in any area where it appears to the court that the child may be, to locate, apprehend and deliver the child to the person named in the order."

20 Article 12, para. 1.

21 Article 12, para. 2.

Although the obligation to order and arrange the return of the child can be compelled only in accordance with the express terms and within the time periods stipulated in the convention, the provisions of Article 18 make it clear that these prescriptions in the convention do not limit the power of a judicial or administrative authority to order the return of the child at any time. Accordingly, even if a court were to find that the child was settled in its new environment and the period of one year from commencement of proceedings had expired, the court would not be compelled under the convention to order the return of the child but could presumably do so, nonetheless, if this action was felt to be in the best interests of the child. [22]

The fact that the child is not in the contracting state to which application for its return has been directed does not relieve that state from all obligations under the convention. Under the provisions of Article 9, where the initial requested state believes the child to be in another contracting state, the former is bound under the treaty to directly and without delay transmit the application to the central authority of the contracting state where the child is believed to be and is bound to inform the requesting central authority, or the applicant, as the case may be of this fact. Similarly, under the provisions of Article 12, para. 3, where a requested state, during proceedings before it, has reason to believe that the child has been taken to another state, the former may stay proceedings and dismiss the application for the return of the child.

The three consecutive Articles — 14-16 — are extremely important in structuring the manner in which the jurisdiction of the requested state is to be exercised. The first two are procedural and the last substantive in nature. Practitioners will be aware of the delays and expense involved in the proof of foreign law. It must be proven as a fact by someone with knowledge of the fact. The pervasive thrust of the provisions of the convention is to expedite matters in an issue of some urgency and great importance. Therefore, the provisions of Article 14 prescribe that in ascertaining whether there has been a wrongful removal or retention, the judicial or administrative authorities of the requested state may take judicial notice of the law of the state of the habitual residence of the child, without specific procedures for the proof of that law or for the recognition of foreign decisions which would otherwise be applicable.

In cases of difficulty or doubt the authorities of the requested state are empowered, prior to making an order for the return of the child, to request the applicant to obtain from the authorities of the requesting state a decision or other determination that the removal or retention was wrongful in terms of the provisions of Article 3. This may be thought to give rise to some difficulty since it might be regarded as asking the courts of the requesting state for an advisory opinion which would be contrary to the usual practice. However, if classified as

---

22 Article 18.

a declaratory judgment, one would be in the realm of increasing commonplace in the type of jurisdiction being exercised by our courts. In any event, it is an obligation assumed under the treaty and therefore to be performed in accordance with its terms. This jurisdictional fact, of course, is vital for the authorities of the requested state who are, generally speaking, discouraged from going into the merits of the case. It is clear from the provisions of Article 16, for instance, that the authorities of the requested state are not to decide on the merits of custody rights until it has been determined that the child is not to be returned under the convention or unless an application under the convention is not lodged within a reasonable time following the receipt of a notice that there has been a wrongful removal or retention in terms of Article 3.

The most anxious consideration and most prolonged discussion in the formulation of the convention involved the issue concerning the circumstances in which the return of the child would not be compelled. The polar positions were clear enough. The convention must accommodate the circumstances where the return of the child would be clearly harmful to the physical and emotional well-being of the child. What one is facing is that unusual case where the removal of the child was justified in fact if not in law. The other polar extreme is where the authorities of the requested state, if left to their own local law and their own perception of the particular facts would not decide in the manner compelled by the convention. This result had to be avoided if the convention was not to run the risk of being rendered nugatory. At what point or points, in between these polar extremes, the line was to be drawn understandably attracted serious and protracted debate, and the resulting decisions both in phraseology and conception reflect the fact of uneasy compromise and not facile agreement.

We have already dealt with some of the circumstances under which return of abducted children is not compelled under the provisions of the convention. On the negative side it is provided in Article 17 that the sole fact that a decision relating to custody has been given or is entitled to recognition in the requested state is not to be a ground for refusing to return a child under the convention. The authorities in the requested state, however, may take into account the reasons given for this existing custody decision in applying the convention. All of these provisions give a very strong signal indicating that the prompt return of the child is compelled subject to few and rather narrow exceptions. These exceptions are set out in the provisions of Articles 13 and 20 and include:

   (i) not actually exercising custody rights at the time of removal or rentention;[23]
   (ii) consent to removal or retention;[24]

---

23   Article 13, subpara. (*a*).

24   *Ibid.*

(iii) subsequent acquiescence in removal or retention;[25]

(iv) there is grave risk that the return of the child would expose the child to physical or psychological harm;[26]

(v) return would place the child in an intolerable situation;[27]

(vi) that the child objects to being returned and has attained an age and degree of maturity at which it is appropriate to take account of its views;[28] or

(vii) if return of the child would not be permitted by the fundamental principles of the requested state relating to the protection of human rights and fundamental freedoms.[29]

The only two stipulated grounds which appear to require elaboration are those in items (v) and (vii). The reference in item (v) would appear to be rather novel as a legislative prescription, but what is meant to be conveyed is that there is no compulsion to return the child if such return would render the child subject to a grave risk of an environment hostile to the advancement of the best interests of the child even though the risk of physical or psychological harm was not present. There is harm which could flow from a negative environment which would not be *ejusdem generis* with physical or psychological harm, but which could make the life of the child so miserable as to render it intolerable. Relief should not be denied to the stout-hearted and physically robust if there is an option which would eliminate the necessity for enduring an environment so unwholesome as to be unacceptable if any other is available. The provisions of Article 20 reflect the well-understood reservation requested by many states in this and other subject areas concerning *ordre public*. It is generally agreed that *ordre public* means a more fundamental objection in the law of the requested state than that it merely has a different rule. It also probably means something more in Anglo-Canadian common law jurisdictions than merely contrary to public policy, although that is the usual approximation as to what is meant.

The debate in the context of this particular international convention arose from the desire to retain something of the qualification of *ordre public* which would permit a refusal to order the return of a child in circumstances which would be repugnant to the essential spirit and morality of the local law while narrowing the exception to a point that would not put the essential purpose of the convention in jeopardy. It was for these critical reasons that the wording was

---

25 *Ibid.*

26 *Ibid.*, subpara. (*b*).

27 *Ibid.*

28 *Ibid.*, para. 2.

29 Article 20.

chosen with great deliberation and care, although even here the selected phraseology was not favoured by a large number of the member states. The applicability of the exception is restricted at least to fundamental principles of the requested state relating to the protection of human rights and fundamental freedoms and not left at large as being contrary to public policy generally. It is not suggested that the formulation is free of difficulty. The polar extremes are clear enough where at one end the exception could be invoked and at the other where it could not. There are the cases in the middle of the spectrum which remain to cause difficulty. There is no mistaking midnight for noon but the precise moment at which twilight becomes darkness is never easy to determine.

7. The Application for the Return of the Child

The procedural provisions of the convention have been formulated to ensure that the launching and processing of an application are made simple and expeditious. It is not fruitful to discuss them without doing so in the context of an institutional construct provided for in the convention and known as the central authority. Before turning to the details of that mechanism, however, we would point out that the essentials of the application are detailed in Article 8 of the convention, which reads as follows:

> Any person, institution or other body claiming that a child has been removed or retained in breach of custody rights may apply either to the Central Authority of the child's habitual residence or to the Central Authority of any other Contracting State for assistance in securing the return of the child.
>
> The application shall contain:
>
> (*a*) information concerning the identity of the applicant, of the child and of the person alleged to have removed or retained the child;
>
> (*b*) where available, the date of birth of the child;
>
> (*c*) the grounds on which the applicant's claim for return of the child is based;
>
> (*d*) all available information relating to the whereabouts of the child and the identity of the person with whom the child is presumed to be.
>
> The application may be accompanied or supplemented by:
>
> (*e*) an authenticated copy of any relevant decision or agreement;
>
> (*f*) a certificate or an affidavit emanating from a Central Authority, or other competent authority of the State of the child's habitual residence, or from a qualified person, concerning the relevant law of that State;
>
> (*g*) any other relevant document.

Although the nature of the information in the application required by Article 8 is quite specific, no special form is required. Indeed, the schedule to s. 47 of the Ontario Children's Law Reform Act, which reproduces the provisions of the convention *verbatim*, does not make any reference to a special form and no form is included. But a special committee was struck at the Fourteenth

Session of The Hague Conference to draft a form of application. The final act of the Fourteenth Session recommended that the special form as drafted by the committee be used for submitting applications but stopped short of making the use of the draft form obligatory.[30]

The matter of language to be used in the application, communication and other documentation is an important and sensitive issue in any multi-lateral and multi-national convention if for no other reason than the expense involved. The convention prescribes that these documents sent to the central authority of the requested state shall be in the original language in which they were drafted, accompanied by a translation into the official language or one of the official languages of the requested state. Where this is not feasible, the original is to be accompanied by a translation into French or English. States are permitted, under Article 24, para. 2, and in accordance with the provisions of Article 42, to make a reservation stating that they object to the use of French or English but they cannot object to the use of French and English.

On ratifying on behalf of the provinces, Canada was not asked to reserve under Article 24 with respect to the use of language and has not done so.

8. Central Authorities

The principle of authorizing and compelling the designation of central authorities as an aid in the administration of an international convention is an established practice with conventions of The Hague Conference on Private International Law. The decision to provide for them in this particular convention was a happy one since the administrative tasks to be performed are numerous, both those that are directed and those that may be performed voluntarily to render the convention more easily and fully effective. No attempt has been made to conceal the fact that there are many gaps in the administrative structure established by the convention. Any *a priori* attempt to fill these gaps would have resulted in a much more detailed legislative scheme than was thought to be justified. It also would probably have meant that some of the predetermined administrative solutions were wrong. Better the details should be left for resolution based on actual experience working with the convention and against a background of good faith and enthusiastic co-operation by participatory states. This type of environment is uniquely congenial to the functioning of central authorities and justifies their use in this sensitive and difficult field of international co-operation. This is particularly true because the provisions of the convention go far beyond the bounds of legal prescriptions.

The provisions relative to the obligation to create central authorities are contained in Article 6 and under them a contracting state is compelled to

---

30 The recommended form appears as Appendix A to this chapter.

designate a central authority to discharge the duties which are imposed by the convention upon such authorities. Article 6, para. 2, does not carry its total meaning on its face. It reads as follows:

> Federal States, States with more than one system of law or States having autonomous territorial organizations shall be free to appoint more than one Central Authority and to specify the territorial extent of their powers. Where a State has appointed more than one Central Authority, it shall designate the Central Authority to which applications may be addressed for transmission to the appropriate Central Authority within that State.

The reference to "Federal States" is to such countries as Canada and the United States and envisages that the constituent units — states, provinces and territories — will designate their own central authority to function within their own geographical and constitutional framework. In these cases the federal administration would be advised, if not required, to have a federal central authority to act in a co-ordinating role for the whole country. This would facilitate the receiving of applications from other countries not familiar with the federal constitutional structure, the directing of applications to the competent provincial and territorial central authority, and the placing of federal government search facilities at the disposal of the applicant, and so on. In passing the legislation implementing the convention, the Ontario legislature provided that the Ministry of the Attorney General shall be the central authority for Ontario for the purpose of the convention.[31] The document of ratification filed by Canada on behalf of New Brunswick, British Columbia and Manitoba also indicates that these provinces had designated the Ministry of the Attorney General as the central authority in their province. The Ministry of the Attorney General for Ontario has assigned a legally qualified practitioner to exercise the functions of this office along with a cluster of other functions arising under provincial legislation dealing with associated matters such as the reciprocal enforcement of maintenance and custody orders.

The reference to "States with more than one system of law" is a reference to a unitary state such as Israel which has one system of the law of divorce, for example, which applies to Jews and another different system of the law of divorce applying to Arabs of the Muslim faith. Conceivably the state might wish to designate subordinate central authorities to deal with custody matters under the convention applicable to the respective constituencies. Similarly, the reference to "States having autonomous territorial organizations" is meant to deal with situations, as in Spain, where there are autonomous regional offices and institutions for purposes of administration. Presumably the convention permits the establishment of adjunct central authorities for these regions.

---

31   Children's Law Reform Act, s. 47(4).

The type of assistance, co-operation and service within the legitimate expectation of applicants can be inferred from the mandated roles of the central authorities under the provisions of Article 7 of the Convention:

> Central Authorities shall co-operate with each other and promote co-operation amongst the competent authorities in their respective States to secure the prompt return of children and to achieve the other objects of this Convention.
>
> In particular, either directly or through any intermediary, they shall take all appropriate measures:
>
> (*a*) to discover the whereabouts of a child who has been wrongfully removed or retained;
>
> (*b*) to prevent further harm to the child or prejudice to interested parties by taking or causing to be taken provisional measures;
>
> (*c*) to secure the voluntary return of the child or bring about an amicable resolution of the issues;
>
> (*d*) to exchange, where desirable, information relating to the social background of the child;
>
> (*e*) to provide information of a general character as to the law of their State in connection with the application of the Convention;
>
> (*f*) to initiate or facilitate the institution of judicial or administrative proceedings with a view to obtaining the return of the child and, in a proper case, to make arrangements for organizing or securing the effective exercise of rights of access;
>
> (*g*) where the circumstances so require, to provide or facilitate the provision of legal aid and advice, including the participation of legal counsel and advisers;
>
> (*h*) to provide such administrative arrangements as may be necessary and appropriate to secure the safe return of the child;
>
> (*i*) to keep each other informed with respect to the operation of this Convention and, as far as possible, to eliminate any obstacles to its application.

The importance placed upon the attempt to obtain the voluntary return of the child is seen from specific reference to it in Article 10 of the convention where it is stated that the central authority of the state where the child is shall take or cause to be taken all appropriate measures in order to obtain the voluntary return of the child. Where voluntary return of the child cannot be achieved then resort must be had to the competent authorities to compel it. For this purpose the central authority may require that the application be accompanied by a written authorization empowering it to act on behalf of the applicant or to designate a representative so to act.[32] The detailed terms of the convention dealing with the institution of central authorities do not say, however, that applications from foreign countries are compelled to go through the federal central authority in

---

32 Article 28.

order to reach the central authority of the competent constituent unit. On the contrary, the provisions of Article 29 make it abundantly clear that the convention does not preclude any person, institution or body claiming a wrongful removal or retention, or alleging a breach of access rights under Article 21 from applying directly to the judicial or administrative authorities of a contracting state, whether or not under the provisions of the convention. The convention does not oust the normal jurisdiction of the courts of the contracting states. The Rapporteur in the official Explanatory Report deals with the matter in these terms:

Article 29 — Direct application to competent internal authorities

The Convention does not seek to establish a system for the return of children which is exclusively for the benefit of Contracting States. It is put forward rather as an additional means for helping persons whose custody or access rights have been breached. Consequently, those persons can either have recourse to the Central Authorities — in other words use the means provided in the Convention — or else pursue a direct action before the competent authorities in matters of custody and access in the State where the child is located. In the latter case, whenever the persons concerned opt to apply directly to the relevant authorities, a second choice is open to them in that they can submit their application "whether or not under the provisions of this Convention". In the latter case the authorities are not of course obliged to apply the provisions of the Convention, unless the State has incorporated them into its internal law, in terms of Article 2 of the Convention.

An obvious advantage of proceeding under the convention rather than independently is the availability of financial assistance under the former and it is to these matters that we now turn.

9. Legal Aid and Costs

That the matter of legal aid should be dealt with in the convention is not at all surprising. That its specific provisions with respect to the entitlement of foreign nationals should have provoked serious differences of opinion, not to mention alienation of affection, amongst member state delegations is also not surprising. The Canadian and American delegations were deeply involved in these particular negotiations and we shared with our American colleagues the view that legal aid should be made available here to the foreign applicant but on terms that would not bestow on foreign nationals a more advantageous grant in aid than is available to our own nationals under the local legal aid plan. This seemed to us all straightforward and anything more generous than this would appear to attract rather serious political difficulties in the forum. Again the matter was settled by compromise, but first the main provisions must be revealed.

Under the terms of Article 25 it is provided that nationals of the contracting states and persons who are habitually resident within those states shall be entitled in matters concerned with the application of the convention to legal aid and advice in any other contracting state on the same conditions as if they themselves were nationals of and habitually resident in that state. So far so good!

Article 26 essentially deals with the matter of costs. The provisions of para. 2 include the following:

> In particular, they [the central authorities] may not require any payment from the applicant towards the cost and expenses of the proceedings or, where applicable, those arising from the participation of legal counsel of advisers. . . .

Obviously the concern was that this provision would enable the applicant to retain counsel of choice with an open-ended brief and to visit the total cost upon the central authority. Accordingly, contracting states were permitted by making a reservation in accordance with Article 42 to declare that they would not be bound to assume any costs referred to in Article 26, para. 2, resulting from the participation of legal counsel or from court proceedings, except so far as those costs may be covered by its system of legal aid and advice. When Canada ratified the Convention with respect to Ontario, New Brunswick and British Columbia, reservations in this form were declared by Canada on behalf of all three since this had been requested by them. No such reservation was made on behalf of Manitoba since that province did not request it. The reservation by Ontario is enshrined in s. 47(3) of its implementing legislation and states that the Crown is not bound to assume any costs resulting under the convention from the participation of legal counsel or advisers or from court proceedings except in accordance with the Legal Aid Act.[33]

The remaining cost provisions of Article 26 stipulate that each central authority shall bear its own costs in applying the convention; that the central authorities and other public services of contracting states shall not impose any charges in relation to applications submitted under the convention; but central authorities may require the payment of the expenses incurred or to be incurred in implementing the return of the child.

Article 26, para. 4, enables the court in a proper case to assess the costs of return of the child or enforcement of rights of access against the person responsible for removing or retaining the child or denying the rights of access. Finally, Article 22 precludes the imposition of security for costs as a condition for being permitted to initiate proceedings.

10. Rights of Access

One of the stated objects of the convention, as we have seen, is to ensure that rights of custody and of access under the law of one contracting state are

---

33   R.S.O. 1980, c. 234.

effectively respected in the other contracting states. But the rights of custody and of access are not accorded equal treatment under the terms of the convention. For example, wrongful removal or retention of a child is defined solely with respect to custody.[34] During the formulation of the convention the Canadian delegation sought to redress the imbalance by proposing that the words "and of access" be added after the word "custody" in the first line of Article 3, para. (*a*). The proposal was defeated by a substantial majority and thus access rights remain relegated to an inferior position under the convention.[35]

Access rights are dealt with specifically in only one place. Article 21 provides that an application to make arrangements for organizing or securing the effective exercise of rights of access may be presented to the central authorities of the contracting states in the same way as an application for the return of the child. The duty is thus imposed on central authorities to co-operate in seeking to make access rights a meaningful reality but no mandatory rules are imposed to achieve this result.

Access rights are not defined under the convention but Article 5(*b*) does provide that they include the right to take a child for a limited period of time to a place other than the child's habitual residence. It is essentially because this right exists even to take the child abroad that it would have been preferable in Article 3 to make the remedy for wrongful removal and retention apply where an access leave is illegally extended.[36]

In s. 20(5) the Ontario Children's Law Reform Act provides that the entitlement to access to a child includes the right to visit with and be visited by the child and the same right as a parent to make inquiries and to be given information as to the health, education and welfare of the child.[37] It will be noted that the legislation stops short of giving the right to make decisions and to intervene with respect to matters of health, education and welfare of the child.

V CONCLUSION

For the legal practitioner not accustomed to working on a regular basis with international treaties and conventions, some aspects of them may appear novel and prove troublesome. For instance, the matter of phraseology may prove an irritation, at best, and, at worst, an obstacle to proper interpretation. The Hague conventions generally, and the abduction treaty therefore, are drafted

---

34 See Article 3, subpara. (*a*).

35 *Actes et documents de la quatorzième session de la Conférence de la Haye de droit international privé* (1982), tome III, "Child Abduction" at 264-67.

36 For a fuller treatment of access rights within the convention see the Explanatory Report of the Rapporteur *ibid.*, at 465 and 466.

37 Children's Law Reform Act, s. 20(5) [en. 1982, c. 20, s. 1].

simultaneously in the French and English languages. In that process, for those who have been exposed to it, it is all too readily apparent that infelicities of expression in one or other of the languages may occur and must be accepted. It must not be assumed that this results from inadequate knowledge of either language by the draftsmen, but it will be appreciated that international treaties are forged in the crucible of compromise. Whatever inartful expression there is results from an attempt to have the two versions of the text as uniform as possible within the obvious strictures of having the words make sense against the background of a multi-legal system. The best choice of term in one language may not be capable of exact reproduction in another tongue.

Ontario practitioners are well aware of the traditional limitations placed by the rules of evidence on the use of extrinsic aids to interpretation such as full admissibility of the legislative history of an enactment. There have been encouraging signs of some relaxation of these strict rules in order to permit reference to reports on whose recommendations the legislation has been based. It is important to stress, therefore, that it is quite commonplace to resort to explanatory reports on the preparation and formulation of international treaties such as those of The Hague Conference in aid of resolving subsequently perceived ambiguities in the text of the convention.

Such an Explanatory Report has been written for The Hague Convention on Child Abduction by Professor Elisa Perez-Vera of Spain, who acted as Rapporteur of the Commission in the Fourteenth Session of The Hague Conference at which the convention was formulated. The Explanatory Report of Professor Perez-Vera dealing with child abduction is included in the bound publication of the conference for the 1980 session. Although reports of this nature are never submitted for the specific approval of members of the conference present at the meeting, they are uniformly prepared with great care and skill and justify reference and reliance. The publication of the proceedings contains a total record of minutes, working papers, draft reports, and so on, leading to the final convention, comprising in all 500 pages (approximately). An index is provided which will lead to any discussion that took place of particular points and thus may throw light on points of difficulty in applying the text of the convention.[38]

---

38 *Actes et documents de la quatorzième session de la Conférence de la Haye de droit international privé* (1982), tome III, "Child Abduction".

APPENDIX A

Recommandation adoptée par la Quatorzième session[1]

La Quatorzième session,

Recommande aux Etats parties à la *Convention sur les aspects civils de l'enlèvement international d'enfants* d'utiliser pour les demandes de retour des enfants déplacés ou retenus illicitement la formule modèle suivante:

Requête en vue du retour

Convention de La Haye du 25 octobre 1980 sur les aspects civils de l'enlèvement international d'enfants

AUTORITÉ CENTRALE REQUÉRANTE OU REQUÉRANT	AUTORITÉ REQUISE

Concerne l'enfant .... qui aura 16 ans le .... 19......

NOTE: Les rubriques suivantes doivent être remplies de la façon la plus complète possible.

I — IDENTITÉ DE L'ENFANT ET DES PARENTS

1 *Enfant*

nom et prénoms ....
date et lieu de naissance ....
résidence habituelle avant l'enlèvement ....
passeport ou carte d'identité No (s'il y a lieu) ....
signalement et éventuellement photo (voir annexes) ....

2 *Parents*

2.1 Mère: nom et prénoms ....
date et lieu de naissance ....
nationalité ....
profession ....
résidence habituelle ....
passeport ou carte d'identité No (s'il y a lieu) ....

2.2 Père: nom et prénoms ....
date et lieu de naissance ....
nationalité ....
profession ....
résidence habituelle ....
passeport ou carte d'identité No (s'il y a lieu) ....

2.3 Date et lieu du mariage ....

II — PARTIE REQUÉRANTE: PERSONNE OU INSTITUTION (qui exerçait la garde effectivement avant l'enlèvement)

3 nom et prénoms ....
nationalité (si personne physique) ....
profession (si personne physique) ....
adresse ....
passeport ou carte d'identité No (s'il y a lieu) ....
relation avec l'enfant ....
nom et adresse du conseiller juridique (s'il y a lieu) ....

III — ENDROIT OÙ DEVRAIT SE TROUVER L'ENFANT

4.1 Renseignements concernant la personne dont il est allégué qu'elle a enlevé ou retenu l'enfant

nom et prénoms ....
profession ....
dernière résidence connue ....
passeport ou carte d'identité No (s'il y a lieu) ....
signalement et éventuellement photo (voir annexes) ....

[1] Extrait de l'Acte final de la Quatorzième session, Partie F.

Recommendation adopted by the Fourteenth Session[1]

The Fourteenth Session,

Recommends to the States Parties to the *Convention on the Civil Aspects of International Child Abduction* that the following model form be used in making applications for the return of wrongfully removed or retained children —

Request for return

Hague Convention of 25 October 1980 on the Civil Aspects of International Child Abduction.

REQUESTING CENTRAL AUTHORITY OR APPLICANT	REQUESTED AUTHORITY

Concerns the following child: .... who will attain the age of 16 on .... 19......

NOTE: The following particulars should be completed insofar as possible.

I — IDENTITY OF THE CHILD AND ITS PARENTS

1 *Child*

name and first names ....
date and place of birth ....
habitual residence before removal or retention ....
passport or identity card No. if any ....
description and photo, if possible (see annexes) ....

2 *Parents*

2.1 Mother: name and first names ....
date and place of birth ....
nationality ....
occupation ....
habitual residence ....
passport or identity card No. if any ....

2.2 Father: name and first names ....
date and place of birth ....
nationality ....
occupation ....
habitual residence ....
passport or identity card No. if any ....

2.3 Date and place of marriage ....

II — REQUESTING INDIVIDUAL OR INSTITUTION (who actually exercised custody before the removal or retention)

3 name and first names ....
nationality of individual applicant ....
occupation of individual applicant ....
address ....
passport or identity card No. if any ....
relation to the child ....
name and address of legal adviser, if any ....

III — PLACE WHERE THE CHILD IS THOUGHT TO BE

4.1 Information concerning the person alleged to have removed or retained the child

name and first names ....
date and place of birth, if known ....
nationality, if known ....
occupation ....
last known address ....
passport or identity card No. if any ....
description and photo, if possible (see annexes) ....

[1] Extract from the Final Act of the Fourteenth Session, Part F.

4.2	Adresse de l'enfant	....

4.3   Autres personnes susceptibles de donner d'autres
informations permettant de localiser l'enfant   ....

IV — MOMENT, LIEU, DATE ET CIRCONSTANCES DU DÉPLACEMENT OU DU NON-RETOUR ILLICITES

....

V — MOTIFS DE FAIT OU LÉGAUX JUSTIFIANT LA REQUÊTE

....

VI — PROCÉDURES CIVILES EN COURS

....

VII — L'ENFANT DOIT ÊTRE REMIS A:

a   nom et prénoms
date et lieu de naissance
adresse
téléphone

b   arrangements proposés pour le retour

VIII — AUTRES OBSERVATIONS

....

IX — ÉNUMÉRATION DES PIÈCES PRODUITES*

....

Fait à ....

le ....

Signature et/ou cachet de l'Autorité centrale requérante
ou du requérant

....

4.2   Address of the child   ....

4.3   Other persons who might be able to supply additional
information relating to the whereabouts of the child   ....

IV — TIME, PLACE, DATE AND CIRCUMSTANCES OF THE WRONGFUL REMOVAL OR RETENTION

....

V — FACTUAL OR LEGAL GROUNDS JUSTIFYING THE REQUEST

....

VI — CIVIL PROCEEDINGS IN PROGRESS

....

VII — CHILD IS TO BE RETURNED TO:

a   name and first names
date and place of birth
address
telephone number

b   proposed arrangements for return of the child

VIII — OTHER REMARKS

....

IX — LIST OF DOCUMENTS ATTACHED*

....

Date ....

Place ....

Signature and/or stamp of the requesting Central Authority
or applicant

....

7

THE YOUNG OFFENDERS ACT: A NEW ERA IN JUVENILE JUSTICE?

Nicholas Bala

The 1982 enactment of the Young Offenders Act[1] (the "Y.O.A.") by the federal Parliament ushered in a new era for juvenile justice in Canada. The Act can best be understood as a culmination of a process of reform, and as a response to the perceived inadequacies of the legislation it superseded, the Juvenile Delinquents Act.[2] This chapter will explore the concerns which led to the Y.O.A. and some of the principal features of the new Act, and will conclude with a brief consideration of some of the problems which have arisen under the new statutory scheme.

I THE JUVENILE DELINQUENTS ACT

When the Juvenile Delinquents Act was brought into effect in 1908,[3] it too was seen as bringing about a new era for youthful violators of the criminal law. In the latter part of the 19th century, as part of a broad movement of reform in Great Britain, the United States and Canada, a number of very substantial changes occurred in the way in which society dealt with its youngest members, for example the creation of a compulsory and publicly funded school system, the enactment of child labour laws, and the creation of children's aid societies.

---

1   S.C. 1980-81-82-83, c. 110.

2   R.S.C. 1970, c. J-3.

3   S.C. 1908, c. 40.

In the field of criminal law, it came to be accepted that children who violated the law should be treated in a manner different from adults, and a separate correctional system for children was gradually established.

Prior to this time, children who violated the criminal law were treated as adults. They were tried in adult court, and if convicted, faced capital punishment or confinement in an adult penitentiary. The only exception was that under certain circumstances children under 14 were able to raise a defence to a criminal charge based on a lack of mental capacity,[4] and thereby escape conviction. Reform efforts began in the late 19th century and ultimately resulted in the Canadian Parliament enacting the Juvenile Delinquents Act, which legislatively recognized the need for special treatment for children and created a juvenile justice system separate from the adult system.[5]

The Juvenile Delinquents Act ("J.D.A.") was heavily influenced by the Positivist School of Criminology, which emphasized that delinquent behaviour was a product of social environment and was susceptible to "treatment" and "correction". The Act was specifically premised on treating the young offender "not as criminal, but as a misdirected and misguided child, and one needing aid, encouragement, help and assistance".[6] Because of the emphasis on getting assistance for the "delinquent" as expeditiously as possible, a very informal and highly discretionary system was established. One of the chief characteristics of the juvenile justice system was its close connection with the child welfare system. One of the prime movers behind the original J.D.A. observed:

> There should be no hard and fast distinction between neglected and delinquent children. All should be recognized as the same class and should be dealt with with a view to serving the best interests of the child. . . .[7]

The J.D.A. had provisions which specifically allowed a child who had been found delinquent to be placed in the care of a children's aid society.[8] It was also a

---

4 The doctrine of *doli incapax* (Latin for lack of capacity to do wrong) provided an absolute defence for a child under the age of 7, while for children aged 7 to 13 it was necessary for the prosecution to establish that the child had sufficient moral discretion and understanding to appreciate the wrongfulness of his act: see J. McLeod, "Doli Incapax: The Forgotten Presumption in Juvenile Court Trials" (1980), 3 Can. J. Fam. L. 251.

5 For an historical background of the enactment of the Juvenile Delinquents Act, see J.S. Leon, "The Development of Canadian Juvenile Justice: A Background for Reform" (1977), 15 Osgoode Hall L. J. 71; and I. Grant, "The 'Incorrigible' Juvenile: History and Prerequisites of Reform in Ontario" (1984), 4 Can. J. Fam. L. 293.

6 Juvenile Delinquents Act, s. 38.

7 W.L. Scott, as quoted in Archambault, "Young Offenders Act: Philosophy and Principles" (1983), 7 Prov. Judges J. 1 at 2.

8 J.D.A., s. 20(1)(*h*).

common practice in many jurisdictions to place children found in need of protection under provincial welfare legislation in training schools and other correctional facilities along with juveniles found delinquent.

The welfare oriented (or *parens patriae*)[9] philosophy of the J.D.A. gave rise to a system where those responsible for making decisions about a child's life were given very substantial discretion to impose dispositions in accordance with a youthful offender's "best interests". Juvenile court judges were given authority to make dispositions based on perceptions of the "child's own good and the best interests of the community",[10] rather than on the seriousness of the offence. Thus, juvenile court judges were able to send youths to training school for such offences as "sexual immorality",[11] truancy and violations of the Tobacco Restraint Act[12] (possession of cigarettes by a person under 16), all in the name of providing what was "best for the child". Conversely, youths who comitted very serious offences and had long records of violations were sometimes placed on probation and left at home, also in the name of their best interests.

Not only judges had a wide discretion, but also juvenile custodial officials; in most provinces youths removed from their homes under the J.D.A. received "indeterminate dispositions". This accorded with the treatment oriented philosophy of the J.D.A. A punishment would involve a definite sentence, but treatment would inherently continue for an indeterminate period until a cure was effected. Correctional officials sometimes determined that delinquents convicted of serious offences could return home after a few weeks in training school, while in other cases juveniles who had committed very minor offences were kept in custodial facilities for long periods. The broad discretionary powers afforded judges and correctional officials resulted in criticisms of the juvenile justice system, both from advocates for children who claimed that in some cases the system could be too harsh, and from those who were concerned about the protection of society and claimed that in other cases the system was "too soft".

---

9   The term *parens patriae* is Latin for "father (or protector) of the country". Historically, the English Court of Chancery exercised a *parens patriae* jurisdiction to protect the interests of minors and mental incompetents. Initially this was largely in regard to property matters, but it came to be a broader jurisdiction, also extending to protection of the person. Superior courts in Canada still occasionally invoke their *parens patriae* jurisdiction to make orders regarding children in situations where there is no express statutory authority for making an order: *Re D.B. and Dir. of Child Welfare for Nfld.* (1982), 142 D.L.R. (3d) 20 (S.C.C.). The term *parens patriae* has also come to take on a broader, non-technical meaning, namely, the state's concern with the promotion of the welfare of children, and it is in this sense that the term is used here.

10   J.D.A., s. 20(5).

11   In the J.D.A., s. 2, the concept of "juvenile delinquent" was defined as a child who violated *any* federal, provincial or municipal law, or who was "guilty of sexual immorality or any similar form of vice". Once found delinquent, a child could receive any disposition under the Act consistent with "the child's own good and the best interests of the community".

12   R.S.C. 1970, c. T-9.

Related to these concerns was some fundamental questioning by sociologists, criminologists and other commentators about whether a treatment based system really "worked". The founders of the juvenile justice system in Canada had hoped that the J.D.A. would "solve" the problem of delinquency. Critics of the system pointed out that despite intensive efforts to "treat" delinquent youths, many nevertheless went on to commit further, more serious crimes. Other critics pointed out that in some programs those who were "treated" seemed to be no less likely to commit further offences than those who were not, and indeed that some youths involved in the juvenile court system seemed positively harmed by the experience.[13] This is not to say that all treatment based programs came to be regarded as ineffective. Rather, there was a growing appreciation that treatment could not easily solve the problem of delinquency. It came to be recognized that some programs were ineffective — some youths were highly resistant to treatment — and that matching delinquents to the most appropriate program was a difficult task.

At the same time, lawyers and other advocates for children began to express concern about a lack of "due process". Originally, most juvenile court judges lacked formal legal education, and few lawyers appeared in this court. The system was very informal and subject to abuse. It seems that some judges were not unduly troubled with what were perceived to be the "technicalities" of the criminal justice system and were prepared to "expedite matters" to allow the desired treatment processes to begin. Juveniles were often detained prior to trial in circumstances where adults would be released on bail, often on the pretext that a youth might benefit from a "short, sharp shock", or because it was felt that adequate care would not otherwise be available. Sometimes fundamental legal rights, like the right of appeal or the right of access to counsel, were effectively denied. Such infringements of legal rights might have been acceptable if it had been demonstrated that the system was really helping young persons, but the concerns about the lack of efficacy of the treatment which the juvenile justice system afforded gave greater weight to the concerns over the infringement of legal rights.[14]

II THE MOVEMENT TO REFORM

All of the factors discussed, the concerns about intermingling of children in need of protection with delinquents, the highly discretionary nature of the

13 This is not the place to review the extensive literature on the efficacy or potential harm of the juvenile court system in Canada: See, e.g., J. Hackler, *The Prevention of Youthful Crime: The Great Stumble Forward* (1978); and S.J. Shamsie, "Antisocial Adolescents: Our Treatments Do Not Work — Where Do We Go From Here?" (1981), 26 Can. J. of Psychiatry 357.

14 For a description of some of the abuses under the J.D.A., see Canada, Department of Justice, Special Committee on Juvenile Delinquency, *Juvenile Delinquency in Canada* (1965).

J.D.A., the potential for infringement of legal rights, and concerns over the lack of efficacy (and indeed potential harm) of the juvenile justice system, produced a period of reform commencing in the 1960s in Canada. This movement to reform the juvenile justice system may in part be viewed as an aspect of a broader development to secure rights for various groups in society, for example for racial minorities, women and the handicapped. It also reflects a growing societal concern with legal rights in a wide range of contexts, perhaps most dramatically illustrated in Canada with the constitutional entrenchment of the Charter of Rights in 1982.

One aspect of the movement to reform the juvenile justice system in Canada was an often tortuous process of parliamentary involvement and federal legislative reform. This began with a major study by the federal Department of Justice, published in 1965, which was highly critical of the existing juvenile justice system and contained recommendations for legislative action.[15] After extensive discussion and debate, involving a range of professionals working with delinquents, and several abortive efforts to exact new legislation,[16] a draft of the Young Offenders Act was put forward in 1981. After parliamentary committee hearings and consultation with the provinces, the statute received Royal Assent in 1982. The Y.O.A. was proclaimed in force on 2nd April 1984, except for the requirements imposing a uniform national age, which came into effect 1st April 1985.

While the process of federal legislative reform was slowly proceeding, the courts and some provincial governments were also taking steps to bring about changes in the juvenile justice system. In the 1960s and 70s, a series of higher court decisions made it clear that the J.D.A. was indeed criminal law, and that a juvenile was only to be subject to disposition under the Act if guilt of a specific offence was established beyond a reasonable doubt. At the same time, the courts also began to move slowly towards a due process model of juvenile justice.[17]

During this same period, most provincial governments began to ensure that judicial appointees had legal training, and to increase the availability of legal aid

---

15 *Ibid.*

16 See, e.g., legislative draft prepared by the Ministry of the Solicitor General, Children's and Young Persons Act, 1967; the Young Offenders Act, Bill C-192, 3rd Sess., 39th Parliament, 1970; Ministry of the Solicitor General, "Young Persons in Conflict with the Law" (1975); Ministry of the Solicitor General "Highlights of the Proposed New Legislation for Young Offenders" (1977); Ministry of the Solicitor General, draft Young Offenders Act, 1979.

17 Some of the leading "due process" decisions in Canada include *Smith v. R.*, [1959] S.C.R. 638; *Re M.*, [1971] 2 O.R. 19 (H.C.); and *R. v. Moore* (1974), 22 C.C.C. (2d) 189 (B.C.S.C.). For even clearer statements about the need for due process in the juvenile courts, see *In re Gault*, 387 U.S. 1 (1967), a decision of the U.S. Supreme Court. For a detailed discussion of the many legal issues which arose under the J.D.A., see L. Wilson, *Juvenile Courts in Canada* (1982); and Bala, Lilles and Thomson, *Canadian Children's Law: Cases, Notes and Materials* (1982).

funding so that more juveniles could obtain legal representation. In many localities "diversion" programs were established so that youths involved in less serious incidents could be "diverted" from juvenile court and dealt with in the community. There were also moves to close some of the large juvenile custodial institutions and send more delinquents to group homes and other community based placements.[18] These were all changes that later received federal legislative sanction, and ultimately funding support through the Y.O.A.

Although changes were occurring in the juvenile justice system in Canada in the 1960s and 70s, one of its prime characteristics remained its tremendous geographical variability.[19] So while some provinces moved towards a system based on diversion, due process, legal representation and community based sentencing, others did not. Further, the age jurisdiction of juvenile court varied from province to province, different provinces having maximum ages of 15, 16 and 17, and effectively limiting the minimum age of criminal accountability to 7, 12 and 14.

III THE YOUNG OFFENDERS ACT: PRINCIPLES AND PROVISIONS

The Y.O.A. can best be understood as a response to the problems arising under the J.D.A., and as a continuation and culmination of a process of reform commenced by the courts and by provincial governments prior to the enactment of the Y.O.A. It must also be recognized that the Y.O.A. imposed a more uniform national approach in regard to many facets of juvenile justice, though still allowing for some local variation in terms of the implementation. The clearest example of the uniformity required by the Y.O.A. is in regard to age; all jurisdictions have 12 as the minimum age of criminal responsibility, while the maximum age of Y.O.A. jurisdiction has been established as the 18th birthday. The Y.O.A. also puts into place a range of legal safeguards to ensure that young persons receive due process, and these apply throughout the country. The greatest scope for provincial variation is in the area of dispositions. Provinces have the authority to decide whether or not to have "alternative measures" (diversion) programs, fine options, community service orders and intermittent custody, and can broadly determine what kinds of custodial facilities they will have.

The Y.O.A. makes clear that while there is to be a special law and a separate justice and corrections system for young offenders, the basis for state

---

18 See J.A. Osborne, "Juvenile Justice Policy in Canada: The Transfer of Initiative" (1979), 2 Can. J. Fam. L. 7.

19 For a detailed description of how the juvenile courts in Canada were functioning in 1982-83, see Bala and Corrado, *Juvenile Justice in Canada: A Comparative Study* (1985). This study emphasizes the tremendous geographical variability under the J.D.A. in terms of provisions, procedures and practices.

action is the imposition of criminal sanctions, not simply the promotion of the welfare of children. As with adults, state involvement in the life of a young person is only justified when a criminal offence is alleged, and duly proven according to law. The criminal law focus is apparent from the shift from indeterminate custodial dispositions (based on detention until the treatment is effective) to determinate custodial sentences (based on notions of punishment and protection of society). The criminal basis of the law is also evident from the fact that the Y.O.A. deals only with violations of such federal statutes as the Criminal Code. Such "status offences"[20] as "sexual immorality" are no longer a basis for coercive state intervention. Provincial governments have largely adopted the Y.O.A. model for dealing with violations of their statutes, though some have retained such offences as truancy or continue to allow child protection applications based on "unmanageability".

The Y.O.A. has an express "Declaration of Principle" which provides:

3.(1) It is hereby recognized and declared that

(a) while young persons should not in all instances be held accountable in the same manner or suffer the same consequences for their behaviour as adults, young persons who commit offences should nonetheless bear responsibility for their contraventions;

(b) society must, although it has the responsibility to take reasonable measures to prevent criminal conduct by young persons, be afforded the necessary protection from illegal behaviour;

(c) young persons who commit offences require supervision, discipline and control, but, because of their state of dependency and level of development and maturity, they also have special needs and require guidance and assistance;

(d) where it is not inconsistent with the protection of society, taking no measures or taking measures other than judicial proceedings under this Act should be considered for dealing with young persons who have committed offences;

(e) young persons have rights and freedoms in their own right, including those stated in the *Canadian Charter of Rights and Freedoms* or in the *Canadian Bill of Rights*, and in particular a right to be heard in the course of, and to participate in, the processes that lead to decisions that affect them, and young persons should have special guarantees of their rights and freedoms;

(f) in the application of this Act, the rights and freedoms of young persons include a right to the least possible interference with freedom that is consistent with the protection of society, having regard to the needs of young persons and the interests of their families;

(g) young persons have the right, in every instance where they have rights or freedoms that may be affected by this Act, to be informed as to what those rights and freedoms are; and

---

20   A "status offence" is one which can only be committed by a person with a particular status, in this case a child. An example was the offence of "sexual immorality" — an aspect of delinquency as defined in s. 2 of the J.D.A. (see *supra*, n. 11); only a juvenile could be convicted of this offence.

(*h*) parents have responsibility for the care and supervision of their children, and, for that reason, young persons should be removed from parental supervision either partly or entirely only when measures that provide for continuing parental supervision are inappropriate.

These principles are intended to serve as a guide to the interpretation of the Act, and are clearly reflected in the substantive features of the Y.O.A.

1. Limited Accountability

While young persons should bear responsibility for their contraventions, they should not in all instances be held as accountable as adults. This important principle is most clearly reflected in the maximum Y.O.A. dispositions, with fines limited to $1,000, and custodial terms limited to three years as opposed to life for adults.[21]

2. Protection of Society

The right of society to protection from illegal behaviour is clearly recognized. Protection of society is expected to come from the apprehension and punishment of young offenders under the Act. Under the J.D.A. dispositions were to be based on the "child's own good and the interests of the community",[22] which allowed courts to place the welfare of a juvenile ahead of concerns about protecting society. The Y.O.A. clearly requires courts to give full consideration to the protection of society when rendering dispositions. This does not mean that courts should necessarily adopt a punitive response when dealing with young offenders, for clearly the long term protection of society demands the rehabilitation of youthful law breakers, and their successful reintegration into society.

One provision of the Y.O.A. which seems intended to protect society is s. 16 which governs the transfer of proceedings into "ordinary court". Under this provision, a hearing is held in Youth Court to determine whether it is appropriate to transfer a young person into the adult system. The effect of transfer is that a young person may face trial in adult court, and, if convicted, may be subject to the same sanctions as an adult. For serious offences this means the possibility of a life sentence served in an adult facility, rather than the maximum of three years served in the juvenile correctional system which a Youth Court might impose. Thus, for young persons who pose a serious threat to society, there is the possibility of lengthy periods of incarceration in order to secure the adequate protection of the community. While transfer under the J.D.A. could only occur if both "the good of the child *and* the interests of the community" demanded

---

21 Y.O.A., s. 20(1).
22 J.D.A., s. 20(5).

it,[23] under the Y.O.A., transfer may occur if the court is of the opinion that this is "in the interest of society. . . having regard to the needs of the young person".[24] This new standard for transfer seems to place greater emphasis on the interest of society, and correspondingly less on the needs of the youth, and therefore seems to require that more attention be paid to the protection of the community.[25]

3. Special Needs

While young offenders require supervision, discipline and control, they also have special needs requiring guidance and assistance. This recognition of the special needs of children is most fundamentally reflected in the existence of a special and separate system of juvenile corrections. This is a system which, at least in comparison to the adult system, seems to emphasize rehabilitation over punishment and confinement.

The concern with special needs is recognized in a number of substantive provisions of the Y.O.A. For example, the Act prohibits the publication of information which might identify a young person who is subject to proceedings under the Act.[26] Section 39 allows a Youth Court Judge to exclude members of the public from the proceedings. The Y.O.A. also restricts access to records concerning proceedings under the Act, and in some cases provides for their destruction.[27] All of these provisions recognize the special susceptibility of young persons to "labelling" if their crimes are widely known, and are intended to protect them from exposure to the public. They also reflect a desire to limit the accountability of young offenders.[28]

The Y.O.A. provides that instead of placing a young offender in a correctional facility, a Youth Court may order that he be detained for treatment, for example in a psychiatric hospital.[29] Such an order can only be made if the young person, and usually his parents, consent. Further, the court must first

---

23   J.D.A. s. 9(1). Emphasis added.

24   Y.O.A., s. 16(1). Under the Y.O.A. transfer can be ordered if the young person who is charged was at least 14 years of age at the time of the alleged offence, and if he or she is charged with one of the more serious indictable offences.

25   See, e.g., *R. v. C.J.M.* (1985), 49 C.R. (3d) 226 (Man. C.A.), which recognizes the increased emphasis that s. 16 of the Y.O.A. places on the protection of society. However, to the contrary see *R. v. B.(N.)* (1985), 21 C.C.C. (3d) 374 (Que. C.A.), which suggests that the standard to transfer may be the same under the Y.O.A. and the J.D.A.

26   Y.O.A., s. 38.

27   Y.O.A. ss. 40-46.

28   Y.O.A., s. 3(1)(*a*).

29   Y.O.A. ss. 20(1)(*i*) and 22.

receive a psychiatric or psychological report indicating that his needs require placement in such a facility, and the facility must agree to accept the young person.

Another provision of the Y.O.A. allows a Youth Court to withhold from the young person a medical, psychological or psychiatric report prepared in connection with the case.[30] This may be done if the court is concerned that releasing the report would be likely to be "detrimental to the treatment or recovery" of the young person, and again reflects a desire to give a judge the discretion to protect the special needs of a young person.

4. Alternative Measures

Where not inconsistent with the protection of society, consideration should be given to taking no measures, or using various forms of non-court diversion. The Y.O.A. has provisions governing the operation of "alternative measures" programs.[31] Whether a particular accused young person is given the opportunity of avoiding the court process initially depends upon a decision by the police or prosecutor[32] to allow a more informal resolution of a matter. Further, the Act attempts to ensure that young persons are not improperly coerced into participating in such processes and that they retain the right to go to court to have their criminal liability properly established before being subject to any sanction.

While the Y.O.A. has provisions governing the operation of such programs, it is up to the provinces to decide whether to implement them. Most provinces have taken steps to establish or expand their diversion programs, but in Ontario the government's initial response to the Y.O.A. has been a refusal to sanction the operation of alternative measures programs, forcing the closure of a number of local projects which were in operation under the J.D.A.

5. Rights and Freedoms

Young persons dealt with under the Y.O.A. are to enjoy all of the fundamental legal rights afforded adults. Further, in recognition of their limited capacities, the Act provides certain special protections of their rights and freedoms.

---

30 Y.O.A., s. 13(6). It may be questioned whether this provision of the Act violates the Canadian Charter of Rights and Freedoms. In particular, if a young person faces sanctions on the basis of a report to which he is denied access, this might constitute deprivation of "liberty" not "in accordance with the principles of fundamental justice" (s. 7 of the Charter) or denial of the right to a "fair and public hearing" (s. 11 (*d*) of the Charter).

31 Y.O.A. s. 4.

32 To the contrary, however, see *R. v. J.B.* (1985), 20 C.C.C. (3d) 67 (B.C. Prov. Ct.), which held that a young person is entitled to some sort of hearing before a decision is made about alternative measures. For a commentary doubting this decision, see the Annotation to *R. v. J.B.* by Bala, in the *Young Offenders Service* (Annotation to Y.O.S. 85-058).

At the time of initial arrest and detention by the police, young persons are to be afforded all the rights given adults under the Charter of Rights, including the right to seek pre-trial release (bail). The Y.O.A. also provides that if questioned by the police concerning an alleged offence, special steps are to be taken to ensure that a young person comprehends his legal rights, including the right to remain silent and to have a parent or lawyer present during questioning.[33] The Act further stipulates that a young person charged with any offence who is unable to obtain counsel and who wishes to be represented, must be provided with counsel paid by the government.[34] Though in practice there have been some difficulties in assuring that all young persons are able to exercise fully their rights to counsel, it is an important provision. Adults have a constitutionally guaranteed right to "retain" counsel.[35] This essentially means adults have a right to have counsel if they can afford it, or if legal aid officials decide to provide counsel. Young persons have a broader right to state provided counsel in any circumstances where they are unable to obtain counsel. Since very few young persons have the financial resources to retain counsel on their own, virtually all young persons have a right to a lawyer paid by the government.[36]

Another example of the special protections for young persons is found in s. 19 of the Y.O.A. A judge accepting a guilty plea from a young person must be informed of the facts of the case and be "satisfied that the facts support the charge". If the judge is not so satisfied, the plea must be struck and a trial conducted.

The Y.O.A. provides that proceedings are to be based on "summary procedures" developed for dealing with less serious charges faced by adults, as opposed to the more complex procedures reserved for dealing with "indictable offences".[37] The rationale for this is that proceedings are to be handled relatively expeditiously. Further, the relatively light maximum penalties which a Youth Court can impose may justify use of the less formal procedures. Thus, while young persons are to enjoy most of the standard features of the criminal process, in a proceeding under the Y.O.A. they are denied access to a preliminary inquiry and a jury trial. Though it seems that this denial of access to the more formal procedure, and in particular to the jury trial, may be justified, at least one

---

33   Y.O.A., s. 56.

34   Y.O.A., s. 11.

35   Charter of Rights and Freedoms, s. 10(*b*).

36   See *R. v. R.H.* (1984), Y.O.S. 84-025 (Alta. Prov. Ct.), where it was held that parents' financial resources are not to be considered when assessing a young person's ability to retain counsel.

37   See Y.O.A., s. 52. Summary procedures are governed by Pt. XXIV of the Criminal Code, R.S.C. 1970, c. C-34, while the procedure for indictable offences is governed by Pts. XV to XVIII of the Code.

Ontario judge has held that this constitutes constitutionally prohibited discrimination on the basis of age.[38] Undoubtedly this issue will ultimately have to be resolved by the higher courts.

6. Minimal Interference

Young persons shall have the right to the least possible interference with their freedom, consistent with the protection of society, the needs of young persons and the interests of their families. The principle of minimal interference is reflected in the provisions of the Y.O.A. for alternative measures (diversion). The Act also provides that young persons convicted of offences may receive various community based dispositions, such as restitution, community service orders or probation. For more serious offenders, the Y.O.A. allows sentencing to "open custody" — places such as group homes and wilderness camps — as well as to "secure custody" — training schools or reformatories.[39]

7. Young Persons to be Informed of Rights

Those involved in juvenile justice are responsible for ensuring that young persons are aware of their rights, including their right of access to counsel. At the time of arrest, the police must inform young persons of their rights. Once in court, the judge also has an obligation to be sure that a young person is aware of his legal rights, and must take certain steps to protect young persons. For example, a judge must inform a young person who is not represented by a lawyer of the right to counsel provided for in the Act.[40]

8. Parental Involvement

The Y.O.A. recognizes the parental role by including provisions for the presence of parents after arrest, for notice to parents of proceedings, for involvement of parents in dispositional decision making and, where appropriate, parental supervision of young persons before trial or after disposition.[41] Though the Act provides that a judge may order the parents to attend the Youth Court if their presence is "necessary or in the best interests of the young person",[42] the parents are not legally accountable for the contraventions of their children, nor are they to decide such issues as whether a young person should

---

38 *R. v. R.L.*, Ont. C.A., 22nd April 1986 (not yet reported), upheld the constitutionality of denying young offenders the right to a jury trial.

39 Y.O.A., s. 24.

40 Y.O.A., see, e.g., ss. 11, 12 and 19.

41 Y.O.A., ss. 7, 9, 16, 20, 22, 28, 56.

42 Y.O.A., s. 10.

have a lawyer or enter a plea of not guilty. While parental involvement is clearly desirable for some young persons, it has been suggested that it may not always be appropriate.[43] There have been cases where parents have improperly pressured their children into pleading guilty to "get things over with", or have appeared to ally themselves with the police in questioning a young person and securing a confession.[44] There have also been concerns expressed in regard to parental involvement in cases involving older youths who may no longer be living with their families.

Although not explicitly stated, a clear principle of the Y.O.A. is that the discretion of decision makers is to be structured, and, increasingly, decisions about young persons are to be made by judges rather than those in the juvenile corrections system. This generally accords with notions of due process; decisions are to be openly made with a possibility of participation by the young person. Thus, the Act stipulates that judges may not impose a more severe sanction on a young person than one which an adult would face for the same offence, while restrictions are placed on the use of secure custody (training school), as opposed to open custody (wilderness camps or group homes).[45] Further decisions about the release of young persons from custodial dispositions prior to completion of an originally imposed sentence are to be ultimately controlled by Youth Courts, and not by correctional officials or parole boards.[46]

In some ways the statements found in the Declaration of Principle of the Y.O.A. may seem inconsistent with one another. Clearly, the Act does not have a single, simple underlying philosophy. Compared to the welfare oriented J.D.A., the Y.O.A. emphasizes due process, the protection of society and limited discretion. Compared to the adult Criminal Code, however, the Y.O.A. emphasizes special needs, treatment and limited accountability for young persons. In many ways, the philosophy of the Y.O.A. may be viewed as ambivalent, but this reflects the attitude of our society towards young offenders, and perhaps more generally towards children and adolescents. On the one hand there is a desire to protect society against potentially violent or unstable youth, and on the other there is a desire to rehabilitate and promote the welfare of young persons who represent society's future. There is also a fundamental tension in

---

43   For the purposes of the Y.O.A., the term "parent" is broadly defined to include "any person who is under a legal duty to provide for" a young person, or "who has in law or in fact, the custody or control of that" young person (s. 2). Where a parent cannot be located, there are provisions for having another adult relative or friend play a protective role for the young person (ss. 9(3) and 56(2)).

44   See e.g. *R. v. S.L.* (1985), Y.O.S. 84-020 (Ont. Prov. Ct.); and *R. v. A.T.B.* (1985), Y.O.S. 85-043 (Ont. Prov. Ct.).

45   Y.O.A., ss. 20(7), 24(3), (4) and (5).

46   Y.O.A., ss. 28-33.

the Y.O.A. between notions of due process, and notions of treatment; in some places the Act gives paramountcy to due process, but there are also places where treatment takes precedence. The underlying tensions and philosophical inconsistencies in the Act reflect the very complex nature of the problem of youthful criminality. There is no simple philosophy that will deal with the problem; there is no single program that will solve the problem. Judges and the various professionals who work with young persons require a complex and balanced set of principles like those found in the Y.O.A.

IV THE YOUNG OFFENDERS ACT: PROBLEMS IN IMPLEMENTATION

Even before the Y.O.A. was proclaimed in force in April of 1984 it was the centre of controversy. In particular a number of provincial governments opposed the raising of the age jurisdiction. In Quebec and Manitoba the maximum age jurisdiction was up to 18 under the J.D.A. In British Columbia and Newfoundland it was up to 17, and in the other provinces it was up to 16.

The Y.O.A. had the effect of imposing a uniform national age of Youth Court jurisdiction. The change to a uniform age was in part a philosophical and political decision: it was felt that young persons throughout the country deserved to be treated in the same fashion. It was also felt that s. 15 of the Charter of Rights and Freedoms — the equality rights provision, which came into effect in April of 1985 — would require a uniform national age. The imposition of a uniform national age inevitably meant that some provinces would have to change their age jurisdiction.

While any maximum (or minimum) age for a juvenile justice system is somewhat arbitrary, Canadian society generally accepts that a young person becomes an adult at 18 for civil purposes, and it seems sensible to use this age for criminal purposes as well. For "hardened" older offenders, there is still the "safety valve" of transfer into the adult system pursuant to s. 16 of the Y.O.A. The age jurisdiction of the Y.O.A. reflects a legal recognition of adolescence — the ages of 12 to 17 — as a distinct period of life, requiring treatment that is different from both childhood and adulthood.

The opposition to raising the maximum age for a youth system was particularly strong in British Columbia, Nova Scotia and Ontario. Some of the provincial concerns were philosophical. There was a belief in Ontario that 16-year-olds should not be dealt with as "children", but rather as adults. Much of the concern, however, was financial. The youth system is generally more resource intensive and expensive to operate than the adult system. The effect of the action of the federal Parliament in raising the maximum age of juvenile jurisdiction was to increase costs for the provincial governments. Further, the Y.O.A. clearly added features to the system which made it more costly for provincial governments to operate. For example, the requirement that the government provide counsel for all young persons wishing to be represented but unable to retain a lawyer clearly increases expenses for the provinces. Though the federal government has paid a portion of these added expenses, the Y.O.A. has cost the provincial governments a substantial amount of money. This has unfortunately led some provinces to a begrudging acceptance of the Act, an acceptance which largely fails to seize many of the opportunities created by the Y.O.A. for innovative responses to the problems of young offenders.

A "minimal compliance" approach to the Y.O.A. seems most evident in Ontario. As noted above, the province has failed to sanction any use of the alternative measures provisions of the Act. Together with Nova Scotia, Ontario has adopted a "two-tier" model of Y.O.A. implementation. Thus, in Ontario, 12 to 16-year-olds are dealt with by a judge in the Family Court, sitting as a Youth Court Judge, with assessment, detention and dispositional services provided by the Ministry of Community and Social Services. These were the agencies responsible for juvenile justice under the J.D.A. Sixteen and 17-year-olds are dealt with by a system carved out of the adult system. They appear before judges of the Provincial Court (Criminal Division) who are nominally sitting as Youth Court Judges. This age group is provided services by the Ministry of Correctional Services, which is responsible for adult offenders; while they are detained separately from adults, sometimes it is only in different parts of a single facility. This two-tier model of implementation has been condemned as inefficient and creating a stark disparity in treatment for older young persons.[47] It may ultimately be struck down as discriminatory under s. 15 of the Charter of Rights and Freedoms and it is to be hoped that the provincial governments involved will reconsider their positions.[48]

Another issue in regard to age has been the raising of the minimum age of criminal responsibility. Under the J.D.A., children as young as 7 could be dealt with in the juvenile court, though between the ages of 7 and 14 it was possible to raise the defence of "doli incapax" — lack of capacity to commit a crime. Further, a few provinces took steps to ensure that young persons under a specified age were dealt with outside the juvenile court process. For example, in Quebec, provincial legislation[49] provided that juveniles under 14 were not to be prosecuted under the J.D.A.; though this action may have been constitutionally

---

47   See Canadian Bar Association — Ontario, *Report of Special Committee on the Young Offenders Act* (6th December 1985).

48   See *R. v. G.W.* (1985), Y.O.S. 86-017 (Ont. Prov. Ct.), where a challenge to two-tier implementation was made; it was not successful as, on the facts of the particular case, there was no "actual evidence" of discrimination.

49   Youth Protection Act, R.S.Q. 1977, c. P-34.1, s. 60 [am. 1981, c. 2, s. 16]. See Bala and Corrado, *Juvenile Justice in Canada: A Comparative Study* (1985), at 17-20 for a further discussion of the age of minimum juvenile court jurisdiction in various provinces.

suspect, very few juveniles under 14 in Quebec were dealt with in juvenile court. Indeed, throughout Canada, the result of various formal and informal policies was that relatively few children under the age of 12 were charged and prosecuted under the J.D.A. Many observers, however, believe that it was a serious mistake to raise the age of minimum criminal accountability for all cases to 12. They argue that we have lost a significant deterrent for offenders under 12. This, however, is the sort of issue which must be studied on a cross-jurisdictional basis. Some provinces appear to have done much better than others in terms of implementing the Y.O.A. in this regard by preparing child welfare authorities for dealing with criminal activity of children under 12. Most notably Quebec seems to have made good progress in dealing with children in this age group who violate the law without having to resort to the criminal system; this province might serve as a model for other Canadian jurisdictions for dealing with this problem.

A disturbing trend which may be developing under the Y.O.A. is the tendency for some Youth Court Judges to interpret the Act in a relatively punitive fashion, emphasizing the need to protect society and punish young offenders, while seeming to ignore the special needs and limited accountability of young persons. There is considerable evidence that in a number of provinces dispositions being rendered under the Y.O.A. are substantially more severe than those which were being imposed under the J.D.A. and that judges are making very limited use of treatment orders and psychiatric or psychological assessments.[50] These problems may be exacerbated by a tendency of some provincial governments to implement the Y.O.A. by providing custodial facilities where only a limited attempt is made to rehabilitate young offenders.[51] Fortunately, some of the appellate courts have been emphasizing the need to consider the lesser maturity of young offenders when imposing a sentence upon them, always bearing in mind their special needs and limited accountability.[52]

It is the author's view that on the whole, the reforms brought about under the Y.O.A. are a distinct improvement over the system in place under the J.D.A. Further, many of the changes seem inevitable in light of the problems and

---

50 See, e.g., Leschied and Jaffee, "Implications of the Young Offenders Act in Modifying the Juvenile Justice System" in Bala and Lilles, *Young Offenders Service* (1985); "Custody, sentences increase under Young Offenders Act", *Globe and Mail*, 6th August 1985; and Victor Malarek, "Court Cannot Force Young Killer to Undergo Therapy", *Globe and Mail*, 20th December 1985.

51 See e.g., *R. v. C.F.*, [1984] 6 W.W.R. 32, reversed [1985] 2 W.W.R. 379 (Man. C.A.), which describes the efforts of the Manitoba government which designated a locked part of a training school and detention facility as a place of "open custody" under the Y.O.A. See also *Re L.H.F.* (1985), 170 A.P.R. 44 (P.E.I.S.C.).

52 See, e.g., *R. v. R.I.* (1985), 44 C.R. (3d) 168 (Ont. C.A.); and *R. v. G.K.* (1985), 39 Alta. L.R. (2d) 355 (C.A.).

developments arising under the old legislation. The Y.O.A. is not, however, a panacea for the problem of juvenile criminality. Clearly there have been difficulties in implementing the Y.O.A., and the effects of the legislation will require careful monitoring.

In the spring of 1986, the federal Parliament enacted some amendments to the Y.O.A.[53] They deal with such matters as record keeping, breach of probation and the publication of identifying information in situations where a dangerous young person is at large. While these amendments should facilitate the work of those who deal with young offenders, they do not mark a major change in the philosophy or fundamental features of the Y.O.A. The federal government has a continuing responsibility for monitoring the implementation of the Act and providing adequate financial support to the provinces so as to allow for a truly new era of juvenile justice in Canada.

---

53   Bill C-106, First Session, Thirty-third Parliament. Third reading 17th June 1986.

8

CHILD PROTECTION LEGISLATION: RECENT CANADIAN REFORM

*Richard F. Barnhorst**

I INTRODUCTION

Throughout Canada in recent years, there has been a tremendous amount of legislative reform concerning the protection of abused and neglected children. Since 1980, nearly every province and territory has amended its child protection legislation. In 1984 alone, Alberta, the Yukon and Ontario passed legislation which addressed some of the most fundamental aspects of the child protection process.

This legislative activity raises questions as to what policies or philosophical approaches are behind the new statutes. One philosophical perspective on child protection legislation can be considered non-legalistic and interventionist. From this perspective parents are viewed as trustees for their children.[1] Children

---

*I would like to thank George Thomson, Professor Michael Wald and the Stanford Law School for their valuable assistance in the development of this chapter.

1 See M. Wald, "State Intervention on Behalf of 'Neglected' Children: A Search for Realistic Standards" (1975), 27 Stan. L. Rev. 985.

are the collective responsibility of the family and the community, not the property of the biological parents.[2] The family is the primary care giver but this responsibility is shared with the state. An important role of the state is to monitor parental child rearing practices and to intervene when the behaviour of the parents interferes with the child's optimal development.[3] This approach emphasizes that decisions made by parents are not always based on what is in the child's interests, early intervention is necessary to prevent future problems for the child, and parents will often resist the use of prevention services by state agencies if such services may be provided only on a voluntary basis.

A key component of interventionist legislation is that broad discretion is granted to child protection agencies and judges. The assumption is that broad discretion is necessary because each case is different and thus flexibility is required. It is also assumed that agencies and judges act in the best interests of children and therefore the need for legal limits on their discretion is minimal. In general, vague, discretionary legislation which permits an interventionist policy to be implemented represents the traditional approach to child protection legislation in North America.

Over the last several years, some legal scholars and law reform bodies have challenged the interventionist approach.[4] They have proposed legalistic, noninterventionist legislative standards which give more deference to family autonomy. This approach to child protection legislation is based on the presumption that child rearing should be left to the discretion of parents unless they fail to provide their children with a clearly and narrowly defined minimum standard of care. Only if the care of the child falls below that minimum standard should the state be permitted to interfere on an involuntary basis. If the care of the child has not fallen below the minimum standard, intervention in the form of services to the family should be a response to the family's own perception of its requirements and should be provided on a voluntary basis. If involuntary intervention is necessary to protect the child, it should be in the manner which least interferes with family autonomy.

---

2 Ontario Social Development Council, "Tomorrow's Child — An Examination of The Children's Act: A Consultation Paper" (1983).

3 M. Wald, *supra*, n. 1.

4 M. Wald, *supra*, n. 1; M. Wald, "State Intervention on Behalf of 'Neglected' Children: Standards for Removal of Children from their Homes, Monitoring the Status of Children in Foster Care, and Termination of Parental Rights" (1976), 28 Stan. L. Rev. 623; R. Mnookin, "Foster Care — In Whose Best Interests?" (1973), 43 Harv. Educ. Rev. 599; Institute of Judicial Administration — American Bar Association, Juvenile Justice Standards Project ("ABA Standards"), *Standards Relating to Abuse and Neglect* (1977); National Advisory Committee on Criminal Justice Standards and Goals, *Report of the Task Force on Juvenile Justice and Delinquency Prevention* (1976).

Legalistic, non-interventionist legislation limits the discretion of agencies and judges through relatively narrow, precise decision-making criteria. It also emphasizes procedural safeguards for parents and children and includes mechanisms for holding agencies and judges accountable for their actions.

The main arguments supporting the legalistic, non-interventionist approach can be summarized as follows:[5]

— Our society's commitment to privacy, diversity of ideas and life-styles and freedom of religion is promoted by allowing families to raise children in a wide variety of living situations and with a wide variety of child rearing practices. A more interventionist approach involves the risk of coercive state intervention being used to "rescue" children of parents who are poor or are members of minority cultures.[6]

— Knowledge is very limited regarding child rearing and the means of achieving long-term change in a child's emotional and psychological development. Studies indicate that it is very difficult to accurately predict future behaviour from observations of child rearing practices or home environment. There is simply no agreement on the "best" or "proper" way to raise a child.[7]

— Except in cases involving seriously harmed children, there is doubt that involuntary intervention will improve a child's situation. There is some evidence that such intervention may actually harm the child. Research indicates the likelihood of negative emotional impact which separation from parents has upon a child, often regardless of the quality of life within the family.[8] Children in care are frequently subjected to several residential placements, especially if they are older and belong to a cultural minority.[9] We are learning much more about the incidence of adoption breakdown[10] and there is little evidence demonstrating the effectiveness of social work intervention, especially such "soft" services as individual and group counselling or parent education programs.[11]

---

5 This summary also appears in R. Barnhorst and G. Thomson, "Policy and Practice in the Child Welfare Area", in *Family Law and Social Policy Workshop Series* (1982).

6 M. Wald, *supra*, n. 1, at 992.

7 *Ibid.*

8 A. Kadushin, "Children in Adoptive Homes", in H. Maas (ed.), *Social Service Research: Review of Studies* (1978), at 49.

9 *Ibid.*; see also H.P. Hepworth, *Foster Care and Adoption in Canada* (1980).

10 A. Kadushin (ed.), *Child Welfare Services* (1980), at 530 and 545.

11 M. Wald, *supra*, n. 1, at 997. However, a recent study which compared home and foster placement found "that the home children seemed to remain at substantial risk in terms of social, emotional and academic development, and that foster care may have been slightly more beneficial than home placement in terms of the children's health and academic performance": see M. Wald, J.M. Carlsmith, P.H. Leiderman, R. deSoles French and C. Smith, *Protecting Abused/Neglected Children: A Comparison of Home and Foster Placement* (1985), at 160.

— Parents should have the uninterrupted opportunity to meet the needs of their child in order to establish the parent-child attachment which many mental health experts believe is critical to a child's growth and development.[12] Disruption of the privacy of the family through state intrusion can prevent the attachment from being established.

— Once the psychological attachment between parent and child has been established, the continuing maintenance of these bonds needs to be safeguarded.[13]

— The law does not have the capacity to supervise fragile, complex parent-child relationships and the state "is too crude an instrument to become an adequate substitute for flesh and blood parents".[14]

In general, these two policy approaches — the non-legalistic, interventionist and the legalistic, non-interventionist — are extremes on a philosophical spectrum and most statutes fall somewhere in between. However, a careful review of a statute can reveal its overall emphasis and thus permit a conclusion as to whether it is essentially interventionist or non-interventionist. The purpose of Part II of this chapter is to review four recent Canadian child protection statutes in order to determine their underlying policy perspective. More specifically, Part II analyzes certain key provisions in the statutes in order to determine the extent to which they embody the legalistic, non-interventionist policy proposed by the critics of interventionist legislation. Part III analyzes the legislative reform process in each of the four jurisdictions in order to determine why they have adopted the policy that is reflected in their legislation.

II CRITICAL AREAS IN CHILD PROTECTION LEGISLATION

In child protection legislation, there are several critical areas which influence the ease or difficulty with which intervention in the family is allowed. The following six areas will be examined in this part of the chapter:

— Principles

— Grounds for Intervention

— Initiation of Proceedings

— Interim Custody of the Child

— Disposition

— Accountability Mechanisms

---

12 J. Goldstein, A. Freud and A. Solnit, *Before the Best Interests of the Child* (1979), at 9.

13 *Ibid.*, at 10.

14 *Ibid.*, at 11.

This part will describe these areas, discuss the kinds of provisions that would reflect a legalistic, non-interventionist approach, and review relevant provisions of four Canadian statutes to determine the extent to which they have adopted a non-interventionist perspective. The four statutes to be reviewed are:

— Ontario's Child and Family Services Act[15]
— Alberta's Child Welfare Act[16]
— Yukon's Children's Act[17]
— British Columbia's Family and Child Service Act[18]

These statutes will be highlighted because, in general, they represent the range of approaches used in Canadian child protection legislation. They are also the products of recent legislative reform activities and thus indicate recent Canadian thinking on child protection policy. All four statutes were passed between 1980 and 1984.

1. Principles

Most Canadian child protection statutes contain some reference to general principles which are intended to apply throughout the legislation. A preamble or declaration of principles can help to clarify the overall policy perspective intended to underlie the legislation. A well-constructed set of principles can be a useful source of guidance for decision makers, such as judges and child protection workers and others trying to interpret the Act, especially in situations not completely covered by more specific provisions throughout the Act. Three basic approaches are evident in the statutes under review:

(a) Best Interests of the Child

British Columbia[19] and the Yukon[20] have taken the approach of including at the beginning of their statutes a brief statement of the overriding importance of the best interests of the child. For example, the British Columbia Act states:

> In the administration and interpretation of this Act the safety and well being of a child shall be the paramount considerations.[21]

---

15 S.O. 1984, c. 55.

16 S.A. 1984, c. C-8.1.

17 S.Y.T. 1984, c. 2.

18 S.B.C. 1980, c. 11.

19 S. 2.

20 S. 2. It should also be noted that, under the heading "General Function of Director", s. 107 states that it is the policy of the Director of Family and Children's Services to supply services "to promote family units and to diminish the need to take children into care or to keep them in care".

21 S. 2.

This general principle provides very little guidance for decisions under the Act. It could be used to support either an interventionist or non-interventionist policy. For example, a non-interventionist policy is based in large part on the rationale that, in general, the best interests of children will be served by a law which clearly respects family autonomy in child rearing. However, a single "best interests of the child" statement fails to identify other principles (for example, family autonomy) which can help determine what is in the best interests of children. By failing to include principles such as the importance of children remaining with their parents, the "best interests" statement may have the effect of encouraging an interventionist approach by judges and child protection workers.

(b) Family Autonomy

In sharp contrast to the British Columbia and Yukon Acts is Alberta's Child Welfare Act. This Act contains a long list of general principles and other "matters to be considered" by decision makers under the Act.[22] The general principles which address the basic philosophical perspective of the Act clearly reflect a non-interventionist approach. They emphasize the importance of not interfering with family autonomy unless necessary to protect the child. When intervention is necessary, the principles state that it should be in the form that least interferes with the rights and responsibilities of parents. Where it is not inconsistent with the protection of the child, services are to be provided by referral to community resources rather than through the court.

(c) Mixed Approach

Basically the same approach is taken in Ontario's Child and Family Services Act. Ontario's declaration of principles gives explicit recognition to the importance of supporting the autonomy and integrity of the family.[23] It states a preference for providing services on a voluntary basis and for using the least restrictive or disruptive means of helping a child or family. However, the Ontario Act also recognizes the "best interests, protection and well-being of children" as a "paramount objective."[24] Therefore, although the Ontario principles generally reflect a non-interventionist philosophy, they also include the best interests approach.

In sum, the principles of the four Acts can be placed along the policy spectrum as follows:[25]

---

22 S. 2.

23 S. 1.

24 S. 1(a).

25 This chart and others throughout the paper are intended to compare only the four statutes being

Non-Legalistic, Interventionist			Legalistic, Non-Interventionist	
B.C.	Yukon		Ontario	Alberta

2. Grounds for Involuntary Intervention

The provisions of an Act which state the grounds on which an agency or court may intervene without the consent of parents in order to protect children is probably the most fundamental part of child welfare legislation. These grounds determine when an agency may conduct an investigation of a family, apprehend a child without a court order and initiate court proceedings, and when the court may order intervention in the form of supervision or removal of a child from the parents. In most Canadian legislation, the grounds are contained in the definition of a child in need of protection.

(a) Broad, Vague Grounds

Most Canadian child protection statutes contain broad, vague grounds for intervention. Typical is British Columbia's brief, five-part definition of a child "in need of protection" which includes a child who is "abused or neglected so that his safety or well being is endangered".[26] Similarly, the Yukon definition includes a child who is "in the care of a parent or other person who is unable to provide proper or competent care, supervision or control over him".[27]

These types of provisions have been criticized by legal scholars for several reasons:[28]

— Terms such as "neglect", "well-being", "improper" and "unfit" are open to a wide variety of interpretations and facilitate arbitrary intervention.

— By failing to specify the harms which justify intervention, vague definitions make it more likely that the child will be harmed by the intervention of the court.

— The failure to identify specific harms prevents a careful weighing of the harms to be alleviated against the harms likely to result from interfering in the parent-child relationship.

— The decision to intervene involves value judgments about appropriate child rearing practices and about where and how a child should grow up. These value judgments should not be left up to the individual values of hundreds of child protection workers and judges.

---

reviewed. It should be noted that statutes in other jurisdictions and model statutes may be more representative of a legalistic or non-legalistic approach, as the case may be. In addition, because of the differences in wording among the four statutes, the placement of the statutes along the policy spectrum is somewhat arbitrary.

26 S. 1.

27 S. 118(1)(*b*).

28 ABA Standards, *Standards Relating to Abuse and Neglect* (1977).

(b) Narrow, Specific Grounds

A legalistic, non-interventionist definition would be one which has very narrow grounds, making it possible for child protection agencies and courts to intervene only in a restrictive range of circumstances. The definition would also include language which describes the grounds in specific and objective terms, thus limiting the range of discretion.

The Ontario and Alberta definitions are in most respects non-interventionist. In particular, they are distinctive among Canadian statutes because, in general, they focus on specific harms or substantial risk of harms caused by the intentional acts or negligence of the parents. For example, the Alberta definition includes:

> the child has been or there is substantial risk that the child will be physically injured or sexually abused by the guardian of the child.[29]

This provision is further clarified and narrowed by a requirement that the physical injury be substantial and observable and by the inclusion of a listing of the types of injuries intended to be covered.[30]

The Ontario and Alberta Acts have also addressed in a detailed way the difficult area of emotional harm. Unlike most Canadian statutes which cover this area by vague, general provisions, Ontario and Alberta have provided specific guidance to decision makers. The Ontario Act states that a child is in need of protection if:

> the child has suffered emotional harm, demonstrated by severe,
>
> > (i) anxiety,
> > (ii) depression
> > (iii) withdrawal, or
> > (iv) self-destructive or aggressive behaviour,
>
> and the child's parent . . . does not provide, or refuses . . . to consent to, services or treatment to remedy or alleviate the harm.[31]

Despite the generally non-interventionist approach of Ontario and Alberta, these provinces also include provisions that are quite inconsistent with a non-interventionist philosophy. The most glaring inconsistency is the Alberta provision which allows intervention if:

---

29 S. 1(2)(*d*).
30 S. 1(3)(*b*).
31 S. 37(2)(*f*).

the condition or behaviour of the child prevents the guardian of the child from providing the child with adequate care appropriate to meet the child's needs.[32]

This part of the definition allows a large degree of discretion by judges and agencies. Harm to the child is not required. Instead a "condition" or "behaviour" must exist which prevents the parents from providing "adequate" care to meet the child's "needs". There is such uncertainty regarding the meaning of this provision that, depending on how the discretion is actually exercised, it could undermine the general thrust of the definition which indicates a concern for narrow, specific and objective grounds for intervention.

In sum, British Columbia and the Yukon are typical of most Canadian jurisdictions in that they provide broad, vague grounds for intervention. Ontario and Alberta are clearly the closest to including a legalistic, non-interventionist definition of a child in need of protection. Thus, in the Canadian context, they are exceptions but they fail to maintain a non-interventionist approach throughout their definitions.

Non-Legalistic, Interventionist	Legalistic, Non-Interventionist
B.C.	Ontario
Yukon	Alberta

3. Initiation of Proceedings

Canadian statutes provide several ways of initiating court proceedings. One is an ordinary application to the court. This simply involves the filing of papers with an allegation that a particular child is in need of protection. Another approach is an "order to produce", a court order to the parents to appear in court. This order is made after the child protection agency applies for such an order. A third approach is apprehension or taking of the child by the agency after obtaining a warrant. Finally, apprehension may occur without the necessity of obtaining a warrant.

A non-interventionist approach to this part of child protection legislation would provide narrow grounds for apprehension. It would require that the least intrusive means of initiating proceedings be used. It would also provide procedural checks on the agency's discretion (for example, requirements to obtain a warrant or court order).

(a) Authority to Apprehend

Regarding authority to apprehend, the British Columbia Act is the most interventionist:

---

32 S. 1(2)(*i*).

> Where the superintendent [that is, the child protection authority] considers that a child is in need of protection, he may, without warrant, apprehend the child.[33]

When this provision is combined with the British Columbia Act's broad and vague definition of a child in need of protection, it is clearly a highly discretionary, potentially very intrusive approach.

In the three other jurisdictions, a warrant is required for apprehension unless certain circumstances exist. These circumstances in Ontario and the Yukon require some immediate or substantial danger to the child.[34] In Alberta, the circumstances are broader and include a child who is "lost" or who has "left the custody of his guardian without the consent of the guardian".[35]

Obtaining a warrant to apprehend in the Yukon and Alberta requires reasonable and probable grounds that the child is in need of protection.[36] However, as noted earlier, the definition of a child in need of protection is much more restrictive in Alberta and thus should result in a less interventionist approach. In addition, the Alberta Act contains general principles which encourage the use of the least intrusive measure. Ontario has basically the same approach as Alberta although its provisions are more specific.[37]

Again, in comparison to the other jurisdictions, Alberta and Ontario are on the non-interventionist side of the spectrum. Between the two, Ontario may be viewed as somewhat more legalistic and non-interventionist regarding the initiation of proceedings:

— As noted above, the grounds for apprehending a child without a warrant may be considered broader and more vague in Alberta than in Ontario.

— Ontario is more specific in its rules governing the various ways of initiating proceedings. Both jurisdictions have adopted the principle of using the least restrictive alternative at this stage of the process. However, the Ontario legislation incorporates a more detailed, hierarchical approach. For example, a court may not order that a child be apprehended unless the agency satisfies the court that the child would not be adequately protected by an order requiring the parents to bring the child to court for a hearing (that is, an order to produce).[38] Instead of this specific approach, the Alberta legislation provides principles at the beginning of the Act, stating that a child should be removed from the family

---

33 S. 9(1).

34 S. 40(6) of the Ontario Act; s. 121 of the Yukon Act.

35 S. 17(9).

36 S. 121(3) of the Yukon Act; s. 17(1) of the Alberta Act authorizes the issuance of an apprehension order.

37 S. 40.

38 S. 40(3).

only when less intrusive measures are not sufficient to protect the child. There may be no difference in practical results under the two Acts (for example, the frequency with which children are apprehended without a warrant) but the Ontario style may possibly indicate a greater concern for ensuring that the discretion of decision makers is structured in the direction of the least intrusive option.

(b) Authority After Apprehension: Medical Consent

Another important element of this pre-court stage concerns the scope of authority of a child protection agency after the apprehension of a child. All Canadian statutes authorize the agency to hold the child until the first court appearance. However, there are various approaches to the issue of providing consent to medical care. In general, where there has not been state intervention, parents have the authority and responsibility to consent to medical treatment of their children.[39] The question in the child protection context is: if a child has been apprehended, does the parental authority regarding medical consents transfer to the child protection agency? A family autonomy statute would not allow such a major interference with parental rights and responsibilities without a hearing and formal determination by a court that the child is in need of protection.

In British Columbia, the superintendent "may authorize emergency medical care and treatment of the child recommended by a medical practitioner".[40] It is difficult to determine whether this provision is interventionist or non-interventionist. The Act does not define "emergency" and the common law is unclear regarding whose consent, if any, is necessary in emergencies.[41] However, if it is assumed that parents would normally have consent authority in an emergency, this provision gives significant power to the superintendent particularly if, in practice, "emergency" is broadly interpreted. Where the basis for the apprehension is a dispute regarding medical treatment for a child, the superintendent can actually decide the issue that would otherwise be decided by the court. The superintendent is in the role of both investigator and judge.

Alberta has responded to this dual role issue to a limited extent but takes an interventionist approach. The director may authorize the provision of "any essential medical, surgical, dental or other remedial treatment . . . without the

---

39 However, it should be noted that some children, especially older children, may have the capacity to consent on their own behalf. Although the law is unclear on this point, it can be argued that the common law requires the consent of children if they have the necessary capacity.

40 S. 10(1)(*b*) [am. 1983, c. 10, s. 21, Sched. 2].

41 See Ontario, Interministerial Committee on Medical Consent, *Options on Medical Consent* (1979), at 27.

consent of the guardian of the child".[42] However, there are two limitations. First, the treatment must be recommended by two or more physicians or dentists, as the case may be. Second, if the child is apprehended because the guardian refuses to permit "essential" treatment, a court order authorizing the treatment is required. The court may authorize the treatment if satisfied that it is in "the best interests of the child". Thus, some checks have been placed on the discretion of the director but these provisions still represent a significant intrusion into parental decision-making authority.

In Alberta, the director also has, at this pre-court stage of the process, the highly discretionary authority to:

> confine the child in a secure treatment institution if the director considers it necessary to do so in order to protect the survival, security or development of the child.[43]

This provision appears to authorize the director to involuntarily commit a child to a locked, psychiatric treatment facility without the consent of the child's guardian, with very loose criteria for the decision and without any form of pre-commitment review. There is, however, a post-admission review by the court within one day of the confinement.

Ontario and the Yukon have taken less interventionist approaches. The Yukon legislation makes a distinction between medical care and medical examination. The director has the power to consent to any necessary medical care or attention for the child "unless a parent . . . has notified the Director that he objects to the Director giving the consent".[44] Thus, there is a recognition of parental rights but the parent has the onus of objecting. It is not clear that the Director has a legal duty to advise the parent of the proposed medical care, nor is it clear what happens if the parent objects and is unwilling to consent to the treatment. Presumably, the matter is decided by the court. The Director may, without the consent of the parent, also consent to "any medical or psychiatric examination or assessment for the purpose of ascertaining the physical or mental condition of the child".[45]

Ontario also makes a distinction between medical treatment and medical examination. The child protection agency, after apprehending a child, is limited to authorizing the child's medical examination, not treatment, where a parent's consent would otherwise be required.[46] The agency may also apply for the

---

42 S. 20(1)(*a*).

43 S. 20(1)(*b*).

44 S. 138(4)(*b*).

45 S. 138(4)(*d*).

46 S. 40(8).

admission of a child to a secure treatment facility.[47] Unlike the situation in Alberta, however, the Ontario child protection agency is an applicant, not the decision maker. The application may be made only in emergencies and the admission criteria are restrictive. The admission decision is made by the director of the secure treatment facility, subject to post-admission review by the court.

(c) Time Limits

Once an apprehension has occurred, the agency must bring the matter before the court or return the child to the parents within a specified time period. A longer time period allows more extensive interference with parental rights and responsibilities without any check on the agency's authority. From a due process, non-interventionist perspective, a short time period is preferable. It gives the parents an early opportunity to be heard and the agency must justify its action before a neutral third party — the judge. Also, it is unusual, at least in Ontario, for the court to make a final determination at the first court appearance. It is likely that the matter will be adjourned and there is at least the possibility that the court will order that the child be returned to the parents during the adjournment period.[48]

The time period is 5 days in Ontario[49] and 7 days in British Columbia[50] and the Yukon.[51] The maximum time in Alberta is 10 days, but the parent may serve the director with a "demand notice" within 5 days of the apprehension, in which case the matter must be heard by the court not more than 1 day after the director is served.[52] If parents are adequately informed of their rights, are assertive and are reasonably articulate or have quick access to legal representation, the right to serve a demand notice may be a helpful tool for parents. However, parents involved in child protection proceedings are often poor, illiterate and hesitant to challenge the child protection authority and thus may not be able or willing to take advantage of the right. Thus, it is likely that, in practice, 10 days may elapse before the matter is brought to the Alberta court.

The positions of the four jurisdictions on matters relating to the initiation of proceedings can be summarized as follows:

---

47 S. 118(1).

48 S. 42.

49 S. 42(1).

50 S. 11.

51 S. 123(4).

52 S. 19 [am. 1985, c. 16, s. 6].

	Non-Legalistic, Interventionist		Legalistic, Non-Interventionist		
Authority to Apprehend	B.C.		Yukon	Alberta	Ontario
Authority after Apprehension	B.C. Alberta		Yukon		Ontario
Time Limits	B.C. Alberta Yukon		Ontario		

4. Interim Custody of the Child

At the first court appearance, it is unlikely that the court will make a determination as to whether or not the child is in need of protection. Some statutes, like those in British Columbia and the Yukon, contain explicit provisions which acknowledge this fact. They provide a two-stage process in which there is first a preliminary determination of whether the agency or the parent should have custody of the child pending the hearing. A date is then set for the second stage, the "child protection hearing", to determine whether the child is in need of protection.[53] Other statutes, like Ontario's, simply state that a hearing is to begin when the matter is brought to the court.[54]

An adjournment may be long and may be only the first in a series of adjournments extending over months or even years. The result is that if on an adjournment, the child remains in or is placed in the care of the agency, the child may be in care for a very long period of time without a formal finding that the child is in need of protection.[55] This "interim" care and custody arrangement creates a status quo which can be difficult for the parents to change, particularly where it has existed for a considerable period of time.

From a non-interventionist perspective, there are several issues to be addressed at this stage of the process. First, are there clear and specific guidelines which encourage the court to leave the child with or return the child to the parents? Second, are there adequate notice and hearing requirements? Third, may the court order the provision of support services to the family so that the child may remain with or be returned to the parents? Fourth, if the court orders that the agency will have interim custody, is the court encouraged to order that the parents may have access to the child during the adjournment period?

---

53 See s. 12 of the B.C. Act and s. 123 [am. 1984, c. 34, s. 5] of the Yukon Act.

54 Ss. 42, 43.

55 J. Tator and K. Wilde, "Child Abuse and the Courts: An Analysis of Selected Factors in the Judicial Processing of 'Child Abuse' Cases" (1980), 3 Can. J. Fam. L. 165.

(a) Substantive Standards

Most of the statutes fail to provide meaningful guidelines to the court on whether the parent or the agency should have interim custody of the child. British Columbia does not include any guidelines. Although the Yukon and Alberta do provide guidelines, they are vague and highly discretionary. For example, in Alberta, the court is directed to make an interim order "that it considers appropriate".[56]

Ontario is an exception. Unlike the other statutes, the Ontario Act contains a relatively high and specific standard which reflects a non-interventionist policy.[57] The standard clearly favours keeping the child with the parents, if possible. Only if it can be shown that there is a substantial risk to the child's health or safety and that the child cannot be protected in the care of the parents, can the court order that the child be placed in the interim custody of the agency.

(b) Notice and Hearing Requirements

The Alberta, Ontario and Yukon Acts have clear and specific requirements regarding holding a hearing on the interim custody issue and on giving notice to the parents.[58] However, the British Columbia Act fails to provide adequate due process for parents in that a hearing and notice to the parents are not required when the matter first comes to court. The Act simply provides that the agency must present a written report to the court and "[o]n presentation of a report", the court may make its order.[59]

(c) Support Services

None of the four Acts explicitly allows the court to order the agency to provide support services to the family so that the child may be in the interim custody of the parents. Ontario, unlike the other jurisdictions, does provide specific authority for the court to make an order granting interim custody to the parents, subject to agency supervision.[60] The court may also attach terms and conditions to such an order, although it is unclear whether this includes the authority to order the agency to provide a homemaker or other support service.

(d) Access

All four of the statutes authorize the court to grant access to the parents when the child is placed in the interim custody of the agency. Although, as

---

56 S. 24(2).

57 S. 47(3). This provision should be read in the context of the Alberta Act's general principles which encourage the use of the least intrusive alternative.

58 See for example, ss. 39, 42, 43 and 47 of the Ontario Act.

59 S. 11.

60 S. 47(2)(*b*).

discussed earlier, the Ontario and Alberta Acts have general principles which would encourage the court to order access, only the Yukon Act has a specific presumption in favour of access.[61]

In summary, on the issue of interim custody, the statutes can be placed along the policy spectrum as follows:

Non-Legalistic, Interventionist		Legalistic, Non-Interventionist
B.C.	Alberta Yukon	Ontario

5. Dispositions

If a court determines that a child is in need of protection, it must also decide what intervention is necessary, that is, whether the child should be placed with the parents, subject to supervision by the agency, or be made a temporary or permanent ward. Canadian statutes do not require separate hearings for determining whether or not the child is in need of protection and for determining the appropriate disposition. However, it is generally accepted that the hearing is bifurcated into these two stages.

From a family autonomy perspective, it is important to keep the dispositional decision separate from the preliminary issue of whether or not the child is in need of protection. As noted in an Ontario discussion paper:

> Evidence relevant to which disposition is appropriate may be prejudicial to the parents and child if considered at the adjudication stage. For example, evidence that the agency has found the "ideal" foster home for the child would be appropriate at disposition but would be irrelevant to the issue of whether or not the child has been harmed . . . within the meaning of the grounds for intervention.[62]

A judge who allows dispositional evidence at the adjudication stage may not be able to keep the matters separate in his/her mind and thus the benefits of the agency's resources may unfairly influence the determination of whether or not any intervention at all is required. Ontario provides a statutory rule which requires that the two types of evidence be kept separate:

> . . . evidence relating only to the disposition of the matter shall not be admitted before the court has determined that the child is in need of protection.[63]

---

61 S. 138(4)(*a*).

62 Ontario, Ministry of Community and Social Services, *The Children's Act: A Consultation Paper* (1982), at 87.

63 S. 46(2).

The other statutes do not address the issue.

In general, Canadian statutes provide some guidelines or factors for the judge to apply at the dispositional stage of the proceedings. From a non-interventionist perspective, a fundamental question is: to what extent do these guidelines or factors encourage placement of the child with the parents? Are there requirements that, before the court may order removal of the child, the agency must establish that in-home services would not provide sufficient protection? If it is necessary to remove the child, does the Act reflect a preference for temporary, rather than permanent, custody orders and for maintaining parent-child contact, if possible?

(a) Best Interests of the Child

One approach is to require that the judge make an order that is in the "best interests of the child". This term may simply stand on its own, or it may be clarified by a specification of factors to consider in a particular case. For example, the Yukon Act includes considerations, such as: the "bonding" existing between the child and parent; the effect upon the child of any disruption of the child's sense of continuity; evidence about who the child relates to as his parent or care-giver; the child's mental, physical and emotional stages of development; a comparison of the risks and merits of the child living with the parents; and the mental, physical and emotional "needs" of the child.[64] The British Columbia Act also lists similar factors for the court to consider although they are not identified as best interests factors and they apply only to permanent orders.[65]

Defining best interests by listing relevant factors is probably better than leaving it undefined because it provides at least some limited guidance to judges as to what it means. However, it is likely that best interests factors in legislation do little, if anything, to encourage the use of the least intrusive dispositional alternative. There are several reasons for this. First, although some factors reflect the importance of considering the positive aspects of the child living with the parents, others may actually encourage placement with "psychological parents" such as foster parents in some cases. Second, applying such factors requires considerable information which is often not available, and predictive ability which judges do not have.[66] Third, even if accurate determinations regarding the factors could be made, there is nothing to indicate their relative weight. Finally, some experience with best interests factors appears to indicate

---

64 S. 132.

65 S. 14(3).

66 R. Mnookin, "Child Custody Adjudication: Judicial Functions in the Face of Indeterminacy" 39 L. & Contemp. Prob. 226.

that their effect has been limited. A review of reported Ontario cases revealed that most courts seemed to be making dispositional orders without much, if any, consideration of Ontario's best interests factors.[67]

(b) Non-Interventionist Direction to the Court

The approaches to disposition in the Alberta and Ontario statutes more clearly indicate a non-interventionist policy and are similar to each other in many ways. As noted earlier,[68] they both contain general principles which apply throughout the legislation and which emphasize respect for family autonomy and a preference for using the least restrictive alternative. They also both provide specific criteria which favour not removing the child from his parents wherever possible. For example, the Ontario Act provides:

> The court shall not make an order removing the child from the [parents] unless the court is satisfied that less restrictive alternatives, including non-residential services and [previous efforts to assist the family]
>
> (*a*) have been attempted and have failed;
>
> (*b*) have been refused by the [parents]; or
>
> (*c*) would be inadequate to protect the child.[69]

If removal is necessary, both Acts encourage the use of a temporary custody order rather than a permanent one. Permanent orders are permitted only where the court is satisfied that the circumstances justifying the finding that the child is in need of protection are unlikely to change within a reasonably foreseeable time.[70]

Another non-interventionist feature of the two Acts is that, unlike other Canadian statutes, a finding that the child falls within the definition of a child in need of protection does not necessarily lead to court-ordered intervention. As the Ontario Act states:

> Where the court finds that a child is in need of protection *and* is satisfied that intervention through a court order is necessary to protect the child in the future, the court shall make one of the following orders . . .[71]

---

67 R. Barnhorst and G. Thomson, "Policy and Practice in the Child Welfare Area" in *Family Law and Social Policy Workshop Series* (1982), at 11.

68 See, *supra*, at 260.

69 S. 53(3). It should be noted that the Ontario and Alberta Acts also contain "best interests" factors for the court to consider: See s. 37(3) of the Ontario Act and s. 2(*h*) of the Alberta Act.

70 S. 53(6) of the Ontario Act and s. 32(1) of the Alberta Act.

71 S. 53(1). Emphasis added.

This provision reflects a non-interventionist perspective because the court is encouraged to go through the thought process of: is intervention through a court order really necessary to protect the child? Is the incident which gave rise to the application merely an isolated incident or is there some evidence that a similar incident is likely to occur in the future? Are there services or other measures to which the parent would consent and which would provide adequate protection for the child? In short, by requiring the court to put its mind to these kinds of issues, this provision encourages a more cautious approach to involuntarily interfering with family autonomy.

Ontario does provide some specific, non-interventionist provisions not contained in the Alberta Act:

— Before making a dispositional order, the court is required to ask the parties what efforts the child protection agency or any other agency has made to assist the child.[72] This should help to inform the court as to whether less restrictive options are feasible.

— Where the court decides that removal is necessary, the Act specifically requires that the court consider whether it is possible to place the child with "a relative, neighbour or other member of the child's community or extended family", instead of with the child protection agency.[73]

— The court is required, before making a dispositional order, to consider a written plan by the agency. Where the agency is seeking temporary or permanent custody, the plan must contain (a) an explanation of why the child cannot be adequately protected while in the parents' care and (b) a statement of what efforts are planned to maintain parent-child contact.[74]

(c) Access

As noted earlier, a non-interventionist statute would, in cases where removal of the child from the family is necessary, indicate a preference for maintaining parent-child contact while the child is in care. Most Canadian statutes, at a minimum, clearly recognize parent-child access as a separate order that may be made by the court. However, the British Columbia and Yukon statutes specifically refer to access only where a temporary, not permanent, order has been made.[75]

To what extent do the various jurisdictions include criteria or guidelines which encourage the making of access orders? The Yukon provides that the

---

72 S. 53(2).

73 S. 53(4).

74 S. 52.

75 S. 13 of the B.C. Act and s. 138(2),(5) of the Yukon Act.

parents be given "reasonable access" when a temporary order is made.[76] Most other statutes, including Alberta and British Columbia, provide no specific criteria or guidelines for the decision.

Ontario states a presumption in favour of access in temporary wardship cases.[77] Where a Crown or permanent wardship order is made, the Ontario Act specifically allows access if the court is satisfied that:

(a) access will not impair the child's opportunities for a permanent placement in a family setting;

(b) the child is at least 12 and wishes to maintain contact;

(c) The child has been or will be placed with a person who does not wish to adopt the child; or

(d) some other special circumstance exists.[78]

(d) Effect of Removal on other Parental Rights: Medical Consent

Most statutes provide that an order of temporary or permanent wardship automatically transfers all parental rights and responsibilities regarding the child to the child protection authority. Thus the agency can consent to medical care of the child. Ontario is an exception. When a child in Ontario is made a temporary ward, the court may order that the parents retain any right they may have to give or refuse consent to medical treatment for the child. However, the court may not make this order "where failure to consent to necessary medical treatment was a ground for finding that the child was in need of protection". In all cases of temporary wardship the parents retain any right they may have under the Marriage Act to give or refuse consent to the child's marriage.[79]

Thus, Ontario, unlike the other jurisdictions, creates the opportunity for the court to preserve some parental autonomy after wardship has been ordered. The policies reflected in the four statutes on dispositional issues can be summarized as follows:

	Non-Legalistic, Interventionist	Legalistic, Non-Interventionist
Substantive Standards	B.C. Yukon	Alberta Ontario

---

76 S. 138(2).

77 S. 55(1).

78 S. 55(2).

79 S. 58. Marriage Act, R.S.O. 1980, c. 256.

	Non-Legalistic, Interventionist	Legalistic, Non-Interventionist
Access	B.C. Yukon Alberta	Ontario
Medical Consent	B.C. Yukon Alberta	Ontario

6. Accountability Mechanisms

One of the general principles of a legalistic approach is that a system of involuntary child protection intervention should be designed to ensure that agencies and courts, are held accountable for their actions.[80] It is important to legalistic accountability that mechanisms be built into the system to review decisions and to review the success or failure of intervention efforts. Implementation of such mechanisms are essential if in order to help ensure that the substantive provisions of the legislation operate in the way in which they were intended.

This section will review four types of accountability mechanisms and the extent to which they have been incorporated in the four child protection statutes: (a) requirement of agency plans; (b) reasons for decisions; (c) periodic court review; (d) standards to be applied at the review.

(a) Agency Plans

Requiring the child protection agency to submit to the court a dispositional plan can help to ensure that the agency has given thought to what it plans for the child if the court orders some form of intervention. It can help to ensure that the court, the parents and the child are reasonably informed as to what the future holds for the child if intervention is ordered and how that compares to what the parents can offer. The dispositional plan can also be a useful basis for assessing the agency's performance at a subsequent review of the case.

Most Canadian statutes, including the British Columbia and Yukon Acts, do not require the agency to prepare and submit a dispositional plan. Alberta and Ontario refer to a plan of care for the child but beyond that there are substantial differences in their two approaches.

The Alberta legislation contains a general provision that states that plans of care should be developed.[81] However, it is limited to situations in which the child is already in care. It does not require that the plan be submitted to the court and it is very limited in the items to be included in the plan.

---

80 See ABA Standards, *Standards Relating to Abuse and Neglect* (1977).

81 S. 2(*k*).

A more specific provision of the Alberta Act does require that the plan be submitted to the court in cases of temporary guardianship.[82] However, it does not require that the plan be considered by the court prior to the dispositional decision, nor does it require the plan in cases of supervision and permanent guardianship orders. The plan, which is to be prepared within 30 days of the temporary guardianship order, does provide a basis for reviewing the agency's performance at a subsequent review of the temporary guardianship order.

In contrast, the Ontario Act has a stronger accountability orientation. It provides that the agency must submit a plan in all cases in which the court makes a dispositional or review order.[83] The plan must be filed and considered before an order is made and the plan must be in writing. Most striking is the detail in which the statute describes the contents of the plan. For example, in addition to the items noted earlier,[84] the plan must include a description of the services to be provided and an estimate of the time required to remedy the situation which caused the child to be in need of protection.[85] This detailed approach should ensure some consistency among reports made in various courts throughout the province. It should also discourage vague, general plans which do little to assist the court in making a disposition or in reviewing the agency's performance in carrying out the disposition.

(b) Reasons for Decisions

Requiring a court to give reasons for a decision is not only fair to the parties, it forces the court to go through the process of thinking more carefully about the basis of its decision. If the decision is appealed, having the court's reasons on the record assists the appeal court in reviewing the appropriateness of the lower court's decision.

The child protection statutes in British Columbia, Alberta and the Yukon do not specifically require the court to give reasons for its decision although they may be required by rules of court not included in the statutes. The Ontario Act specifically requires the court to give reasons and sets out in some detail what the court must address.[86]

The relevant provision of the Ontario Act highlights the importance of the plans of care for the child by requiring the court in its reasons to state all proposed plans and the specific plan adopted by the court. This should ensure the implementation of the earlier requirements that, before making an order, the

---

82 S. 29(3).

83 S. 52.

84 *Supra*, at 274.

85 S. 52(*a*),(*c*).

86 S. 49.

court must consider the agency's plan for the child. The provision should also help to ensure that the generally non-interventionist philosophy of the Act is implemented. In keeping with the Act's preference for leaving children with their parents, the court is required, in cases involving removal, to establish on the record why it is departing from the preferred approach.

(c) Periodic Court Review

A basic means of ensuring the appropriate implementation of the court's order is to provide for periodic review by the court. Court review can be a check on both agency and parental performance and can serve as an incentive to both the agency and the parents to conform their behaviour to the court's expectations.[87] From an accountability perspective, some of the issues to be addressed are: are all court orders subject to review by the court? Are the reviews automatic or only when applied for by one of the parties? Is the right of the parent to initiate a review more limited than the agency's? What criteria govern the court's decision on review?

The statutes in British Columbia, Alberta, Ontario and the Yukon provide for the review of the three basic types of dispositional orders. However, only Ontario provides for mandatory reviews.[88] In that province, the agency must apply for a review of supervision orders and temporary wardship orders before they expire.

There are some variations among the statutes regarding the parent's right to apply for a review. British Columbia and Alberta allow the parent to apply for a review of supervision orders and temporary custody orders.[89] However, only the child protection agency may apply for review of a permanent order. The Yukon allows the parents to initiate a review of temporary and permanent custody orders but not supervision orders.[90] Ontario allows the parents to initiate a review of all three orders.[91]

These differences regarding the review of permanent orders are significant because they indicate that child protection agencies in Alberta and British Columbia are less likely to be held accountable to the court for their implementation of these orders. Furthermore, the parents' inability to initiate a review of a permanent order severely restricts the parents' opportunity to regain custody of their child. Such a restriction seems particularly inappropriate in cases where a stable placement for the child has not been made.

---

87 See ABA Standards, *supra*, n. 80.

88 S. 60(2),(6).

89 S. 13(6) of B.C. Act and s. 30(1) of the Alberta Act.

90 Ss. 129.1 [en. 1984, c. 34, s. 7], 133(1) [am. 1984, c. 34, s. 9], 145(1).

91 S. 60(4).

In some of the statutes, other limitations are placed on the parents' right to apply for review. For example, in Alberta the director may apply for review at any time but the parents are limited to applying once during the term of the supervision order or temporary custody order.[92] Similarly, in Ontario, the agency may apply at any time but the parents must wait six months unless they can persuade the court that a major element of the agency's plan is not being implemented.[93] British Columbia and the Yukon do not place these kinds of restrictions on parents.[94]

The reasoning behind such restrictions appears to be a concern that parents may use the review mechanism frivolously. Frivolous applications unnecessarily consume the time of courts and agencies, may prevent the agency from getting on with the implementation of the order and may cause disruption and uncertainty for the child.

(d) Standards at the Review

The substantive standards to be applied at the review by the court are of critical importance. British Columbia and the Yukon take the general approach of requiring that the applicant must show a "change of circumstances" in order to have the order varied.[95] Alberta and Ontario are more specific.

In reviewing a supervision order or temporary guardianship order under the Alberta Act, the court is required to consider the following matters:

— whether the circumstances that caused the child to be in need of protective services have changed;

— the protective services that have been provided to the child or the family of the child;

— whether the director has followed the plan filed with the court for the care of the child;

— whether a guardian has complied with the order.[96]

From an accountability perspective, a flaw in the Alberta Act is that it does not provide criteria for the court when considering an application by the agency to terminate permanent guardianship. The Ontario Act requires the court to consider the kinds of matters included in the Alberta legislation in reviewing all orders, including permanent orders.[97]

---

92 S. 30(1)(*b*).

93 S. 60(7),(8).

94 S. 13(6) of the B.C. Act and ss. 144(1) [am. 1984, c. 34, s. 10] and 145(1) of the Yukon Act.

95 S. 13(6) of the B.C. Act and ss. 144(3) and 145(3) of the Yukon Act.

96 S. 30(2).

97 S. 61(3).

In terms of accountability, the advantage of the approach taken in Alberta and Ontario is that it directs the court to certain specific matters related to agency and parental performance, rather than leaving the court with wide discretion in determining what is relevant. It is particularly significant that the court is required to compare the current circumstances with those that justified the finding that the child was in need of protection, rather than simply determining at the review what is "best" for the child.

In sum, the policies reflected in the four statutes regarding accountability mechanisms can be represented as follows:

Non-Legalistic, Interventionist			Legalistic, Non-Interventionist
B.C.	Yukon	Alberta	Ontario

7. Summary

The following chart provides an overview of the four statutes in relation to all of the key provisions discussed in this part of the chapter:

SUMMARY OF KEY PROVISIONS

		Non-Legalistic, Interventionist		Legalistic, Non-Interventionist	
1.	Principles	B.C.	Yukon	Ontario	Alberta
2.	Grounds for Intervention	B.C. Yukon			Ontario Alberta
3.	Initiation of Proceedings				
	— Authority to apprehend	B.C.		Yukon Alberta	Ontario
	— Authority after apprehension	B.C. Alberta		Yukon	Ontario
	— Time limits	B.C. Alberta Yukon		Ontario	
4.	Interim custody	B.C.	Alberta Yukon		Ontario

SUMMARY OF KEY PROVISIONS (Cont'd.)

	Non-Legalistic, Interventionist			Legalistic, Non-Interventionist	
5. Disposition					
— Substantive standards	B.C.	Yukon		Alberta	Ontario
— Access	B.C.	Yukon Alberta		Ontario	
— Medical consent	B.C. Yukon Alberta			Ontario	
6. Accountability Mechanisms	B.C.	Yukon	Alberta		Ontario

III THE LEGISLATIVE REFORM PROCESS

The review of legislative provisions in Part II of this chapter revealed some clear differences among the four highlighted child protection statutes, all of which were passed between 1980 and 1984. British Columbia and the Yukon have enacted legislation which can be classified as essentially interventionist. In general, these two statutes, in comparison to those of Ontario and Alberta, contain broad and vague grounds for decisions, few provisions which encourage minimum interference with families, and few accountability mechanisms. Thus, these statutes give considerable freedom to judges and child protection workers in using their discretion throughout the child protection process. However, between the two, the Yukon Act reflects somewhat more concern for respecting family autonomy and for addressing issues in a more detailed, legalistic manner.

Ontario and Alberta have followed more of a non-interventionist policy. They both, in general, include substantive provisions emphasizing the importance of family autonomy and the least intrusive alternative. However, in certain areas, Ontario uses more specific, detailed provisions and, in general, is more consistent in its application of a legalistic, non-interventionist philosophy. In particular, Ontario's legislation shows greater concern for holding judges and child welfare professionals accountable for their actions, especially in its provisions regarding plans of care, reasons for decisions and rights of parents to initiate court reviews.

This part of the chapter will discuss the process of legislative reform in each of these jurisdictions in an attempt to determine why the different approaches to child protection legislation have been taken. It is beyond the scope of this paper to provide a detailed account of the legislative reform process in each jurisdiction.[98] Instead, the focus of this part will be limited to several specific factors that seem to have influenced whether a jurisdiction adopted an interventionist or non-interventionist stance:

— Pressure for reform

— Key government actors

— Key non-government actors

— State of previous legislation

— Research

— Public consultation

This part ends with several conclusions about the development of child protection statutes in Canada.

1. Pressure for Reform

(a) Alberta[99]

Alberta was the only jurisdiction in which scandals or serious abuses in the child welfare system created significant pressure for legislative reform. In 1979 reports of mistreatment of children in the care of the Department of Social Services and Community Health were receiving widespread publicity. Media reports and an investigation by the Ombudsman criticized the government for such incidents as:

— children being subjected to solitary confinement in "quiet rooms";

— as a behaviour modification technique, a boy being forced to eat dog food laced with tabasco sauce;

— a girl being forced to sleep in her own urine soaked sheets in an attempt to stop her bed wetting; and

— a boy in a foster home being punished by having his head shaved.

These incidents became major media and political issues and created enormous pressure for something to be done. Finally in 1980, the minister appointed a Board of Review, chaired by Justice James Cavanagh of the Court of

---

98 For a detailed account of the process in B.C., see M. Callahan and B. Wharf, *Demystifying the Policy Process: A Case Study of the Development of Child Welfare Legislation in B.C.* (1982). Regarding the Ontario process, see R. Barnhorst, *The Development of Child and Family Policy in the Legislative Process* (forthcoming).

99 The main sources for the information about Alberta in this part of the chapter are "Redefining Child Justice", *Alberta Report*, 14th November 1983, at 6-13; *The Child Welfare System* (the report of the Cavanagh Board of Review) (1983); and interviews with government officials in Edmonton, Alberta in January 1985.

Queen's Bench, to study the child welfare system in Alberta. After 3½ years of investigation, the Cavanagh report was released. It called for much more legalistic and non-interventionist legislation and, in some areas, made very specific recommendations for implementing the new approach.

The Cavanagh report and the steady revelation of abuses provided direct, clear evidence that care provided by the government was less than adequate and that many children may be better served if left in their families. Thus, in Alberta an atmosphere was created in which a non-interventionist approach would be favourably received.

(b) Ontario[100]

In the mid-1970s, the children's services system in Ontario was being widely criticized both within and outside government. The system was disorganized and unmanageable and becoming increasingly difficult to fund in a period of financial restraint. In 1977 the government took the first step in responding to the criticism by reorganizing the administration of children's services under a new department called the Children's Services Division of the Ministry of Community and Social Services.

Legislation was only one of several tools used by the ministry to attempt to respond to the need to improve the system of children's services. There was no evidence of serious problems caused by the child protection legislation, and most of the new comprehensive children's legislation which was finally passed had very little to do with the problems that led to the creation of the new division. However, repeated public comments by senior government officials that comprehensive legislation would eventually be forthcoming created widespread expectations of legislative reform. Thus, clearly "something had to be done" but no one inside or outside of government had a clear idea as to what the legislation should provide.

(c) British Columbia[101]

In the early 1970s it was generally recognized both within and outside government that British Columbia's Protection of Children Act was badly out of date, having remained essentially the same since its enactment in 1901.[102]

---

100 The information about Ontario in this part of the paper is based primarily on my experience as the director of the children's legislation project in Ontario.

101 The main sources for the information about British Columbia in this part of the paper are M. Callahan and B. Wharf, *supra*, n. 98 and interviews with government officials in Victoria, B.C. in January 1985.

102 S.B.C. 1901, c. 9. Various minor amendments were made between 1901 and 1968. Some significant amendments were made in 1968 regarding child abuse reporting and limitations on the length of temporary wardship.

Among the problems identified were:

— vague and archaic language;

— no means of ensuring that the child's voice would be heard in the court process;

— a conflict of interest for the superintendent of child welfare between his roles as guardian and advocate for children; and

— outdated provisions for immigrant children.

To a large extent, these were technical problems related to modernizing the legislation. In general, the problems were not related to the six critical areas discussed in Part II of this chapter. However, it is noteworthy that one of the concerns regarding archaic language was that the grounds for intervention were from another era and highly moralistic in tone. In addition, there was concern that the legislation caused an over reliance on court action to assist parents.

Another factor that created pressure for legislative reform was the establishment of a royal commission. In 1973 the recently elected New Democratic government appointed Justice Thomas Berger as chairman of a royal commission to conduct a comprehensive study of all aspects of family law in the province. Many members of Cabinet were interested in such a study. The minister responsible for social services, who was formerly an activist social worker, was particularly interested in developing comprehensive children's legislation.

One of the commission's reports entitled "Children and the Law" contained recommendations addressing a wide range of areas: the status of children born outside marriage; a children's Bill of Rights; children with "special needs"; child protection; custody, access and guardianship; and adoption.[103] A comprehensive model act covering these areas was prepared by the commission as a supplement to the report.[104] Regarding the six critical areas discussed in Part II of this chapter, the commission recommended an approach which was basically interventionist. However, the approach was clearly less interventionist and more legalistic than the 1901 act which was under review. The commission proposed broad grounds for intervention, including a vague definition of emotional neglect; recognition of the fetus as a child; introduction of "best interests of the child" as the statutory test for dispositions; wide discretion for the court in deciding whether to place an unmanageable child in a "confined setting"; limitations on dispositions to take account of the child's "sense of time"; and new accountability mechanisms (for example, plans of care).

---

103 See British Columbia, *Fifth Report of the Royal Commission on Family and Children's Law* (1975).

104 See British Columbia, *A Supplement to the Fifth Report of the Royal Commission on Family and Children's Law, The Children's Act, 1976, Draft Model Act* (1975).

The commission documented widespread dissatisfaction with the existing children's legislation and its several reports created the expectation that new, comprehensive legislation would be forthcoming. However, shortly after the commission finished its work a provincial election was held in which the New Democratic Party was defeated by the Social Credit Party.

(d) The Yukon[105]

In the Yukon, there were primarily technical reasons for reforming the law. In 1982, four factors led to the interest in developing new children's legislation. First, several provisions of the existing legislation were considered to be archaic. Second, the Yukon had no legislation in certain areas affecting children (for example, custody and guardianship). This was recognized as a major gap by government officials. Third, the territorial government was concerned about two legislative developments at the federal level. The federal government would soon be passing new young offenders legislation and territorial legislation would have to dovetail with the federal act in several areas. In addition, the Canadian Charter of Rights and Freedoms had recently been introduced and the Yukon would have to amend many statutes, including those affecting children, in order to comply with the Charter. Fourth, a family law professor from Dalhousie University was available and was willing to spend a sabbatical year helping to develop new children's legislation for the Yukon.

In sum, there was non-interventionist pressure in Alberta, forms of philosophically neutral pressure in Ontario and the Yukon. The pressure in Ontario was primarily administrative in the sense that the major concern was to reorganize the administration of children's services. In the Yukon the pressure was technical. In British Columbia it was both technical and interventionist. These pressures cannot in themselves explain the various legislative outcomes, but they did set the stage for the interaction of other influential factors.

PRESSURE FOR REFORM

British Columbia	Yukon	Alberta	Ontario
technical; interventionist	technical	non-interventionist	administrative

---

105 The information about the Yukon is based on an interview with Professor Alastair Bisset-Johnson and a paper by him entitled "Protecting Children in the North", an expanded version of a paper given at the Fifth International Congress on Child Abuse and Neglect, Montreal, Quebec (September 1984).

2. Key Government Actors

(a) British Columbia

The British Columbia policy process was dominated by a senior administrator, the deputy minister, who had been appointed shortly after the election of the Social Credit government. The new deputy had been in the Ministry of Human Resources for 19 years in a variety of administrative capacities. Faced with the pressure to develop new child welfare legislation, he produced a short, skeletal act with technical assistance from a government lawyer.

The deputy wanted to limit government intervention with families, both voluntary and involuntary. He felt that the earlier legislation inappropriately presumed a large state role (that is, that the state would do "all things for children") and that it gave the impression of an adversarial, rather than co-operative, relationship between parents and the state.

On the other hand, it is reasonably clear that the deputy wanted a sparse act in order to facilitate his ministry's administrative control and to minimize judicial influence over the system. He felt that it was a mistake to get "too specific" in legislation. In his view specificity reduced the ministry's flexibility and made it likely that the legislation would require frequent amending. In order to maintain flexibility, he preferred to rely on administrative manuals and policy directives prepared by the ministry. In short, it appears that the deputy was opposed to the detail and precision of a legalistic statute. The statute he developed gave him the flexibility he sought and in some respects favoured administrative convenience over due process (for example, the provision that allows interim custody to be decided on the basis of a written report).[106]

(b) Ontario

In sharp contrast to British Columbia, Ontario's key government actors were two lawyers in the policy branch of the Social Services Ministry — the director of the legislation project and an associate deputy minister ("ADM"). When work began on the legislation, the project director had been with the ministry for a little over a year. He had strongly held views about how children's legislation should be changed. His experience in representing children and parents in child protection cases and his reading, writing and teaching on children and the law led him to be very critical of the existing legal system for children and families. In particular, he felt that professional service providers and judges had too much discretion and that substantive legal rights and procedural safeguards were needed.

---

106 *Supra*, at 269.

The project director worked closely with the ADM on the legislation until the ADM's departure from the ministry early in 1982. The ADM was also new to government work, having come to the division at the time of the creation of the Children's Services Division in 1977. He was a well-known, highly respected Family Court Judge with a reputation for innovative reform. Formerly, he had been a family law professor. In general, he and the project director shared the same legal rights, non-interventionist philosophy towards child welfare reform. Neither had a particular commitment to the existing, professionally dominated service system. The administrative reorganization of children's services in Ontario provided a unique opportunity for these key actors to develop a new, legalistic statute to govern the children's services system.

(c) Alberta

In Alberta, a lawyer headed the government's legislative policy development process. This senior planner had been with the department for 10 years. Prior to coming to the department, she had been a prosecutor in juvenile court. Her experience in juvenile court had influenced her attitude towards child welfare policy. She felt that social workers had too much discretion and she agreed with Cavanagh's view that the child welfare legislation should be reformed in a more legalistic direction. She had long felt that legislative reform was needed but her efforts to initiate changes had been blocked by senior department officials. She welcomed the opportunity presented by the appointment of the board of review.

It is unclear whether the Alberta legislation would have been as non-interventionist if the senior planner had not been required to respond to the Cavanagh Board of Review. However, her generally legalistic, reformist attitude combined with two other factors to push the legislation in a legalistic, non-interventionist direction: (1) the pressure generated by the scandals and the subsequent Cavanagh report, and (2) a close working relationship with the department's minister who was very supportive of the Cavanagh report.

(d) The Yukon

A key government actor in the Yukon was the visiting law professor from Dalhousie University. Prior to coming to Canada, he had taught law in England. He worked closely with the director of child welfare and a lawyer from the legislative counsel's office.

The law professor, in particular, seemed to hold a view which emphasized the psychological impact on children of the court process and of dispositional decisions. He appears to have been less concerned than the lawyers in Ontario and Alberta with the need to protect family autonomy and the potential harm to children of vague, discretionary provisions.

In a paper which reviews the new Yukon legislation, the law professor seems to reject a non-interventionist policy on the ground that it fails to adequately balance the rights of parents against the needs of the child:

> One of the premises of Goldstein, Solnit and Freud's work (*Before the Best Interests of the Child*) was a policy of minimum state intervention which was to be restricted to the most blatant cases of physical abuse. Whilst this theory of deferring, in most cases, to parental autonomy in matters of child rearing has been offered as an aspect of children's rights, it is important to realise that parental rights and those of their children may be related but are not identical.[107]

His basic policy position on state intervention in the family seems to be at least partially summed up as follows:

> Hard decisions about children do not become easier over time and the best that one can do is to make strenuous efforts to supply services to quickly return the child to the family but where this fails, the "gordian knot" may, in a small but regretable number of cases, have to be cut without undue delay. Parents do not own their children and concept of the trust, which may be breached, is perhaps an appropriate analogy.[108]

In sum, in all of the jurisdictions, key government actors held views which were reflected in the statutes on which they worked. It is also clear that lawyers working for the government played key roles in three of the four jurisdictions.

KEY GOVERNMENT ACTORS

British Columbia	Yukon	Alberta	Ontario
senior administrator	lawyer	lawyer	lawyers

3. Key Non-Government Actors

(a) Ontario

Unlike the other jurisdictions, child protection agencies in Ontario are private, non-profit corporations rather than a direct arm of a government department. The 51 children's aid societies and the Ontario Association of Children's Aid Societies were very vocal and critical of both the non-interventionist philosophy and many of the specific provisions of the legislative proposals contained in a government consultation paper. These organizations were also supported by other members of the child welfare sector (for example, the professional association of social workers).

---

107 A. Bisset-Johnson, *supra*, n. 105, at 6.
108 *Ibid.*

These representatives of Ontario's child welfare sector clearly had some influence. In draft legislation which followed consultation on the initial proposals, the government softened its non-interventionist approach. This softening was most notable in the removal of a family autonomy principle from the declaration of principles and in the broadening of the grounds for involuntary intervention.

However, two other sets of non-government actors counterbalanced the child welfare sector's influence to a considerable extent, particularly once the draft legislation was reviewed by the standing committee of the legislature. First, two legal advocacy organizations and a few individual lawyers provided a small but important base of support for the ministry's initial proposals. Second, the standing committee of the legislature had influence. Most of its more significant recommendations regarding the child protection provisions were adopted by the government. The committee's report, in general, sided with the views of the non-government lawyers rather than the child welfare professionals. It recommended that the new legislation should reflect a policy position that would be closer to the government's initial, non-interventionist proposals.[109]

(b) British Columbia

Several groups outside government responded to a draft Bill circulated by the British Columbia government. These groups included the British Columbia Association of Social Workers, the British Columbia Federation of Foster Parent Associations, the Coalition on Children, Youth and the Law[110] and the two schools of social work.

In general, the draft Bill was not well received by these non-government groups. They criticized it as inadequate and not related to the royal commission's report. Many of the submissions called for broader government intervention and more comprehensive legislation, like that proposed by the royal commission. The six critical legislative areas discussed in Part II of this chapter were not a primary focus of the submissions. However, some respondents wanted a child's being "out of control" to be a basis for intervention. Others specifically recommended that certain royal commission proposals be included such as the definition of emotional neglect, the requirement of a plan of care, and recognition of the best interests of the child as a paramount consideration.

---

109 Legislative Assembly of Ontario, *Recommendations by the Standing Committee on Social Development on The Child and Family Services Act: Draft Legislation* (1984).

110 The Coalition is "a committee of the Social Planning and Review Council of B.C. . . . which consists of lay persons and professionals concerned about the rights, dignity and status of children in B.C." (*Athena*, a publication of the Coalition on Children, Youth and the Law, 6, Nov. 1980, at 1).

Despite the generally negative reaction to the draft Bill, the Bill that was introduced in the legislature was very similar to the draft Bill. The submissions made by interested groups clearly had had very little impact.

The Berger Commission, as noted earlier, was an important actor early in the process and did help to create pressure for change. However, the commission had long been disbanded by the time policy decisions were being made and the legislation was being drafted. People connected with the royal commission, such as the Superintendent of Child Welfare, were still present, but had no influence. On the other hand, the commission's report seemed to have some limited influence as evidenced by the inclusion of some of its proposals in the government's draft Bill (for example, recognition of the best interests of the child as a paramount consideration).

It appears that the election of the Social Credit government in 1975 considerably weakened the impact of the New Democratic Party-appointed Berger Commission and of those inside and outside of government who supported the commission's recommendations. As one government official stated, it would be difficult "to put forward something that looked like they were just carrying on what the New Democratic Party had done".[111]

Similarly, the legislature had no significant impact on the content of the legislation. The Bill that was introduced remained essentially unchanged throughout the legislative process.

(c) Alberta

The major outside influence in Alberta was clearly the Cavanagh Board of Review. The board not only intensified the pressure for change created by the well-publicized scandals in the child welfare system, but it also made strong recommendations for a more legalistic and non-interventionist legislative approach. These recommendations had a powerful and direct influence in shaping the content of the new legislation.

The Bill introduced by the government shortly after the release of the Cavanagh report was generally quite consistent with the Cavanagh recommendations. Several responses to the Bill were submitted to the Department of Social Services and Community Health from groups outside government. The most prominent perspective was that of social workers, with many submissions being made by professional associations (for example, Alberta Association of Social Workers) and academic social workers (for example, University of Calgary). Among the major points raised in the public submissions were:[112]

---

111 Cited in M. Callahan and B. Wharf, *supra*, n. 98 at 26.

112 Alberta, Department of Social Services and Community Health, *Summary of Briefs in Response to Bill 105* (1984).

— support for the emphasis on the family but also a concern that the Bill was too family-centered and did not make the interests of children paramount or at least a higher priority;

— concern that the Bill implied that the role of the social worker is intrusive rather than supportive;

— strong support for the use of the least intrusive measure;

— concern that the grounds for intervention were too narrow (for example, concern that truancy was omitted as a basis for intervention); and

— some concern that the Bill was too sweeping in authorizing medical treatment without the consent of the guardian where a child has been apprehended.

The consultation process did not result in any significant changes in the Bill. Similarly, the small minority of opposition members in the legislature had no impact.

(d) The Yukon

In the Yukon, no individual or group outside government stands out as being particularly influential. Unlike the other jurisdictions, professional associations do not appear to have been active participants. Indian organizations seem to have been the major participants but had little impact on the content of the critical legislative areas discussed in Part II of this chapter, particularly after the Bill was introduced in the legislature.

KEY NON-GOVERNMENT ACTORS

British Columbia	Yukon	Alberta	Ontario
		Cavanagh Board of Review	Child welfare professionals, lawyers, legislative committee

4. State of Previous Legislation

(a) British Columbia and the Yukon

In British Columbia and the Yukon, the legislation being reformed was archaic in many respects. Although some significant amendments were made in British Columbia in 1968 (for example, child abuse reporting provisions), there had been no comprehensive review of the legislation since its enactment in 1901. Thus, a major task involved in the law reform efforts in British Columbia and the Yukon was simply to bring the language and concepts of the previous legislation up to date. For example, the previous British Columbia and Yukon Acts did not have a provision authorizing voluntary care agreements between parents and the child protection authorities, a provision which is found in most modern child welfare statutes.

(b) Ontario

In Ontario, the Child Welfare Act had undergone significant amendment twice in the 17 years preceding the release of the government's 1982 proposals for comprehensive legislative reform.[113] Furthermore, the 1978 amendments moved the Ontario legislation in more of a legal rights direction (especially with respect to children's legal rights) than any other jurisdiction in the country. For example, the 1978 amendments introduced the right of children to court-ordered legal counsel and the requirement that the consent of older children must be obtained for a voluntary care agreement to be valid. The 1978 amendments also were fairly specific, providing detailed sections on issues which were addressed only generally, if at all, in most other Canadian child welfare statutes.

(c) Alberta

Alberta's legislation was, in general, similar to Ontario's pre-1978 statute. Thus, it was relatively up-to-date, although its grounds for intervention contained some archaic language (as did Ontario's). For example, a "neglected child" included one "who is being allowed to grow up without salutary parental control or under circumstances tending to make him idle or dissolute".[114]

These differences in the legislative history of the statutes being revised may help to explain some of the differences among the new statutes. British Columbia and the Yukon were grappling with issues that had already been resolved in the other two jurisdictions. Even if the pressure in British Columbia and the Yukon had been for a non-interventionist statute, it is unlikely that the policy makers would have made the leap from an archaic statute to a highly detailed, legalistic statute like Ontario's. Such a revolution in law is unusual and law reform is much more likely to take place in a gradual, incremental manner.[115]

Ontario took more of an incrementalist approach. Although the 1978 amendments did not address the difficult, critical issues addressed in the 1984 legislation, they did lay the groundwork for more legalistic, non-interventionist and accountability oriented reform. Perhaps this factor, combined with the

---

113 Child Welfare Act, R.S.O. 1980, c. 66 [repealed by the Child and Family Services Act, 1984, c. 55, s. 208]. Extensive amendments to the Child Welfare Act were made in 1965 and 1978.

114 Child Welfare Act, R.S.A. 1980, c. C-8, s. 6(*e*)(viii).

115 See E. Lemert, *Social Action and Legal Change* (1970).

philosophical orientation of the key actors in Ontario, helps to explain the fact that, compared to the Alberta statute, Ontario's Act is more precise and consistent in its legalistic approach.

In sum, the four jurisdictions were beginning their legislative reform efforts from very different statutory starting points. The state of the previous legislation, when combined with other factors (for example, key actors and pressure for reform), probably helped to produce the different legislative outcomes.

STATE OF PREVIOUS LEGISLATION

British Columbia	Yukon	Alberta	Ontario
archaic	archaic	modern	modern, legalistic

5. Research: Legislative Models

All four jurisdictions conducted research as part of the policy development process. Legal research in the form of reviewing law reform proposals and statutes from other jurisdictions was the primary research activity.

(a) British Columbia

Although "some language" from other statutes was used, no statute or proposal served as a basic model for the legislation in British Columbia. The deputy minister felt that there were problems with every proposed or existing statute reviewed, including the royal commission's draft act. In particular, he found that most of the proposed or existing legislation was too broad, giving the impression that the drafters were "trying to write social policy".

(b) The Yukon

The Yukon Act appears to have been at least partially influenced by the law reform proposals made by Goldstein, Freud and Solnit in *Beyond the Best Interests of the Child*.[116] The law professor, a key actor discussed earlier, specifically refers to this book in his paper on the key features of the new legislation. He emphasizes certain concepts proposed by Goldstein, Freud and Solnit, including: the importance of "bonding" between the child and parent or caretaker; the child's "sense of time"; and that children should not remain in a "legal limbo" for long periods of time. In addition, he notes that the legislation's

---

116 (1973).

basic policy statement on the purpose of services provided under the Act was based on a similar policy section of the English Children and Young Persons Act, 1963.[117]

(c) Ontario

Ontario's awareness of recent legislative models was very influential in guiding the development of its legislative proposals. Three sources were most influential: the American Bar Association's tentative standards on child abuse and neglect,[118] two law review articles written by Professor Michael Wald,[119] and *Before the Best Interests of the Child*,[120] another more recent book by Goldstein, Freud and Solnit. These materials were generally consistent with the legalistic, non-interventionist direction of the legislation project.

(d) Alberta

The Ontario proposals were made public during the time that the Cavanagh Board of Review was conducting its investigation in Alberta. Some of the major Ontario proposals were adopted as a model by the Cavanagh board (for example, basic philosophical principles and grounds for involuntary intervention).

The government's senior legislative planner acknowledged that both the Ontario proposals and the ABA Standards were of particular significance to her work in developing the legislative bill. However, it is noteworthy that Alberta did not choose to apply the legalistic approach of Ontario and the ABA Standards throughout its new legislation, although it would have been quite consistent with the Cavanagh recommendations. Regarding the critical areas discussed in Part II, the legislation maintains a generally non-interventionist, legalistic approach in those areas specifically addressed by Cavanagh. However, in other critical areas not addressed by Cavanagh, such as the court's decision on interim custody and the scope of state authority after apprehension, the legislation departs from the legalistic course and resorts to a more discretionary and interventionist approach.

In sum, it appears that the existence of proposals or models which were compatible with the general philosophical direction of key actors was an important force in shaping the specific content of three of the new statutes. The

---

117 1963 (U.K.), c. 37.

118 ABA Standards, *Standards Relating to Abuse and Neglect* (1977).

119 M. Wald, "State Intervention on Behalf of 'Neglected' Children: A Search for Realistic Standards" (1975), 27 Stan. L. Rev. 985; "State Intervention on Behalf of 'Neglected' Children: Standards for Removal of Children from their Homes, Monitoring the Status of Children in Foster Care, and Termination of Parental Rights" (1976), 28 Stan. L. Rev. 623.

120 J. Goldstein, A. Freud, and A. Solnit, *Before the Best Interests of the Child* (1979).

proposals provided a blueprint for implementing a general policy position and, in varying degrees, were adapted to fit the requirements of Ontario, Alberta and the Yukon.

RELIANCE ON LEGISLATIVE MODELS

British Columbia	Yukon	Alberta	Ontario
no	yes	yes	yes

6. Public Consultation

It is not simply coincidental that only in Ontario did the public consultation process have a significant impact in terms of shifting the policy content of the government's initial legislative proposals. Only in Ontario, as noted earlier, were the child protection workers relatively independent of the government and, unlike the other jurisdictions, they were publicly vocal and negative in their reaction.

Apart from the greater independence of the child welfare sector in Ontario and the legalistic substance of the proposals, there were two other differences in the various consultation processes which may have contributed to the hostility among children's services professionals in Ontario.

(a) The Consultation Document

Alberta, British Columbia and the Yukon sent out draft legislation for public comment. The drafts were written in the usual "legalese" of statutes and were accompanied by virtually no explanation. In contrast, Ontario distributed a long (184 pages) consultation paper which raised issues, identified possible solutions, discussed the advantages and disadvantages of the possible solutions and made recommendations in fairly specific terms.[121] In short, the Ontario consultation document was much easier to read and laid out quite clearly the rationales for its recommendations. By making the document's contents easily understandable and by openly revealing the underlying reasoning (for example, concern about the potentially arbitrary judgment of social workers), the Ontario policy makers probably increased the likelihood of alienating the professional service providers. Finally, the use of a discussion paper rather than draft legislation was more likely to give the impression that the government had not yet made up its mind and was genuinely interested in feedback on the proposals.

---

121 Ontario, Ministry of Community and Social Services, *The Children's Act: A Consultation Paper* (1982).

(b) Scope of the Proposals

Even if there had been significant opposition in British Columbia and Alberta, it is likely that the opposition would have been limited to a fairly narrow range of professional service providers — mainly those involved in child protection.[122] The legislative proposals in these two provinces were, in terms of scope, traditional child welfare statutes which primarily affected professionals in the child welfare sector. Although the Yukon's proposals were somewhat broader in that they included areas such as custody, guardianship and establishment of parentage, Ontario's approach provides a more striking contrast. The Ontario consultation paper encompassed not only the usual child protection and adoption matters, but also controversial issues such as intrusive medical procedures and behaviour modification procedures, admission of children to mental health and mental retardation institutions, juvenile corrections and confidentiality of records. The Ontario policy makers applied their legalistic approach to these other areas as well, thus alienating not only child welfare professionals but also nearly every other professional children's services group in the province (for example, medical doctors, psychologists, social workers working in settings other than child protection agencies and child care workers). The cumulative effect of the widespread opposition was to create great pressure on the government to make compromises throughout the subsequent draft legislation, including the child protection part.

PUBLIC CONSULTATION

	British Columbia	Yukon	Alberta	Ontario
Impact	minimal	minimal	minimal	moderate
Consultation document	draft Bill	draft Bill	draft Bill	discussion paper
Scope of legislative proposals	very narrow	broad	narrow	broad
Child protection agencies	government operated	government operated	government operated	private but government funded

7. Summary

The following chart summarizes the policies embodied in the four statutes and the factors identified that help to explain why the policies were adopted in each of the jurisdictions.

---

122 However, it should be noted that the Alberta Act includes provisions relating to secure treatment.

SUMMARY OF OVERALL POLICY

Non-Legalistic, Interventionist			Legalistic, Non-Interventionist
B.C. Yukon		Alberta	Ontario

SUMMARY OF FACTORS IN LEGISLATIVE REFORM PROCESS

	British Columbia	Yukon	Alberta	Ontario
1. Pressure for reform	technical,	technical interventionist	non-	administrative interventionist
2. Key government actors	senior	lawyer administrator	lawyer	lawyers
3. Key non-government actors			Cavanagh Board of Review	Child welfare professionals, lawyers, legislative committee
4. State of previous legislation	archaic	archaic	modern	modern, legalistic
5. Reliance on legislative models	no	yes	yes	yes
6. Public Consultation				
— Impact	minimal	minimal	minimal	moderate
— Consultation document	draft bill	draft bill	draft bill	discussion paper
— Scope of legislative proposals	very narrow	broad	narrow	broad
— Child protection agencies	government operated	government operated	government operated	private, but government funded

IV CONCLUSION

Although the discussion in this part does not constitute an exhaustive analysis of the legislative reform process in the four jurisdictions, it does provide a basis for drawing some conclusions regarding factors that affect both the general philosophy and specific provisions of Canadian child protection statutes.

First, many variables are involved in the development of child protection legislation. No single variable is determinative but rather it is the combination of variables in a particular jurisdiction which determines where on the intervention spectrum its legislation will be.

Second, in general, the most important policy work is done before a Bill is introduced in the legislature. Legislatures did not play a significant role in shaping the content of the Bills. In Ontario, the legislative committee did exert pressure regarding the draft legislation and the government incorporated many of the committee's recommendations into the Bill that was subsequently introduced. However, even here, the legislative committee did not go beyond the basic parameters that had been set by both the draft legislation and the earlier consultation paper. In short, the Ontario legislature played an important role in forcing compromises (most notably, toward a return to the earlier proposals) but it did not make major changes or establish a different policy framework for addressing the issues. Thus, one lesson seems to be that it is important for those interested in shaping policy to be involved in the policy development process at a very early stage.

Third, the initial and most influential policy work is usually done by people who work for the government. In fact, who those people are is probably the single most critical factor in explaining why a statute embodies an interventionist or non-interventionist approach. In all the jurisdictions reviewed, the attitudes, experience and training of key government actors were critical to the direction and style of the legislation. A government's general policy objective is typically so broad (for example, to protect children and support families) that the people in government working directly on the legislation have considerable room to manoeuvre. They make numerous, important policy decisions on matters not clearly dictated by the government's official policy position. For example, these key government actors will decide which research or legislative models to accept or reject.

Fourth, lawyers play important policy making roles in government. However, it would be inaccurate to suggest that there is a single, legal perspective which they all bring to the policy development process. The above discussion shows that some significant differences may exist. For example, the Yukon's law professor approached his work from a distinctly less legalistic and more interventionist perspective than his counterparts in Ontario and Alberta. In addition, there is some evidence that the Ontario lawyers were more committed to a non-interventionist philosophy than was the key legal policy maker in Alberta.

Fifth, it is clear that the types of pressure for legislative reform can have a significant effect on the content of legislation. As noted earlier, the reform pressure sets the stage or creates an atmosphere in which other important variables interact. If the pressure is relatively neutral in terms of philosophy, as it was in Ontario and the Yukon, the policy makers have considerably more leeway. Thus, who occupies the policy making roles becomes even more critical. If the forces for change create pressure for a distinct philosophical approach, the policy makers have less leeway. For example, it would have been extremely difficult for the key government actor in Alberta to have produced essentially interventionist legislation in the face of widespread media coverage of the child welfare scandals and the subsequent Cavanagh report. Once again, however, the importance of the attitudes, training and experience of key government actors is evident. If the key government actors in Alberta had been the Ontario lawyers, it is likely that they would have produced a more consistently non-interventionist statute that would still have been in line with the recommendations of the Cavanagh report.

Sixth, non-government actors can be influential, depending on the context in which the legislation is being developed. For example, Justice Cavanagh's Board of Review was clearly influential in Alberta whereas a similar body, Justice Berger's royal commission, was not nearly as influential because of the change in government shortly after the completion of its report. Similarly, child welfare professionals had some limited impact in Ontario's public consultation process because of certain contextual factors, such as their relative independence from government and the absence of any scandals or issues which could have created widespread political support for the legislative proposals.

Finally, depending on the type of pressure for reform and who the key actors are, other minor factors may contribute to pushing the legislation in a more or less interventionist direction. For example, the state of the previous legislation can be relevant. The former archaic, discretionary and interventionist statutes in British Columbia and the Yukon made it less likely that these jurisdictions would produce modern, legalistic and non-interventionist statutes. However, such a radical shift may have occurred if, in these jurisdictions, there had been child welfare scandals and a board of review, as in Alberta, and strongly non-interventionist lawyers in key policy positions, as in Ontario.

part III

FUTURE DIRECTIONS IN CHILD AND FAMILY LAW

9

EVIDENTIARY CONCERNS IN CASES OF CHILD SEXUAL ABUSE*

Janne M.N. Burton**

---

*This chapter, bearing the title "But Who Protects the Children? A Critical Analysis of the Criminal Justice System of Canada from the Perspective of the Child Victim of Sexual Assault", took second prize in the Seventh Annual Lieff Competition, 1985, sponsored by the Canadian Bar Association — Ontario, Family Law Section.

**The author gratefully acknowledges the advice and guidance of Professor Nicholas Bala in the preparation of this chapter.

I INTRODUCTION

When a young person in Canada is charged with an offence, she[1] encounters a court system legislatively designed to accommodate the special needs of the young.[2] When, however, a young person is found to be the victim of a sexual assault,[3] she encounters a court system designed for adults, where, with notable exceptions, her credibility is doubted and her profound embarrassment ignored.

In sexual abuse cases, the victim's testimony is crucial. Often there is no other evidence of the perpetrator's guilt. Yet forcing the child victim to describe several times, and ultimately in public, the details of a sexual encounter aggravates her emotional trauma. The common law presumptions that a child's testimony is suspect and the consequent built-in safeguards denigrate her testimony and further exacerbate the harm.

This chapter argues that a child victim of sexual assault should not be forced to testify personally at criminal trial. Rather, her testimony should be replaced by a videotape of a pre-trial examination conducted under strictly controlled conditions by a child sexual abuse expert. This expert will supplement the videotape examination with in-court testimony.

Part II discusses the problems inherent in the present system — the credibility hurdle for the child complainant, the number of valid cases dropped, the potential destruction of the victim's family and the imbalance of the rights of the accused and those of the child victim. Part III addresses the pertinent criminal and evidence law in Canada. Part IV outlines possible solutions in theory and in practice. Part V recommends a proposed reform for Ontario and possibly all of Canada. Part VI examines the proposed reform in light of rights guaranteed under the Canadian Charter of Rights and Freedoms, and concludes that it is possible to balance the rights of the accused and of the victim without offending the rights of a defendant to a fair trial.

---

1 Feminine gender pronouns are used generically in reference to child victims throughout this chapter; masculine gender pronouns, in reference to perpetrators. This generalization is based on fact — most victims are female and most perpetrators male; see *Sexual Offences Against Children* (1984), hereinafter cited as Badgley, at 196-98 and 215.

2 Young Offenders Act, S.C. 1980-81-82-83, c. 110, s. 2(1).

3 The terms "sexual assault" and "sexual abuse" are used interchangeably in this chapter, and when appropriate refer also to incest in the clinical sense. "Child sexual abuse is a sexual act imposed on a child who lacks emotional, instructional, and cognitive development. . . . [I]ncestuous child sexual abuse encompasses any form of sexual activity between a child and a parent or stepparent or extended family member (for example, grandparent, aunt or uncle), or surrogate parent figure (for example, common-law spouse or foster parent)." From Suzanne M. Sgroi, *Handbook of Clinical Intervention in Child Sexual Abuse* (1982), at 9 and 10.

II THE EXISTING PROBLEMS

The principal problem for a child victim of sexual assault in the existing criminal justice system is the potential for psychological harm. Section 1 examines this trauma from two viewpoints: (a) there is great potential for harm built into the system, and (b) there is no proof of harm. Section 2 discusses briefly the resultant crisis to a family after the revelation of sexual assault. Section 3 refers to the possibility of a child being left "in limbo", with little or no response to her complaint. Section 4 speaks to the imbalance of rights of the accused and child victim.

1. Possible Trauma to Child Victim Resulting from Criminal Court Proceedings

"The behavioural science literature is bereft of research listing assumptions about ways in which the legal system induces and enforces trauma in child victims."[4] Where this issue has been addressed at all, two opposing viewpoints have emerged: (a) that the criminal justice system exacerbates the trauma already suffered by the victim as a result of the sexual abuse; and (b) that "the opportunity to 'have their day in court' would be cathartic and symbolically put an end to the episode in [the victims'] minds".[5] Following is a discussion of the inherent harm and inherent healing assumptions.

(a) Inherent harm

"[T]he very safeguards of the rights of the accused may produce the greatest trauma for the child."[6] One author, David Libai, identifies the components of legal proceedings which psychiatrists have identified as capable of putting the child victim under prolonged mental stress and of endangering her

---

4 Mary Wells, Unpublished Paper presented at the International Congress of Child Sexual Abuse, Montreal (September 1984). At the time of writing, Ms. Wells was Co-ordinator of Support Services, Metropolitan Chairman's Special Committee on Child Abuse, Toronto. The author is grateful to Ms. Wells for making this paper available to her. See also Gail S. Goodman, "The Child Witness: Conclusions and Future Directions for Research and Legal Practice", in "The Child Witness" (1984), 40 J. Soc. Issues 157 at 167-69.

5 Wells, *supra*, n. 4.

6 David Libai, "Protection of the Child Victim of a Sexual Offence in the Criminal Justice System" (1968-69), 15 Wayne L. Rev. 977 at 979.

emotional equilibrium:[7] repeated interrogations[8] and cross-examinations, facing the accused again, the official atmosphere of the court, acquittal for want of corroborating evidence to a child's trustworthy testimony, and conviction of a parent or relative.[9]

Libai's opinion is suported in subsequent literature. In her 1982 article, Jacqueline Y. Parker writes, "The documentation for his assertions has recently grown both in quantity and quality".[10] Parker goes on to describe the short and long-range psychological effects of the sexual assault itself coupled with the effects of its aftermath.[11]

Dr. Heinz Brunold, reporting the results of his study of adult women who had suffered sexual abuse as children, states: "Several women asserted that the investigations by the police or in court had made a considerably worse impact on them than the offence."[12]

In an article describing Israel's judicial response to sexual assault on its children and the reasons for this response,[13] Judge David Reifen points out that a child's recovery from the trauma of the assault can be threatened by the requirement, up to a year after the event, to testify in court and relive incidents better forgotten.[14]

The Metropolitan Chairman's Special Committee on Child Abuse in Toronto takes the position that, properly handled, criminal justice intervention has an important role to play in the community response to child sexual abuse, a positive value in itself.[15] This viewpoint and the resulting program are described

---

7 *Ibid.*, at 984.

8 The Metropolitan Chairman's Special Committee on Child Abuse, *Child Sexual Abuse Protocol* (1984), at vii. The Special Committee points out that without a co-ordinated, co-operative approach, ". . .in the space of several days, a child could be interviewed by a teacher, a public health nurse or school social worker, one or more child welfare workers, several police officers, plus medical and legal personnel". The Special Committee is, as of the date of publication, named the Metropolitan Toronto Special Committee on Child Abuse and in June 1986 released the second edition of the *Protocol*.

9 Libai, *supra*, n. 6, at 984.

10 Jacqueline Y. Parker, "The Rights of Child Witnesses: Is the Court a Protector or Perpetrator?" (1981-82), 17 New Eng. L. Rev. 643 at 649.

11 *Ibid.*, at 649-53.

12 Heinz Brunold, "Observations After Sexual Traumata Suffered in Childhood" (1964), 4 Excerpta Criminologica 5 at 7.

13 David Reifen, "Protection of Children Involved in Sexual Offences: A New Method of Investigation in Israel" (1959), 49 J. Crim. L.C. & P.S. 222. Judge Reifen was Chief Judge, Juvenile Courts of Israel.

14 *Ibid.*, at 223.

15 Discussion between Lorna Grant, Executive Director, Metropolitan Toronto Special Committee on Child Abuse, and the author.

later in this chapter. However, in her paper presented at the International Congress of Child Abuse in Quebec in September 1984, Mary Wells, then Co-ordinator of Support Services for the Special Committee, and a recognized expert in this field, identified potential fears of the child victim, especially the victim of an incestuous relationship:

that she will be called a liar;[16]

conversely that she will be believed and thus be responsible for sending the offender to jail;[17]

that she will be responsible for the family's loss of income, thereby bringing her mother's anger on herself and the community's derision on her family;[18]

that she will be identified in the media;[19]

that the offender may hurt her in the courtroom;[20] or yell at her,[21] or look at her in a frightening way;[22]

that defence counsel will yell at her, say she is lying, confuse her or frighten her in some way;[23]

that the Crown Attorney and the judge will be angry at her "if she does something wrong";[24]

that she will forget, get confused, vomit or be unable to talk.[25]

Ms. Wells goes on to explain why the child's fear of being called a liar may be well founded. She cites from an article by Judith Lewis Herman which explains that the roots of the disbelief in children's reports lie in Freud's pronouncement that children lie about sexual abuse.[26] This "tenacious prejudice"[27] has become deeply ingrained in the culture. Not only the lay public, but

---

16 Wells, *supra*, n. 4.

17 *Ibid.*

18 *Ibid.*

19 *Ibid.*

20 *Ibid.*

21 *Ibid.*

22 *Ibid.*

23 *Ibid.*

24 *Ibid.*

25 *Ibid.*

26 A possible explanation for Freud's shift from his original contention that childhood sexual trauma formed the basis of his female patients' neuroses to his later view of his patients' *fantasies* of childhood sexual activity forming the cornerstone of his theoretical system can be found in Lucy Berliner and Mary Kay Barbieri, "The Testimony of the Child Victim of Sexual Assault" in "The Child Witness" (1984), 40 J. Soc. Issues 125 at 127.

27 Wells, Unpublished Paper presented at the International Congress of Child Sexual Abuse, Montreal (September 1984).

professionals, medical and legal, have dismissed children's complaints as fantasy. Physicians have been known to assert that children can contract venereal disease from clothing, towels or toilet seats.[28] Ms. Herman notes that *Wigmore on Evidence*, a prestigious and influential text, contains, in the 1934 supplement to the second edition, a doctrine impeaching the credibility of any female, especially a child, who complained of a sex offence. This edition goes on to warn that women and girls are predisposed to bring false accusations against men of good character, and that these accusations might convince unsuspecting judges and juries.[29] Herman also cites a study proving that Wigmore had falsified or omitted information. For example, in his discussion of incest he reported, as examples of pathological lying in children, the cases of 7 and 9-year-old girls who had accused their fathers of sexual assault. He omitted reporting the original clinical reports documenting the 7-year-old's gonorrhea and the 9-year-old's vaginal infection which caused swelling of such severity that the doctor could not make a physical examination.[30] "Wigmore's assertions, supposedly based upon medical expertise, remained unchallenged for decades in the legal literature, and still retain great prestige and influence in the courtroom."[31]

Jean Piaget, the Swiss psychologist and expert in child development, supports the contention that young children fantasize. His experiments indicate that up to about age 7 or 8, a child "distorts reality in accordance with his desires and his romancing".[32] And later in the same text, "wherever the mind feels no actual need for accommodating itself to reality, its natural tendency will be to distort the objects that surround it in accordance with its desires or its fantasy, in short to use them for its satisfaction".[33] Between the ages of 6 and 7 children believe that lying is wrong only in relation to the punishment it can produce;[34] that it is wrong because it will not be believed;[35] and that lies to adults are naughtier than to children, because adults are "bigger" or "older" and because "a gentleman is worth more than a child".[36]

Eight to 10-year-olds begin seeing lies as inherently wrong,[37] and between 9 and 12 the concept of the destruction of trust through lies evolves.[38]

---

28 *Ibid.*, citing from Judith Lewis Herman, *Father-Daughter Incest* (1981), at 11.

29 Herman, *ibid.*

30 *Ibid.*

31 *Ibid.*

32 Jean Piaget, *Moral Judgment of the Child* (1932), at 160.

33 *Ibid.*, at 161.

34 *Ibid.*, at 165.

35 *Ibid.*, at 167.

36 *Ibid.*, at 169.

37 *Ibid.*, at 166.

38 *Ibid.*, at 167.

Newer theoretical notions counter Piaget's claims that children's thinking is entirely tied to developmental "stages". In a recent article, Gail S. Goodman writes that most developmental researchers now recognize that a child's knowledge of or familiarity with "to-be-remembered" information profoundly affects memory performance. A child's knowledge about a certain domain of information, the cognitive skills he or she brings to a particular task, and the emotions experienced during the event and during attempts to remember are likely to influce both memory and report.[39]

The credibility issue has been addressed by commissions and committees studying child sexual assault. The Metropolitan Chairman's Statement of Principles contained within the *Protocol* states categorically that children do not lie about this experience; in fact they are much more likely to falsely deny than to falsely report its occurrence.[40] Of some 2,000 youngsters assisted by a California sexual abuse team between 1971 and 1975, not one was found to be lying.[41] The Badgley Commission,[42] after citing more balanced recent Wigmorian thinking on the veracity of children, adds "that in the context of child sexual abuse, children's alleged 'disposition to weave romances and to treat imagination for verity' is strongly refuted by the research findings obtained in its several national surveys".[43]

The Badgley Commission illustrates the findings of the police, hospital and child protection surveys. The proportion of cases reported as "confirmed/founded" was:

---

39 Gail S. Goodman, "Children's Testimony in Historical Perspective" in "The Child Witness" (1984), 40 J. Soc. Issues, c. 9 at 18.

40 *Child Sexual Abuse Protocol* (1984), at iii. See also Berliner and Barbieri "The Testimony of the Child Victim of Sexual Assault", in "The Child Witness", *ibid.*, at 127.

41 The Metropolitan Chairman's Special Committee on Child Abuse, Information Brochure, at 2. Under "Assumptions Regarding Intervention and Treatment", the brochure quotes from "Child Sexual Abuse Newsletter" (August, 1981), published by Social Planning and Research, United Way of the Lower Mainland, Vancouver, B.C. "In the 2,000 families referred to the Giarretto Program in San Jose for child sexual abuse, every father eventually admitted that the complaint made by the child was true. In a survey of 137 cases regarded as questionable by the Michigan State Police because supportive evidence could not be found, only one child's testimony was not borne out by a polygraph . . . examination. In that one case, the child's 'lie' was to have reduced the number of years of her victimization."

42 Formally named the Committee on Sexual Offences Against Children and Youths, appointed by the Minister of Justice and the Attorney General of Canada and the Minister of National Health and Welfare. The report of the Committee is *Sexual Offences Against Children* (1984).

43 Badgley, *ibid.*, at 373. The surveys specifically referred to here are the National Police Force Survey, described at 16, the National Hospital Survey, at 19, and the National Child Protection Survey, at 18.

Police Force   94 per cent
Hospital   92.5 per cent (approximate)
Child Protection   45.5 per cent

The Commission notes the unexpected finding of the Child Protection Survey[44] that over half of the children known to child protection workers were not believed. Perhaps the time taken to seek the assistance of each of these three classes of agencies explains the discrepancy. The average time spans from incident to reporting are illustrated in table form later in the same chapter. About 74 per cent of the cases were reported to police and 68 per cent to hospitals within one week, but only 32 per cent to child protection agencies within that time. Conversely, only 3.3 per cent and 5.2 per cent of the reports came to police and hospitals respectively after one year, but a full 32 per cent of the cases came to the attention of child protection agencies over one year after they occurred.[45] The types of cases reported may further explain the credibility gap. If the perpetrator is a stranger or if there has been an injury, police and/or medical assistance will be sought quickly. However, intra-familial cases may come to the attention of child protection workers in another context, possibly long after the abuse. All evidence supporting the complainant may be lost by that time.

How then to reconcile the psychological stance that children do fantasize or lie with the findings of agencies working with a specific group of youngsters? Perhaps the answer is best put by one child psychologist:

> A child will certainly fantasize, but only about things of which she has some knowledge. She will not likely imagine sexual intercourse without having some understanding about the sex act or the nature and function of sex organs. Therefore, if a young pre-schooler reports intercourse, one must ask what opportunity a child of this age has had to learn about it other than through direct experience. The fact that many in this age group blurt out the details in an unabashed way suggests they know so little that they are not even aware it is considered wrong. The major concern with an older child is not that she will fabricate, but that she will fail to report the event at all because, in the normal course of acquiring information about sex, she will have also learned that it is a more or less taboo topic. Of course it is conceivable that a child might falsely report sexual abuse, but the child stands to gain little by it, and most children gradually become implicitly aware of this. In any case, a skilful examiner, knowledgeable about child mental health, should be able to sort out inconsistencies and fabrications from the truth.[46]

As the studies in this chapter demonstrate, child victims of sexual assault have been required historically to surmount a greater credibility hurdle than the

---

44 Badgley, *ibid.*, at 224-25.

45 *Ibid.*, at 228.

46 As related to the author in one of several interviews with Jane H. Hamacher, Ph.D., Psychologist, Grey County School Board. The author gratefully acknowledges the generous assistance of her long-time friend, Dr. Hamacher.

victims of other crimes, greater even than women complainants of rape. Recent studies point out, however, that this historical belief in children's propensity to fabricate sexual experiences has been quite wrong. Notwithstanding these recent data, the erroneous belief is still pervasive in our culture.

This chapter has examined the veracity issue in some depth because it is at the root of many potentially traumatizing elements of the criminal justice process. It results in repeated interrogations, police accusations that child protection workers or parents coach the child,[47] the possibility of the court's refusing to hear her testimony under oath, and finally vigorous cross-examination which is "very effective in totally demoralizing the child and is sometimes effective in shutting her up".[48] The child may also be further hampered by her inability to articulate verbally. If she has initially told her story to a worker through anatomically correct dolls or drawings, she may be prevented from doing so in criminal court because of the physical layout of the courtroom itself.[49] She therefore must be assisted prior to giving testimony, but may become too well prepared, giving rise to the coaching accusations.[50]

"Kids are so powerless; no one believes them."[51] "Without [the commitment of all systems responsible for serving children to act without doubt or delay] the balance of power will remain forever in the hands of those adults who choose to violate the bodies and spirits of children."[52]

Another important factor to be considered when studying potential inherent trauma in the criminal justice process is the investigative interrogation of the complainant. Of course, if criminal charges are contemplated, the police must be called in. But whether the officer selected to investigate the allegations will be specially trained to question children depends on the community in which the investigation takes place. Leroy G. Schultz, a Missouri Probation and Parole Officer, writes,

> Interviewing the immature victim can involve a dilemma in which the gathering of information itself may induce or contribute to emotional damage of the victim. Emotional damage hinges on the manner in which the interview is conducted. Under these conditions the

---

47 As related to the author by Paula Mallea, at that time Lawyer, Children's Aid Society of the City of Kingston and County of Frontenac, whom the author thanks for her time and advice.

48 As related anonymously by a children's aid society worker who specializes in sexual abuse cases, and who accompanies child witnesses to criminal court.

49 *Per* Ms. Mallea, *supra*, n. 47.

50 For a brief discussion of the problems inherent in prosecuting sex abuse cases where the child is the only witness, see "The Testimony of Child Victims in Sex Abuse Prosecutions: Two Legislative Innovations" (1985), 98 Harv. L. Rev. 806 at 807.

51 Ms. Mallea, *supra*, n. 47.

52 *Child Sexual Abuse Protocol* (1984), at v.

interviewer needs skill in interviewing adults and children, as well as a knowledge of psychodynamics, and the interviewer must know when to stop interviewing because of possible damage to the victim.[53]

He goes on to say,

The investigator should avoid grilling, coercing, showing authority or giving advice. It is these aspects of interviewing which induce possible trauma in the child victim, and are characteristic of the techniques emloyed by police and attorneys.[54]

It appears that in Ontario there is a great discrepancy in the knowledge and experience of investigators. At one end of the spectrum, a police force, urban or rural, may choose to follow the guidelines published by the Special Committee on Child Abuse in Metropolitan Toronto.[55] These guidelines advocate sensitivity to the child's emotions, intellectual abilities, verbal abilities, surroundings during the interview,[56] and so on. At the other end of the spectrum is the police force which dispatches a large, male, uniformed (complete with billy club) officer to interview a 4-year-old girl.[57] The officer may be well intentioned and kind; however, his uniform can terrify a child and become a barrier to any effective communication. It is entirely within the discretion of each police force to decide how complainants of sexual assault are to be treated.[58]

It is beyond the scope of this paper to address the breakdowns in communication, confusion about responsibilities, duplication of effort, and conflicting expectations and pressures created by simultaneous Family Court and criminal court proceedings experienced by many public workers serving children. The reader is referred to other excellent sources[59] for this information. However, these are important issues to be considered when thinking about their impact on the young victims who may end up lost in the system and even more confused by the behaviour of adults.

---

53 Leroy G. Schultz, "Interviewing the Sex Offender's Victim" (1959-60), J. Crim. L.C. & P.S. 448 at 451.

54 *Ibid.*, at 452.

55 Mary Wells, *Guidelines for Investigative Interviewing of Child Victims of Sexual Abuse* (1984).

56 *Ibid.*, at 3-4.

57 As related anonymously to the author by a child protection worker. The event occurred in 1984 in a medium sized Ontario city.

58 The author has arrived at this opinion after speaking informally to several sources throughout Ontario.

59 Marion E. Lane, *The Legal Response to Sexual Abuse of Children* (1982), prepared for The Metropolitan Chairman's Special Committee on Child Abuse; R.C. Holmes, "The Police Role in Child Abuse" in John M. Eekelaar and Sanford N. Katz (eds.), *Family Violence: An International and Interdisciplinary Study* (1978), at 417; W. Johnson and J. Thompson, "Child Abuse: The Policeman's Role: An Innovative Approach" in *Family Violence*, at 428.

In summary, automatic disbelief in the child complainant's report of sexual abuse, coupled with her probable powerlessness to withstand the tough questioning she will encounter at least once in a criminal proceeding, may cause greater psychological harm than that caused by the assault itself.

(b) No inherent harm

The other view is that child witnesses either experience no lasting or serious harm in the criminal justice system,[60] or can be empowered by the experience.[61]

The Badgley Commission addressed this issue briefly in its National Child Protection Survey. The report states,

> In two in [sic] three cases (67.5 per cent) in which sexually abused children had been involved in criminal court proceedings, child protection workers reported no information concerning whether in their judgment these children had been harmed by this legal intervention. About one in ten (9.8 per cent), a proportion higher than that reported for cases appearing before child welfare courts, was deemed to have been harmed.[62]

The Commission recognizes that the findings concerning whether children have been harmed are incomplete.[63] It found that in many cases workers had either not been involved in the trials or were uninformed about what had happened to these children on a long-term basis.[64] Of the cases coming to the attention of child protection services having any form of court intervention, three in four had resulted in criminal court proceedings.[65] The Commission comments that the lack of appreciation by child protection workers of the effect on children is a serious omission in the scope of services provided.[66]

Nevertheless without reference to this or any other research on the possible resultant trauma, the Commission strongly recommends that all Canadian children speak on their own behalf at legal proceedings.[67]

The Metropolitan Chairman's Committee has reached the conclusion that including the child victim in criminal justice intervention can endow the child with a sense of mastery and integrity.[68] However, it has done so only after

---

60 Schultz, *supra*, n. 53, at 450.

61 *Protocol*, *supra*, n. 52, at v.

62 Badgley, *Sexual Offences Against Children* (1984), at 612.

63 *Ibid.*

64 *Ibid.*, at 614.

65 *Ibid.*, at 607.

66 *Ibid.*

67 *Ibid.*, at 67.

68 Wells, Unpublished Paper presented at the International Congress of Child Sexual Abuse, Montreal (September 1984).

addressing very carefully the harm it sees can be done and implementing techniques to prevent that harm.[69] The Committee does not deny the potential for inherent trauma; rather it sees the court process as potentially cleansing to the child *if the procedures are carried out in a sensitive manner*, and if the child is given assistance in overcoming her anxiety.[70]

In summary, several experts and authors have addressed the issue of possible harm to the child victim of sexual assault. It has been stated often that there is little or no empirical data on the subject.[71] One study[72] did compare the long-term reactions of witnesses and non-witnesses; however, a difficulty with studies of legal process trauma is the lack of information on any personality defects existing prior to the sexual assault and/or court experience.[73] Nevertheless, several authors and workers express the opinion that "the criminal justice system, seeking sound, indisputable evidence, descends on the child and family with terrifying force",[74] and that the "intervention may harm the child by forcing her to submit to the questioning of many people and perhaps to testifying against her father".[75] Other studies either address the harm potential only briefly[76] or recognize it and conclude that it can be overcome by giving the child the necessary coping strategies.[77]

2. Crisis in the Family

All revelations of sexual abuse can result in family turmoil and anguish. One family's experience illustrates this point. The parents suddenly discovered that three of their four children had been assaulted by a trusted family friend.

---

69 Opinion of the author. The Metropolitan Chairman's Committee offers advice throughout its literature on methods of meeting the emotional needs of the child victim and her family. It is submitted that implicit in this advice is the message that without proper handling, the child could suffer more trauma.

70 Wells, *supra*, n. 68.

71 Wells, *ibid*; Libai, "Protection of the Child Victim of a Sexual Offence in the Criminal Justice System" (1968-69), 15 Wayne L. Rev. 977 at 981; Goodman, "The Child Witness: Conclusions and Future Directions for Research and Legal Practice", in "The Child Witness" (1984), 40 J. Soc. Issues, No. 2, 157 at 167; Letter to the author from Selwyn M. Smith, M.D., Psychiatrist-in-Chief, Department of Psychiatry, Royal Ottawa Hospital, Ottawa, Ontario.

72 Libai, *ibid.*, at 982.

73 *Ibid.*, at 983.

74 Henry Giarretto, "Humanistic Treatment of Father-Daughter Incest", in R.E. Helfer and C.H. Kempe (eds.), *Child Abuse and Neglect* (1976), at 144.

75 Michael S. Wald, "State Intervention on Behalf of Neglected Children: Standards for Removal of Children from Their Homes, Monitoring the Status of Children in Foster Care and Termination of Parental Rights" (1976), 28 Stan. L. Rev. 625 at 656, n. 141.

76 Badgley, *Sexual Offences Against Children* (1984), at 612.

77 Wells, *supra*, n. 68.

Their hurt, anger and confusion were exacerbated by a child protection worker's refusal to believe the events as described by the mother. The horror was worsened by a question put to the 5-year-old by an examining physician at the local hospital's emergency department inquiring whether she "enjoyed it".[78]

When the perpetrator is a family member, the trauma may be even greater. "It is evident that typical community intervention in incest cases, rather than being constructive has the effect of a knock-out blow to a family already weakened by serious internal stresses."[79] The three main players in the most common family drama — the daughter, father and mother — have all experienced ambivalent emotions before the disclosure: the daughter, a mixture of anger, bewilderment, anxiety, and love for her father,[80] and guilt, shame, fear of anger, and anger towards her mother for failing to protect her;[81] the father, guilt, self-disgust,[82] denial,[83] and jealousy towards his daughter's friends;[84] the mother, if she knew or suspected,[85] the psychological effects of colluding with other family members to keep the family secret.[86] The sons of the family do not escape the emotional effects of this secret; often they are either ignored by their father or suffer his hostility.[87]

Allegations of sexual assault occasionally arise for the first time in the context of custody or access battles between separated parents. Usually it is reported that the abuse has occurred during access visits.[88] The circumstances surrounding these reportings lead many professionals to suspect their veracity. Whether the child in question is truly abused or is being encouraged to lie (and does so to gain a parent's approval), she is a victim of one parent or the other.

---

78 As related anonymously to the author. These events occurred in the summer of 1984 in a community a short distance from Metropolitan Toronto.

79 Giarretto, *supra*, n. 74, at 148.

80 *Ibid.*, at 146.

81 Ingrid K. Cooper, "Decriminalization of Incest — New Legal-Clinical Responses", in Eekelaar and Katz (eds.), *Family Violence: An International and Interdisciplinary Study* (1978), at 518.

82 Giarretto, *supra*, n. 74, at 148.

83 Cooper, *supra*, n. 81, at 520.

84 Giarretto, *supra*, n. 74, at 147.

85 Early literature indicates that a denying mother often knew of the incestuous father/daughter relationship and therefore colluded in it: Cooper, *supra*, n. 81, at 520. But see Jane F. Gilgun, Ph.D., "Does the Mother Know? Alternatives to Blaming Mothers for Child Sexual Abuse" (Fall 1984), Journal of the Centre for Women Policy Studies 2.

86 Cooper, *ibid.*, at 520.

87 *Ibid.*

88 For a full discussion of the consequences of allegations of sexual abuse during custody litigation, see the materials prepared for the "Symposium on Custody Litigation", presented by the Law Society of Upper Canada, Department of Education, 6th June 1986; Jeffery Wilson, Barrister and Solicitor, Program Leader.

The Metropolitan Chairman's Committee emphasizes that the quality of response in the first 48 hours after disclosure determines the eventual outcome for the child.[89] It goes on to comment, however, on the extremely limited scope and number of services equipped to provide the immediate and intensive intervention desperately needed by the victim and other non-offending family members.[90]

3. Valid Cases Dropped

It is beyond the scope of this paper to determine whether charges should be laid in *all* cases of sexual abuse of children. The reader is referred to other sources for opinion on the proper way to proceed.[91] Research has shown, however, that there are instances where charges should be laid and are not. There are several reasons for this situation:

failure of members of the medical profession to report suspected or confirmed cases, or reluctance to give information that provides medical evidence;[92]

lack of evidence;[93]

denial by the accused;[94]

child, witness or spouse unwilling to testify;[95]

credibility of complainant questioned;[96] and

age of the child.[97]

Personal accounts in the Badgley report support the above findings. Although parents found the police to be supportive,[98] often nothing could be done

---

89 *Child Sexual Abuse Protocol* (1984), at vii.

90 *Ibid.*

91 Cooper, *supra*, n. 81, at 523-27; Badgley, *supra*, n. 76, at 617; Giarretto, *supra*, n. 74, at 149-58.

92 Holmes, "The Police Role in Child Abuse", in Eekelaar and Katz (eds.), *Family Violence: An International and Interdisciplinary Study* (1978), at 422.

93 Badgley, *Sexual Offences Against Children* (1984), at 607: 72.7 per cent of the cases drawn from the National Child Protection and Ontario Surveys. Lane; *The Legal Responses to Sexual Abuse of Children* (1982), at 59.

94 Lane, *ibid.*: 3 in 12 cases.

95 Badgley, *supra*, n. 93, at 607: 16.7 per cent. This, however, is a key factor in Lane. In half the cases charges were not laid because of denial of the complainant or hostility of the mother: see at 59-60.

96 Badgley, *ibid.*, at 607: 12.1 per cent.

97 *Ibid.*: 5.6 per cent.

98 *Ibid.*, at 167-69.

beyond a warning to the individual suspected. Frustration, confusion and anger with the system are apparent throughout these accounts.[99]

It is important to note the reasons for lack of evidence in these cases. By its very nature sexual assault, especially of a child, occurs in secret. There are no witnesses. Often the passage of time between occurrence and investigation eliminates the possibility of there being any physical evidence, such as semen, on the child. Relatively few victims suffer physical injuries requiring medical attention.[100] Minor physical injuries heal before the investigation. In short, it is a crime difficult to prove.

Police forces, Crown Attorneys and child protection agencies make the decisions whether to lay charges in all cases of assault of children. Unless an effort has been made in a community to adopt a team approach to the legal and protection responses to its abused children,[101] these agencies will continue to work in relative isolation,[102] and occasionally in an atmosphere of mutual antipathy.[103] Too often police and child protection workers are confused about their roles in the investigative process.[104] Occasionally the conflicting philosophies and practices will leave the child "in limbo", at serious risk[105] or feeling abandoned to a hostile family.[106] It is not surprising that the cited studies have strongly recommended strengthening or revising the services provided to child victims.

4. Imbalance of Rights

Fundamental to our criminal justice system are the rights of an accused to make a full answer and defence, face his accuser, cross-examine the accuser in the presence of the trier of fact[107] and decline to testify.[108]

---

99 *Ibid*. The author has heard expressions of similar emotions from members of AFTERMATH —
  for families of sexually abused children, an organization that has offered support and education
  to families, professionals and the general public since July 1985.

100 *Ibid*., at 210-13, where it is reported that results of various surveys show more victims suffer
  emotional than physical harms.

101 Similar to that devised in Metropolitan Toronto.

102 Cooper, "Decriminalization of Incest — New Legal-Clinical Responses", in Eekelaar and
  Katz (eds.), *Family Violence: An International and Interdisciplinary Study* (1978), at 521.

103 Holmes, *supra*, n. 92, at 422.

104 *Ibid*., at 423; Lane, *supra*, n. 93, at 26-29 and 64-65.

105 *Protocol*, *supra*, n. 89, Foreword.

106 Giarretto, "Humanistic Treatment of Father-Daughter Incest", in Helfer and Kempe (eds.),
  Child Abuse and Neglect (1976), at 144.

107 Canadian Charter of Rights and Freedoms, s. 11(*d*). This paragraph is adapted from Joyce
  Miller's article "Abused Children as Witnesses: Softening the Trauma" (1984), O.L.W. 12. The
  author acknowledges Ms. Miller's kind assistance in the research of this chapter.

108 Charter, s. 11 (*c*).

Also fundamental is the right of a victim to a crime to seek the protection of the same system. However, it is difficult to ascertain any rights of the child victim (or any other victim) beyond this. Once the allegation has been made, the child is at the mercy of the procedures employed in her jurisdiction. If she is fortunate, she will be treated with sensitivity; if not, she will encounter procedures designed for adult complainants and laws founded on the premise that all children fantasize even after swearing to tell the truth.[109]

III THE PERTINENT LAW IN CANADA

The current criminal law concerning sexual offences against children has recently been analyzed by the Badgley Commission and published in its report. This chapter draws primarily from that source and from the comments made therein. Because of the ready availability of that single source, the comments in this chapter will not be in great detail, but will allude only to those issues discussed, *supra*, in Part II and to the reform proposed, *infra*, in Part V.

1. Criminal Code[110] — Sexual Offences

The specific provisions of the criminal law do not, of course, contribute directly to the central issue of this discourse — potential trauma to the child/victim/witness in criminal proceedings. The Badgley report does, however, point out some interpretations and oversights in the law which could indeed prove most distressing to a child in court. The following problems with the Criminal Code are demonstrative of the pitfalls a child may encounter.

(a) Legal Definition of "Assault" and "Consent"

The precise meaning of "sexual assault" in s. 246.1[111] remains to be judicially defined. It is unknown at this time if this section will exclude those acts where an accused invites a child to touch him or her, but neither touches nor threatens to touch the child in return. The now repealed offence of indecent assault on a female was interpreted judicially to exclude just that situation.[112] Applying this thinking, courts will reason that there has been no assault and therefore no sexual assault. It appears possible, therefore, for an adult man or

---

109 *Horsburgh v. R.*, [1968] 2 C.C.C. 288 at 320 (S.C.C.).

110 Criminal Code, R.S.C. 1970, c. C-34. Bill C-133, An Act to amend the Criminal Code and the Canada Evidence Act, which received first reading in the House of Commons on 10th June 1986, addresses some of the problems described in this Part.

111 En. 1980-81-82-83, c. 125, s. 19.

112 *R. v. McCallum*, [1970] 2 C.C.C. 366 (P.E.I.S.C.), and *R. v. Baney*, [1972] 2 O.R. 34 (C.A.).

woman to invite a child to fondle his or her genitalia, to neither threaten nor touch the child in doing so, and to be completely outside the criminal law sanctions.

It is known, however, that sexual assault has been held to exclude the fondling of a woman's breasts. There has been a judicial finding that a woman's breasts are secondary sex characteristics only and have no more sexual meaning than a man's beard. Therefore, according to this judicial thinking, it is no sexual offence to fondle them.[113] A child as well as a woman would have no recourse in law if her breasts had been fondled.

Section 246.1(2) provides,

> Where an accused is charged with an offence under subsection (1) or section 246.2 or 246.3 in respect of a person under the age of fourteen years, it is not a defence that the complainant consented to the activity that forms the subject-matter of the charge unless the accused is less than three years older than the complainant.

A strict interpretation of this provision allows a capable person under 14 to give a valid consent to being threatened, harmed, wounded, maimed or disfigured by someone less than three years older.[114] For example, a group of 14-year-old girls could fondle the genitalia of a 12-year-old boy with his consent, injure him, and plead 246.1(2) as a defence of consent to a charge under section 246.2.[115]

Without commenting on which of these cases would reach the criminal courtroom, it is not difficult to imagine the bewilderment of any of the three victims of the above-described acts while attempting to understand how the law protects him or her.

(b) Incest: Section 150[116]

The very narrow definition of this offence applies to only blood relatives and must include sexual intercourse. It therefore excludes the sexual fondling by a mother of her daughter or son; the oral sex engaged in by a father with his

---

113 *Chase v. R.* (1984), 40 C.R. (3d) 282 (N.B.C.A.). In a recent decision, *Gardynik v. R.* (1984), 42 C.R. (3d) 362 (Ont. Co. Ct.), Lovekin J. of the then County Court of the judicial district of Durham refused to follow *Chase*. Lovekin J., delivering his judgment in an appeal from the Provincial Court decision, states, at p. 369: "[*Chase*] fails to give the proper scope to the term 'sexual assault' that . . . the legislature intended it to convey when it holds that 'sexual' refers only to 'the sexual organs or genitalia'. Parliament has spoken and we have a new offence, sexual assault, and the term 'sexual' properly refers to a component of sexuality".

114 Badgley, *Sexual Offences Against Children* (1984), at 309.

115 En. 1980-81-82-83, c. 125, s. 19.

116 Am. 1972, c. 13, s. 10; 1985, c. 19, s. 21.

daughter or son; it excludes sexual intercourse between stepfather and step-daughter; or between foster father and foster daughter; and it excludes the buggering of a son by his father.

It is not denied that these offences are addressed elsewhere in the Criminal Code, but not always with the same sanctions as those for incest.[117]

One aspect of the offence of incest is potentially traumatic for a child victim. There is a technical requirement under s. 150(3) that a court find a victim guilty of the offence and find she committed incest under restraint, duress or fear before it can discharge her.

> Even though I am no longer a child or a youth (I am 40), I would like to report sexual abuse as a child. The first rape occurred when I think I was approximately 18 months-old [sic]. I was too little to speak and tell my mother. A second rape occurred when I was between two and three. From three to age seven, I was raped routinely, especially in the summer when I could not be kept in the house. The rapist was my father.[118]

If that father had been arrested and charged with incest (he was not; he died begging forgiveness from his sister, a nun, for having abused her as a child; and he had probably molested at least 7 of his other 11 children)[119] this child would have been found guilty in a court of law unless she could have met the restraint, duress or fear requirements of s. 150(3)! If she was old enough to partake in the legal proceedings and understand the court's finding, surely her emotional turmoil would have been exacerbated by a public finding of guilt on her part.

2. Evidence of Children

The pertinent current legislation is contained in s. 16(1) and (2), Canada Evidence Act[120] and ss. 60 and 61, Young Offenders Act.

In criminal court a crucial issue is whether a child under 14 will be deemed competent to testify under oath. If she is the sole witness to the sexual asault, and usually is, her sworn testimony will be vital to securing a conviction. Consequently she must meet the test prescribed by the Ontario Court of Appeal[121] — she must understand the moral obligation of telling the truth; she need not, however, believe in any supreme being[122] or that in taking the oath, she is telling any supreme being that what she says will be true.[123]

---

117 For example, sexual intercourse with a foster daughter carries a two-year sentence (s. 153(1)) as opposed to the 14 years for incest (s. 150 (2) [re-en. 1972, c-13, s. 10]).

118 Badgley, *supra*, n. 114, at 163, from Personal Account 9.

119 *Ibid.*

120 Canada Evidence Act. See Bill C-113.

121 *R. v. Fletcher* (1982), 1 C.C.C. (3d) 370 (Ont. C.A.).

122 *Ibid.*

123 *Ibid.*

If she does not meet this test, the court may examine her to determine if she possesses sufficient intelligence to give evidence and understands the duty to speak the truth.[124] If she meets this test, she may be affirmed to give unsworn evidence. Any evidence she gives must be corroborated for a conviction to follow.[125]

These legal tests have almost blurred in meaning; it is difficult to ascertain a great difference between understanding "a moral obligation to tell the truth" and "the duty of speaking the truth". A judicial interpretation, however, could mean that the child is excluded from swearing. If she is the only source of evidence, the case is dismissed.

The Young Offenders Act provides that evidence of children under 12 shall be given under solemn affirmation only — thereby requiring corroboration. Thus, the same evidence given under oath by a child in criminal court will require corroboration in Youth Court.[126]

Under the current law of the evidence of children, an 11-year-old who has been sexually assaulted by an 18-year-old and a 17-year-old may be able to testify under oath in criminal court, but will require some other evidence to corroborate her allegation in Youth Court. (This hypothetical, of course, is based on the assumption that the 17-year-old accused is tried in Youth Court under the Young Offenders Act and not in criminal court with his co-accused.)

3. Corroboration

The statutory requirement of corroboration of a child's evidence has been discussed in section 2, *supra*. It remains here to reiterate its necessity in Canadian law based on the assumption that children's testimony, sworn or unsworn, is inherently untrustworthy.[127]

The fine points of the nature of corroboration, the required quality and examples of corroborative evidence in sexual assault cases, are surveyed in the Badgley report.[128] It is important to note that the Criminal Code reforms of January 1983 removing the corroboration requirements for sexual assaults did not necessarily do so for the offences of buggery[129] and sexual intercourse with an underage female.[130] Over and above this, there remain s. 586, Criminal

---

124 Canada Evidence Act, s. 16(1).

125 *Ibid.*, s. 16(2).

126 Badgley, *supra*, n. 114, at 370. But see Jeffery Wilson and Mary Tomlinson, *Wilson: Children and the Law*, 2nd ed. (1986), at 323-24.

127 *Horsburgh v. R.*, [1968] 2 C.C.C. 288 (S.C.C.).

128 Badgley, *Sexual Offences Against Children* (1984), at 377-79.

129 S. 155.

130 S. 146 [am. 1972, c. 13, s. 70]. See Badgley, *supra*, n. 128, at 380.

Code, and s. 16, Canada Evidence Act, which require corroboration of all unsworn evidence of children. This requirement can only add to the emotional trauma of the incest victim referred to in section 1, *supra*, who, in addition to her legal guilt, must be able to corroborate her claim of "rape" by her father. Perhaps it could be considered sufficient that she admit her crime, thereby implicating her father by association.

4. Recent Complaint

Historically, the common law has taken a sceptical view of the testimony of complainants of sexual offences. Consequently, the very technical doctrine of recent complainant evolved. Only a virtually spontaneous allegation of a sexual offence, made at the first "reasonable" opportunity could overcome the inference that the victim's allegation was either totally or substantially untrue.[131] The abrogation of this doctrine in January 1983[132] appears on its face to apply only to the new sexual assault offences and not to all other sexual offences (incest, unlawful sexual intercourse) to which it applied at common law.[133]

It is often true, however, that a child will not report a sexual offence until long after its occurrence.[134] There are many reasons for this, very valid reasons to a young child. However, a court may impugn her evidence simply because she did not tell someone immediately.

5. Previous Sexual Conduct

The January 1983 amendments to the Criminal Code provided safeguards against unjustified inquiries into a complainant's past sexual conduct or sexual reputation when the accused is charged with a form of sexual assault as defined in the then new s. 246.[135] The amendment did not, however, extinguish the common law assumption that chastity and veracity are linked for the other sexual offences where consent is at issue. Two offences falling outside the amendments are incest and sexual intercourse with a female under 14.[136]

---

131 Badgley, *ibid.*, at 387.

132 See Criminal Code, s. 246.5 [en. 1980-81-82-83, c. 125, s. 19].

133 Badgley, *supra*, n. 128, at 389.

134 *Ibid.*, at 189-93. It is Dr. Hamacher's experience that children will report sexual abuse during counselling for other problems. Ms. Mallea referred to the possibility of waiting until the child is older to take legal action. In this way it might be possible to overcome the evidentiary problems experienced by a young child. However, as Ms. Mallea pointed out, a danger in taking this route is a possibly successful Charter defence under s. 11(*a*) or (*b*).

135 En. 1980-81-82-83, c. 125, s. 19. See Badgley, *ibid.*, at 408.

136 *Ibid.*, at 408-409.

It is possible, therefore, under current Canadian legal doctrine to cross-examine an 11-year-old complainant of incest about her sexual activities with a person other than her father. It is an unlikely scenario, but it is theoretically possible.

6. Public Access to Hearings

There is a deep tradition in the common law systems that criminal trials should be open to public scrutiny. The legal rights of the accused are best protected in this way. The individual is up against the full power of the state; open trials prevent the state from falsely accusing a person, trying him in secret and removing him from society.

Against this tradition is another — that in some exceptional circumstances, a trial or a portion of a trial may be held *in camera* to protect, *inter alia*, portions of the testimony of a witness.[137]

In 1979, the Ontario Court of Appeal[138] held that embarrassment alone to witnesses testifying as to sexual behaviour was insufficient ground to hold a trial *in camera*. The court stated: "But [embarrassment] alone is not reason to suppose that truth is more difficult or unlikely or that the witness will be so frightened as to be unable to testify. In this case there was no suggestion that the latter might be so."[139] The witnesses in this case were teenage complainants of unlawful sexual intercourse, indecent assault and gross indecency. It is unlikely that a strict application of the Court of Appeal's test would spare even very young complainants the acute discomfort of testifying in public.

7. Hearsay

> Hearsay evidence is testimony in court, or written evidence of a statement made out of court, the statement being offered as an assertion to show the truth of matters asserted therein, and thus resting for its value upon the credibility of the out-of-court asserter.[140]

> A three year-old [sic] asks her daddy if milk comes out of his pee-pee. He says no, and then tells his wife. She later asks her daughter about it, who replies, "Well milk comes out of Susie's dad's pee-pee and it tastes yucky."[141]

On a charge against Susie's father for sexual abuse, the mother's testimony about the child's statement is clearly inadmissible hearsay. It cannot be admitted in court to prove the truth of the matter asserted. Susie's father, in law, has the

---

137 Criminal Code, s. 442(1) [re-en. 1980-81-82-83, c. 110, s. 74].

138 *R. v. Quesnel* (1979), 51 C.C.C. (2d) 270 (Ont. C.A.).

139 *Ibid*, at 275.

140 McCormick, *Evidence*, 2d ed. (1972), at 584.

141 Badgley, *supra*, n. 128, at 393.

right to directly challenge the credibility of this child, that is, to cross-examine her on her personal knowledge of the event in question. Current legal doctrine states that only by cross-examining her personally can he overcome the dangers inherent in all recountings of past events: inaccurate perception, inaccurate memory, poor communication ability, and insincerity.[142]

There are exceptions to the hearsay rule, but none which would make the above statement admissible. All exceptions, save admissions and former testimony, contain two characteristics:

1. "[T]here are circumstances surrounding the making of the statement which guarantee its trustworthiness and so dispense with the need for an oath and cross-examination . . ."; and

2. "[S]ome grounds of necessity exist resident in the unavailability of the declarant or the inconvenience in requiring his attendance".[143]

The exceptions pertinent to this discussion follow.

(a) Business and Professional Records

At common law, the Supreme Court of Canada broadened this exception to the hearsay rule. It allowed admission of "records . . . made contemporaneously by someone having a personal knowledge of the matters then being recorded and under a duty to make the entry or record . . . as *prima facie* proof of the facts stated therein".[144]

The Canada Evidence Act, s. 30(1) and (12), states:

> 30.(1) Where oral evidence in respect of a matter would be admissible in a legal proceeding, a record made in the usual and ordinary course of business that contains information in respect of that matter is admissible in evidence under this section in the legal proceeding upon production of the record.
>
> (12) In this section
>
> "business" means any business, profession, trade, calling, manufacture or undertaking of any kind carried on in Canada or elsewhere whether for profit or otherwise, including any activity or operation carried on or performed in Canada or elsewhere by any government, by any department, branch, board, commission or agency of any government, by any court or other tribunal or by any other body or authority performing a function of government . . .
>
> "record" includes the whole or any part of any book, document, paper, card, tape or other thing on or in which information is written, recorded, stored or reproduced. . . .

---

142 R.J. Delisle, *Evidence Principles and Problems* (1984), at 202.
143 *Ibid.*, at 219-20.
144 *Ares v. Venner*, [1970] S.C.R. 608 at 626.

This section was interpreted by a criminal court in Ontario.[145] In that case, the witness, an F.B.I. fingerprint expert, was prepared to give his opinion that fingerprints taken on arrest were the same as those in the F.B.I. records. He had no personal knowledge of the making of the fingerprints but did have extensive knowledge and experience in the recording and storing of fingerprint records. Callaghan J., in allowing admission of the F.B.I. fingerprint record in order to provide identity of the accused, reasoned:

> Section 30 was placed into the *Canada Evidence Act* in 1968. . . . It would appear that the rationale behind that section for admitting a form of hearsay evidence is the inherent circumstantial guarantee of accuracy which one would find in a business context from records which are relied upon in the day to day affairs of individual businesses, and which are subject to frequent testing and cross-checking. Records thus systematically stored, produced and regularly relied upon should, it would appear under s. 30, not be barred from this Court's consideration simply because they contain hearsay or double hearsay.[146]

Part V of this paper will argue for the admissibility of the videotape of a child's testimony under an extension of this exception to the hearsay rule.

(b) Exceptions where Declarant or Testimony Unavailable

At common law, there are several instances where declarants cannot testify in court but their prior statements are allowed as evidence.[147] Originally, the exception required that the declarant be deceased,[148] but this is no longer always necessary. For example, in *Ares v. Venner*, the nurses' notes were ruled admissible although the nurses themselves were in the courtroom during the trial.[149]

The statutory and common law discussed in this part addresses some of the technical difficulties in Criminal Code sexual offences, the evidentiary problems child witnesses may encounter, and exceptions to the hearsay rule which will be applied in the reform recommended in Part V.

IV POSSIBLE SOLUTIONS

Several jurisdictions and authors have devised plans to assist the child victim as actual or potential witness for the prosecution in criminal trials. In some cases the systems are in place; in others, they are theoretical models. This chapter looks at both.

---

145 *R. v. Grimba* (1977), 38 C.C.C. (2d) 469 (Ont. C.A.).

146 *Ibid.*, at 471.

147 Delisle, *supra*, n. 142, at 232.

148 *Ibid.*

149 *Ares v. Venner, supra*, n. 144, at 626.

1. Youth Interrogator

In 1955, within a few years of Israel's attaining independent statehood, the Knesset[150] passed the "Law of Evidence Revision" (Protection of Children)[151] after much consideration of the basic rights of the defendant "as well as the principles of Mental Hygiene to protect the child".[152] It is to be noted that Israel has a common law system of law,[153] and has no written constitution.[154]

The law contains the following major points:

1. No child under 14 years shall be investigated, examined, or heard as a witness in an offence against morality, save with the permission of a youth interrogator.

2. A statement by a child as to an offence against morality committed upon his person, or in his presence, or of which he is suspected, shall not be admitted as evidence, save with the permission of a youth interrogator.

3. For the purpose of the law, a youth interrogator shall be appointed after consultation with an appointment committee. This committee shall consist of a judge of the juvenile court, who will act as chairman, an expert in mental hygiene, an educator, an expert in child care, and a high ranking police officer.

4. Evidence as to an offence against morality taken and recorded by a youth interrogator and any minutes or report of an examination as to such an offence prepared by a youth interrogator are admissible as evidence in court.

5. Where evidence as referred to above has been submitted to the court, the youth interrogator may be required to re-examine the child and ask him a particular question, but he may refuse to do so if he is of the opinion that further questioning is likely to cause emotional harm to the child.

6. A person shall not be convicted on evidence by a youth interrogator unless it is supported by other evidence.[155]

As can be seen, the two major innovations are the removal of all children under 14 as witnesses in sexual assault cases, unless the youth interrogator decides the child may appear,[156] and the placing of all investigation of the child

---

150 Parliament of the State of Israel.

151 Reifen, "Protection of Children Involved in Sexual Offences: A New Method of Investigation in Israel" (1959), 49 J. Crim. L.C. & P.S. 222 at 224.

152 *Ibid*.

153 David Reifen, *The Juvenile Court in a Changing Society* (1972), at 76.

154 Libai, "Protection of the Child Victim of a Sexual Offence in the Criminal Justice System" (1968-69), 15 Wayne L. Rev. 977 at 1004.

155 Reifen, *supra*, n. 153, at 72.

156 A 1962 amendment to the law provides that if a child is testifying and becomes emotionally upset, the court on the youth interrogator's advice can order that such testimony be discontinued: Reifen, *ibid*., at 75.

victim into the hands of trained personnel. It should be noted that a conviction is possible only if there is evidence corroborating that of the complainant.

The Israeli law is silent about personal qualifications of youth interrogators, but the Appointment Committee,[157] "following the spirit of the law"[158] chooses people trained in the dynamics of human behaviour and interviewing techniques: clinical psychologists, psychiatric social workers, psychiatrists, probation officers and child care workers.[159] Youth interrogators are not necessarily government employees, are paid a fee for services, and often perform this role as a second job.[160]

The statute anticipated potential antagonism between the police and the youth interrogators in the investigative stage of the criminal process.[161] As a consequence, the investigation of these crimes was not left up to the two bodies' abilities to co-operate. Direct examination of the child is exclusively the province of the youth interrogator.[162] It is implicit that the police remain responsible for all other aspects of an investigation.

In practice, police and youth interrogators work as a team.[163] Youth interrogators never wear uniforms, do not interview a child in a police station unless absolutely necessary, and exercise full control over the entire investigation, including medical examinations,[164] identification lineups,[165] and contacts with the police.[166]

The youth interrogators of course are aware from the beginning of the investigation that the information they gather must be of sufficiently high quality to be admissible in court[167] and to withstand cross-examination.[168] The information gleaned is recorded in notes rather than by any electronic means.[169]

Experience with this system has been positive. The youth interrogators are capable, using their professional, understanding techniques, of acquiring much

---

157 Consisting of the persons specified in point 3, *supra*.

158 Reifen, *supra*, n. 151, at 224.

159 Libai, *supra*, n. 154, at 996.

160 *Ibid.*

161 *Ibid.*, at 997.

162 *Ibid.*, at 997-98.

163 *Ibid.*, at 999.

164 *Ibid.*

165 Reifen, *supra*, n. 153, at 73.

166 Libai, *supra*, n. 154, at 1000.

167 Reifen, *supra*, n. 153, at 73.

168 *Ibid.*

169 *Ibid.*, at 74. This 1972 book contains the most recent information available at time of writing. The author has written to Dr. Libai in Israel in an attempt to update the description of this system.

more information than police officers using their traditional interrogation methods.[170] The trauma of the court experience appears to have been reduced.[171] The child's family, if necessary, can be assisted by the youth interrogator in understanding what has happened to their child so they can lend much needed support instead of criticism.[172] The police, who initially had entertained many doubts about this system, have come to "support it wholeheartedly".[173]

The Israeli system appears to be designed primarily for victims of sexual offences other than incest. It is not clear whether it is used in incest cases; the legislation does speak of "an offence against morality";[174] nevertheless, none of the descriptions speaks of intra-family sexual abuse.

2. Special Police Officers

In three jurisdictions surveyed by David Libai[175] specific police officers are designated to interrogate the child. Copenhagen, Stockholm and Chicago use similar systems, with the investigations being carried out in an informal, relaxed atmosphere,[176] usually in the child's home,[177] using terminology and vocabulary at the child's level, and "being patient and sympathetic and letting the child do most of the talking".[178]

Copenhagen and Stockholm police forces employ special and highly trained policewomen of advanced education who have the exclusive mandate to interrogate the child.[179] They do not assume the function of a psychiatric social worker or of a child care worker.[180] The interview with the victim is tape recorded, giving the advantage of recording manner of telling, emotional state of the child, spontaneity of statements, leading questions, decisive or ambigu-

---

170 Reifen, *supra*, n. 153, at 74.

171 *Ibid.*, at 75-76. In his article, *supra*, n. 154, David Libai noted, at 982, n. 18, that he and Judge Reifen were at that time conducting an empirical study of the Israeli system. Information on the results of this study have not yet been received by the author.

172 Reifen, *ibid.*, at 78-79.

173 Reifen, "Protection of Children Involved in Sexual Offences: A New Method of Investigation in Israel" (1959), 49 J. Crim. L.C. & P.S. 222 at 229.

174 Reifen, *supra*, n. 153 at 72.

175 Libai, "Protection of the Child Victim of a Sexual Offence in the Criminal Justice System" (1968-69), 15 Wayne L. Rev. 977 at 986.

176 *Ibid.*, at 989.

177 *Ibid.*, at 990, n. 47. Sweden is an exception. It has found the police station more amenable to tape recording the examination.

178 *Ibid.*, at 990.

179 *Ibid.*, at 989. The Swedish system applies to children under 14 years of age; the Danish to under 12-year-olds: at 989, n. 45.

180 *Ibid.*, at 989.

ous accounting of events, and authentic, original telling.[181] Also, the specialization of the interviewer and the tape recording allow the prosecutor, other police officers and various expert witnesses to acquire a direct impression of the child's story, thus saving her from repeated recountings.[182]

In order to overcome court suspicion about police practices, pre-trial investigations (including out-of-court identification of the accused)[183] are supervised by legislatures, police authorities and the judiciary.[184]

The Scandinavian legal systems have few rules of evidence, none against hearsay, and only the rudiments of cross-examination.[185] These systems therefore have no difficulties admitting the sworn testimony of the special policewoman who supports her evidence with the tape recording.[186]

The Chicago model is similar, yet different in significant ways.

The Youth Division of the Chicago Police Force is composed of ex-patrolmen and ex-detectives, in fact, any police officer who expresses an interest in youth work.[187] There are no special educational requirements to qualify for this division.[188]

Notwithstanding the written rules, child victims are routinely first approached and interviewed by uniformed patrolmen. If deemed necessary, a detective with no special training in interviewing children will then question the child. The police *may* then bring in the special officer who will require a third telling of the event.[189] While in theory special officers should aid all sexual assault investigations from the beginning, in reality they are not even notified[190] in a large percentage of cases. The investigating detectives generally consider themselves as capable as youth officers at interviewing child victims.[191]

The Chicago system also fails to address the possibility of police influence on the child in the pre-trial identification of the accused. There are no built-in

---

181 *Ibid.*, at 990.

182 *Ibid.*, at 991.

183 In Stockholm the lineup is conducted by the policewoman and a detective, with the defence counsel allowed to be present. The persons in the lineup confront a one-way glass, and the child is reassured that these people cannot see her: *ibid.*, at 994, n. 65.

184 *Ibid.*, at 992.

185 *Ibid.*, at 1004-1005.

186 *Ibid.*, at 992.

187 *Ibid.*, at 988.

188 *Ibid.*, at 988-89.

189 *Ibid.*, at 988.

190 *Ibid.*, at 988, n. 43.

191 *Ibid.*, at 988.

safeguards to eliminate suggestive influences on the child to choose a certain suspect.[192] The youth officer's testimony is therefore as suspect in court as that of any other officer. Libai elaborates on this point:

> Because of detectives' interest in concluding their investigation successfully, and the privacy and secrecy in which the police operate, courts are suspicious of police investigations. The gap in the court's knowledge of what really occurs in pretrial, non-judicial interrogations leaves room for allegations of unfair police practice. Judges search for impartial evidence in support of one of the parties at the trial in regard to questions of admissibility and credibility of evidence recorded out of court.[193]

Because there is no formal notetaking method in the Chicago model, the victim will be required to repeat her allegations yet again — to the examining physician and to the prosecutor.[194] The child herself testifies at the preliminary hearing and at the grand jury hearing.[195] Illinois guarantees the right of every defendant to confront witnesses against him, regardless of any adverse mental effect that such confrontation may cause a child.[196]

3. Special "Child Courtroom"[197]

This has not yet been adopted by any jurisdiction,[198] but is included for completeness.[199]

This model employs a "child examiner" similar to Israel's youth interrogator but with the additional responsibilities of videotaping the interview and of supplementing the recording with a detailed written social profile of the complainant.[200] The child examiner accompanies the child throughout the judicial process.

The trial will take place in a specially constructed "child courtroom".[201]

---

192 *Ibid.*, at 994.

193 *Ibid.*, at 991-92.

194 *Ibid.*

195 *Ibid.*, at 1005.

196 *Ibid.*, at 1006.

197 *Ibid.*, at 1014.

198 Dustin P. Ordway, "Parent-Child Incest: Proof at Trial Without Testimony in Court by the Victim" (1981), 15 U. Mich. J.L. Ref. 131 at 139, n. 39.

199 See Libai, "Protection of the Child Victim of a Sexual Offence in the Criminal Justice System" (1968-69), 15 Wayne L. Rev. 977 at 1002-1032, for a detailed description of the suggested model.

200 *Ibid.*, 1002-1003.

201 *Ibid.*, at 1014. A variation of this proposal is advocated by Parker whose article includes draft state legislation creating the office of Child Hearing Officer (CHO) — an attorney specially trained to protect the well-being of young witnesses in all criminal and civil judicial processes. Under this model, whenever a child 16 or under is required to give sworn testimony in court, he

The proposal is an attempt to balance the mental health needs of the child with the American constitutional requirements for a fair trial.[202] The child is located in a special "judge's room", surrounded by only four people: the judge, the prosecutor, defence counsel and the child examiner. The accused, jury and spectators are seated on the other side of a one-way glass. The accused and his counsel communicate via microphone and earphones.[203]

This model has been criticized for its additional demands on judicial resources, for failing to protect the child from the traumatic experience of adversarial cross-examination, and for failing to add expertise to the analysis of the child's story.[204]

An alternative to the above model, and similar to it, proposes taking the complainant's testimony at a special hearing after the apprehension of the accused but before the trial.[205] Defence counsel would receive all relevant evidence, including a transcript of the child's story[206] and at the special hearing be given an opportunity to cross-examine in full.

The special hearing would be videotaped; the videotape of the hearing would be admitted in evidence at trial as an exception to the hearsay rule similar to a dying declaration. An answer to an objection based on hearsay is found in the conditions attached to the recording of the videotape: an opportunity to cross-examine was afforded the accused at the time of recording, and the tape itself affords the trier of fact an opportunity to observe the child's demeanor during testimony and cross-examination. If a need to cross-examine further were to arise subsequently at trial, the court could so order, subject to the opinion of the child examiner on the possible effects of further cross-examination.[207]

The advantage to the child of this model is that it allows her to testify early and to begin to put the offence behind her as soon as possible.

4. Videotape

The author of a proposal only for victims of parent/child incest[208] advocates appointment of a specially trained "social services worker, who would

---

or she would do so in a Child Hearing Courtroom (CHC), a specially constructed facility similar to that proposed by Libai: see Parker, "The Rights of Child Witnesses: Is the Court A Protector or Perpetrator?" (1981-82), 17 New Eng. L. Rev. 643 at 664-73.

202 *Ibid.*, at 1015.

203 *Ibid.*, at 1017.

204 Ordway, *supra*, n. 198, at 139, n. 39.

205 Libai, *supra*, n. 199, at 1028.

206 The article does not explain why counsel would not receive a copy of the videotape itself.

207 Libai, *supra*, n. 199, at 1030-31.

208 Ordway, *supra*, n. 198, at 132.

provide the child's only contact with the legal system and who would bring the child's recorded testimony into court."[209] This model is also based on the Israeli system, whereby the worker would be one trained primarily in the behavioural sciences, and secondarily in pre-trial and trial procedures.[210] The expert would protect the child by limiting access to her. The expert, rather than the prosecutor, on determining the safety and justification of so doing, would have the power to compel the child to testify, taking into consideration the child's wishes and the burden of proof. As a rule, though, under this model the child "should be kept out of court".[211]

The expert would have total control of the pre-trial examination of the child and of recording any interviews. If after the initial examination legal action is initiated, the recording would be made available to both parties who could then submit questions to the expert and observe any subsequent interview with the child.[212]

At trial, the audio or video recordings of the child's testimony would be played in lieu of the child's personal testimony.[213]

If further questions arose at this time, they could be submitted to the expert to be asked of the child. Either party would be free to call the expert as a witness.[214]

This model builds in several safeguards. First of all, the expert knows from the beginning that objectivity is crucial; the dual role of the expert is to help the child and to assist the trier of fact in rationally deciding whether to believe the child.[215] The shift of power from the prosecutor to the expert is necessary to prevent undermining the proposed reform. However, in order to maintain an ongoing professional relationship with the prosecutor, the expert must be reasonable when deciding whether, in extraordinary circumstances, a child may testify. And there are always the alternate remedies of dismissal and compelling testimony where assertion of a privilege not to testify threatens the defendant's right to a fair trial.[216]

It appears that this proposal has not been adopted in its entirety by any jurisdictions. However, several states[217] in the United States have passed legisla-

---

209 *Ibid.*, at 139.

210 *Ibid.*, at 139 and 140, nn. 41 and 42.

211 *Ibid.*, at 139, n. 40.

212 *Ibid.*, at 140. The article does not specify whether this observation would be one-sided, i.e., whether the child would be aware of these parties.

213 *Ibid.*, at 140.

214 *Ibid.*

215 *Ibid.*, at 140, n. 42.

216 *Ibid.*, at 139. n. 40.

217 For example, Arizona (Ariz. Rev. Stat. Ann. para. 12-2312 (1982)), Florida (Fla. Stat. Ann.

tion permitting admission of videotaped testimony of child victims of sexual abuse. Other states are allowing child victims to testify via closed circuit television from a room close to but separate from the courtroom.[218]

5. Amendments to the Rules of Evidence

The Badgley report takes the strong position that Canadian children can enjoy the full protection of the law only by speaking effectively on their own behalf at legal proceedings arising from allegations of sexual abuse.[219] The Commission advocates no special rules of testimonial competency with respect to children; rather, it recommends that a child's testimony be weighed by the trier of fact in the same manner as that of any other witness in the proceedings.[220] It recommends amendments to the Canada Evidence Act, the Young Offenders Act and all provincial and territorial evidence acts to reflect the above.[221] Over and above this, it recommends that a child who does not have the verbal capacity to reply to simply framed questions be precluded from testifying,[222] and that the court "shall instruct the trier of fact in the need for caution in any case in which it considers that an instruction is necessary".[223]

In further support of the above recommendations, the Commission studied corroboration requirements in Canadian law.[224] Based on the statutory reforms to sexual offences in recent times and the fact that these reforms do not reflect any change in the conventional assumptions about the credibility of children;[225] and based also on the Commission's research results showing the high number of "founded" cases,[226] the Commission takes the position that the veracity of

---

para. 918.17 (West Supp. 1981)), Montana (Mont. Code Ann. para. 46-15-401 (1981)), New Mexico (N. M. Stat. Ann. para. 30-9-17 (1981 Supp.)), Texas (Vernon's Texas Ann. C.C.P., art. 38.071. 9 Texas Session Law Service 1983, 3828). See Parker, *supra*, n. 200, at 679 for a discussion of these and other statutory amendments to the rules of evidence. See also "The Testimony of Child Victims in Sex Abuse Prosecutions: Two Legislative Innovations" (1985), 98 Harv. L. Rev. 806, for a thorough review of U.S. videotaping and hearsay statutes designed to ease the burden that the judicial system places on the child victim.

218 Kentucky (Ky. Rev. Stat. para. 421.350(3) (Supp. 1984)); Texas (Tex. Crim. Proc. Code Ann. para. 38.071(3) (Vernon Supp. 1984)); California (ABC Television, "World News Tonight" broadcast 15th November 1984).

219 Badgley, *Sexual Offences Against Children* (1984), at 67 and 371-72.

220 *Ibid.*, at 372 and 373. This is also the recommendation of the Fraser Report, *Pornography and Prostitution in Canada*, Recommendation 81. See Bill C-113.

221 Badgley, *ibid.*, at 373.

222 *Ibid.*

223 *Ibid.*, at 374.

224 *Ibid.*, at 377.

225 *Ibid.*

226 *Ibid.*, at 224.

children is no better and no worse than that of any adult and that consequently, there should be no special requirement for corroboration of an "unsworn" child's evidence.[227]

Because of the unlikelihood of any out-of-court statement about sexual abuse falling into one of the recognized exceptions to the hearsay rule,[228] and after once again addressing the credibility of children in the hearsay context, the Commission recommends acceptance of child victims' out-of-court statements on a case-by-case basis.[229] Accordingly, it recommends amendments to the Canada Evidence Act, all provincial and territorial evidence acts and the Quebec Code of Civil Procedure[230] to provide that:

> 1. A previous statement made by a child when under the age of 14 which describes or refers to any sexual act performed with, on, or in the presence of the child by another person.

> 2. Is admissible to prove the truth of the matters asserted in the statement.

> 3. Whether or not the child testified at the proceedings.

> 4. Provided that the court considers, after a hearing conducted in the absence of the jury, that the time, content and circumstances of the statement afford sufficient indicia of reliability.

> 5. "Statement" means an oral or recorded assertion and includes conduct that could reasonably be taken to be intended as an assertion.[231]

These are but a few of the many recommendations[232] made in this extensive report. They do, however, speak most directly to the testimonial roadblocks encountered by child witnesses.

6. Sex Abuse Team

In 1981 in Toronto, the Metropolitan Chairman's Special Committee on Child Abuse was established with a mandate to "develop improved methods of co-ordination and delivery of services to abused children and their families".[233]

---

227 *Ibid.*, at 382. See the Fraser Report, *supra*, n. 219, Recommendation 82, for a similar recommendation.

228 For a discussion of a legislated exception to the hearsay rule, see Sheryl K. Peterson, "Sexual Abuse of Children — Washington's New Hearsay Exception" (1982-83), 58 Wash. L. Rev. 813. In *State v. Ryan*, 103 Wash. 2d 165 (1984), the Supreme Court of Washington found Washington's new hearsay exception to be constitutional. See also *State v. Myatt*, 697 P. 2d 836 (Kan., 1985), for a similar decision of the Supreme Court of Kansas which cited with approval then current analyses in the legal literature of hearsay exceptions in child sex abuse cases.

229 Badgley, *supra*, n. 219, at 399.

230 R.S.Q. 1977, c. C-25.

231 Badgley, *supra*, n. 219, at 399-400: see Fraser, Recommendation 83, for an opposing point of view.

232 Badgley, *ibid.*: see chapter 3 of Badgley for an overview of the report's recommendations.

233 *Child Sexual Abuse Protocol* (1984), Foreword, at i.

Although the Committee's mandate is to address all forms of abuse, sexual abuse was identified as a focus for action.[234] As part of its research, the Committee drew on a decade's worth of experience of similar teams in San Jose, California, and Seattle, Washington.[235]

Membership on the Special Committee includes senior representatives of the children's aid societies, police, health and education professionals, and the metropolitan and provincial governments.[236] The Committee takes the position that only through collaborative action can a successful response to child sexual abuse be maintained.[237] After extensive research, intensive working sessions, the preparation of several working drafts, and consultations, the Special Committee ratified its final document, the *Child Sexual Abuse Protocol*, in November 1983.[238] The *Protocol* reflects the initiatives taken in the following areas: investigation/protection/prosecution, crisis support/treatment, prevention/detention, and training.[239]

In her unpublished paper presented at Montreal to the International Congress of Child Abuse in September 1984, Mary Wells outlined the belief of the Committee that the model adopted seeks not only to "alleviate the harm inflicted on the child, but actively pursues a goal of endowing the child with a sense of mastery and integrity". The Committee believes that testifying personally may be "cathartic and symbolically put an end to the episode in their minds".[240]

However, the Special Committee emphatically does not believe the child should face the legal system alone. It recognizes the potentially trauma producing aspects of the legal process[241] and uses the team to guide the child through the obstacles.

The Committee believes that "[e]very situation involving child sexual abuse must be assessed individually to determine the best interests of the child involved".[242] The following principles are used as a guide towards that goal:

---

234 *Ibid.*

235 *Ibid.*, at iv, note referring to the Harborview Sexual Assault Center in Seattle and the Child Sexual Abuse Treatment Program in San Jose. See also Rona Maynard, "Sexual Abuse Team: A New Way to Help the Child", *Chatelaine*, November 1984, 93 at 208.

236 See the brochure published by the Metropolitan Chairman's Special Committee on Child Abuse, "Developing a Comprehensive Response to Child Sexual Abuse" (May 1984), hereinafter cited as "Response".

237 *Protocol*, *supra*, n. 233, Foreword, at i.

238 *Ibid.*, at ii.

239 "Response", *supra*, n. 236.

240 Wells.

241 "Response", *supra*, n. 236.

242 *Protocol*, *supra*, n. 233, at iv.

1. Children reporting sexual abuse should be presumed to be telling the truth and bear no responsibility for their involvement, regardless of time or circumstances.

2. The use of a child by an adult for sexual purposes is an abusive and criminal act which should be investigated and prosecuted as such.

3. Conviction of offenders, however, is not enough. Without appropriate treatment, the risk of re-offence remains high.

4. Effective response requires the full co-operation and co-ordination of all systems. Specialization of core personnel is necessary to promote sensitivity, consistency and collaboration.

5. Following disclosure of sexual abuse, the child victim and adult offender should be separated immediately. In intra-familial situations, every effort should be made to remove the offender from the home, rather than the child.

6. Attention must be given to the development of specialized crisis and treatment services for the child victim and non-offending family members.

7. Early detection and prevention provide the ultimate key to ending the destructive consequences of child sexual abuse.[243]

The *Protocol's* detailed guidelines and procedures outline the step-by-step approach to each case, always with the above principles in mind, from receipt of reports of the abuse, through interviews with the child, assistance through whichever court she encounters, and finally follow up after disposition.[244] Some highlights of these procedures are:

the police and children's aid societies have sexual abuse specialists who co-ordinate the investigation of the complaint; they act as a team, with the children's aid society specialist taking on prime responsibility for protection of the victim and the police specialist taking on the investigation of the offence and the identification of the offender;

the team conducts a detailed interview with the child in a neutral setting; considering the needs and best interests of the child and depending on rapport with her, either the police or children's aid society specialist acts as primary interviewer;

the team encourages communication through use of age appropriate language, anatomically correct dolls, drawings, and so on;

the interview is audiotaped in all cases and videotaped where circumstances permit.[245]

---

243 *Ibid.*, at iv-viii.
244 *Ibid.*, Table of Contents.
245 *Ibid.*, at 1-5.

The purposes of taping the complainant are: to avoid several re-interviews, to inform the accused and his counsel of the case against him, to encourage an early guilty plea, to ascertain the capacity of the child to testify in court, to refresh the memory of the child witness in court, and to provide independent evidence in child welfare proceedings.[246]

In intra-familial sexual abuse, the Committee recommends consideration of prosecution under s. 75 of the Child and Family Services Act[247] as an alternative to the Criminal Code. This route provides the advantages of expeditious completion of proceedings, less trauma to the victim, more immediate access to treatment, and the possibility of defence counsel's willingness to encourage early guilty pleas if the dangers for sex offenders in federal penitentiaries could be avoided. Also, in Provincial Court, Family Division, there are limits on public access and media exposure, and cases are heard by judges more attuned to the sensitive nature of family problems. "This route could combine mediation, conciliation and treatment with the legal leverage of a potential fine, jail sentence and probation order."[248] The difficulties with the use of this provincial legislation alone are the possible interpretation that the offence has been decriminalized, and the inability of the police to arrest and hold the accused for a "no contact" condition of bail.[249]

Where the child must appear as witness, it is a specialized Crown's responsibility to prepare the child for court, preferably by meeting the child at least once, as early as possible in the weeks prior to the preliminary hearing or trial, with the child's counsel (if any), and a support person or the police or children's aid society team in attendance.[250]

Ms. Wells advocates giving the child some strategies to cope with the courtroom experience:

identification of fears connected with the court process;

information about the courtroom's physical features;

identification to an ally to accompany the child to court;

encouragement to focus her attention on non-threatening or supportive people (her mother, the Crown attorney, the judge) or things (a clock, a small doll, a lucky coin) while testifying.

---

246 *Ibid.*, at vi. Alexis Singer, at the time of writing Program Liaison, Child Sexual Abuse Protocol to the Special Committee, informed the author that it is the Committee's goal to limit the recountings. The author is very grateful to Ms. Singer for her generous assistance and guidance.

247 Child and Family Services Act, S.O. 1984, c. 55.

248 *Protocol, supra*, n. 233, at xv.

249 *Ibid.*

250 *Ibid.*, at 13.

She would also request the crown attorney to be of assistance by standing in a position to block the child's view of the defendant (except at the point where she identifies the accused).[251]

The above models, then, range from those requiring legislative changes to those working within existing legal systems while taking fresh administrative approaches.

V RECOMMENDED SOLUTION

The proposed model is two-pronged, requiring both provincial and federal legislative reform. It draws on the thinking and experience of the solutions described in Part IV, *supra*, and selects those characteristics most appropriate for the Canadian setting. It addresses the central problems of the credibility hurdle for the child, the lack of sensitivity at the investigative stage, and the family's need for immediate counselling.

It is recommended that an Ontario-wide program be instituted as soon as possible. Metropolitan Toronto has created an effective[252] approach. However, both urban and rural communities in the remainder of the province[253] have no co-ordinated programs to alleviate the suffering of their sexually abused children. It is not an effective use of funds, time or human resources to require each community to work out its own program in a piecemeal fashion. It is argued, therefore, that the appropriate legislative bodies should address their minds to young citizens who have been sexually victimized by adults, and devise a caring, supportive, concerned solution to assist these individuals through the criminal court system.

It is the thesis of this chapter that not all children will benefit from testifying in court, that it is possible that some will be traumatized, and that as a society we must look at the plight of the child victim of sexual abuse and decide whether that child has any rights in the legal system. If so, how should her rights be balanced with those very valid rights of an accused perpetrator?

---

251 Wells, Unpublished Paper presented at Montreal to the International Congress of Child Abuse (September 1984).

252 An assessment of the effects of the comprehensive response is currently under way.

253 The author conducted an extremely informal survey of two small cities and one rural community. Each contact informed her that there was no well thought out, co-ordinated program addressing investigation of child sexual abuse in that particular community. One child protection worker stated that she had given a copy of the *Protocol* to the police chief in her community. The police chief was "uninterested". Since that time, Lorna Grant, Executive Director, Metropolitan Toronto Special Committee on Child Abuse, informs the author that numerous communities throughout Ontario have adapted the *Protocol*. Also, New Zealand and the Republic of Ireland have used it as a model for developing procedures in their communities.

It is also the position of this chapter that incest and sexual assault on our children should remain a criminal offence. The solution does not lie in proceedings under the current child welfare legislation or in guilty pleas to reduced charges. Rather, our society, that is our provincial legislature, should publicly state that the abuse of our children is absolutely unacceptable, that perpetrators will be prosecuted under the Criminal Code, and that child victims will be protected and assisted in every possible way.

Ontario can benefit from the experience and thinking of other jurisdictions and authors. It is recommended that the Metropolitan Toronto system be adopted and applied throughout the province, with the exceptions, additions and changes outlined below.

1. Creation of the Office of Child Sexual Abuse Expert

Only by legislation can Ontario demonstrate a policy which states clearly that all agencies responsible for children must co-operate with one another. The new child sexual abuse expert would provide one focus in each community in all investigations of allegations of sexual abuse of children. The Crown, children's aid society and police roles would be simultaneously defined, so that the antagonism between these agencies would no longer present a bar to proper investigations, and if necessary, prosecutions.

The model recommended is most similar to that described in Part IV, section 4, *supra*. The foundation for this approach is the Israeli office of youth interrogator. The qualifications are: general training as a behaviourist, additional specific training as a sexual abuse expert, and legal training in order to fulfil the role of *objective* information gatherer and assessor of the child complainant's credibility. The presumption that child complainants of sexual assault are telling the truth must be balanced with well thought out tests of veracity.

The legislation would mandate the expert with the *sole responsibility* for the examination of the child. Police and children's aid society, health and education workers would all be required to contact the office of the expert immediately on receipt of information of sexual abuse. Ideally, the first (and only) contact a child will have with the legal system will be with the expert.

The police will carry out all aspects of the investigation other than the examination of the child. The children's aid society will continue to be responsible for the child's welfare generally.

The timing of the examination of the child will be at the discretion of the expert. As recognized by the Special Committee, the first 48 hours are crucial in the determination of the final outcome;[254] thus the detailed examination should

---

254 *Child Sexual Abuse Protocol* (1984), at vii.

be early enough in the process to allow the complainant to tell her story. Balanced with the desirability of an early recounting is the necessity of eliminating several recountings. The suspected perpetrator and the Crown need time to prepare and submit questions to the expert to be asked of the child. Perhaps the solution lies in two videotaped examinations of the complainant: one within 48 hours of disclosure, the second several days later — a supplementary examination wherein the Crown and suspect question the child through the expert.

The detailed interviews should always be audiotaped and, if at all feasible, videotaped. The advantages of this have been described in Part IV, section 2, *supra*. The expert should control the equipment — a child might be rendered speechless by a technician in the room.[255] There can be safeguards to overcome suspicion of tampering with the tape — a large clock with a second hand in the background would clearly indicate any editing. The interviews could be observed by the Crown and defence counsel from behind a one-way glass.

The videotape would serve the purposes described in the *Protocol*.[256] It may have one additional purpose, however, it may replace the child's testimony in court.

2. Creation of an Exception to the Hearsay Rule

In order to admit videotaped testimony, amendments to the Canada Evidence Act will be required. It is therefore recommended that the Federal Parliament legislatively create an exception to the hearsay rule, an exception analogous to the common law exception for dying declarations. The amendment would create a presumption of incapacity to testify for child victims of sexual abuse under a specified age. The requirement of necessity would thus be met. The second test, that of trustworthiness, would be met only if the examination of the child were conducted in the carefully controlled setting described above, by a person, the child sexual abuse expert in Ontario, whose mandate is to remain objective.

During the investigation, the expert would protect the child by limiting access to her and taking on full responsibility for medical examinations and all questioning. Notwithstanding this control and in order to maintain objectivity, the expert should not make the decision whether to prosecute, nor be consulted by the police or Crown in that decision. The expert is to protect the child, gather information and present that information in court if called upon to do so.

If the case does proceed to criminal trial, the expert has the discretion to decide whether the child is allowed to testify personally. The factors to consider

---

255 As related to the author by Ms. Mallea.

256 *Supra*, n. 254, at vi.

will be the expert's professional assessment of the child's emotional stability, the wishes of the child, the possible cathartic benefit to the child, and of course, the age of the complainant. It is suggested that the enabling legislation provide the following guidelines to the expert:

(a) Ages under 12[257] — presumption of incapacity:

Child complainants of sexual assault under 12, will be able to testify through the medium of the videotape. It will remain possible, however, for children in this age group to testify in person if they wish to, provided they exhibit the competence to do so, and provided the expert believes the benefits to the child who takes this route will outweigh possible trauma.

(b) Ages 12 to 14[258] — presumption of capacity with discretion to the expert to exclude:

Young people in this age group will testify on their own behalf unless, in the discretion of the expert, the risk of trauma to a particular victim is too great; if that is the case, the procedure for the under 12-year-olds will be followed.

If at trial the expert sees any child under 14 becoming distressed, he or she will have the authority to discontinue the child's testimony and revert to the videotape which would be admissible under an amendment to s. 30 of the Canada Evidence Act. Whether or not the complainant testifies in person, the expert can be called and cross-examined by either side.

This proposed hearsay exception is similar to the business and professional records exception currently recognized.[259] A strict interpretation of s. 30 of the Canada Evidence Act allows admission only of business records made by a person in the ordinary course of business, and replacing *that person's* oral evidence. As noted, *supra*, in Part III, however, s. 30 has been judicially broadened to allow the evidence of a witness who, while very familiar with the record-keeping practices of a particular organization, did not actually make the record.[260] The proposed reform requires the admission into evidence of a videotaped record. This record will have been subjected to frequent testing and

---

257 The ages are chosen somewhat arbitrarily for purposes of discussion, but not without reason. One reason is for consistency with the Young Offenders Act which defines a child as a person under the age of 12 and a young person as over 12 and under 18: s. 2. The second reason for choosing age 12 as a "watershed" age is psychological. As one author declares, "A consensus now exists among psychologists that qualitative changes in cognitive skills in the direction of adult thought begin at the age of twelve to thirteen." See Stuart J. Baskin, "State Intrusion into Family Affairs: Justifications and Limitations" (1973-74), 26 Stan. L. Rev. 1383 at 1395, n. 16.

258 Fourteen is chosen for consistency with the common law that a person of that age has capacity to testify.

259 See the discussion in Part III, *supra*.

260 *R. v. Grimba* (1977), 38 C.C.C. (2d) 469 (Ont. C.A.).

cross-checking, will have been relied on by several government agencies, and will be a "tape . . . on or in which information . . . is recorded, stored or reproduced".[261] The business record will contain not the observations of a potential witness but the actual testimony of a key witness. The videotape evidence would be supported by the sexual abuse expert's personal testimony. The proposed amendment to s. 30 amounts to a minor extension of the current judicial interpretation of that section.

The proposed reforms would benefit victims, their families and the accused in several ways.

Discussing her sexual experience with a supportive, non-judgmental adult will begin a healing process rather than extend the trauma for the victim.[262] The child will learn to accept that although she may have participated (especially in incest situations), she is not guilty.[263] She will benefit from the expert's knowledge of the underlying causes of intra and extra-familial child abuse.[264] With carefully developed, convincing evidence, the number of guilty pleas may rise, thus sparing the victim the ordeal of testifying.[265] However, if there is a trial, the complainant can be spared the acute embarrassment of describing, in public, the details of where she was touched and how.

Reform would benefit families of both intra and extra-familial sexual assault. The expert, whose knowledge and experience will be especially beneficial here, will be able to explain what has happened and lend support. This will be particularly important in incest cases, where the confusion and disruption to the family resulting from the child's disclosure may lead the non-offending members to blame the child. The expert will counsel these family members to assist them in understanding that it is not the child who has caused the disruption but the perpetrator, and that the child is in very great need of their support.

The accused who goes to trial may benefit from his counsel's ability to cross-examine an adult child expert with more vigour than is sometimes advisable with a child witness.[266]

One author expresses the opinion that reform of this type will produce more reliable evidence than the victim's personal in-court testimony.[267] The

---

261 Canada Evidence Act, s. 30 (12).

262 Ordway, "Parent-Child Incest: Proof at Trial Without Testimony in Court by the Victim" (1981), 15 U. Mich. J.L. Ref. 131 at 141.

263 According to Dr. Hamacher, "Very young children have a different sense of justice than adults. From what we know of moral development, we can predict that if there is 'punishment' (i.e., abuse resulting in physical harm or fear), then the young child will feel she must have done something to deserve it. The concept of innocent victim takes a long time to develop."

264 Ordway, *supra*, n. 262 at 141.

265 *Ibid.*

266 Lane, *The Legal Responses to Sexual Abuse of Children* (1982), at 82.

267 Ordway, *supra*, n. 262, at 141-42. This opinion is based on that expressed by, *inter alia*, L.

victim's ability to remember and communicate relevant facts will be enhanced by the calm atmosphere of the interview session and by the expertise of the interviewer in communicating with children. The expert's supplemental testimony will assist in the understanding of the victim's story and in the assessment of her credibility.[268] Also, as mentioned in the description of a similar proposal in Part IV, section 4, *supra*, the Crown and defence will have several opportunities before the trial to submit questions, and again at trial if the need arises.

The implementation of these reforms will be costly, especially to the Ontario Government. However, the investigative work is currently being carried out by the police and/or children's aid society. The expert would relieve these workers of this task.

We must ask ourselves, "At what cost do we do nothing?"

VI DEFENDANT'S AND VICTIM'S CHARTER RIGHTS UNDER THE PROPOSED REFORM

Notwithstanding the advantages discussed above, the proposed reform must be considered in light of the Canadian Charter of Rights and Freedoms and the rights conferred therein.

The long-standing rights at common law of a defendant to the presumption of innocence and a fair trial have been entrenched in the supreme[269] law of Canada, the Charter. These rights are addressed particularly in s. 7 and s. 11(*d*):

> 7. Everyone has the right to life, liberty and security of the person and the right not to be deprived thereof except in accordance with the principles of fundamental justice.
>
> 11. Any person charged with an offence has the right . . .
>
> (*d*) to be presumed innocent until proven guilty according to law in a fair and public hearing by an independent and impartial tribunal.

As with all other rights and freedoms, the above-described rights are subject to s. 1:

> 1. The *Canadian Charter of Rights and Freedoms* guarantees the rights and freedoms set out in it subject only to such reasonable limits prescribed by law as can be demonstrably justified in a free and democratic society.

Every accused person, then, has the right to publicly make a full answer and defence. Only through these rights can a defendant withstand the power of the state. The rights balance the power.

Berliner and D. Stevens in their then unpublished paper, "Advocating for Sexually Abused Children in the Criminal Justice System 2" (November 1976).

268 Ordway, *ibid.*, at 141 and 142.

269 Constitution Act, 1982, s. 52.

It is submitted, however, that under the present legal doctrine of Canada, the child victim has no rights, or whatever rights she has are not enforced. "Victims and witnesses do not receive even a fraction of the protections and defences that are accorded an accused. Typically, the interests of the victim and witnesses are subordinated to what are regarded as more important interests."[270] Part III of this chapter looked at the problems with the Criminal Code, the rules of evidence and the common law of children's evidence. The young victim is forced into legal machinery designed for adults at the investigative stage, and designed to presume her a liar at the trial stage. Notwithstanding that it is the accused who faces loss of liberty and whose rights must therefore be rigorously protected, it is the child victim, who faces possible permanent psychological damage, whose rights are not being addressed.

Although the child witness is often submitted to a prolonged ordeal in court, other events have frustrated the effective prosecution of sex offenders. Charges are not laid for the various reasons outlined in Part II. Where prosecution is initiated, the case may be ultimately dismissed because of one of the evidentiary problems in Part III.

It is submitted that the reform proposed by this paper would alleviate these problems while protecting the Charter rights of the accused. The reform would bring the prosecution of child sexual abuse cases in line with the thinking of Simonsen J. of the Manitoba Court of Queen's Bench in a sexual assault case:

> The competing forces at work . . . must balance the rights of the accused against the interests of society, which obviously include the interests of the victim. Society has an interest in having crimes reported and in developing a legal system which encourages such reporting.[271]

The principal argument against the proposed reform would be the loss to the accused of the right at trial to cross-examine the complainant, to test the credibility of that person's story, a right it would be alleged is guaranteed by ss. 7 and 11(*d*) of the Charter. Canadian courts have held, however, that neither s. 7 nor s. 11(*d*) confers on an accused a specific right to confront the witnesses against him.[272] An Ontario court has held that s. 7 is not offended by the use of s. 643 of the Criminal Code which permits the Crown to adduce at trial evidence of a witness taken at the preliminary inquiry where the witness was absent from Canada, notwithstanding that the missing witness was a complainant in a sexual

---

270 William F. McDonald, "Towards a Bicentennial Revolution in Criminal Justice: The Return of the Victim" (1975-76), 13 Am. Crim. L. Rev. 649.

271 *R. v. Bird* (1984), 40 C.R. (3d) 41 at 54.

272 *R. v. Clarke* (1982), 3 C.R.R. 271 (B.C.S.C.), and *R. v. Pawliw* (1984), 13 W.C.B. 200 (B.C.S.C.).

case and her credibility may have been most important.[273] Murray J. of the British Columbia Supreme Court decided in a murder case[274] that s. 637(*b*) of the Criminal Code,[275] authorizing an order appointing a commissioner to take the evidence of a witness who is out of Canada, is not inconsistent with s. 7. The decision goes on to state that s. 7 guarantees a fair trial, but does not guarantee that every rule that governs that trial, when examined individually, must be fair to the accused. Only a rule that is so unfair that it will result in an unfair trial will be struck down.

In the cases discussed herein, there were procedural safeguards protecting the rights of the accused. In two of the cases,[276] preliminary inquiries provided the opportunity to cross-examine the complainant. In the third case,[277] the accused was afforded the opportunity, in court, to speak against granting the order under s. 637(*b*) of the Criminal Code. Counsel argued that the order should be refused as the jury at trial would not be able to observe the demeanor of the witness. The British Columbia Supreme Court found that that difficulty is easily overcome by videotaping the examination in chief and cross-examination of the witness.[278] The reform proposed in this chapter provides procedural safeguards whereby the accused is given the opportunity to put questions to the complainant through the mouth of the child sexual abuse expert before and, if required, during the trial. A carefully made videotape will allow the trier of fact to observe the demeanor of the witness.

The procedures followed in other jurisdictions in the criminal prosecution of child sex abuse cases demonstrate that other free and democratic societies do not find it contrary to fundamental justice to admit carefully taken evidence without granting an opportunity to examine the complainant at trial. It is submitted that the reform advocated herein is reasonable in every way and can be demonstrably justified in a free and democratic society.

VII SUMMARY

The state, in most communities, currently intervenes in child sexual assault cases with investigative and trial procedures which are inappropriate to the needs of the victim, her family and society. These procedures can exacerbate the trauma of the victim and fail to address the multitude of problems surrounding

---

273 S. 643 [am. 1974-75-76, c. 93, s. 76]. See *R. v. Balkwell*, Ont. Co. Ct., 28th April 1983 (not yet reported).

274 *R. v. Pawliw, supra*, n. 272.

275 S. 637 (*b*) [am. 1985, c. 19, s. 149].

276 *R. v. Clarke, supra*, n. 272, and *R. v. Balkwell, supra*, n. 273.

277 *R. v. Pawliw, supra*, n. 272.

278 *Ibid.*

these cases. This chapter suggests an effective solution which is consistent with the rights of the accused to a fair trial, and begins to heal the emotional wounds suffered by the victim.[279]

---

279 This summary is adapted from the Conclusion in Ordway, "Parent-Child Incest: Proof at Trial Without Testimony in Court by the Victim" (1981), 15 U. Mich. J. L. Ref. 131.

10

LEGISLATING FOR THE BRAVE NEW CHILDREN

Bernard M. Dickens

I INTRODUCTION

The incidence of infertility in society appears to be increasing.[1] Its causes are many, ranging from the natural reduction in fertility that comes with advancing age to industrial,[2] environmental and ecological effects. Women's and perhaps men's ability to have children when they marry or remarry later in life is lower than when they are younger. Life-style causes such as venereal infection are often cited to explain the rise in infertility, but medically prescribed drugs and devices, such as intrauterine contraceptive devices, can cause pelvic inflammatory disease and other conditions as significant in reducing fertility. Fertility itself is differently defined in medical, social and, for instance, demographic sciences. Some individuals are chronically infertile (primary infertility),

---

1   See generally Population Information Program, Johns Hopkins University, *Population Reports* (1983), series L, no. 4.

2   See N.M. Chenier, Canadian Advisory Council on the Status of Women, *Reproductive Hazards at Work: Men, Women and the Fertility Gamble* (1982).

but others are infertile at some times only (secondary infertility). A woman who had a voluntary contraceptive sterilization after completing her childbearing preference in marriage may be infertile in a second marriage in which she wants a child. Due to advancing skill in reproductive medicine, a number of alternatives have recently become available to assist people of absent or reduced fertility, adding to the options of childlessness and adoption.

Biomedical advances have also given fertile individuals reasons not to have their own children. Prognostic evidence may show the risks to her life and health a woman may bear in a future pregnancy. Genetic knowledge may show the risk of a child conceived in the future being grossly abnormal and severely handicapped, or of a pregnancy ending in spontaneous abortion.[3] Many fertile couples who want children may decide that they should not have their own children. The prospects of children being available for adoption are lower than they used to be, however, due to such causes as effective contraceptive methods reducing the rate of unwanted pregnancy and birth, the widespread acceptability of single women rearing their own children, legal access to abortion services and, for instance, assistance adolescents may receive to keep their children.

Accordingly, a demand has arisen for medicine to address and resolve the difficulties increasingly experienced in the conception, birth and rearing of healthy children. Further, couples whose own children would be at great risk of being genetically handicapped seek means by which unaffected partners can have healthy children the couples can rear in their families, and seek medical means to achieve their purpose. Pressure has arisen in infertility clinics and elsewhere to permit couples experiencing infertility or risks of dysgenic reproduction (the birth of a genetically handicapped child) to be like couples who are not reproductively disabled, and who have normal children.

Medicine has responded to this pressure by the development of a number of techniques. The law has responded to these techniques more slowly, since a time lag usually separates developments in medicine, biotechnology and social demand for services from their legal accommodation. Legal responses to medical means to achieve families tend to be particularly slow and cautious, since the family is a social institution to which the law is customarily reverential and in which experimentation and innovation are discouraged. The law is influenced by conservative religion in distinguishing what are considered to be natural and unnatural practices and their consequences.[4] Protection of genetic lines through legal concepts of legitimacy and succession through legitimate

---

3   See generally the U.S. President's Commission for the Study of Ethical Problems in Medicine and Biomedical and Behavioral Research, *Screening and Counseling for Genetic Conditions* (1983).

4   See M.A. Glendon, *State, Law and Family: Family Law in Transition in the United States and Western Europe* (1977).

heirship represents an important traditional value in the law. Creation of families through employment of third parties' sperm and ova (gametes) or of surrogate mothers at first appears bizarre, unnatural and legally unacceptable.

The technique of artificial insemination by donated sperm (A.I.D.) has been undertaken for many decades, and the service is covered under Canadian provincial health plans as routine medical treatment for infertility and for risk of dysgenic birth. The law no longer speaks of such donation as adultery,[5] but where the distinction exists between legitimacy and illegitimacy, the children of proven A.I.D. are held to be illegitimate, with all of the legal disadvantages they bear in their social families due to that status. The fact of A.I.D. is frequently concealed, because children born to married women are legally presumed to be their husbands', and no one has an interest to rebut that presumption. New means of genetic diagnosis and prognosis depend, however, upon tracing of genetic ancestry, so that the health care of children born of A.I.D. may be harmed if their genetic parentage is concealed.

The law has to come to terms with the births of children by means which invoke the imagery of Aldous Huxley's *Brave New World*. Legislating for these Brave New Children may be undertaken upon a variety of theoretical bases which it is the aim of this chapter to review. Underlying the options is the perceptive observation made in 1966 regarding artificial insemination by donor, which has proven true in that case, and which shows clear signs of being true regarding other reproductive technologies, that:

> Any change in custom or practice in this emotionally charged area has always elicited a response from established custom and law of horrified negation at first; then negation, without horror; then slow and gradual curiosity, study, evaluation, and finally a very slow but steady acceptance.[6]

II MEDICAL AIDS TO REPRODUCTION

A number of conditions of infertility may be treated by routine management of patients themselves. Diet control and hormone treatments may be undertaken, the latter at times inducing superovulation resulting in multiple pregnancy. Where a woman has, for instance, blocked fallopian tubes, surgical or microsurgical repair may be undertaken so that pregnancy may occur in the natural way. It is an interesting feature of such surgical treatments that medical specialists who undertake them have not been asked to ensure that their patients would be good parents, and that they are partners in stable unions. In contrast, those involved in techniques of artificial reproduction are frequently expected to act as guarantors of their patients' social acceptability as parents.

---

5 Compare *Orford v. Orford* (1921), 58 D.L.R. 251 (Ont. S.C.).

6 S.J. Kleegman and S.A. Kaufman, *Infertility in Women* (1966), at 178.

There are three medical techniques available when infertility cannot be treated so as to permit natural fertilization to occur. These are:

(a) artificial insemination, in which sperm are artificially introduced into women's reproductive tracts, normally by syringe, with the intention that they will have the same effect as if introduced by normal sexual intercourse. The sperm may be those of a husband (A.I.H.) or of an unrelated donor (A.I.D.);

(b) *in vitro* fertilization (I.V.F.), in which ova and sperm are combined in the laboratory (a "test tube") and consequently fertilized ova (embryos) are either placed in the reproductive systems of the donors of the ova or are transplanted into those of other women; and

(c) *in vivo* fertilization by artificial insemination or natural intercourse followed by removal of fertilized ova by a washing or flushing technique and their transplantation to the reproductive systems of other women.

When children conceived and gestated through these techniques are born, they may remain in the custody of the women who bear and give birth to them. Even when the ova came from other women and were fertilized by I.V.F. or *in vivo*, the law follows its historic view that a woman who gestates and delivers a child is its mother: *mater est quam gestatio demonstrat*.[7] The process of gestation and delivery constitutes authentic motherhood by biological and social tests, and this is not reduced by the fact that genetic motherhood by ovum donation resides in another woman. Further, if the mother is married, the child will legally be presumed to be her husband's, even if the fertilizing sperm came from another man.[8]

If a woman conceives a child by natural means, by A.I.D., by I.V.F. or otherwise, for the purpose of surrendering it upon birth, she may be considered a "surrogate mother". This expression is strictly a misnomer, since she undertakes authentic mothering before birth even if the embryo she gestates was formed from another woman's ovum. Usually, so-called surrogates are inseminated artificially with the sperm of men whose wives cannot bear children due to their infertility, liability to chronic spontaneous abortion or, for instance, heart conditions rendering their pregnancies life-threatening. Upon birth, the children are surrendered to the donors of the sperm. The men are biological fathers of the children, and may not have to adopt them to form a legal relationship. Adoption may be undertaken for the purpose of giving the children their fathers' surnames, however, and in any event wives of such men may want to regularize their relationships to the children they will rear through seeking step-parent adoption.

---

7   J.K. Mason and R.A. McCall Smith, *Law and Medical Ethics* (1983), at 46.

8   In some cases the presumption is rebuttable.

A surrogate motherhood arrangement is not dependent upon medical assistance, since it may be undertaken by condoned adultery, meaning natural intercourse with consent of the surrogate and her husband and of the intended father and his wife. There are obvious reasons, of course, why this type of insemination may be unacceptable to conscientious individuals. The alternative of artificial insemination is not necessarily dependent upon medical assistance either, since A.I.D. is not clearly "the practice of medicine" which by provincial legislation[9] can be undertaken only by licensed physicians or others, such as nurses, specially approved for the purposes. Numerous instances are known in which non-qualified people have achieved insemination by artificial means, by use not only of syringes but also, for instance, turkey-basters. There are physiological risks in the procedure which may make it unwise in untrained hands, and it might be best managed with counselling and explanations which only qualified persons can give. There is some resistance, however, to the medicalization of natural processes surrounding pregnancy, and in principle artificial insemination may be no more the practice of medicine than natural insemination. Compelling reasons may have to exist to justify its placement in medical hands.

III GENERAL LEGAL ATTITUDES TO ARTIFICIAL REPRODUCTION

It is trite to observe that modern contraception has separated sexual intercourse from reproduction and modern biomedicine has separated reproduction from sexual intercourse. The law expressed in judicial and related attitudes remains uncomfortable in dealing with the human realities of sexual reproduction, however, and is no more comfortable in approaching asexual reproduction. Reflecting conservative principles, the law has been reluctant to condone deviations from a limited range of sexual proprieties, and until recently considered asexual reproduction deviant. In the first case in a common law jurisdiction to consider A.I.D., an Ontario judge in 1921[10] stated in *obiter* that it constituted adultery. Although modern courts reject this view,[11] not least because, with freezing of sperm, the donor may have died long before the insemination, and because the medical practitioner or nurse inseminating a woman may be female, legal analysts of A.I.D. continue to ask if it involves adultery when other analysts consider the question absurd.

In 1956, the Canadian Bar Review published an exchange on A.I.D. between Dean Tallin and, as he later became, Dean Hubbard.[12] The former

---

9 See for instance Ontario's Health Disciplines Act, R.S.O. 1980, c. 196, s. 45(*f*).

10 See *Orford v. Orford, supra*, n. 5.

11 An influential turning-point was the Scottish case of *MacLennan v. MacLennan*, [1958] S.L.T. 12 (Ct. of Sess.); see also *Strnad v. Strnad*, 78 N.Y.S. 2d 390 (S.C., 1948).

12 (1956), 34 Can. Bar Rev. 1, 166, 425, 628.

asserted that in law the practice constituted adultery. Dean Hubbard took the view which has since prevailed of denying this, but he nevertheless described A.I.D. as "this abhorrent practice"[13] and as a "detestable practice"[14] which was "a perversion of the natural order . . . immoral *per se*".[15] It may be asked whether conduct assessed in 1956 as immoral *per se* may be seen more sympathetically only three decades later. It is interesting to reflect that the deliberate conception of children inescapably doomed to suffer gross genetic abnormalities, and of fetuses predictably fated to be spontaneously aborted or stillborn, when A.I.D. might produce normal children, has not been described by lawyers as immoral *per se*, although geneticists and other conscientious persons may consider it to be so.

Where legislation has not eliminated or narrowed the distinction between legitimate and illegitimate children, those born by A.I.D. are considered to be illegitimate, subject to legal suppression of the fact of A.I.D. through the presumption of a husband's paternity of his wife's child.[16] Judicial attitudes to the concept of surrogate motherhood have been hostile and at times quite intemperately expressed,[17] but the law's reactionary disposition is not invariably obstructive of the new reproductive technologies. When I.V.F. permits a woman to bear her husband's child, the technology causing her pregnancy is of no legal account. Induction of superovulation and fertilization of many of the ova recovered, resulting in multiple implantation and multiple pregnancy, and freezing of unimplanted ova (cryopreservation) followed by, for instance, their transfer to other women, engage little if any of the law's traditional doctrines. Similarly, *in vivo* fertilization and embryo recovery by flushing and subsequent embryo transfer attracts little of the law's attention. The issue of the legal status of the embryo *extra uterum*, for instance, remains unresolved,[18] and its deliberate wastage seems to offend no legal provisions except perhaps within the contractual agreement between the gamete donors and those undertaking fertilizations. Ambivalence surrounds the issue of whether the embryo *extra uterum* is governed by principles of property law.[19]

---

13   *Ibid.*, at 425.

14   *Ibid.*, at 438.

15   *Ibid.*, at 450.

16   On the tenacity of this presumption in the face of clearly contradictory facts, see *Bolduc v. Lalancette-St. Pierre*, [1976] C.S. 41 (Que. S.C.).

17   It is of interest that the most extremely expressed English judgments have not been released: see (if you can) *A. v. C.*, Ont. H.C., 20th June 1978, affirmed Ont. C.A., 18th July 1978 (unreported).

18   See B.M. Dickens, "The Ectogenetic Human Being: A Problem Child of our Time" (1979-80), 18 U.W.O. L.Rev. 241.

19   A U.S. federal judge allowed a legal claim for damage to property to go to a jury in *Del Zio v. Presbyterian Hosp.*, 74 Civ. 3588 (S.D. N.Y., 1978), unreported but discussed in W.H. Winborne (ed.), *Handling Pregnancy and Birth Cases* (1983), at 230-36.

It appears that if the law is to take a systematic approach to artificial reproduction, it will be through legislation.[20] The welfare of children these technologies will increasingly create requires a more positive approach from the law than classification of children born of donated sperm as illegitimate, and condemnation of surrogate motherhood agreements as void as contrary to public policy.[21] Courts governed not just by precedents but also by conventional distaste of unorthodox sexual conduct are proving incapable of developing a cohesive jurisprudence to protect the best interests of the Brave New Children.[22]

Judgments in family matters have arisen overwhelmingly in disputes between spouses over custody, in disputes over paternity and related maintenance obligations, and for instance in disputes over legitimacy and inheritance rights. The emphasis has been upon adultery and fidelity to genealogical lines of succession, giving priority to intentions of deceased testators rather than to well-functioning relations among members of social families. A contrast between this old family law and the new family law necessary to accommodate reproductive technology may be that the old law did little more than condemn certain parents, whereas the new law may positively welcome children, and aim to serve their family and social interests. As with elimination of the distinction between legitimate and bastard children, the new law is founded upon legislation.

IV LEGISLATIVE MODELS[23]

The placement of children within families receives legal recognition according to a small number of models. These models fall under different degrees of regulation. One model is that of A.I.D. itself, although, as will be described below, this is a purely negative model. The available models are: natural reproduction: unregulated but recognized; adoption: regulated and recognized; and artificial insemination (by donor): unregulated and unrecognized.

---

20 See the two-volume Ontario Law Reform Commission *Report on Human Artificial Reproduction and Related Matters* (1985), which analyses existing law and makes comprehensive recommendations for legislation.

21 In this regard, the U.K. *Report of the Committee of Inquiry into Human Fertilisation and Embryology* (the Warnock Report), H.M.S.O. Cmnd. 9314 (1984), is quite inadequate in that it recognizes that ". . . there will continue to be privately arranged surrogacy agreements" (para. 8.19, at 47) but makes no provisions for the welfare of the resulting children. Contrast the Ontario Law Reform Commission's *Report, ibid.*

22 See, for instance, the Supreme Court of Michigan in *Syrkowski v. Appleyard*, 362 N.W. 2d 211 (1985), reversing the state Court of Appeal's decision at 333 N.W. 2d 90 (1983), which upheld a trial judge who interpreted legislation so as not to accommodate a surrogate parenting arrangement.

23 For an elaboration of these models, see B.M. Dickens, "Surrogate Motherhood: Legal and Legislative Issues", in A. Milunsky and G. J. Annas (eds.), *Genetics and the Law III* (1985), 183 at 185-93.

1. Natural Reproduction

Natural reproduction is a capacity adults can exercise with little regulation by the law.[24] The Criminal Code sets a minimum age of consent to intercourse at 14 for females,[25] and above that age adolescents are offered protection against sexual exploitation by provincial legislation on child abuse. Incest prohibitions govern sexual intercourse (but not asexual reproduction) within defined blood relationships. Involuntary sterilization may be authorized for minors and mentally retarded persons when it is therapeutically necessary, but contraceptive sterilization without individual consent is governed by the limits set by the Supreme Court of Canada in the *Eve* case.[26] Beyond limits of this nature, however, individuals are free to engage in sexual relationships which may result in pregnancy and the birth of children.

The law in principle does not tell individuals when they may conceive children naturally, by whom they may do so, by what reproductive means they exercise their natural procreative capacity nor which of their natural children may live in their homes as children of their families. Their legitimate children are recognized at birth, and for some purposes before birth,[27] with no formal act of legal recognition. The state is passive rather than active regarding birth registration in that facts of paternity are accepted with no requirement of evidence that the man named as father is the biological parent.[28]

The state's permissive and passive approach to natural reproduction may be a phenomenon only of the present time in Canada. Alternative instances exist of states taking strongly pro-natalist positions, urging and actively encouraging reproduction for the purpose of building population size, the labour force and, for instance, military power for defensive or other uses.[29] Similarly, countries considering themselves overburdened by population growth have so strongly urged contraceptive sterilizations and abortions that their voluntary acceptance in individual cases has been doubted. Canadian jurisdictions may wish to

---

24 See generally B.M. Dickens, "Reproduction Law and Medical Consent" (1985), 35 U. T. L.J. 255.

25 R.S.C. 1970, c. C-34, s. 146(1) [en. 1972, c. 13, s. 70]. But see *R. v. Roche* (1985), 20 C.C.C. (3d) 524 (Ont. C.A.), providing a defence of mistake of fact where a consenting girl aged 13 was honestly believed by the defendant to be 15.

26 Judgment pending on the appeal against the decision in *Re Eve* (1981), 115 D.L.R. (3d) 283 (P.E.I.S.C.): see generally B.M. Dickens, *supra*, n. 24, at 265-71.

27 See E.W. Keyserlingk, *The Unborn Child's Right to Prenatal Care: A Comparative Law Perspective* (1984).

28 See *supra*, n. 20, at 65-73.

29 See B.M. Dickens, "Comparative Legal Abortion Policies and Attitudes Toward Abortion" in M.W. Shaw and A.E. Doudera (eds.), *Defining Human Life: Medical, Legal, and Ethical Implications* (1983), 240 at 259-61.

exercise greater control of natural reproduction, through encouragements and discouragements, and perhaps more direct controls. Control of the reproductively disabled alone, through control of artificial reproduction, may be questionable, however, under s. 15 of the Canadian Charter of Rights and Freedoms, which provides for non-discrimination on grounds of physical disability.

2. Adoption

In contrast to natural reproduction, adoption is highly regulated by legislation and judicial scrutiny.[30] Standards of eligibility to adopt children have become exceptionally high, because of the dearth of adoptable children. Standards may be lowered for so-called "hard to place" children, such as those affected by severe physical or neurological abnormalities. For normal children available for adoption, however, prospective parents have to come close to ideal standards before they are likely to be awarded a child. Formal exclusion criteria of eligibility have had to be eased in recent years, under the impact of provincial human rights codes and the Canadian Charter of Rights and Freedoms.[31] Accordingly, public agencies placing children for adoption may not discriminate in their publicized criteria of eligibility on grounds of marital status, or, for instance, physical or mental disability. Nevertheless, it may be doubted that agencies and courts addressing the best interests of individual children placed for adoption will depart far from a traditional vision of a "normal" family. The fact that many children live and thrive in non-traditional families is unlikely to influence patterns of adoption placement in the foreseeable future.

Adoption applications are divisible into those made by former strangers to the children eligible for adoption, and those involving partners of the children's natural parents, or family members such as a sister of a child's disabled or deceased mother. These latter (for example, step-parent) adoption applications receive considerably reduced judicial scrutiny, since, were they to be rejected, the children would remain in their *de facto* parents' homes and would constitute members of their adult guardians' families. Accordingly, because it would probably be contrary to a child's interests to obstruct regularization of relations with for instance the parent's marital partner, the child's placement in the newly constituted family is usually considered a *fait accompli*, and judicial scrutiny is slight and accommodating.

In contrast, an adoption application by a person formerly unrelated to the eligible child would be scrutinized in some detail. Notwithstanding formal removal of discriminating legislated provisions which in themselves might violate the Canadian Charter of Rights and Freedoms and/or the provincial

---

30   See *supra*, n. 20, at 111-17.
31   See *ibid.*, at 112, n. 13.

human rights codes, public or quasi-public adoption agencies and the courts asked to approve adoptions are likely to address such issues as an applicant's age, health, marital status and history, family structure and stability, employment status and economic means. More refined assessments may consider the physical, material, emotional and psychological environment in which a child may be reared, including scrutiny of the applicant's personality, motives, tolerance, compatibility, congeniality, and philosophical, religious, political, educational and child-rearing convictions.

The adoption model would expose applicants to infertility programmes to intense scrutiny, reaching a level which would be intolerable to apply to persons of ordinary reproductive capacity. The level of examination applied in fact in existing infertility programmes may provide evidence of what is acceptable practice.

3. Artificial Insemination (by Donor) (A.I.D.)

A.I.D. is quite widely undertaken in Canada,[32] but it provides a model only in the sense that it is not legally prohibited. It is not generally regulated by legislation,[33] and its consequences are suppressed or evaded rather than positively recognized and accommodated. In Ontario, for instance, the Vital Statistics Act requires that, when a woman gives birth having lived with her husband when the child was conceived, the husband's particulars shall be entered in the Statement of Live Birth under the column headed "father".[34] This indicates that the birth register functions as a social rather than a true genealogical record, since the provision applies when pregnancy resulted from use of donated sperm. The A.I.D. model is a permissive or *laissez-faire* model of legislative non-intervention, in which parties to artificial reproduction are free to arrange their affairs within the limits of the inadvertent law.

A couple having recourse to A.I.D. often employ sperm of a donor who matches the husband in body build and colouring, in order to increase the chance of the child appearing to be his. Registration of the child's fatherhood in his name is consistent with the couple's intended public presentation of the child. Similarly, the sperm donor intends not to be registered as the father of his genetic offspring, so that suppression of his name suits his own preference. Accommodation of birth by donated sperm in accordance with all the actors' intentions is found equally in birth by ovum donation, where fertilization is undertaken *in vitro* with sperm of a husband or donor. The woman gestating and delivering the child would be considered the "mother".[35]

---

32   For Ontario practice and statistics, see *ibid.*, at 17-24.

33   For legislation in Quebec and Yukon Territory, see *ibid.*, at 374-75.

34   Vital Statistics Act, R.S.O. 1980, c. 524, s. 6(4).

35   See *supra*, n. 7.

This pattern of use of existing law is less accommodating, however, of other forms of artificial reproduction. If a widow gave birth to a child conceived through use of her deceased husband's frozen sperm, and birth occurred later than 300 days after his death, she might be considered as an unmarried woman, and be unable to have her late husband named as the child's father, although that would be biologically true.[36] In a surrogate motherhood transaction involving a married woman, her husband's name might have to be recorded as father of the child, leaving the intended father to seek a separate judicial declaration of paternity before he could gain a right of custody. He might also have to adopt his child before a birth certificate could be issued naming him as his child's father. Further, where the child was produced from his wife's ovum but borne by another woman, the wife might have no means of obtaining a judicial declaration of maternity,[37] and would have to adopt her biological child in order to gain a right of custody. Accordingly, the absence of specific legislation leaves parties to modern means of artificial reproduction to the random effects of laws designed for other purposes.

A major inadequacy of present legislative regimes is that, even when they accommodate the preferences of active participants in artificial reproduction, as in the case of A.I.D., they do not necessarily protect the children consequently born. Legal confusion at the birth of a child might impair secure placement with those intended to be responsible for its protection and rearing, for instance when a surrogate mother gives birth in a hospital and the biological father and his wife seek custody of the child intended to be surrendered to them. A larger problem concerns children born of donated sperm and/or ova, whose medical care and later reproductive counselling may be dependent upon knowledge of their genetic parentage. The absence of means of tracing at least genetic profiles of biological parents may place them at a disadvantage and perhaps at risk.[38] The adoption model may expose children to disadvantage, but it usually permits discovery of at least a birth mother's characteristics;[39] the practice of birth through donated sperm or ova reveals a default of legislative attention that exposes an increasing number of children to the risk of grave disadvantage to health.

---

36 But see *supra*, n. 20, at 70-71.

37 Paternity declaration proceedings might have to be made available *mutatis mutandis* to women in order not to discriminate on grounds of sex in breach of s. 15 of the Canadian Charter of Rights and Freedoms.

38 See generally G.J. Annas, "Fathers Anonymous: Beyond the Best Interests of the Sperm Donor" (1980), 14 Fam. L.Q. 1.

39 See F.C. O'Donnell, "The Four-Sided Triangle: A Comparative Study of the Confidentiality of Adoption Records" (1983), 21 U.W.O. L. Rev. 129.

V CONCEPTUAL APPROACHES

If it is accepted that legislative intervention is justifiable to regulate the practice of artificial reproduction, it may be founded upon different concepts reflecting different orientations. Three general approaches have been distinguished,[40] namely: the static approach, the private ordering approach, and the state regulation approach.

1. The Static Approach

The static approach is socially and psychologically static, in that it is conservative in orientation. It may base itself upon principles of biology or of social form, or of both where they are not incompatible. Biology confines acceptable social units to those that are genetically coherent, so that use of donated sperm or ova would be discouraged and surrogate motherhood including ovum donation might be penalized. Biological parenthood would determine personal status and recognition, so that genetically unrelated persons would lack rights of general inheritance and be eligible only for specific bequests identifying them by name or strictly drawn description.

Social form centres upon family solidarity and stability. It would limit legitimacy of reproduction to married couples by providing that spouses can properly bear children only of each other. The approach to asexual reproduction would be unsympathetic, except when *in vitro* fertilization would permit a woman to bear her husband's child. That practice would not be available, however, to permit sperm, ovum or embryo donations. The static approach may impose hardships upon children born outside its permitted limits, but it reflects a sense of social and sexual order which reflects some religiously inspired visions of natural propriety.

2. The Private Ordering Approach

The private ordering approach, in contrast, would not only permit individuals to pursue reproductive practices of their own choosing, but would give them the means to achieve their preferences by determining which people are to be legally recognized as parents of the resulting children. It might lead to libertarian extremes and accommodate commercial transactions in the donation of sperm, ova, embryos and surrogate services. Certain practices might offend the individual conscience, of course, but the toleration of A.I.D. practices over many decades in Canada, including insemination without medical mediation,

---

40   See W. Wadlington, "Artificial Conception: The Challenge for Family Law" (1983), 69 Va. L. Rev. 465; and *supra*, n. 20, chapter 4.

and the emergence of *in vitro* fertilization services without legal regulation,[41] indicate that privately ordered reproductive practices can be left legally unhampered, even when not specifically accommodated. The private ordering approach is compatible with a philosophy of reduced governmental involvement in private matters and of deregulation of health services.

3. The State Regulation Approach

The state regulation approach may offer a middle ground between the prohibitive excesses of a rigidly static approach and the permissive excesses of private ordering. There are two orientations of state regulation, the punitive and the inducement approaches. Punitive regulations may implement a static approach, through instruments of penal sanctions, for instance against commercial surrogate motherhood arrangements,[42] and through civil disabilities, for instance illegitimacy and non-recognition of relationships resulting from prohibited reproductive conduct. As against this, however, the inducement approach may use the instrument of recognition more positively, as a carrot and not a stick, in order to offer benefits aimed to induce those employing artificial reproduction to conform to approved practices. These might include their prior recourse to medical and social counselling, which will require them to receive information regarding what they propose to undertake, to reach informed decisions, and perhaps to identify and make agreements on matters of important concern. Another method may be to offer medically reliable services at specially approved centres, where sperm donors are carefully screened against, for instance, venereal disease and acquired immune deficiency syndrome (AIDS), and where social and other counselling is offered or alternative medical services to overcome infertility are available.

Since such practices as using artificial insemination and making surrogate motherhood agreements can be undertaken without medical intervention and can be hidden from social scrutiny, the possibility of suppressing them by penal or civil non-recognition sanctions appears low;[43] they may be driven underground by these means, however, to the prospective disadvantage of the children in fact born of them. Some advocate the repression of offensive reproductive conduct by criminal sanctions,[44] and more neutral commentators raise serious concerns about implications both of unorthodox reproduction and of state

---

41   In Ontario, a number of I.V.F. centres have been promised funding of their services from the provincial health insurance plan.

42   See for instance the United Kingdom's Surrogacy Arrangements Act, 1985, c. 49.

43   See *supra*, n. 21.

44   The Surrogacy Arrangements Act, 1985, *supra*, n. 42, followed the Warnock Report, *supra*, n. 21.

repression of unorthodoxy.[45] Many fear that the sins of the parents may be visited upon their children by ill-considered legislation, which may be clear about the family values it aims to protect but less sensitive to the values of individual liberty and of child protection it may jeopardize or sacrifice.

Whatever concept or orientation is applied by legislation which aims to affect artificial reproduction, a number of specific issues must be addressed. Some of these issues transcend any particular reproductive technique, while others relate more specifically to individual means of artificial reproduction. A number of issues which legislation should address are reviewed below.

VI TRANSCENDING ISSUES

The Canadian Charter of Rights and Freedoms, s. 15, provides for equality before and under the law, and for equal protection and benefit of the law "without discrimination based on . . . mental or physical disability". Since legislation rarely limits reproductive freedom of the naturally fertile and then does so in indirect rather than direct ways, concerning the young and the mentally impaired, it must be asked whether legislation can directly limit reproductive opportunities of those affected by a physical or genetic disability.[46] Provincial legislatures considering the imposition of limits upon procreative pursuits of the reproductively disabled must decide whether to employ the "override" provision in s. 33 of the Charter, or to rely upon s. 1 of the Charter, which subjects s. 15 rights to "such reasonable limits prescribed by law as can be demonstrably justified in a free and democratic society".

Provincial human rights codes may provide for non-discrimination in access to public facilities on grounds of marital status. It must be asked whether limiting access to public hospitals' infertility services to legally married couples offends such provisions, and whether provincial legislatures will exempt such limitations from the operation of the provincial human rights codes.[47]

Limitations upon individuals' recourse to artificial reproduction may be based upon the concept of "the best interests of the child". It may be in the best interests of society, of course, that children not be born to particular individuals or by particular reproductive means. It must be inquired, however, whether a decision that a particular child not be conceived can be justified because that

---

45 See M.A. Somerville, "Birth Technology, Parenting and 'Deviance'" (1982), 5 Int. J.L. & Psychiatry 123.

46 See generally J. Robertson, "Procreative Liberty and the Control of Conception, Pregnancy and Childbirth" (1983), 69 Va. L. Rev. 405.

47 See the preference to confine artificial reproduction to married couples expressed in the Vice Chairman's dissent in the Ontario Law Reform Commission, *Report on Human Artificial Reproduction and Related Matters* (1985), at 287-88.

decision is in the best interests of the very child intended not to be born. The question raises the paradox presented in the so-called "wrongful life" action,[48] in which a handicapped child claims damages for having been born. Opponents of the wrongful life action claim that it cannot be in a child's best interests not to have been born.

Birth registration may seek to maintain fidelity to biological parenthood, or to serve the purposes of social appearance of parenthood. Provincial legislation and practices appear to serve neither goal well, since A.I.D. births are rarely if ever recorded as such, and the original birth registration survives a child's adoption; although a new birth certificate is issued naming the adoptive parents and the original registration is sealed, the register may be opened in certain cases.[49]

Restrictive provincial legislation may cause residents to go to other jurisdictions for birth and birth registration or for adoption of children. The restrictive province must address the recognition it will afford the lawful practices of administrative agencies and courts of other jurisdictions which apply principles different from and more lax than its own.

Possible claims by children to genetic information of their biological parentage must be addressed, for instance, by determining whether or not genetic data will be preserved. Such preservation would require women to inform physicians of the biological parentage of the children they bear. The latter may also require that physicians retain information, or, for instance, that they include such data in children's medical records. This may require that A.I.D. be brought under the control of physicians, for instance by being legislated to be the "practice of medicine" controlled by the provincial College of Physicians and Surgeons. Alternatively, such colleges may be expected to make their own provisions for this purpose, for instance in their definitions of the disciplinary offence of professional misconduct, which may be expressed in provincial regulations promulgated under parent legislation governing medicine.

Consideration must be given to whether, if artificial reproduction is to be permitted by positive legislation, it will be on medical grounds only, such as infertility or genetic risk, or whether it will be permitted on social grounds, such as the absence of an approved partner of the opposite sex. Where medical grounds alone are permitted, it must be determined whether artificial reproduction will be approved only as a means of last resort, whether it will be allowed as

---

48   See W.H. Winborne (ed.), *Handling Pregnancy and Birth Cases* (1983), at 393-419.

49   See generally F.C. O'Donnell, *supra*, n. 39, and S.E. Simanek, "Adoption Records Reform: Impact on Adoptees" (1983), 67 Marq. L. Rev. 110.

a treatment of medical choice when other methods may be attempted (e.g., microsurgical reconstruction of damaged fallopian tubes), or whether it will be an option available simply at a patient's request.

When artificial reproductive means are to be available subject to legislated conditions, it must be considered whether an appeal is to be available to a tribunal or a court of law against an adverse assessment, or whether the court's review jurisdiction may be made available. Appeals against medical diagnostic or prognostic assessments are not usually justiciable, although second medical opinions may be sought. Assessments based upon social or other criteria and prognoses may be more amenable to appeal or review.[50]

VII ISSUES IN SPERM, OVUM AND EMBRYO DONATION

It must be decided whether genetic and related testing (for example, for AIDS) of donors will be required to be in accordance with legislatively prescribed criteria, or whether the medical profession will be entrusted with appropriate standard setting.[51] A middle-ground may exist in implementing standards through regulations made under statutory power. A difficulty with rigid standards is that medical developments and evolving knowledge may render them irrelevant or inadequate.

It must be determined whether genetic donors and children will be able to trace either personally identifying or non-identifying health information about each other (see the discussion *supra* in Part VI).

However this is resolved, it must be considered whether, and, if so, how responsibilities and rights between biological parents and children to be reared in others' families will be severed.

The status of donors' biological children under the law of wills and intestacy will need to be determined if tracing is possible.

If legislation is enacted on access to medical records, wills, intestacy and comparable matters, it must be determined whether it is to have only a prospective effect, or whether it can operate retrospectively.

Provincial permission for commercial sperm, ova and/or embryo banks or services may have to be considered. Options include prohibition of sales and purchases, toleration of cost-recovery fees by services established, for instance, in public hospitals, permission of licensed services charging approved fees, and permission of private enterprise facilities.

---

50 On the available means of challenge in Ontario, see *supra*, n. 47, at 159-60.

51 On standards, see Health and Welfare Canada, *Report of the Advisory Committee on the Storage and Utilization of Human Sperm* (1981).

It must be determined whether standards for preservation of sperm, ova and embryos by freezing (cryopreservation) will be set by legislation or regulations,[52] or be left to cryopreserving agencies. Since the science of freezing and thawing is advancing, standards may need to be capable of development, however set.

Frequency of employment of individual donors may be limited by legislation or regulation, or by standards of professional or commercial practice. Frequency may be related to distribution, since smaller centres may serve a geographically limited socio-economic class, with increased chances of children of a single donor later meeting and marrying; facilities serving a wider geographical area can avoid such concentration of distribution, and use individual donors more frequently. This issue is related to provincial permission for commercial sperm, ova and/or embryo banks and services discussed *supra*.

Time limits may be proposed for cryopreservation of sperm, ova or embryos, such as ten years from donation or the estimated end of the donor's reproductive capacity. While such proposals have been made, some consider them arbitrary and of no benefit.

VIII ISSUES IN IN VITRO FERTILIZATION

The protection of the embryo *in vitro* and in cryopreservation by criminal law is under consideration by the Law Reform Commission of Canada;[53] analysis indicates that destruction would not currently violate Criminal Code provisions on murder, manslaughter, abortion or child destruction, but that provisions on theft and mischief may be applicable.[54] It is a matter of provincial law whether child welfare legislation applies before birth, and, if so, at what stage of fetal or embryonic development.

Subject to the above, legislation may attempt to clarify who is responsible for and can exercise control over the embryo *extra uterum*. This may include responsibility for and control of the disposition of blighted embryos and of others not destined for implantation. Legislation may impose solutions, or require parties to resolve issues by contractual agreements.

Legislation may attempt to control the clinical practice of I.V.F., for instance by providing that more ova may not be recovered from a woman than, upon successful fertilization, will be implanted in her or another recipient. It may be observed, however, that no plan can ensure prevention of a surplus embryo.

---

52   *Ibid*.

53   Under its Protection of Life Project.

54   See *supra*, nn. 18 and 19.

Legislation may attempt to regulate research on embryos *extra uterum*, for instance by total prohibition, by permitting research intended to promote their individual viability, or by permitting research intended to reduce implantation failure and other causes of infertility, to reduce cancerous growths or other specified conditions, or to advance more general knowledge of human reproduction and health. Alternatively, it may be preferable to leave control of research to the guidelines and procedures to be developed by, for instance, the Medical Research Council of Canada. A jurisdiction limiting research may have to determine whether to make use of knowledge gained elsewhere in breach of its own standards.

Legislation may determine whether an embryo *in vitro* or in cryopreservation constitutes a "life in being", analogous to a child *en ventre sa mère*, for the purposes of the legal rule against perpetuities;[55] alternatively, the issue may be left for resolution by the courts.

IX ISSUES IN SURROGATE MOTHERHOOD

Initially, an assessment must be made of surrogate motherhood itself. It may appear as a profoundly offensive and immoral practice which should be prevented because, for instance, it violates the sanctity of the family or exploits women by inducing them to offer their reproductive capacities for money. It may alternatively appear acceptable when it is not commercialized and permits a woman with, for instance, no uterus or a history of chronic spontaneous abortion or life-threatening pregnancy to rear her husband's child; if she can ovulate, the child may be conceived *in vitro* and be her own genetic child. A limitation upon surrogate motherhood for convenience or vanity may be that a medical reason for it must exist. It may serve the best interests of a child of a woman affected by, for instance, diabetes or phenylketonuria (PKU) to be gestated outside her own uterus — a harmful environment which, without the greatest of care, will cause the child irreparable neurological and other injuries. However surrogate motherhood is assessed, the possibility of such arrangements is now widely known as a reproductive option,[56] and children will probably continue to be born in consequence of such arrangements.[57]

A jurisdiction must determine whether, for instance, to seek by legislation to prohibit the bearing of a child for the purpose of surrender upon birth to

---

55   See C. Sappideen, "Life After Death — Sperm Banks, Wills and Perpetuities" (1979), 53 Aust. L.J. 311.

56   See, for instance, L. Andrews, *New Conceptions: A Consumer's Guide to the Newest Infertility Treatments, Including In Vitro Fertilization, Artificial Insemination, and Surrogate Motherhood* (1984), and K. White, *What to Do When You Think You can't Have a Baby* (1982).

57   See *supra*, n. 21.

another, to prohibit any payments for such a practice, to prohibit commercialization of the practice by banning payments beyond reasonably incurred expenses, to tolerate the practice subject to prior approval of its financial or other terms (see *infra*), or to have no express legislation and leave the practice to fall under the general law on, for instance, determination of paternity and adoption. A simple prohibition may make adult actors liable to prosecution, and leave children born of agreements to fall under the general law.

In addition to or instead of the above, a jurisdiction may prohibit the establishment of agencies and the publication of advertisements for purposes of arranging surrogate motherhood agreements, or it may seek to control agencies and advertisements. A jurisdiction may similarly control the involvement of professionals such as gynecologists, psychiatrists, lawyers and social workers who may appear to promote such agreements.

If agreements are to be permitted and accommodated by legislation, it must be determined if parties can settle terms simply among themselves, anticipating for instance spontaneous abortion, death of intended social parents and abnormality of the child; whether particular provisions will be prohibited or mandatory; and whether a system of administrative or judicial scrutiny of prospective arrangements will be implemented. If payments are allowed, they may distinguish between payment for reasonable costs actually incurred, lost earning opportunities, and pain and suffering in pregnancy and delivery. Scrutiny of terms may be proposed through a child welfare agency, subject to judicial appeal or review. Alternatively, scrutiny may be undertaken by a court, such as a family court, for instance through a "surrogate adoption" procedure.[58]

If agreements can be approved after scrutiny, it must be determined if they can be monitored and enforced. Determination of parentage after birth may have to be allowed, in order to show whether a child was in fact produced by an agreement. Compelling a pregnant woman to conform to the terms of an agreement, for instance on her diet or prenatal care and welfare, may be the type of specific performance courts have traditionally declined to order in contracts of personal service because of the difficulties involved in supervising such contracts. Remedies for breach of agreement may be required to be specified in the agreement itself as genuine pre-estimates of loss, or they may be determined *ex post facto* by the courts.

An issue of major sensitivity is whether, following the birth of a child, legislation will permit it to be taken from an unwilling surrogate mother and given into the custody of the originally agreed social parents. Seizure and transfer can be supervised by the courts, as it is in custody disputes and child protection proceedings. To permit the taking of a child to whom a surrogate

---

58   See *supra*, n. 47, at 233-36, and B.M. Dickens "Surrogate Motherhood: Legal and Legislative Issues" in A. Milunsky and G.J. Annas (eds.), *Genetics and the Law III* (1985), at 208-209.

mother has emotionally bonded before birth may be unacceptable; it may be preferable for the intended social parents to bear the risks of her unwillingness to surrender the child at birth. As against this, a surrogate may decline to surrender the child not due to bonding, but because she wants a sizable money payment. Unenforceability of surrender by judicial action may thus open the way to ransom, baby selling and unscrupulous commerce.

Where a surrogate mother is married, legislation may have to rebut legal presumptions of her husband's paternity, and permit evidence to be acquired and recognized of the intended social father's paternity in fact or, where donated sperm were used, in law.

Legislation may have to address implications of surrogate motherhood, with the mother's own ovum and with an embryo created from an intended social mother's ovum, upon the operation of wills and on intestacy law. When a person leaves a bequest to a daughter's child, the intention may be to benefit a social grandchild of the testator's but not a child conceived to be surrendered to another family.

Revenue authorities may seek legislation to classify various payments to surrogate mothers, distinguishing, for instance, out-of-pocket expenses from payments constituting income.[59] Further, entitlement to child allowance deductions from statements of income may have to be allocated between surrogate mothers and social parents, since the latter will probably pay the childbirth expenses of the former.

Maternity leave provisions of contracts of employment may have to be reconsidered, since employers who bear the expenses of their employees' family development may object to subsidizing employees who earn fees as surrogate mothers.

X CONCLUSION

Not all of the issues raised above need to be determined by legislation. Common law evolution through case-by-case judgments may be adequate to deal with many issues, such as whether a child born in consequence of negligent genetic screening of a sperm or ovum donor can succeed in a claim for wrongful life.[60] Nevertheless, many issues arising in the practice of artificial reproduction are not amenable to systematic or consistent accommodation by a legal system dependent only upon declaratory or *ex post facto* judgments of the courts. The issues are of such social significance, and potentially of such major impact upon

---

59   See J. Maule, "[U.S.] Federal Tax Consequences of Surrogate Motherhood" (1982), 60 Taxes 656.

60   See *supra*, n. 48.

children to be born, that a responsible society must address them through specific, informed and perceptive legislation. We cannot evade the challenge of legislating for the Brave New Children.

11

THE FUTURE OF THE FAMILY, THE LAW AND THE STATE

*J. W. Mohr**

I INTRODUCTION

If we take seriously what we hear, have heard before, will hear again, what has become part of our daily dose informing us that wives are being beaten, children assaulted, sexually abused and abducted; that families break up at an unprecedented rate, responsibilities for maintenance are flagrantly abandoned; and that the best we can expect from the law is that it functions like an International Red Cross in this war of all against all; that the law too is mainly adversarial and, after some attempts at conciliation and mediation, has to adjudicate and bring to bear its own violence on the family; that the State throws ever increasing resources into this battle to hold the lines, but without success, since by now almost half of those entering the battle of marriage will be losers — if we take all this seriously, as I am afraid we must, then we do have to ask the question why it is that we want to maintain the war, why somebody should speak on the future of the family with the presumption that there is going to be one.

We take the answer for granted — most of the time. When asked for reasons, we tend to trot out the platitudes of the family being the backbone, and yes, the future of society (which is now in question too). We speak of love and learning, of sharing and caring, and so on and so forth. It is all too familiar.

There is a curious form of schizophrenia here, a split and dissociated mind, not recognized because it is assumed to be normal, which tells us on the one side that the family is the place of all evil and on the other that it is the source of our deepest needs and expectations. Both can be convincingly demonstrated, but we keep the two sides separate, and when we speak in terms of the law we tend to give public visibility to one side only. In this perspective and with this vision our despair has a ring of reality whereas our hopes and aspirations sound like a string of banalities.

---

*This chapter was previously published as an article in (1984), 4 Can. J. Fam. L. 261.

It is noteworthy that although divorce has been increasing, marriage has not gone out of style. Young people getting married are well aware of gloomy predictions. This, however, does not prevent them from having the same hopes they always had. If anything, more so. Even those who have gone through the mill once, or even twice or more often, re-form the same hopes and aspirations. And few take it lightly. Those who try to ward off the evil by avoiding certification, by avoiding anything which smacks of the law soon find that the need for trust, stability and permanence creeps up on them and cannot be easily shaken off. The law, in any case, has caught up with them and holds them to be married not only as a narrow common law assumption but statutorily so for most purposes which have weight.

The revolution in family law which has occurred during the past decades shows itself now (as most revolutions eventually do) to have been an adaptation to what was going on in our minds and between us. Always a bit late, to be sure. As the Jesuit philosopher Bernard Lonergan once said about the Church, the law too arrives at the place of action always a bit late and out of breath. Few still believe that the impossibility or even difficulty of obtaining a divorce keeps families together, although, as Thomas Huxley observed, many a theory survives long after its brains have been knocked out. The reforms to the Divorce Act, recently proclaimed, have been long overdue, and, in the main, they only legitimate actual practices.

Family law, as far as it can go in our present understanding of what law is and what it signifies, has adjusted to our minds as far as substantive law and legislation is concerned. The real problems have not decreased. If anything, they have increased. We are now attacking the very meaning and purpose of our traditional formal processes, embedded as they are in the adversary system. Thoughtful observers of the reform process now recognize that we do not have a family law any more, that this is a misnomer. All we have left is a "law of persons", a law which not only conforms with our present basic notions of being independent, autonomous persons, but a law which conforms to its own self-understanding of being a law for just such persons. Every person now is an island unto him/her/itself and the law will protect his/her/its territory. It is ironic that at a time when we begin to realize that this understanding of law is deeply flawed, we entrench it in a charter and fashion family law accordingly. But there is no family of independent, autonomous persons. There are no such people. This understanding of law could never accommodate dependent persons and had to make them legal non-persons such as married women, idiots and children.

Married women have now become legal persons and are finding out that their responsibilities are as real as ever but their newly acquired rights are often illusory. Hardly anybody would defend any more the "unity of personality" of husband and wife, although we reject the concept of fault for this very reason: we cannot disentangle who did what to whom and on whose bidding. To conceive of a single parent as an independent person is just as much a fiction, this time not in law but in reality.

Idiots — and this is the word the law commonly used — are now torn between being normalized in law but not in social reality. The law did not use the term idiot in its disparaging sense, but in its touching original sense as a self unto itself which, because its interdependence was threatened, needed the protection of a higher order, the *parens patriae*.

The battle around our legal definitions of children still goes on wanting to make them independent and autonomous so that they too fairly fit into our legal conceptions of persons, but reality again resists. The little critters seem to want to be dependent and so do the not-so-little ones even when they resent it and their parents resent their resentment. Ironically, at the same time as the law tries to increase children's autonomy, it increases parental responsibility in the private law field to the breaking point. When the break is achieved, the State will take care. The covenant has become a contract with many specific performance claims; status, which was the state we were in, is finally absorbed by the State through a notion of law which tries to tell us that we are independent equals even when we are blatantly neither.

II FAILURE OF PRESENT LAW TO RESOLVE FAMILY PROBLEMS

Although the dissolution of a concept of family in family law seems to have followed rather than preceded the increasing dissolution of families in social reality, this is not true for the law as a whole. If we look to areas such as property and contract (the important ones as any lawyer will tell you) we can see that the underpinnings of any important notion of family have been taken out long before and replaced by notions such as the corporation — a curious extension in law of the natural person — or the corporate State with its ever increasing domain of public and administrative law. Many of the functions of the family, not as a nuclear remnant, but as a social and communal form, have been taken over by corporations and the corporate State. That by 1984 we refuse to see those as our true families is sheer perversity. We can see, after all, that we have no real independent means to support our lives, these come from the corporations, and that the private law system which promises us party autonomy cannot cope with the real problem of autonomous parties and has to turn to the State for enforcement and support.

Even in what we now see as more humane and familial forms of dispute resolution, such as conciliation, mediation and arbitration, we know that we have to transform these ideas into services which have to be provided. Who will provide them? The demand for reconciliation has been part of the Divorce Act[1]

---

1   R.S.C. 1970, c. D-8 [repealed and substituted by 1986, c. 4, s. 32].

since its inception. It has never been treated seriously. Procedures for non-adversarial sorting out of family problems have not been a part of the traditional family law regime and are still rarely a part of the present one. Even the Unified Family Court, by no means universal in Canada, can only cut down to some extent the jurisdictional fragmentation and the tensions and incompatibilities that exist between adversarial and non-adversarial procedures. The Unified Family Court remains embedded in a legal system which takes adversarial stances and adjudication as the hallmark of its reasoning. It is also the end of its reasoning as the massive problems of non-compliance with maintenance orders show, as well as the continuing problems in custody and access. The main reason that the private law system still appears to be functioning is that people get disillusioned or run out of money, or both. The stress is shifted to the public law system and increasingly to criminal law.

As the impotence of the family to cope with problems is finally expressed in family violence, the impotence of law to cope with problems is finally expressed in the violence of state measures. I do not only mean criminal law proper which is resorted to more and more in family matters, but the ever increasing creations of criminal prohibitions and sanctions in welfare statutes. For instance, the revised Child Welfare Act of Ontario,[2] in many ways a model for new approaches to child welfare legislation, lists about 18 offences starting out with the familiar "Everyone who. . ." and ending up with fines of up to $10,000 or three years' imprisonment or both. Like King Kanute, or for that matter family members who cannot cope with the problems they face, we try to beat what threatens us into submission. And the circle becomes truly vicious. Family members who are afraid of their anger have now nobody to turn to because social workers and doctors have not only lost any implicit privilege they have had in using their judgment, they are now under threat of prosecution and punishment. Everybody else shall report without having to face those they accuse. Only lawyers have privilege. The State will take care. It is our neighbour's keeper.

It is all understandable. We know the familiar questions: "What would you do if. . ?" and then comes a hard case, but hard cases we know make bad law. Consider a recent report of a committee on the enforcement of maintenance orders. It reeks of coercion. Again, it is understandable if one considers the flagrant and widespread attempts to frustrate such orders or just to ignore them. But the report does not ask why otherwise responsible people default on their basic responsibilities, how further enforcement will influence their relationship to their children, or whether anger and violence will increase.

---

2   R.S.O. 1980, c. 66 [repealed by the Child and Family Services Act, 1984, c. 55, s. 208].

III THE FUTURE OF THE FAMILY

I have gone on to speak of the past and the present rather than of the future, to speak of law rather than the family. The fact is that like the couple about to be married, I can see no intrinsic problem in the future of the family. It seems to me that the deep need people have and the yearning for intimate, lasting relations are as obvious as ever and most of the problems discussed here are a sign of their frustration rather than their disappearance. There is no problem I can see that is not already present in biblical accounts or in the great myths which have to be rediscovered and faced from generation to generation. What we seem to have lost is the very sense of generation — the only future there is. But if this were so, why would we worry about the future at all? It is ironic that at a time and a place as in this society now, when we have more earthly goods than we ever had, we claim that we cannot afford children or, when we cannot resist this luxury, leave it at one or two, the second becoming a decreasing fraction in statistics. The problem is not abortion. I doubt that pro-life ideologists have any more children than their pro-choice counterparts. Catholics, as far as I know, have no more children than protestants or atheists for that matter; people in so-called free societies have no more than those under ostensive state control, whether those states limit having children as in China or reward it as in East Germany.

I mention this because conditions do, of course, influence the way families constitute themselves, the way they live and the way they understand themselves. These days, at least in public discourse, we seem to express ourselves mainly in economic terms. But although we relate economic conditions to problems in the family, economists rarely consider the family. I for one look forward to the Interim Report of the Macdonald Commission which is now due, to see whether there is any mention of the family, whether a report on the economic union and development prospects of Canada will in fact consider family union and prospects for family development. The Vanier Institute and many other groups concerned with family and community have brought it to their attention.

One can appreciate how much even language has changed when one considers that the very word "economy" literally means the rules of the household, the way families go about their business. Much of this business has, of course, been taken away from the family and officialized. From childbirth, which happens mostly in hospitals, to dying, which mostly happens at the same place, much that has been important to and in families is now carried out by experts. And experts can teach us just about anything, except how to live in our particular family. They can fix just about anything, replace and substitute everything, except our own intimate, lasting relations.

In spite of daycare facilities, schools, treatment centres and Family Courts, the work of feeding, cleaning and clothing children still rests with the family and is time-consuming, exhausting and expensive. Rational economic man, and now woman too, who, as economics tells us, maximizes his own economic benefits, must obviously reject having children. Then why do we have them? Every parent wonders about that from time to time and will concede that it is irrational. Moreover, to split production from consumption, to split the material from the emotional and spiritual leaves us with no concept of care that has any lasting meaning. On this, both Locke and Marx agree and the Canadian Catholic Bishops have recently reconfirmed it on the basis of much older teachings. The ideological consequences of most positions which now mark and divide the world are the same: Familism is obliterated by individualism as well as "State-ism". Or, as some would express it, the family has no place in Late Capitalism or State Capitalism.

Nevertheless, if we are to speak of the future of the family in any serious sense in the context of law and the State, we must raise the question of a coherent family policy which can bridge the gap between private and public law, between private commitment and public services. We recognize, do we not, that taxation, welfare and labour laws, economic, income, and welfare regulations have a greater impact on our families than what we call family law and that their failures can produce more breakdowns and pathologies than any family service can cure.

Why is it that we have no coherent family policy, no commission on family union and development prospects in Canada? The need surely is obvious. How long will we continue to ascribe the massive breakdowns in and of families to individual pathologies which we settle on a case-to-case basis? Even with conciliation, mediation and protection and even with lessening the exacerbation and polarization of problems in what we call family law, we miss the point.

How long until people recognize that the very state and the very law to which they go for support and protection are organized in a way which can only deal with individuals in competition. Neither state nor law can address in any meaningful sense continuing, interdependent human relations. Almost every-body who has faced or observed the process of break up with some honesty knows this. At best, counsel and counsellors are helpful in steering clients through legal and bureaucratic pitfalls which other counsel and counsellors have set up. At worst, counsel and counsellors get them more deeply entangled, increasing the anger and the hostility. There are many who know this now. But this knowledge remains inert because it is laden with a sense of personal shame and failure, either accepted or projected onto the other, or repressed in a vague notion that this is the way things are.

Even the Canadian Charter of Rights and Freedoms, which promises to give us rights and freedoms and tells us that those can only be limited by the law and by whatever means the State finds reasonable, says nothing about the realities of responsibility and care, the only meaningful way in which rights and freedoms can be expressed. Rights talk and freedom talk is poor family talk. Families don't unite around them, they break up over them.

If one raises the question of a family policy, one is immediately asked what one means by family. And then one gets the list of nuclear family, extended family, one-parent family, reconstituted family, successive families, homosexual families, groups and communes, family images along religious, ethnic and class lines and so on and so forth. Of course we live in a pluralistic society, of course families come in all forms, shapes and sizes. But are the basic values by which they live all that different? Is there any group which will deny that families need a home, an income base and the ability to care for children? Is there anybody in this pluralistic society who will deny that it is basically better for families to work together than to be separated? And I do not just mean broken; this is only the end stage. Is there anybody who will deny, if there is any commitment to family at all, that it is better for a family to live under conditions in which they can share their liveliness rather than just their tiredness as is so often the case now; that family should claim a priority on time and energy and not just live on leftovers; that the economy is there to support the family and not the family to support the economy; that we achieve because of family and not in spite of it. If family is only a haven in a heartless world, it must soon become disheartened in a world which cannot be a haven. Otherwise we can say, as Abby Hoffman once did: "God is dead and we did it all for the kids".

There are plenty of shared values, not in an abstract or formal sense where they indeed differ, but in what we know to be true in our everyday practices. Pluralism would be no obstacle if we could take seriously the self-understanding which every family has, whether it can express it or not, admit it or not. Families have always come in all shapes, forms and sizes. This is not the problem. What is intrinsic to family does not change even though forms and conditions and understandings do. There has been a Jewish family which has endured in spite of biblical post-office divorce, no less than the Christian family for whom this, apparently and for some time only, has been forbidden. It is ironic that what is often in a formal sense advertised as the Christian family would exclude, on almost all counts, the Holy Family as we know it from the New Testament. The last request of Socrates to the jury who condemned him to death was to look after his children, not to support them, but to hold them to the values which he had espoused. "If you do this, I shall have had justice at your hands, both I, myself, and my children."[3] It is rumoured that he was nagged by his wife but even this is as it should be for someone who spent so much time with his friends. Even a Clifford Olson bargains for his family which only enrages but does not touch us.

---

3   Plato, *Apology*.

As we turn to public and administrative law and to criminal law to shore up our families, it may help to listen to a contemporary Hungarian writer to see whether it sounds at all familiar to us in apparently different circumstances.

> I question, explain, prove, disprove, comfort, threaten, grant, deny, demand, approve, legalize, rescind. In the name of legal principles and provisions I defend law and order for want of anything better to do. The order I defend is brutal though fragile, it is unpleasant and austere; its ideas are impoverished and its style is lacking in grace. I can't pretend to like it. Yet I serve it, it's law, it works, it's rather like me, its tool. I know its ins and outs. I simplify it and complicate it, I slow it down and speed it up. I adapt myself to its needs or adapt it to my needs, but this is as far as I will go. I repudiate the heroes of the Fresh Start, with the pedantic recommendations and mawkish visions; I repudiate their blueprints for a *perpetuum mobile*, which for the time being (but only for the time being) has to be started with a crank and operated under the strictest supervision. I repudiate the high priests of individual salvation and the sob sisters of altruism, who exchange commonplace partial responsibility for the aesthetic transports of cosmohistorical guilt or the gratuitous slogans of universal love. I refuse to emulate these Sunday-school clowns and prefer — and I know my limitations — to be the skeptical bureaucrat that I am. My highest aspiration is that a medium-rank, utterly insignificant civil servant should, as far as possible, live with his eyes open.[4]

People do not learn love, respect and caring through the police or police-like agencies, nor through the courts or prisons or welfare offices or even children's aid societies, as necessary as these are under present circumstances and as valiantly as individual workers try, be they policemen, legal counsel, judge, prison guard or caseworker, who deserve our understanding and respect for the impossible tasks we give them. They too soon come to the limits of their endurance, are "burnt out", or resort to violence, official violence which is hardly recognized as such, except by those to whom it is applied. Can it be otherwise?

To repeat and to summarize: If we speak of the future of the family, or even its present and presence, we cannot on the one hand continue to speak in sanctimonious terms and on the other hand ignore all the basic conditions families need to exist. We can see now very clearly, if we want to see at all, that the need and the desire of people to form families is undiminished even in an age of narcissism and self-gratification. We can also see now that our efforts of family law reform were largely efforts to resolve a legal past which in its form no longer holds for most people. And although we have eliminated a series of glaring legal injustices, especially to women and children, injustices which also demeaned men, we have lost any coherent notion of family and can now only think in terms of legal rights and obligations of individuals which are mostly illusory in a family context and therefore have to be claimed through or from the State. Maybe this is all the law we have can do; but if this is so, then it will have to

---

4   George Konrád, *The Case Worker* (1974), at 168.

throw more and more responsibility on the corporate, administrative State because too many individuals either cannot or do not want to adhere to the edicts of the law.

If this is so, then we better start divorce proceedings from formal family law as we are already doing in stressing conciliation and closed mediation. But although these will diminish some of what the law itself exacerbates, they will not diminish the real problems which are created by our social conditions. Many women and children will still be poor, as they are now, and all will be poorer. And men, who are less visibly poor on the basis of income statistics, know that this too is illusory if they are to live up to their responsibilities; if not, they have to pay in terms of their self-respect, altogether too high a price. So the State has to provide and the *parens patriae* which we have questioned for the few will be for the many. Some will say that this is what the modern State has always wanted, to be the parent of us all and to hold exclusive power, no matter what kind of ideology it espouses. God is not dead, He has just disguised Himself. And the law, which was to protect us from the State because it espouses justice and not power, has delivered us to it.

Before we continue divorce proceedings between the law and the family and go cap in hand to the corporate State, we should try to practice what we preach. We have passed the stage of conciliation which, as our experience in family law tells us, only settles minor and temporary disagreements. True, adjudication would be disastrous at this stage because we have not yet assessed fully enough the future prospects of the family or the law, except that they both will survive in one form or another because they are perennial. So mediation would be a good approach because in mediation we have to recognize that there are mutual claims and that these claims can only be met if we recognize the differing bases of claims which cannot be reconciled in a satisfactory maner by a base-less compromise, only by a new base. What we seem to ignore in "mediation", as we speak of it today, is that mediation in any real sense demands a medium no less than adjudication which is mediated through law.

As the process leading up to adjudication sharpens and accentuates adversarial features of the particular case, so that winning and losing can be determined on the basis of rules, mediation must seek common interests which can modify particular demands. Law, as we understand it today, insists on specificity of facts which fit abstract rules; its rationality is instrumental, the kind of rationality which Freud once claimed he used only for minor decisions in his life. Law purports to settle cases once and for all; not much in our lives can be settled that way; only death does that. Mediation, in a different understanding of law, is no less of a legal process than adversarial adjudication. In fact, it is what most lawyers do most of the time in their offices when they draw up agreements rather than destroy them as they do in court. Mediation, nevertheless, demands a different mind-set. It must keep in the foreground continuing relationships rather than separate individuals, contexts rather than particular claims. Maintenance, custody and access *are* continuing relationships and form a context. They are therefore least likely to be settled by the mind-set of adversarial adjudication. Children are the continuing common ground *par excellence*; this is their basic best interest.

Family has to recognize that there is no future in being the romantic image of individuals, — man, woman, or child — who see the other only as an extension of themselves and their needs without a concrete notion of the commonality of fairness and justice which the maintenance of self and other demands as the very condition for the duration and endurance of love in its biological, psychological, social and spiritual expression. Fairness and justice themselves in any concrete sense can only appear in lasting relations. It is only there that they cannot be faked or substituted. This is what is meant by "natural justice". Although it cannot be generalized and formalized into law as rules, it is forever the fount and the legitimacy of living law.

"Natural justice" does not come from nature, nor from individuals, nor the State, try as it may to specify individual and State rights. Fairness is embedded in customs and mores, in our understandings of the forms and ways we live together. Justice speaks to our understanding of *human* nature. Justice illuminates customs and mores but cannot be found in them. Justice is a categorical imperative, as Kant has called it, which lives in us but is not of us.

The difference between justice and fairness is Job's dilemma which all the efforts of mediation could not resolve. He looked to fairness as a measure of justice until he was told that it was not, that there was more to it than that. Family and its extension in community is for most of us the highest court of the land and its judgment the most serious we can countenance. Fairness is a necessary but not sufficient condition to realize justice. Neither is law.

Law has to recognize that if its own form and rules supersede and become unhinged from fairness and justice, or what traditionally we have called morality which now is a dirty word, it will indeed be sounding brass and tinkling cymbal. When it does not recognize a promise without a consideration which does not even have to be considerate, when it treats a wrong as if it were between strangers, when property is exclusive and not the base of relation, when trust means that we don't trust, the law cannot claim respect and it too must resort to coercion and violence after it has exhausted rituals which have largely become meaningless. This is indeed the end of the law as Marx has prophesied, as he has the end of the State.

But neither the State nor the law can wither away in a Hobbesian world, even if the war of all against all, which justified law, is transformed into one of class against class which rejects law as the property of the propertied class. In both cases, in the end there is the Leviathan which devours us with or without the teeth of law. Form cannot disappear from function, reflection from action, nor will from power, nor power from the State, nor will from the law. But whose will shall be done? This is the question in family, law and State, a question we are trying to hide under utopian notions until it explodes into violence.

Family is not neutral, neither is the law, nor the State. Neither are we, as neutralized and neutered as we may have become seeking our fulfilment in the kingdom, the power and the glory — now and forever. The covenant has been converted into a contract with the State under the Rule of Law, and family has been set aside as some kind of private place, a castle or bastion in the war of all against all. As the understandings of the covenant disappeared from the contract, this contract, which has been called social, is visibly breaking or being broken. What remains? The barely disguised power of the State.

But State and law are abstract terms. Who hides behind them? Some say the powerful and the wilful. But the few could not remain either powerful or wilful if they would not provide a hiding place for the many and bind some by greed and others by need. The will to power is denied in the family and in the State until it can no longer be hidden and then the law has to do the bidding for both. But as the family is not a private place in a public State, family law cannot separate itself into private and public law.

If we think in terms of family, we must have a notion of law and equity for its operations, a notion of fairness for its relations, and a notion of justice for situating family in us and the world. Love is truly not enough, at least not what we loosely tend to call love. When we think in terms of law we must find a measure which expresses the meaning and order in human affairs and holds us to the quest for justice. When we think in terms of the State we must remember that the State is first and foremost a state of mind and that its instrumental rather than its expressive function is a personification as is the corporation. In our tradition and tradition of law it was indeed a person — the sovereign, sanctified "by the grace of God". The death of God disempowers the sovereign as a *corpus mysticum* and only the Leviathan remains and overshadows the corporate, contractual State which is now dying too. But a State as the formal expression of our common state of mind, forcing us to face up to our commonality, cannot disappear without all of us doing the same, simply or severally and now maybe, altogether.

The future of the family in the context of law is thus also the future of law in the context of the family and its extension to community and society. From Aristotle's *Politics* to Locke's *Two Treatises of Government*, the family is the basic, material metaphor for any kind of statehood and its expression in law. Family, in whatever form we may conceive it, has to first understand itself in terms of some kind of lawfulness which should not be altered, only fulfilled, rather than in terms of a disembodied humanism which ascribes hardness and harshness only to law. Families are the law for most of us most of the time. We may break its rules, conventions and understandings, but not without consequences which either make us change our behaviour or our very notions of self, other and family. I am arguing for the legalization of families. (I take love as a given in this context.)

Law, in whatever form we may want to shape it, has to regain features of the family. All important notions of law we learn in family first and foremost. Few non-lawyers tend to recognize this and most lawyers tend to forget it. Property: "It's mine, you can't play with it". This is the law we have. If you don't observe it, it's a crime. What does family say: "You don't need it now, let Nicky play with it". This is not the law we have. Contract: "You promised me. . . ." Go, tell the child you did not mean it. This is the law. We may well claim "consideration", a tangible acknowledgment, as part of the promise. But if it was not a part of the bargain, family better keep the promise. This is not the law. "He has hurt me" — tort or crime? However we may interpret it in family, and we invariably must, we better make sure we control our prejudices as well as the legalism of the combattants. There must clearly be a constitution and a division of powers (that's not my job) and jurisdiction (you have to ask your mother) as well as procedures for conciliation, mediation and arbitration, and yes, adversarial adjudication. There is not a single basic concept or practice law students learn which they have not experienced in the family before, although they are exhorted not to mitigate legalism by familism, to take their measure from the worst and not the best case, to put mistrust over trust.

This is why it is so difficult to change the law in any fundamental sense because it incorporates the structure of our most intimate experiences — and our attitudes towards them. Law is curiously absent not only from our conception of family but also from our educational experience outside law school, and except for criminal law (the poorest form of law), it hardly enters the public imagination. Good and evil which have become homeless have displaced right and wrong in the public imagination as well as in our family images. Blackstone, or an equivalent work, is hardly part of our books at home, neither is the Code Napoleon or the Code Civil which, it is said, replaced the Bible in forming language.

In short, I argue for the re-humanization of law, a task far too large for lawyers alone; but then, it has always been said that the law was far too important to be left to them. It is my experience and my belief that the potential for human knowledge in law is enormous and can be discounted only at our peril. The law as superstructure will hopefully wither away; if not, it ought to be kicked. But the law as a base which alone can face us with our contradictions can never disappear. We had better "dis-cover" it.

In the meantime, it will be said, we have to deal with broken families and the argument that there are too many now "to be dealt with" will not convince experts of the family, of the legal, political or other persuasions. In fact, the majority of families which break up do so without contest, use experts only when necessary and do not depend on legal coercion. All families break up and recombine in one way or another. Children arrive and leave; there is death and mobility and ever-present change. This needs to become visible in our concerns about the future of the family. When we deal with a question such as maintenance we ought to know what it is we want to maintain and we should not talk about custody and access at all without being horrified by our very talk. Who wants to have a child in custody, joint or otherwise and who really wants access to a child as if it were a piece of property; and if so, why should anybody, including the law, assist such demands. It is not just a question of words; they structure our discourse and consequently our lives. We do have to deal with the abuse of wives and children but what can we possibly mean by their "use". This becomes even more clear when we address the "sexual abuse" of children. We have little meaning left of the "uses" of sexuality except self-gratification hemmed in by deeply felt values which we can only express through horror stories. And how can we be so sure that our official interventions, which are not just human responses, but have to be structured, decrease even the limited horror which hits families, whether they are together or broken, otherwise stable or unstable. In cases of violence or violation we have to do the best we can, as with those injured in war. There is a place for experts, who have to show, however, that they do more good than harm.

All this speaks of necessity but not of desire except in a negative or perverse way. No future can be built on it. Neither the family nor the law can live on necessity without desire, on scarcity without surplus. Desire cannot be just the leftover after necessity is mastered. When wants are constantly converted into needs, all that is left is a fetishism of the production or consumption type. There is no freedom left and no personhood possible. The question of the future becomes immaterial, there can only be an eternal recurrence of the same. This is the basic threat which now threatens us.

Is it really beyond our imagination to reform our images of family, to take them and our desires for duration and endurance seriously, to reform the law in the image in which we have been formed, to shake off the image of the war of all against all, the war of class against class, sex against sex, age against age, religion against religion and all this combined in State against State? And the reciprocal image of sameness, conformity, mass and sheer numbers aggregated as power/knowledge which equally oppresses and destroys us? Is it really beyond our capability to stop finding solutions and start making our patent solutions problematic, solutions which always appear new but always turn out to be the same, as the daily news does, the daily newspaper which gives us paper news far removed from our daily lives which it pre-empts?

We all know better than that when we happen not to play trivial pursuit.